The Way Things Ought to Be

RUSH
H. LIMBAUGH, III

The Way
Things
Ought to Be

POCKET BOOKS
New York   London   Toronto   Sydney   Tokyo   Singapore

POCKET BOOKS, a division of Simon & Schuster Inc.
1230 Avenue of the Americas, New York, NY 10020

ISBN: 0-671-75145-X

First Pocket Books hardcover printing October 1992

30 29 28 27 26 25 24 23 22 21 20

POCKET and colophon are registered trademarks of
Simon & Schuster Inc.

Printed in the U.S.A.

This book is dedicated to my parents, whose love and devotion made me the terrific guy I am.

ACKNOWLEDGMENTS

WRITING A BOOK IS AN UNDERTAKING THAT CANNOT BE APPRECIATED until you actually begin work on it. One must summon forth a resolve and commitment not normally needed in everyday life. This is especially true for people like me, who don't write books—or anything else for that matter—for a living. In light of the fact that my writing experience was quite limited, I was determined nevertheless to actually write the book, rather than farm it out to a ghost writer. Still, I needed to make use of assistance in areas I considered crucial to completing the project.

I chose as my collaborator John Fund, an editorial writer for the *Wall Street Journal* and a friend who shares my ideas and beliefs. This was crucial, for John's primary role was to interview me on tape, then write the first draft from the transcriptions of the interviews. His performance was masterful. He was able to divorce his own ego and personality from the process and concentrate on drawing me out, which he did flawlessly. He gave freely of his time and always rearranged his day to accommodate mine. Additionally, he served superbly as a researcher when I couldn't remember where I had read or seen something. If it was to be found, he found it.

Editing and the first re-write occurred after Fund had submitted the first drafts of chapters. Here the help of my brother, David Limbaugh, was indispensable. He is a profound conservative thinker, and a much better writer than I will ever be. Many of his suggestions have been incorporated, making the final product better than it would have been.

There are others whose contributions are also greatly appreciated. John Bell Williams, who has his own radio program in Birmingham, Alabama, wrote the lyrics to all the Bungee Condom spots used on my radio program and reprinted here. Robert Wohlfeld is the author of the lyrics to both "The Philanderer" and "Kenna-Day-O" song parodies that are so popular on my radio program. Rob Carson of Columbia, Missouri, created the hilarious House Bank and House Post Office commercial parodies, and Dick Rich, a friend in New York, wrote the Feminazi Trading Card bit.

There are also numerous people at WABC-AM, New York, whose assistance is perhaps unknown to them, so I will note it here. General Manager Don Bouloukos and John Mainelli, the Program Director, are due a tremendous amount of gratitude. A positive state of mind, and (quite simply) a good mood, are essential to being one's best, and Bouloukos and Mainelli provide an atmosphere each day at WABC that allows for this. In fact, Mainelli's cooperation during the entire four years my radio show has originated from WABC has been instrumental in the success of all the projects I have taken on.

Kit Carson, my celebrated Chief of Staff, is also due a tremendous amount of thanks for absorbing so many of my day-to-day decisions during the period of time I spent writing this book. The ability to delegate so many aspects of my business life to one so competent as he freed me to concentrate as much as I needed and wanted to on the book. In this regard, I would like to offer my thanks to my secretary, Kathy Dellacava, who signed on in the middle of the project and received a true baptism under fire in getting up to speed with everything.

Most important, however, is Ed McLaughlin. Had he not taken the risk of giving me a national radio program, and allowing me to do it as I feel it should be, none of this would be happening. Ed's contributions are detailed in this book, but I would be remiss if I failed to say a simple "Thank You" to him for his vision and patience. The same goes to our partners in the radio program, John Axten and Stu Krane. I am convinced that I am associated with the absolute best there is.

ADVISORY

By the time you have wisely purchased this tome (book, for those of you in Rio Linda, California) most critics will have undoubtedly savaged it. In many cases, their reviews will have been written before the book was published. How do I know this? Because I do. Also because my esteemed and brave editor, Dame Judith Regan, was harassed for months prior to the publication of the book by people who castigated her for even offering me the opportunity to write the book and thereby giving me this forum. Repeated efforts were made to dissuade her from actually publishing this book, and I owe her at least a condo in Los Angeles for ignoring these hysterically shrill, cacophonous protests. In practically all cases, the people who were vilifying her had not ever heard my radio show or read one word I had written. What they had read was critical newspaper and magazine articles, and they had formed their opinions accordingly. But they needn't have gone to even that trouble. All they needed to know is that I am a conservative, and as such, I am politically incorrect. So beware: there are people out there—Communists, Socialists, Environmentalist Wackos, Feminazis, Liberal Democrats, Militant Vegetarians, Animal Rights Extremists, Liberal Elitists—who will try to prevent you from reading this book.

I considered advising you to place the jacket sleeve from a similiar-size copy of the Bible over this book, which would place you in less jeopardy. But I then remembered that you wouldn't

legally be allowed to read it in a school or during a commencement ceremony or many other public places, because God is
unconstitutional. Besides, reading what would appear to be the
Bible in public would cause you to be accused by some civil
libertarians of attempting to force your religious views on them.
So forget that idea. Just please be aware that reading this book in
the wrong public places could result in its being set on fire or
your being pelted with rotten vegetables. Don't be frightened.
Read it anyway. Be courageous and brave, as is Dame Judith
Regan, and don't be intimidated. Smile when they stick their
noses in the air and harumph. Laugh when they confront you
and ask you why you are reading fascism. Ignore them when they
call you a fat slob. Chuckle when they blame you for hunger in
Ethiopia. Smirk smugly when you are accused of prosperity.
When they accuse you of insensitivity, cry fake tears and say that
your parents are making you read the book. Everybody knows
that parents are the real problem, because they voted for Reagan.

For those of you among the Liberal Elite who take a stab at
reading this book, be forewarned. Everything in this book is right
and you must be prepared to confront that reality. You can no
longer be an honest liberal after reading this entire masterpiece.
Throughout the book you will be challenged, because you will
actually be persuaded to the conservative point of view. Whether
you can admit this in the end will be a true test of your mettle as a
human being.

Now get to it.

CONTENTS

CONTENTS

Contents

INTRODUCTION

I DECIDED TO WRITE THIS BOOK TO TELL A BIT ABOUT MYSELF AND MY radio show and where I stand on the important political and social issues affecting our society today. However, I encountered a recurring problem: most of the issues involve current events. What seemed catastrophically important one week may have been diminished in importance the following week by other events. In writing this book I experienced the frustration of feeling that my observations were often obsolete within a week of completing a chapter.

Then it dawned on me that I was allowing myself to become too immersed in specific events whose ephemeral nature made it impossible to achieve "cutting edge" relevance, especially by the time the book would be published. I was carving out for myself an impossible task, and indeed, an unnecessary one.

In considering this issue of timeliness it dawned on me that political analysts, commentators, and pundits must offer their observations through the analysis of events within the time frame of those events as well as after the event. My specialty is analyzing and commenting on events as they occur and play out. This is impossible to accomplish in the format of a book.

Although most of the events discussed in this book have come and gone, the analysis and commentary is timeless and instructive, as well as funny when appropriate. In truth, events are simply vehicles which allow commentators, philosophers, and analysts the opportunity to illustrate their beliefs and define themselves. In that regard, the events I discuss in this book serve superbly as opportunities for me to express my soul, my heart, my passion and humor. Accordingly, dear readers, you will find a flawless blend of sincerity, profundity, seriousness, humor, and irreverence, just as can be found on my radio show. You will have to read the entire book to experience the total flavor, for not every chapter contains all these elements.

I believe in specific ideas and I believe that those ideas have consequences. I believe in the individual, in less government so as to allow that individual maximum freedom to create and achieve; that societies which are founded on restraining the government rather than the individual are optimum; that the individual is smart enough to solve his own problems and does not need to depend on big government for resolution of all his problems; that my belief in individuality and limited government does not preclude me from advocating the requisite amount of governmental authority to ensure law and order in our society; that our ability to enjoy peace vis-à-vis other nations is directly related to our military strength; that the best that we can hope for in an imperfect world will most likely be achieved by maximizing individual economic and political freedoms and, conversely, that social utopia cannot be achieved through governmental largesse and socialistic redistributions of wealth; that compassion is defined not by how many people are on the government dole but by how many people no longer need governmental assistance; that political and economic freedom are inextricably intertwined; that society owes its citizens equality of opportunity but cannot guarantee them equality of outcome; that strong, wholesome family values are at the very core of a productive, prosperous, and peaceful society; that those values cannot be instilled by government but can indeed be sucked dry and eliminated by well-intentioned but destructive governmental programs; that human life is sacred and that God placed man in a position of having dominion over nature; that environmental awareness is

2

healthy, but that apocalyptic environmentalism based on disinformation and hysteria is destructive to society and man's best interests; that racial relations will not be enhanced or prejudice eliminated by governmental edict; that there is one God and that this country was established with that foundational belief; that our morality emanates from our Divine Creator, whose laws are not subject to amendment, modification, or rescission by man; that certain fundamental differences between men and women exist in nature; that men and women are not at war and that their relationship should not be redefined by those who believe that we are; that the meaning of the establishment clause of the First Amendment should not be stretched beyond its intended dimensions by precluding voluntary prayer in our public schools; that the United States of America was founded on the beliefs I have just enunciated and that it is the greatest nation in the history of the world; and that the USA is the greatest nation, not because Americans are inherently superior but because its government was founded on principles which seek to allow maximum individual achievement.

I also believe that the dominant media culture is composed of liberals who seek to push their view on society without admitting they are doing it. I believe conservatives are indeed the silent majority in this country and that they prove that every four years at the polls.

Finally, I believe that certain liberals have become painfully aware that they do represent the minority position in society. That they are losing, so to speak. They have read the writing on the wall and have made subtle adjustments in order to reposition themselves for another run at reestablishing control.

These subtle adjustments have taken the disguised form of popular, sentimental political causes which are difficult for people to oppose, such as environmentalism, animal rights activism, and feminism. Although each of these groups superficially advocates the specific programs within their particular causes, a common broadsweeping theme underlies all of these "movements." Unmistakably, that theme is anticapitalism, secular humanism, and socialism.

In this book I discuss these various disguised liberal movements and how their agendas are affecting our society. I believe that in order to combat the misinformation that is so prevalent on our political landscape today we have to remain informed and alert to the things that are occurring. The best way to do that is to read, listen to, or watch me.

Nineteen ninety-two has been quite a year. Things are changing so fast that by the time this book is on the shelves, you and my publisher will be clamoring for another. Well, just tune in to my award-winning radio show for an ongoing supplement to this book. You will not even be charged extra. Also, by that time, my television show will begin airing, and what you miss during the day you can catch at night.

Writing this book has been one of the most difficult things I have ever done. I am fortunate in that I love my work so much that it really isn't work to me. One of the reasons is that I have the freedom and responsibility to be entirely myself on the radio. That, coupled with my having done it for so long, makes it seem easy, almost instinctive. However, I had never written a book. I hadn't even asked those who had how they had done it; I just considered it something that other people did. Let me tell you, it is overwhelming. Many thought my task would be as simple as dictating my thoughts into a tape recorder, having them transcribed, then published, and voilà!—a book. Not so. As is the case in everything I do, I became obsessed with doing the best I could, which meant writing the book, not just dictating it. My self-expectations are demanding, primarily because of the success I have found doing the radio show. I expect myself to do everything as well. But how, when you are doing something for the first time, such as writing a book? Well, you just do it, you persevere and WORK.

The payoff, as it always is, has been profound and rewarding. When sitting writing a book of 100,000-plus words, one must think. I am convinced that few people really do think, although they believe they do. Thinking is demanding and tiring. It is exercise for the mind, and for that reason alone writing this book has been invaluable. I thought my task would be to remember all the marvelous and wonderful things I had said in the past, organize them, and put them on paper. There was some of that, but what really propelled me was the discovery of things I had not thought of or realized before, new analogies, different ways to be persuasive on a point. Gathering my thoughts and compiling the data has been like a review course in life, with myself as the teacher. Who better, after all? It was a beautiful thing.

Now, having said all this, I realize that some of you will nevertheless be offended when you read certain parts of this surefire best-seller. Believe me when I say that my purpose is not to offend. In fact, it bothers me when someone is honestly offended because I don't consider myself an offensive guy. I am just a harmless, lovable little fuzzball.

So, take some advice. Lighten up. We should all laugh more at ourselves. I don't need to improve much in this area, but admit it, many of you people do. Many of you take things far too seriously in most cases. Come on, laugh at yourselves, folks. And if you can't laugh at yourself, turn these pages and laugh at me laughing for you.

GOING NATIONAL

So there I was, at KFBK, Sacramento, minding my own business and enjoying for the first time almost everything life had to offer. It was January 1988. I had lived in Sacramento just a little over three years and I was reflecting on how I had finally put it all together despite the vagaries of the broadcasting business. I was happy and content and had more good friends and more relevance to my life than ever before.

I had received inquiries from other radio stations around the country about working for them but none really excited me because I didn't want to move again and, for all intents and purposes, start over again. I was thirty-seven, and for the first time in my life I actively appreciated where I lived. I was no longer a passing personality but rather a functioning, practicing, and participating member of my community—aspects of life which were new to me. And I loved it all.

Now, let me introduce you to Bruce Marr. Bruce is a radio consultant who was in my corner from the first day we met at KFBK. Were it not for him I would probably have lost the battle (in my early days) over whether to have guests on my show. Bruce insisted to the management that I was one of the few hosts who didn't need guests. He became a sounding board for me. I sought his advice often, because I trusted him.

In mid-January I received a mysterious call from someone claiming to represent a prominent San Francisco family who was interested in syndicating my program nationally. I asked Bruce to meet with the person on the phone and determine if there was anything to it. He met with the guy and thought it was worth another meeting, which happened, but I rejected the idea because the group was just too ideologically driven. They wanted my program to be oriented toward saving the country from whatever commie-lib evils they thought existed, and, as I explain in detail in the chapter on show philosophy, this was a big red flag.

However, this little meeting proved to be a catalyst in my thinking. The old ambition, which was only slightly dormant, was awakened and I began talking with Bruce about the possibility of going national, which to me was the pinnacle. He said that if I was serious (which he thought I should be, since it was his opinion that I had what it took "to be a network guy"), he would mention me to some guy in New York who used to be with ABC. "If anybody can put this together," he said bravely, "this guy can."

Yeah, yeah.

So, I kept on enjoying life, which was getting even more interesting because the anniversary date of my contract was coming up. March 1, I think it was. Anyway, it would be the beginning of the third and final year. Basically, I could escape the contract with thirty days' notice should I accept an offer from a station in one of the Top 5 markets. For whatever reasons, and fortunately for me, the management at KFBK had other priorities and allowed the third year of the contract to begin as written, with no attempt to renegotiate or extend the deal. I say "fortunately" now, but at the time I was perplexed and a little angry at their attitude.

Toward the end of February, Bruce Marr told me that he had arranged a meeting in San Francisco with "the only guy who can put this deal together." I said, "What deal?"

"Whaddya mean, what deal?" He was incredulous. "Going national with your show!"

This was The Plan: we would drive to San Francisco in separate cars and have dinner with this Big Guy, then Bruce would leave and after dinner I would consume adult beverages with this Big Guy and attempt to show him just why I was worthy of national syndication.

The Big Guy was Ed McLaughlin, a broadcasting legend who had just retired as president of the ABC Radio Networks and who had started up his own entrepreneurial company syndicating the *Dr. Dean Edell* radio show. He was interested in expanding and, known to me, already knew much about me. KFBK had recently been sold by the local newspaper family in town to Group W, Westinghouse Broadcasting, and Ed was one of the many who had considered buying it. As such, he had visited Sacramento and listened to the station and heard me and—well, you can figure out the rest.

The upshot of all this is that Ed and I got on well and he laid out for me what had to occur in order for the project to come together, which I will get to in just a moment. First, he and I had to make a deal, which we did, but I must tell you it was one of the most agonizing things I ever endured. I always thought that when The Call, The Opportunity, came, I would be filled with total happiness and feelings of euphoria. I didn't. I was scared. Here I was, all content in Sacramento, now contemplating the biggest move I could make, and I had no idea whether I was making the right decision, demanding the right things, or agreeing to the right money. I had never used an agent and didn't feel confident starting then, so I agreed to the basics and my legal eagle brother, David, flew in and assembled the details of the contract and improved on what I had negotiated for myself. While it took you about fifteen seconds or so to read about this, it took us nearly three months to get it done, and I mean to tell you it was anything but fun.

I have to back up a bit here, because I have just raced by the anniversary date of March 1, and what happened there is somewhat critical because I had to escape the KFBK contract. In February, Ed had nothing firm to offer me because there were still a bunch of dominoes which had to fall in the right order. And Ed McLaughlin was the only person who could have done what indeed happened.

8

He asked me to sign an option contract which gave him the first right to my services from March 1 through the end of the year. Otherwise he couldn't proceed. This contract was presented to the KFBK management on March 1, 1988, and served to inform them that I intended to leave and would give them the required thirty days' notice. This did not sit well. But it was inevitable.

Now, here is what had to happen for this national show to get on the air. First, there was that little item in my contract which would allow me to leave only if I accepted an offer from a station in one of the Top 5 markets. This became Ed's responsibility, since he was the syndicator of the program. He first had to find a Top 5 market station to air the program, which was no easy feat since this was to be a national program, not a local one, and the Rule of All Rules in radio is that if a show is not local it is not wanted. The Local Local Local Problem, we called it. Unlike TV, radio stations want all local programming so that the issues are local, the callers are local, and the phone numbers are local. Most stations, but not all, *will* take national programs at night because there is much less at stake. Far fewer people listen to radio at night, so advertising rates are comparatively small to what can be charged during daytime programming, so it becomes cheaper to take a show off a satellite than to hire local hosts.

This would probably be a good time to interject just what a monumental challenge this was. We were planning to do what virtually everyone at any meaningful radio station in the country said was impossible: syndicate a controversial, issues-oriented program during the middle of the day. When I say that no one gave us a chance, I am not exaggerating. ABC Talk Radio had tried it with an impressive lineup of hosts, but all in all, it had never taken off. The key, however, was not that it had failed, but why it had failed, which will be explained shortly.

It so happened that ABC's noon–2 slot, then occupied by Owen Spann, was going to open up in August. Ed knew this and his plan was to get that time from ABC for our partnership, so that it would be ours, not ABC's, and put me in that slot. Which was fine and dandy, except that none of the fifty-six stations carrying ABC programming in that time slot were in the Top 5 markets.

This was a crucial moment in all this, for if Ed was unable to make the deal with ABC for the noon–2 slot, we didn't have a delivery system for the show. Ours was truly a small business. We had no studios of our own, we had no satellite time of our own, no sales force of our own to sell advertising, and no support staff of engineers and call screeners. This meant we had to originate from a station where all these elements were in place, and that station had to be in New York if we were to have any chance of succeeding. This was so for a number of reasons, but the main one was financial. It is just a fact that national advertisers and their agencies will not consider advertising in a show which is not aired in the nation's largest market, so we either had to be on the air in New York, or find a way to get our spots aired in New York.

Enter now WABC in New York, which was undergoing a change in philosophy and management just at that moment. As the flagship station of the entire company, they were carrying some of the programming offered by ABC Talk Radio and it wasn't working as well as they had hoped. They were in the process of dropping all network programming in favor of Local Local Local programming, and one of the time slots to become available was the 10 A.M.–noon slot.

Ed pitched me to the new management for the 10–noon slot. This was not a slam dunk, either, because those New Yorkers were unfazed and unimpressed with whatever success I'd had in Sacramento. Sacramento? What's that? But he pressed on. I met the WABC people, assured them I was not some hick off a pumpkin truck, and convinced them I had the urbanity and sophistication to be accepted in New York.

But let me tell you what really swung the deal. I must go back to the fact that Ed and I were a small company, and when forming the partnership I had no capital to invest. I had no money to speak of, so my contribution came in another way. The only way this was going to come together was for me to do two shows: the 10–noon show on WABC, which would be a Local Local Local show, and then the national show from noon–2, which WABC would not air. The kicker was that I did the WABC Local Local Local show for nothing, in one sense. Zero compensation. Looked at another way, however, I was compensated handsomely: WABC furnished, at no charge, the studio, engineers, telephones, and call screeners for both shows. They also agreed to air our national commercials in the 10–noon Local Local Local show, which meant we could promise New York to advertisers.

In all the days I had imagined what it would be like to finally hit the pinnacle and go national, I never even conceived of anything like this. But I also didn't imagine I would be a partner in the show, rather than an employee. I knew, for the first time, what being a small businessman was really all about.

As I look back on it, and I do quite often, I am more and more amazed that it actually happened. But fate is a strange thing, and so is luck. Because this is the only way we could have succeeded to the degree we have. And what we have done is basically to revive AM radio from the dead, so our success is profound.

Let me go back to why ABC Talk Radio wasn't working. They were offering an entire day's lineup of programming, asking, in essence, that stations take not one program but four or five. Now, when meaningful stations in large markets aren't keen on taking any syndicated programming, why on earth would anyone think they would take a whole day's worth? ABC had figured this out and was in the process of divesting themselves of the whole daytime talk network, although this was not known publicly at the time we were starting up. This is why they made the deal with Ed to give us the noon–2 slot for my show. We used the ABC sales department to sell our commercials and they earned a commission on all sales, so they still had a financial stake in the slot.

I began the WABC local show on July 4, the day after the United States gunned down an Iranian civilian jetliner in the Persian Gulf. So I had an automatic issue to talk about.

On August 1, the EIB (Excellence in Broadcasting) Network premiered with its fifty-six radio stations and a total audience of 250,000 people, of whom over half came from WABC. (We counted the audience from the WABC Local Local Local show since I was the host and since our national commercials aired in it.) Eventually we were able to ease out of the New York Local Local Local show, which was a relief and a major accomplishment. In truth, I soon resented having to do two shows,

11

especially since my focus was on the national show. That, after all, was why I had made the move in the first place.

Later, after the show gained popularity, we were able to expand it to three hours. A surprising number of our affiliates went along with our change very quickly and agreed to take our third hour. This was much easier said than done, because all of them had existing shows of one kind or another during that hour and we had to convince them that it was in their financial best interests to carry our third hour. Because revenue is derived from selling advertising, our revenue potential immediately expanded by fifty percent because we had fifty percent more inventory (time) to sell.

New York is a TOUGH market for radio. Before I came to New York, I had only been there once, for three days on a business trip. I didn't know what to expect from working there. I always thought that when you went to the New York market you had earned it. The mere fact that I had broken into the nation's largest market would somehow mean I would be treated as something special. I have never been more wrong in my life.

The fact that I had been king of the hill in Sacramento was as irrelevant to everybody in New York as the color of my shoes. It wasn't just the audience that wasn't at all interested in who I was. Newspaper stories appeared predicting that of all the guys appearing on WABC, I was the least likely to succeed.

One of my major problems with the New York audience was that I am not argumentative. And life in New York is one long argument. You get in a cab, and you don't just tell the guy where you're going, you have to argue with him about the route. The level of aggression in this city was something I'd never experienced before.

My first day on the air in New York, I began with a monologue on the day's headlines and then opened up the phones to callers. But no one responded to what I had just said. They would talk about something they'd heard on some other show the previous day or even months ago. They called to make speeches. They called to yell and taunt me into losing my cool.

This went on for at least three months and caused me to experience serious doubts about my ability to hit that pinnacle I have referred to here. I was pouring my heart and soul into the

Local Local Local show but still there was no response of any substance. New Yorkers are, despite what you may think of them, highly sophisticated in several ways, one of which is their awareness of their importance as the nation's Number 1 market. They are acutely aware that they can make or break people in entertainment and they require you to prove your worthiness.

But back to the nature of the callers. I do not engage in combat radio. There is no confrontation, no conflict between myself and the callers, yet that is what most callers on WABC expected and seemed even to want. I was just a guy trying to have fun on the radio and instead I was listening to callers telling me how cheap and no good I was and why I should go back to where I came from. This was not a beautiful thing.

Only later did I realize that this was due to the power of Bob Grant, the king of talk radio in New York City since the early 1970s. Before WABC changed philosophy and hired all local hosts, Bob's was the only local show, and it was the only show that had any audience. A Number 1 audience. He is WABC. Bob Grant is a pioneer. He is one of the few talk show hosts who has lasted in combat radio. He defined it and spawned countless imitators all over the country. Nobody does it better than he does and his ratings are proof. He *is* New York and the Tri-State area, both in manner and approach. If New York is an argument, and it is, then Bob Grant's show is New York every day. And he's been doing it for twenty years, the last seven at WABC. It stood to reason then that anyone calling a WABC talk show would expect to get involved in a brouhaha. They were just so conditioned by the omnipresence of Bob Grant that it was going to take a while for me or anyone else even to be noticed, much less to be accorded any respect and individual identity.

New York represented a real challenge for me. Don't get the idea I didn't like the city. I fell in love with New York the very first day. The physical and geographical adjustment was one of the easiest in my life. I love not having to drive and park a car. I love being able to get things delivered to the door. I love the restaurants and the cultural life. My problem was adjusting psychologically to New York. I had been a big deal in Sacramento. You could say I was a huge whale in a sauna. I came to New York and I immediately became a nothing, a zero. I wasn't a viable host. I didn't even exist. This was tough because I had been under the impression that a move to New York meant precisely that I had become somebody. It seemed that nothing I had accomplished meant anything. It was also tough coming from a town where I had just begun to enjoy life more than I ever had. Now, none of the ingredients in that recipe for happiness were in my life. I had just kissed them off for the proverbial Shot At The Big Time. Many times I thought I was going to fail.

There was one moment I'll never forget. I was beginning to get a lot of press in the small markets that comprised the original fifty-six. John Mainelli, the WABC program director, would post on the bulletin board all newspaper stories about me and the show published in these markets. One of the first was a huge story from Lancaster, Pennsylvania. A couple of days after it was posted, the general manager of WABC walked by my desk and said to me: "You think this impresses me? So, you're a big guy in Lancaster. Big deal. Well, what do you want, to be a big guy in Lancaster or a big guy in New York, because you can't do both. You're kidding yourself if you think we'll ever carry your national show here. I don't give a hoot what they think in Lancaster and neither does anyone else in New York. You better figure it out because you can't do both." A beautiful thing.

I led a completely bifurcated existence. The ratings for the New York Local Local Local show were good, but I had no feedback to tell me I was connecting with listeners. There were just some numbers on a piece of paper. But I stuck with the Local Local Local show. Life is full of things you would rather not do. But you have to do them, and you often come out stronger as a result. What made the local show bearable was that things were looking up elsewhere.

Within three months we had a hundred stations on the national show. Naturally, someone with my awesome talent and bravado was bound to bowl people over in cities that had never had a high-powered talk show host. The problem was that many of these stations had managers who became very nervous whenever somebody complained about my show.

I remember a station in South Bend, Indiana, that was being besieged with phone calls attacking me. "TAKE THIS GUY OFF THE AIR. I'M NEVER LISTENING AGAIN," was among the

14

more polite messages they were getting. In South Bend, they weren't used to getting those kinds of calls. So the station called and said they couldn't handle it. They were taking my show off the air.

I jumped into action. I didn't care if it was only South Bend, Indiana; this program was not going to lose radio stations. I couldn't let word get out that radio stations were dropping the show after a few weeks. I had to convince the station that they were hearing from an unrepresentative sample. What they were hearing wasn't surprising. If you buy a car and you don't like it, what do you do? You call the dealer and demand he do something about it. If you like the car you buy, what do you do? You drive it. You don't call and tell them how much you enjoy driving it.

I went on the air the day after the South Bend station told us they were going to pull the program. "Ladies and gentlemen in the South Bend area," I began. "A concerted effort to censor this show has begun. As we speak, a few angry liberals, precious guarantors of the First Amendment that they claim to be, are calling the station demanding that this show be taken off the air. They're claiming to represent huge numbers of people, far more than they actually are. If you love this show—and you know you do—you must let the station know. Otherwise, we will be canceled and you will have to drive to Fort Wayne to hear the program." Well, not only was the South Bend station swamped with calls from South Bend, they were getting them from all over the Fruited Plain. The station kept me on.

I took that same approach with a number of stations. Manchester, New Hampshire, was one. In Santa Barbara, California, a different tack was necessary. In late 1988, the station in Santa Barbara was going through its usual Christmas sales promotions. They would get local advertisers to buy spots in which the store would wish listeners the best of the holiday season. One of the places that was going to buy some spots that year was a rib joint named Woodie's Barbecue. Then I happened to mention the word *feminazi* on my program for the first time.

Woodie immediately called the station and told them he would never buy any ads on a station that allowed someone to use the term *feminazi*. The station called us. They weren't mad, they were just amused. "Wait a minute, this isn't funny," I said. "I'm not here to lose advertisers. We are here to build advertisers and make their advertising work. This will not happen. I don't care if it's just a two-hundred-fifty-dollar order. I'm going to do something about this."

The next Monday I went on the air and said, "Ladies and gentlemen, I was informed last Friday that Woodie's Barbecue in Santa Barbara, California, has decided to drop its Christmas advertising plan with its local station because I have used the term *feminazi*. Now, there are two ways I could deal with this. I could cry about it and I could shout about how unfair it is for Woodie to do this. Then I could petition the government to make up the two hundred fifty dollars that the radio station will lose because Woodie is being unfair. Or . . . I could approach this the conservative way. I could face it squarely like a man and fix it.

"Obviously, I've chosen the second option. This is what I would like you to do. If you have plans to go to lunch or dinner this week, go to Woodie's Barbecue. I understand Woodie's food is great, and we need to show him that he's making a mistake by not being part of the EIB Network revolution. Do me a favor, and tell him why you're there. Let's make it our goal that Woodie runs out of food by this Thursday."

Well, people flocked in, as I knew they would. He was laughing about it, and he even ran an unauthorized ad in the newspaper which said I had endorsed his place. I knew that trouble like this, if it spread, would doom our effort because we had so many strikes against us being a network (not a Local Local Local) show.

I share all this with you for many reasons. I am proud— extremely proud—of the accomplishments. They are significant. There were obstacles that we really hadn't anticipated and we hurdled them. We did what all the experts said couldn't be done. Mostly, I am grateful to both Bruce Marr and Ed McLaughlin, without whom the unique circumstances which made this possible would not have existed. The real risk taker was Ed. He put money into this, whereas I didn't. If it failed, he was out the money and perhaps some of his reputation. I had comparatively little risk because this wasn't supposed to work anyway. If it failed, the least I could do was return to the home of my single greatest happiness, having given it my best shot.

But the best thing of all to have happened in all this is that my father was able to realize he had not failed as a parent before he passed away. From the moment in 1970 that I announced I was quitting college and moving to Pittsburgh to be a DJ he was convinced I would not have the tools and education to prosper as he so hoped I would. He was never confident that his influence, presence, and love were all I really needed, which I guess is natural for all parents to feel.

Because of failing health he never heard me host a talk show until 1989, when my national show was picked up by KZIM in our hometown of Cape Girardeau. He died on December 8, 1990. It wasn't until the final year of his life that I was able to convince him I was going to do just fine. I think *the* moment came during my first appearance on ABC's *Nightline* on November 8, 1990. There I was on national television discussing the deployment of troops to the Persian Gulf with Ted Koppel and syndicated columnist Mark Shields. No jokes (Dad didn't see anything funny about politics and always thought I was distracting from my true abilities when I ventured into irreverence), just serious discussion of the issues. My mother told me the next day what his reaction was.

"He just turned and stared at me and said, 'Millie, where did he learn all that? Where did he get it from?' He was just so proud, Rusty. I wish you could have seen his smile."

Well, I learned it from you, Dad. I got it from you. I'm just so happy you finally realized it.

MY SUCCESS IS NOT
DETERMINED BY WHO WINS
ELECTIONS

DURING THE SPRING OF 1986, WHILE STILL WORKING FOR KFBK IN Sacramento, I did my program for a week from the ABC studios in Washington, the only time since 1984 I have had guests on my show. One of the people I interviewed was George Will, the syndicated columnist, one of the many people who unknowingly provided me guidance and inspiration to better myself.

I was in awe and asked him a question which conveyed my feelings. I asked him if he ever took time late at night, after the family had retired, to turn out the lights and sit down with an adult beverage and just contemplate what he had become to people, to dwell on what his life and work meant to so many. He immediately got impatient and said no. I queried further because I couldn't believe that someone as widely read and quoted as he was didn't pause occasionally to ponder and take some sense of satisfaction, some pleasure from it. He steadfastly maintained with increasing frustration that I was way off target. He wasn't rude or impolite, just insistent. I continued to probe the point and he finally said, "Look. I have a job. I don't have time to sit around and think about how good I am at it. I was lucky. I had good parents who made me read books. I use my talent, I use my skill. I just do it."

The interview concluded and I still didn't believe him. It seemed to me unbelievable that someone so profoundly successful didn't take time to savor it or even be aware of it. Today, however, I know exactly what he meant.

For most people, success does not occur overnight. Rather, it builds slowly and there are many times along the way where some actually lose ground. For most successful people, achievement is the result of intense, dedicated hard work and there is often little if any surprise or amazement associated with it. It becomes a matter of fact. It is. Life goes on within that context. Indeed, success breeds new opportunities for success which must be concentrated on. I always considered my career like a football field. Each new success meant I had gained so many yards, with the final achievement represented by gaining all 100 yards and scoring a touchdown. This is not so. You know what happens? The field gets bigger. There are more yards to gain and touchdowns to score. Ambition and drive keep the successful person focused on what's ahead, not on what has happened.

It has always puzzled me that so many people want to know *why* my radio program is a success. In all candor, why is no big deal to me. I just accept the fact that it is and concentrate on improving it, which means maintaining an environment and atmosphere where I can be myself.

Practically from the beginning I have been asked by reporters to explain the show's success. I never thought about why and in truth I was afraid of finding out. My fear was that the discovery would cause me to become a caricature of myself; that is, I would try to be myself rather than just be myself.

My big break in life and in business came in 1984 in Sacramento. This was the first time in seventeen years—seventeen years! —that I was allowed to be myself. So simple, yet so crucial, and I have learned much from this realization. I was no different a person in 1984 than on all those other occasions I had been fired. Oh, I was a little older and more mature, but my personality, sense of humor, and philosophy about doing a radio program were the same. The difference was that for the first time in my career I wasn't doing it someone else's way. Folks, you will never be your best doing it someone else's way, particularly if you utilize talent, as opposed to learned skills. I am convinced that you have absolutely no idea how good you can be—at whatever you want to do. You don't know because you are trapped in situations where you either can't or are afraid to be yourself.

It took me a little while to figure this out. It didn't occur to me in a flash. Only when I began to try to answer the incessant question of why the program was successful did I stumble onto the real reason. In truth, there are many reasons why the show is hot, and I will touch on them in this chapter, but the key, again, was getting the chance to be myself.

I have always viewed radio as an entertainment medium, part of show biz. One of the early reasons radio interested me was that I thought it would make me popular. I wanted to be noticed and liked. Consequently, many of my initial years on the radio were spent pursuing the dream of stardom. The business aspects of radio couldn't have been less interesting to me, and I often wonder if I might have found success sooner had I learned early on that radio stations didn't exist in order to gratify my ego.

When I sat down in the summer of 1988 to plot the success track of my show as it went national, I never gave any consideration or weight to my political and social views. Honestly. I thought I would have to be the best entertainer I could be.

I never imagined my show would prosper in large part because I was a conservative. In fact, I always thought that my politics would be irrelevant to the success of the show. I just thought I had to do great shows, and I never associated political views with greatness in show business. As an example, name one great entertainer who is great in large part because of his or her politics, other than me. Heh, heh, heh. I didn't think you could. Remember, entertainment is not the breeding ground for successful politicians or commentators.

Well, guess what. I was terribly, terribly wrong. From the day the show began on August 1, 1988, it was obvious to all of us at the EIB Network that something we hadn't anticipated was going on. People were going crazy over this show, primarily because of my political point of view. As it turns out, I had underestimated just how liberal many people consider the dominant media culture in America to be. Here, finally, was someone on the radio saying what they felt, what they said to their friends and family. They were rejoicing, to be blunt. But that wasn't all. The audience thought this was some of the best entertainment they had heard on radio in a long time, particularly from a conservative. Frankly, I have always been perplexed by this notion that conservatives aren't funny. The fact is that there aren't too many funny liberals out there, save for most comedians. Most liberals are too busy mired in misery and hand-wringing and doing what they can to spread it.

So, there it was, this unique blend of humor, irreverence, and the serious discussion of events with a conservative slant. Nowhere else in the media today will you find all these ingredients in one presentation. I would love to tell you that this was the result of a brilliantly conceived and flawlessly executed strategy, but it wasn't. It was just me being myself. I like to have fun, I like being irreverent, and I am dead serious about the things I feel passionately.

The show has evolved but remains structurally and philosophically the same. The show is devoted exclusively to what I think. I do not attempt to find out what the people of the country are thinking. It is the height of presumptuousness for anyone hosting a radio show to think he or she can discover what the people who live in their neighborhood, city, or country think by virtue of what happens on their show.

People often confuse the role that callers play in a great talk show. The primary purpose of callers on my show is to make *me* look good, not to allow a forum for the public to make speeches. I, after all, am the reason people listen, because I have taken the risk of setting my show up that way. When I decide to turn over some of the responsibility for audience acquisition and maintenance to a caller, I must be confident that the caller can accomplish it, or that there is enough there to permit me to save the day should the caller bomb. This is crucial, folks. Two minutes of a boring caller is the same as playing a song nobody likes. What do you do when a song you don't like is played? You go looking for a song you do like.

Callers are not allowed to read someone else's opinion, or even their own. They must be passionate or interesting enough to hold the audience. If they are judged unable to accomplish this, they are politely refused permission to go on the air. Now this may sound cruel and heartless, but it is not. Remember, this is a business, not some boring public service foray. I must attract an audience, not send them off to other stations. The maximum number of people from the audience that will even attempt to call a talk show is 1 or 2 percent, which means that 98 percent are listening. It is to them that the program must be directed. Caller-driven shows, by definition, are aimed at such a small percentage of the audience that even if you please them all, you fail.

The attitude I take with me into the studio each day is crucial to the success of my excursions into broadcast excellence. I do not look upon my show as a chance to advance an agenda. I do not view it as an opportunity to register more Republican voters or to expand the number of conservatives in the country. I don't view my radio show as a forum for conservative activism of any kind. I walk into the EIB studios and sit down behind that golden EIB microphone every day at noon wanting to do the best damn radio show I can do. When it is over I want people to say, "Wow, that was a great show!" And I want them to be back listening the next day, and the day after that. Forever. I want them listening to all three hours every day. Remember this above all else: My success is not determined by who wins elections, my success is determined by how many listeners I have.

It is imperative you not misunderstand this, however. You might be wondering if this means that I don't really care about my beliefs, that I am simply using them to attract like-minded people. Wrong-o. To the contrary, they are my heart and soul, the essence of my being, and I never betray them or misrepresent them in the pursuit of audience, other than when I am doing satire and parody. I will admit that as the show has evolved I have become aware of the increasing importance of my views in acquiring and holding the audience, and it is for this reason that I present my views with the utmost responsibility and sincerity. I am quite aware that millions of people invest their trust in my honesty, and I will not ever be cavalier about that. Still, I am first a broadcaster, bound by the dictates and requirements of broadcasting, as I take to the air each day. The important thing to remember is that I also have the freedom to be myself, which means that sharing my passions and beliefs, as well as my commentary on events, is a very close second on the list of reasons why I choose to be on radio and TV.

I also do not believe I should use my show for activism. It is, after all else, still entertainment. I want it to be that way. I don't go out and adopt campaigns and hype them. I am not into demonstrating my influence in politics. I certainly don't try to stir up emotions among my audience. Contrary to the fears of many in the mainstream media who I think are actually jealous that they don't have the impact they wish they had, radio talk show hosts cannot and do not invent public emotion.

Take the congressional pay-raise fight of 1989. Early that year Congress tried to raise its own pay without actually voting on the issue, by attaching it as an inconspicuous rider to another piece of legislation. This outraged the public, and a *caller* (not a host) to a Detroit radio show suggested that voters send in tea bags to their members of Congress to recreate the Boston Tea Party. The idea spread throughout the country and tea bags poured in. People didn't need to be told by radio talk show hosts that they should be mad about this—they already were. Congress backed down from the pay raise, but only for ten months. By November of 1989 they had passed the raise in the dead of night, and talk radio hosts weren't able to stop it.

Once in a great while an issue will come up that I feel strongly about and I decide to get involved. The House Bank was one of those. Here was a group of people in Congress who had arrogantly abused privileges no one else in America had. I resolved to press for the release of all the names of those who kited checks at the House Bank. It so happened that the public was already energized on the issue and the House leadership finally caved in and released the names. *Newsweek* magazine later said in its Conventional Wisdom box that, although I was a blowhard, I had forced the House to its knees on the Bank scandal. Nonsense. The American people did that, I just helped amplify their outrage.

I am amused when opponents refer to me as "The Most Dangerous Man in America." I like that so much I have stolen it from them and now use it myself. Why am I dangerous? Simple.

Because I am right and because I am having fun being right. Liberals are convinced I'm creating a cadre of robots out there who don't think for themselves, when in fact it's the exact opposite. As I've discussed elsewhere, liberals don't believe people are capable of thinking for themselves. They therefore assume I have this Svengali-like hold over my audience's thoughts and point hysterically to the fact that I assure my audience that if they listen to me every day, they will no longer need to read newspapers or watch TV.

On Fridays, I remind my audience that the weekend is coming. "The weekend is upon us, folks, so head on into it with abandon. Relax and forget everything and have a great time. I will stay informed for you. I will devote my weekend to keeping track of all relevant events so that you won't have to. On Monday, if you're here, I'll tell you not only what happened over the weekend that was of any importance but, as an added bonus, I'll tell you what to think about it as well." This parody of what elite liberals in the media do, without admitting it, drives the left-wingers nuts. For it is they, you see, because they think people are such dimwitted fools, who feel it necessary to spoon-feed them with the proper versions and details of events, all the while denying that they do it.

All this having been said, I must now admit something. As my and the program's political relevance expanded I became enamored of putting it to use. The question was how, since I refuse to use the entertainment forum of my radio show to advance agendas or causes. Well, I thought about it for quite a while because it would be a major step to take, and one which could be greatly misunderstood and perhaps even harm the image of the radio show if it was not executed properly.

THE NATIONAL CONSERVATIVE FORUM

Ultimately, I decided that if I was going to get involved in issues and agendas, it would have to be outside the radio show. And that is how the National Conservative Forum was born—as a means of putting that idea to work. The first meeting—and I hope there will be many more—was held in Long Beach,

California, on July 27, 1991. It was an all-day affair. The morning consisted of thirty-minute speeches by invited participants, and the afternoon session was a roundtable discussion among all of us. The speakers were former Secretary of Education Bill Bennett, General Thomas Kelly, Brent Bozell of the Media Research Center, Gary Bauer of the Family Research Center, nationally syndicated columnist Mona Charen, and Judge Robert Bork. For the roundtable in the afternoon, we added Congressman Bob Dornan, since we were doing this in his district.

This was done under the auspices of the Rush Limbaugh Institute for Advanced Conservative Studies, our in-house think tank of the EIB Network. The discussions were based, of course, on the current issues of that time. In the morning session, Judge Bork spoke about his confirmation process and his views on *Roe v. Wade.* Bauer addressed the issues of family; Bennett dealt with culture, education, and drugs; Charen spoke about being a conservative woman in light of the feminist movement. Bozell did a tremendous job of detailing the media bias that conservatives are up against.

This event cost a lot of money; one of the things we want to do in the future is bring down the cost. I paid the speakers whatever fee they asked, as well as their travel expenses and hotel accommodations and limousine service. But I never would have asked them to do it for nothing. These are people whose time is valuable, and speech making is one of the ways in which they make a living. And I'd rather be straightforward about it: I didn't want them to owe me anything when it was over, and I didn't want to owe them anything. I certainly wasn't going to ask them for any favors, especially since we were flying blind—this was our first one, and we didn't know how many people would show up.

People said to me: "Rush, you could have done that on the air, you could have had the same discussion and it wouldn't have cost you a penny." Of course I could have. But the point is, Bill Bennett and Robert Bork and Bob Dornan and Mona Charen and all the rest are always seen on television, always heard on the radio, and almost never seen in person. People who would like to get to know them never get a chance to do that. When they give speeches or lectures, it's mostly at think tanks or on university campuses. The main idea of the Forum was to bring these people to the average American, the average American voter out there.

In the morning session, some of the speeches went as long as thirty-five or forty minutes, and not one person in the audience left. This was one of the most dynamic, satisfying days in my life—being around these mostly young, affluent people who were listening with such rapt attention. Since we had such a large audience, we had video screens set up so that people could get close-up views. We also had a director and two or three cameras filming the proceedings at different angles, so that we now have a videocassette of the event, which we sell.

In the roundtable discussion after lunch, we talked about the Clarence Thomas nomination and some of the issues in California politics related to Pete Wilson's governorship, which had just started at the time. We also had quite a robust discussion on blacks and the conservative movement, and we lamented the fact that there wasn't more black participation in the conservative wing of the Republican party. I quoted that wonderful saying Jack Kemp has: Conservatives define compassion not by the number of people who receive some kind of government aid but rather by the number of people who no longer need it.

We also praised Kemp as the one member of the Bush administration who has actually made an effort to go into the inner city and look for people to whom he could talk about getting the conservative message out to these people. Because I cringe, as all of us do, at the constant accusations that we conservatives are fascist, racist, selfish, that we've got ours and we don't want anybody else to get a fair shake.

We do not believe that the American economy is a zero-sum game—in other words, if I have more, that means someone else will have less. What we said in that forum is that we believe in a growing pie. Just because I have a certain slice of the pie or you have a certain slice of the pie does not exclude anybody else from it by design. Unfortunately, the opposite view is held by many people in the West today. They do think it is a zero-sum game, that there's only so much to go around and that it has to be shared more fairly. They do not comprehend expanding wealth or creating wealth; they view it as limited and finite and want to redistribute it. It pains us greatly when we are not able to get the message across that the great prosperity so many people in this country enjoy is available to everybody—if you are just taught how to avail yourself of it, how to believe in yourself, how to be self-sufficient, and how to escape government dependency.

As we were discussing all this, and trying to come up with ways to get the message out more effectively, there was suddenly a burst of applause from the audience. We couldn't see what was going on because we were on the stage at a giant conference table, with the television klieg lights in our faces. So I got up and walked to the front of the stage to take a look. Nine or ten black couples were standing up, saying: We're here, we're the kind of people you're looking for. And they were getting a standing ovation from all the people around them. It was incredibly heartwarming. If you talk to any of those black men and women, or anyone who was at that forum and heard the discussion about conservatism and black America, none of them will tell you that conservatives want to exclude people from prosperity.

It is simply exasperating that this notion has been allowed to take hold of people's minds in so many parts of the country. The liberals, you see, do not want to confront conservative ideas; they just attack conservatives as a group, and particularly their motives. If you believe what they say about us, you would think that if someone like Bill Bennett, or Jack Kemp, or myself were driving through South Central Los Angeles and looking at the slums and the poverty, we would go: Oh, man, this is great— they've got nothing, so that means we get more. It's simply preposterous. We all want to live in a great country. And for the country to fulfill its potential, you need individuals to be the best they can be—not the government taking care of people.

Anyone who attended the National Conservative Forum could not fail to get this message. This is one example of how I am trying to involve myself in the conservative movement outside the arena of my show. The other reason I did not want to engage in this on the air—although I have no doubt that it would have been interesting—is that it would have typecast the show as an instrument of conservative politics, and it would have made the show a political target.

Admittedly, my primary purpose with my talk program is to service the requirements necessary for success in radio. As I have stated elsewhere, the show must always come first. Therefore, my first task is to entertain, to provide a reason for as *many people as possible*, not just conservatives, to listen to my program. However, this is not to disparage or downplay the significance of my conservative beliefs or their importance to the success of my program.

My theory is that by interweaving a conservative message with an entertaining, innovative radio program, I can make a greater impact on people and demonstrate by example a human side to conservatism. I can help prove that the human attribute we refer to as a sense of humor is not unique to liberals, and can hopefully help make conservatism palatable to many who heretofore have rejected it as a callous political philosophy which is without compassion.

Please do not misunderstand me. There is no hypocrisy involved here. I am talking only of presentation and technique, not of substantive issues. On my program, I unequivocally assert my conservative views. I state my beliefs with conviction and I don't mislead or deceive my audience in order to gain a greater market share.

Make no mistake that I attribute my success in great measure to the reality that mainstream Americans are in fact conservative. They are crying out for a media voice—someone to consistently articulate their beliefs and defend their unabashed patriotism and loyalty to American tradition.

Just because I do not perceive my radio program as the proper forum to "change the world" does not mean that I am unwilling to directly contribute to the cause of restoring traditional American values into the mainstream of our society.

That is why I inaugurated the Conservative Forum—to provide an opportunity for like-minded individuals to congregate and to exchange ideas among themselves and with the leaders of the conservative movement, with a view toward restating and reaffirming our American traditions.

PEOPLE: THINK FOR YOURSELVES
OR
DEMONSTRATING ABSURDITY
BY BEING ABSURD

I HAVE ALWAYS BEEN CONCERNED THAT TOO MANY PEOPLE ARE credulous, too willing to accept all of the propaganda that is showered on them daily by the media and politicians. That's why I try to provoke my audience into thinking for themselves, and not blindly accepting all they are spoon-fed by the media, myself included. How do I do this? Psychologically. Each Friday I urge people to pursue their weekend with reckless abandon, and not to worry about keeping up with the news, because I will do it for them. They need only tune in to my show on Monday and I will tell them about any important events which took place over the weekend and, as a bonus, will also tell them what to think.

This bewilders and confuses my critics, who shriek and moan that I am attempting to take over the country and poison people's minds. Nope. That is what *they* do, with their political correctness and dominance of the media. My little offer to think for people motivates them to do just the opposite: to think for themselves. Kind of like Ross Perot saying he never wanted the presidency, that he wouldn't give three cents for the job. We all know what happened. Millions of people literally begged him to run . . . just as he had planned. See how it works? In fact, I want people to think for themselves and not believe everything they hear or read . . . except what I say or write.

As I've said elsewhere in this book, I often illustrate my points with real-life examples; stated another way, I like to demonstrate the absurd by being absurd. One vehicle I use sometimes to demonstrate the absurd is the Update feature of my show. Other times I demonstrate the absurd through my monologue or in bits I do on the show.

THE RUSH UPDATES

A lot of people have wondered where the Updates on my show originated. In the Update feature of my show, I share with the audience an item from the news on any one of a variety of cultural and political topics. Each Update is introduced by an Update theme which I have chosen for that particular topic. Often, but not always, the Updates are satirical in nature. There are Updates on The Homeless, Animal Rights, Feminazis, Governor Mario Cuomo, Condoms, Victims, and several other topics.

The Updates were born six months after I began hosting my radio show in Sacramento in 1985. Six hundred sons and daughters of rich Democrats were going to march from Los Angeles to Washington in what was billed the Great Peace March for Global Nuclear Disarmament. Because I felt that the peace movement was inherently anti-U.S., yet was reported as substantive and morally correct by a willing and sympathetic media, I determined that I wanted to comment on it each day, to be persuasive and passionate about my views. For some reason, I just decided off the top of my head to introduce each day's commentary with a hokey peace song. I remembered seeing and laughing at Slim Whitman's vocal portrayal of "Una Paloma Blanca" in one of those irritating, two-minute TV commercials offering Slim's Greatest Hits on the pan flute. Music to use your Ginsu knife by. I found the tune, mixed some bomb sound effects in with it just to tweak any long-haired, maggot-infested, dope-smoking peace pansies who might hear it. And voilà! The Peace Update was born.

The Way Things Ought to Be

Well, after about six weeks I heard that an Ohio minister had called a news conference. He said that he had found a satanic message in the theme from the TV show *Mister Ed*. He wanted that theme banned because it was poisoning the minds of America's youth. When asked what was satanic about the Mister Ed theme, this minister claimed that when you played it backwards on a turntable, the part that goes, "A horse is a horse, of course, of course," turned into "s-s-s-satan, s-s-s-s-satan."

I thought this was too good to pass up, and I resolved to find a satanic message in "Una Paloma Blanca," that song of peace, hope, and charity I'd been playing. The next morning, a Tuesday, I told my listeners that I came before them that day with a heavy heart. I told them that I had tried to be righteous, honest, and truthful. I had never knowingly led them down the wrong path. But I had to confess that I had now been unwittingly co-opted by, yeo, EEVIL.

Friends, I said, I don't know if I can continue as your host. I have subjected you to an unspeakable abomination. I have poisoned this program, but I cannot tell you exactly how. It's buried in the song "Una Paloma Blanca." Even if I rid this show of this evil, can I ever in the eyes of God be truthful and honest with you again? If I didn't know this time that I was co-opted by evil, it might happen again. I told my audience that I expected to resign from the program by the end of the week.

I went into a break, then opened the phones. My call screener came out and asked me how long I was going to go on with this gag. He said callers were taking it seriously, saying that I must have been spreading devil worship and that I hadn't been fair to them. They all wanted to know what I had done. He urged me to fess up to the joke before Friday.

I waited two days, until Thursday. Then I went on the air and said that the demands of listeners to know the evil I had subjected them to were overwhelming. Ladies and gentlemen, I suggest that those of you who are weak in your faith not listen. Turn to another station. It will be at least five minutes before you can tune back in, then it will be okay. But I warn you, if you listen to this and your faith is weak, I won't accept responsibility.

I then played Slim Whitman's song. Backwards. The devil himself was lurking in the record grooves. "Tell me, where did

31

you get a turntable that plays backwards like this?" the devil's voice asked. "My disciples and I have been waiting for this for years. We can only find them in ministers' homes and we don't like going there very much. Well, I promise I'll never forget you now that I've found you. Good to know you. We'll be talking again." The music faded away into silence. The phones were going crazy. My sides were splitting with laughter. By absurd parody, I had illustrated the folly of the Ohio minister's claims.

The first call came in. A woman. "Rush, don't you know what you've done? Rush, you've been saved. You've exorcised the devil. God spoke to you, Rush. Don't resign. You've been saved." I stopped the call, and asked the call screener if there were more people like that on the phone. She said all six lines were filled with them.

The next caller said, "Rush, Rush, I have every one of Slim Whitman's records. Should I burn them?" I told him, yes.

The funniest call that came in was from Rio Linda, the benighted armpit of Sacramento. This guy called in from his front porch. He had been listening to me ever since I came to Sacramento, and he hated me. He had been waiting to prove me wrong for months. He was convinced that I was a hypocrite, a liar, and a phony. Now he had his evidence. "Hey, I don't believe this crap you've been saying about Slim Whitman," he began. I asked him how he could say that, seeing that I had gone through torture for a whole week over it. "I don't believe any of it. You can't fool me. You think we're all stupid out here." I politely told him that I had risked my career to inform him of what had been happening with the record. He interrupted me. "Listen, pal, you're not dealing with idiots out here. I have that record. You understand? I have it. And my turntable don't play backwards, but I ain't no fool. I just put that needle on the end of the record and spun it backwards. There ain't no message in that song. What do you got to say to that?" By this time I was laughing so hard I had to turn off the mike. I took a deep breath, put the caller on again, and asked him what year his turntable had been made. "What do you mean, you're just trying to weasel out of it." I told him no, and repeated the question. He said it was 1979 or 1980.

"Ah, that's the problem," I said. "You see, turntables made

before 1983 don't have the disgronificator." "What the hell is this disgronificator?" my Rio Linda caller asked. "It's new laser technology, sir. It expands the dynamic range and allows you to clip the high end of the trebles and the low end of the bass, and expands the midrange where the satanic message is located. You can only hear it on a new turntable." "You mean to tell me that if I went and bought a turntable made after 1983, I could spin that record backwards and hear that message. Is that what you're saying?" I told him that he should ask for the disgronificator circuitry and if the turntable had it he would be able to hear the devil's message. He said he would try asking for one.

By this time I had lost my composure. I forgot to tell him to go down to the local Philco electronics store, where they could make him a special deal. I would then have known whether he actually tried to buy one. I would love to have known if he really fell for the joke.

A year later we repeated the whole bit, only this time we were honest about the gag. We told them exactly how the joke worked. Even then many people believed it, and I had to reassure several callers that the devil had not taken over the Rush Limbaugh show.

So, that was the auspicious beginning of my Updates, which have now expanded to cover a multitude of topics I consider worthy of comment, lampooning, or observation. The Updates rarely grow into the type of episode I just described, but they are all intended to make a point about a political or cultural topic that is newsworthy at the time.

WHAT TO DO WITH UGLO-AMERICANS

I first suggested that we do something about Uglo-Americans back when I was doing radio in Kansas City. There, the Country Club Plaza wanted to go upscale, and as the leases of places like Woolworth's and the local bowling alley expired, they weren't renewed. In their place came stores like Saks Fifth Avenue. The management was obviously not interested in having average people around, so I suggested they ban Uglo-American people from the shopping center. You can imagine how this idea was received. When I got to Sacramento, I noticed how conscious many people were about their physical appearance. I decided that California's narcissistic environment was the perfect place to reintroduce my anti–Uglo-American campaign.

I told my audience on KFBK in Sacramento that there are Uglo-American people everywhere.

These are not just people of average ugliness, mind you. We're talking shocking, revolting, vile ugliness. It's everywhere, though you can find Uglo-Americans most often in bowling alleys.

Uglo-Americans tend to hang around together. They also tend to marry one another. And as a result they tend to have, you guessed it, Uglo-American children.

How many times have you been somewhere, say at a shopping mall, and noticed an Uglo-American walking toward you? Admit your reaction. You give thanks you are not married to her and you feel sorry for the person who is. Then you see that person's Uglo-American spouse walk out of the restroom and you watch the two of them stroll off together. You give thanks all over again that you are not an Uglo-American, because of whom you would likely marry.

Now imagine yourself walking into a shopping mall and you want to go into a store. But hanging around outside the store on benches are a bunch of Uglo-Americans. They often go to malls and just sit around all day.

I don't know about you, but when I see a bunch of Uglo-American people I tend not to want to go near them. I shift directions. If they're standing in front of a store, I generally will walk by. Now if that's my reaction, no doubt I'm not alone. If others are doing the same thing, then this economic recovery is in jeopardy. Having so many Uglo-American people hanging around during peak shopping hours is probably causing a lot of people to delay their shopping.

My suggestion is that, for the good of the country, we ban all Uglo-American people from the streets during daylight hours. Now you will no doubt ask how in the world this can be enforced. It will be tough to determine exactly who is an Uglo-American. That's a good question. But I think we should try it the way we handle most things in this country. We do things the easy way first, and then if that doesn't work, we impose more drastic measures.

I suggest that we make the ban voluntary. Uglo-American people know who they are. They can decide that it's best that they stay home that day. If just a few break the curfew that's all right. It's when they gather in groups that we have problems. I propose that someone propose guidelines for the ban to the city council at its next meeting.

Well, the reaction to my anti–Uglo-American campaign was predictable. People called in and asked if I'd ever heard of a guy named Hitler, because he advocated things like that. Some people really believed me. One woman called and was glad I had brought the subject up. She had a daughter who was "as Uglo-American as sin" and was worried that her daughter would never get married and never leave the house. I felt very sad for her and decided to admit to the audience that it was all a gag.

Little did I know that a few years later some government officials would actually believe that Uglo-American people had to be protected under our civil rights laws. Early in 1992, the Santa Cruz, California, City Council debated a bill banning anyone from discriminating on the basis of looks. A San Francisco supervisor proposed the same thing.

The ordinances would have prohibited the denial of any job or housing on the basis of someone's "height, weight, or personal appearance." People claiming they were discriminated against could take their case to a mediator and then file a civil lawsuit for damages.

All this just goes to prove that nothing I satirize is immune from eventually being taken seriously by some pompous left-wing radicals. They will then turn right around and try to pass a law against it. I'm going to be careful about what I propose in the future. I hate to give these big-government people new ideas for targets.

RUSH H. LIMBAUGH, III

TAXING THE POOR

On April 1, 1992, I did the following bit on my show:

Ladies and gentlemen, as many of you know who've heard this morning's Rush Update, it is time to get serious and it is time to get tough about tax policy in this country. I don't know about you, but I see the size of the deficit at 400 billion dollars and I look at ways to cut it. And we could cut spending and of course we need to do that, but there clearly is a need for more revenue. If you cut the entire defense budget you raise 290 billion and that still leaves you 110 billion to close the deficit. We can't, and shouldn't, cut all of defense and we can't cut all of middle-class entitlements. We can't cut all of anything.

And we can't continue to rob the rich. We have been punitive against the rich in this country. Everybody talks about the savings and loan problem and blames the huge deficit on it. Well, we've got the savings and loan problem because we sought to punish the rich. You know how we did it? We had the 1986 Tax Reform Act and what did it do? The 1986 Tax Reform Act devalued real estate. You know how? By eliminating the tax incentives for investment in real estate.

No longer were people motivated to invest in real estate in order to escape punitively high tax rates. Instead we said, now we'll make the top marginal tax rate 28 percent and will remove a great part of the depreciation deduction.

Well, that's all fine and good in theory, ladies and gentlemen. However, the big problem is that people had been playing by and relying on the old rules for a long, long time and had invested year after year after year in real estate. And it's simple supply and demand. The more you invest in real estate, the more people who want it, the more people who are trying to get in the market, and the greater the demand, up goes the price.

Prior to the '86 Tax Reform Act it had always been considered wise to invest in real estate. Even the S&L's, by the way, when they were deregulated and granted the freedom to invest, began to invest in real estate. Plus, they accepted real estate for collateral on many loans they made. Then came the '86 Tax Reform Act and removed the incentives for getting into real estate. As a result, activity in the real estate market declined and the value declined with it. And so the banks immediately became undercollateralized across the board. If someone defaulted, there was insufficient collateral to satisfy the loan.

The savings and loans that invested in real estate took another hit as the value of their real estate investments plummeted. By a simple stroke of the pen the federal government caused gargantuan losses to fall upon these institutions and others who invested in or who accepted mortgages on real estate.

Now who were the people hurt? The people hurt were white-collar people. There is little doubt that the origins of our recent recession can be traced to the '86 Tax Reform Act. You could say that this recession was an upper-bracket recession.

You may say that, well, the rich deserved it. Folks, the rich don't deserve it. We are just coming out of a recession where a great deal of unemployment and suffering occurred in the name of punishing the rich. Let me show you some of the hypocrisy that's going on. Lars-Erik Nelson, in a column about Jerry Brown in the New York *Daily News*, makes an excellent point. Jerry Brown is out campaigning and complaining about the S&L bailout. He's running around to union and construction workers and demagogue-ing the issue on the S&L bailout by saying that because we're bailing out the S&Ls, little guys are getting shafted. "We ought to take whatever money we're using to bail out the S&Ls and use that money for social programs or help the unemployed or help the chronically ill or whatever the other buzzwords are."

But the fact is that the very union people Jerry Brown's out there trying to fool were the prime casualties of these policies designed to punish the "rich." Why? Because those with money invested in and developed real estate. Who actually performs the construction work on real estate that's being developed? Construction workers. And they are members of what? Construction unions.

Because the S&Ls were deregulated, real estate remained high in value and that's where people invested their money. And then the rug was pulled out from under them and everybody suffered—not just the rich!

As I have said for the longest time, what this recession needs is a good dose of inflation in real estate and a lot of problems would be solved. This is undeniable. If you choose to believe this class-warfare propaganda that the S&L was nothing but a bailout for the rich, think about this. Who invested in S&Ls? You. Individual people. You thought your accounts were insured up to $100,000 and one of the purposes of the bailouts was to make as many individual citizens whole as possible. They're covering amounts even beyond the $100,000.

This is a prime example of what I've been talking about all along. If you're tired of bailing out the S&Ls, then send the money back that you've got. Let's be honest here.

So we want to raise taxes on the rich? No, the rich have been punished enough. And it doesn't just stop with the S&Ls. The activity in which the rich engage is what ends up employing people in this country. Yet we've got a liberal Democratic Congress and a bunch of Democratic presidential candidates who are saying we should punish the rich even more. They don't use the word *punish*, of course, but that's what they mean; that's what they want you to think is going to happen: that the rich are going to get punished.

Instead of trying to tear down achievers in this country, instead of trying to tear down those who have made it, instead of trying to punish those people for working hard and excelling, what we ought to be trying to do is to teach other people how to do it. We ought to be trying to motivate others to give it a shot rather than to be pacified by indictments of the rich and promises that they will be made to pay their fair share.

The Way Things Ought to Be

That's what the Democrats always play on: the envy button; and this time they were pushing it so far as to incite the revenge of the proletariat. When people go home and watch ABC's *World News Tonight* and see that Jerry Brown and Slick Willy are going to punish Wall Street, their mashed potatoes aren't going to need any gravy that night because the gravy is what they just heard on the news.

All right, well everybody says then let's raise taxes on the middle class. Well, well, how can we do that? One of the reasons we have a recession is that the middle class doesn't have any money. Why? Because they have been taxed at a confiscatory rate. Because all of you middle class people are out there loving your rump roast when you hear the rich are gonna get really attacked; you're the ones really being attacked as well.

Taxes go up on everybody. And taxes have to go up on the middle class 'cause that's where the bulk of the money is. So you're taxed—you don't even know how much. You don't have any idea. Consider the sales tax you pay, the gasoline tax, your state and city taxes. When you add all those up, it's no wonder you can't afford to send your kids to college. Instead of supporting your own kids, you're supporting a giant bloated pig in Washington, D.C., and you're just trying to get your face into the nipple so that you can get some of it back. We've all become a bunch of little piglets trying to get to the mother pig and then trying to squeeze in and get our share.

The middle class, coupled with the rich, make this country work. Now, what's slowing this country down? What is the equivalent of putting the oars in the water and just dragging them along or of shutting down three of the four jet engines on a Boeing 747? I'll tell you what it is. The poor.

The poor and the lower classes of this country have gotten a free ride since the Great Depression when it became noble to be poor. Look at how we treat the homeless: we celebrate them, make romantic figures out of them. We make movies about them and teach them to dine in dumpsters.

My friends, we have the wealthiest poor in the world. If

you want to look at poverty and suffering, go to India, Ethiopia, Vietnam, China, Cambodia, and the former Soviet Union.

The poor in this country are the biggest piglets at the mother pig and her nipples. The poor feed off of the largesse of this government and they give nothing back. Nothing. They're the ones who get all the benefits in this country. They're the ones that are always pandered to.

Now you might be saying, Rush, this is so cruel, this is so hard-hearted. But think about it for a minute: over half this population receives some kind of government check. It's getting so bad that even liberal Democrats in New Jersey realize we can't keep it up. They have just passed a law over there within the past three months telling welfare mothers they can no longer procreate with impunity. If you have another baby, it's your responsibility, we are not paying for it because we can't. We have been encouraging poverty by subsidizing the increasing numbers of the poor. And Democrats love giving money away to the poor because it makes them dependent upon the Democrats and helps to ensure their reelection.

And do the poor pay anything back? Do they pay any taxes? No. They don't pay a thing. They contribute nothing to this country. They do nothing but take from it. There are people who are putting into this economy. There are people who are working hard every day, playing by the rules and contributing. They are the givers. Who are the takers? The poor.

It's time to get serious about raising taxes on the poor. It's time that the wealthiest poor in the world started paying their fair share instead of being treated like a bunch of helpless soulless waifs who can only survive with a big government providing them things. It's time to make the poor no longer objects of sympathy, but people whom we should assist in overcoming their poverty status.

There's no reason that we have to have the level of poverty in this country that we have. Tax them. Let's balance this budget on the backs of the poor. Show them what life is like for the rest of us and encourage them. Now I know what you're saying. You're saying, But, Rush, what do we do if we can't collect the money they owe?

What if we don't—what if they just can't pay? The poor in this country have an average of three television sets in their houses. Let's go and get two of them. The poor in this country all have cars. Let's repossess them. We already have an agent for selling them. It's called the Resolution Trust Corporation. If they're clunkers, if they're old cars which are polluting the planet, we need to get rid of them anyway.

We need to get them off the streets and get them off of booze. We need to stop giving them coupons where they can go buy all kinds of junk. We just don't have the money. They're taking out. They continue to take out, they put nothing in. And I'm sick and tired of playing the one phony game I've had to play and that is this so-called compassion for the poor. I don't have compassion for the poor. Because I think they can do something about it.

What if we all decided to be poor? What if we all said, I don't want to pay taxes, I'll just be poor and rely on the Democrats. And I'll derive my happiness by watching the news and hearing about how the rich are going to be punished for making me the way I am. Yeah. I'm sorry, ladies and gentlemen, but it's time somebody said this. The poor have become like social security recipients: a hallowed, protected class. You can't talk about them without somebody attacking your very soul, your being, your integrity.

Well, how many people out there want to be poor? How many of you would recommend to your children that they strive for poverty? None of you.

We need to encourage people to contribute to the economy, not to sit around basking in self-pity. We need to help them get out of the situation, rather than glorifying and perpetuating it. Encourage them to become economically equal members of this society, rather than a collection of sycophants sidling up to the pig and looking for the biggest nipple they can find.

How do we do this? *Self-reliance* is the key. We've got to

instill that in the poor, rather than a dependency mentality fostered by the Democrats. We're wasting capable, productive members of our society by making it noble to be poor.

Look at Jerry Brown. How has Jerry Brown gotten credibility for himself? By being a phony poor person. Jerry Brown's family is loaded. What does he do, he goes over there and sits around with Mother Teresa. Sits around with other poor. So we're supposed to think, Oh, man, he cares, he's taken a vow of poverty. That's not wise, that's not compassionate, it's stupid. If you're going to go hang around a bunch of poor people the worst thing you can do is join them. The best thing you can do is try to help them out of it. Don't go over there saying, I feel so sorry for you, I'm going to sleep in this sleeping crate with you tonight. That may make Jerry Brown feel good and assuage his guilt, because he has shown he "cares"; but it doesn't do a solitary thing for the poor.

What have we accomplished with all this pseudocaring? We still have as many poor people. Yet we are encouraged by such "leaders" as Jesse Jackson to reduce ourselves to the lowest denominator; to emulate the poor, rather than encouraging them to emulate those who produce.

Sympathy never brought anyone prosperity or happiness. These public displays of sympathy are not for the poor, but to make those expressing it look good.

That's what I like about liberals. They have a monopoly on caring. We care more than you care. That's what liberals say. And because of that they're more moral. Well, I don't buy it. We have the poor and we have poverty in this country precisely because of the liberal approach, which has been proceeding full steam in this country since the Great Society.

Now, realize one thing: I meant everything I said, save for the bit about actually taxing the poor. Other than that, I was dead serious and honest, yet the suggestion to tax the poor should have sent up red flags to the audience. Following that segment, you wouldn't believe the number of calls I got from people who thought I was serious about my suggestion that we tax the poor. Many people are far too quick to believe anything that sets off their hot buttons. My April Fools' joke illustrated how quick people are to take offense even when I am obviously—at least I thought it was obvious—being absurd. Of course, I don't believe the poor should pay more taxes. The only way they can escape poverty is to have a chance to keep what they can earn. America does have the richest poor in the world, but that doesn't mean there isn't a lot of misery in this country.

We do, however, have to wean people off the government pig. The country is losing its self-reliance and becoming a subsidy hog. But, of course, that is not the fault of the poor. The blame for that can be laid at the feet of liberals who use the plight of the poor to advance their goal of dominating society.

First, you should not believe what you hear or read simply because it confirms your preconceived notions. A lot of people believe whatever bad news about the environment they hear, simply because they've been taught that the planet is in imminent danger. There was a serious message intended with both of my stories. Both involved absurd suggestions which were believed by a surprising number of people, because much of the content of both messages, particularly the Tax the Poor routine, made total sense and in fact were good ideas. My hope is that people will be discerning and attentive. If, however, they choose to believe totally in me, don't worry. They'll be okay because I am, after all, almost always right, 97.9 percent of the time. I do it for our future. Thank you. It's a beautiful thing.

THE STATE OF THE UNION

THE THANKSGIVING WEEKEND OF 1991 WAS THE FIRST ONE IN A LONG time which I didn't spend traveling. This meant that I had a chance to watch more consecutive days of television than I had in many moons (a little Indian lingo, there). I was appalled, shocked, depressed, then finally enraged at what I saw and heard. I was fuming, livid. Upon returning to the golden EIB microphones the following Monday I delivered a monologue which was devoted to sharing my emotions and thoughts about the bilge and psychobabble I had seen over the weekend. I submit it here, for the ages.

Ladies and gentlemen, I've hit my boiling point. Like that character in the movie *Network*, "I'm mad as hell and I'm not going to take it anymore." I have about had it being told that the plight of the homeless is my fault. I'm sick and tired of turning on my TV and being told that the AIDS crisis is my fault too, because I don't care enough. I'm tired of hearing about how we're not spending enough on AIDS, even though we're spending more money on it than we do in the war on cancer.

The Way Things Ought to Be

In this five-hundredth-anniversary year of Columbus's voyage, I'm tired of hearing him trashed. I don't give a hoot that he gave some Indians a disease that they didn't have immunity against. We can't change that, we're here. We're the best country on earth and I'm sick and tired of people trying to change history so as to portray this country as an instrument of evil. It isn't true. I'm sick and tired of hearing Western culture constantly disparaged. "Hey, hey, ho, ho, Western culture's got to go," is the chant at Stanford University. What would Stanford be if the pioneers that are so reviled today as imperialists, racists, sexists, bigots, and homophobes hadn't fought their way across a continent to California?

The American middle class is just plain tired and worn out. They get blamed for everything in this country. They are taxed more than ever, and now they have to put up with lectures about how we have to ship billions of dollars to the former Soviet Union so they can eat this winter, even though it's cold there every winter and the people there have been hoarding food in their cellars for months. As if that's not enough, the American people are sick and tired of hearing that they have to pay the Russians to dismantle their nuclear weapons.

I'm sick and tired of turning on the television every Thanksgiving weekend and looking at news reports of how rotten a Christmas season we're going to have. There's no news in that. Every year they go out and do the same story. They report the American people aren't spending as much, that "this year they're not wasting money." Well, excuse me. The American people never waste money. To say this is the first year that consumers are looking for a deal is stupid. They look for a deal every day, not just every Christmas. No one I know goes in and throws money around. "Americans are shopping more carefully these days," the news media tells us. The reason they're doing that is because we've been in the deepest recession in years, taxes are going through the roof, and we have people like Richard Gephardt, the House Majority Leader, telling us that the American people expect too much from Congress.

The truth is that the American people wish Congress would leave them alone. In 1990, they ganged up with President Bush and promised to reduce the deficit by imposing the largest peacetime tax increase in history. Now they're screaming again for more taxes and the deficit just hit $400 billion a year. The members of Congress are now back in their districts begging for our votes. The *nerve*. People I talk to are paying their medical bills by exceeding their credit card limits. Members of Congress exempt themselves from the laws they impose on us, pass their midnight pay raises, overdraw their accounts at the House Bank, and then take a junket to some exotic Caribbean island with some lobbyists. Then they dare tell us that it's our fault for wanting to keep more of the money we earn and not surrender it in taxes.

Working people are striving against the odds to make it in this country, and all the government can do is view them as a revenue target. While picking their pockets the government has the audacity to foist a guilt trip on them to boot. They're made to feel responsible for everything. Look at AIDS. A terrible disease, but it is largely behaviorally spread. Yet all we hear is that "people aren't doing enough about it."

There's one simple thing that could be done about it. People could STOP———AROUND! Instead, the kids of God-fearing parents are handed condoms at school and told, "We know you are just a bunch of little minks, that we can't stop you from exploring your sexuality and doing wrong and dangerous things. So here, take this condom and protect yourself." In many school districts, parents aren't even allowed a say in the matter. Well, if the schools are serious, what they ought to do is convert the study hall to a giant bedroom with beds and clean sheets. Have the principal and the school nurse demonstrate to every couple how to use a condom, then observe them to ensure they do it right. Hell, we may as well go all the way. In fact, if the schools are so certain that kids are going to do this, what they ought to do is find disease-free hookers and bring 'em in. Teach a little supply and demand.

The Way Things Ought to Be

We're getting to the point where the tax producers will someday be outnumbered by the tax eaters of society. Those who choose to accept the responsibilities of life have had enough of being told that they should give more to those who don't shoulder those responsibilities. We're supposed to feel sorry for this group and that group. For the down-trodden. For native Americans. For those who suffered because Columbus landed. What about feeling sorry for those who *are* living, who pay the taxes? Those are the people NO ONE ever feels sorry for. They are asked to give and give until they have no more to give. And when they say "Enough!" they are called selfish. The TV news keeps rerunning stories about the decade of greed we had in the eighties. You could shut down every TV station in America and rerun the news from five years ago and it wouldn't be any different. Everything is the fault of the people who don't give enough. This despite the fact that charitable contributions during the "avaricious" eighties climbed at an astonishing rate. But that's not enough.

Then we have the spaced-out Hollywood left eating beans and rice to focus attention on the evils of capitalism. We are told that there is an inequitable distribution of food and other products under capitalism. Wrong. That's not the problem. The world's biggest problem is the unequal distribution of capitalism. If there were capitalism everywhere, you wouldn't have food shortages. If capitalism is the problem, how is that the U.S. is the only nation in the world that can feed itself and still feed much of the rest of the planet? That won't last much longer though. The American farmer is being put out of business by a bunch of people who are more concerned with the rights of animals than they are with assuring that the American people have enough food at an affordable price. We're told that cows are our biggest enemy. I say, pass the burgers.

In schools we're teaching kids about tribal Africa instead of Aristotle. We're not teaching anything else very well. Our kids get lower scores on math and English tests every year. As a result, kids from backwater European and Asian countries are outperforming our kids left and right in school because we're hung up on teaching feel-good history and worthless social gobbledygook.

I could go on about the insanities that are loose in this country, all of it tolerated just so a bunch of aggrieved weirdos who don't fit in can feel better about themselves. They control many of our institutions, our universities, our major media outlets. They all have cushy jobs, they never seem to get fired or laid off.

Dan Rostenkowski, the House Ways and Means Chairman, says, "We will all have to sacrifice to fix our nation's problems." Congressman, what the hell do you think everybody's been doing because of your policies and your ideas? The people who work in this country have been sacrificing, and for a lot of people who aren't related to them. And now you want to increase the sacrificing by raising taxes? Congressman, can you or anyone else show me where any society in human history has taxed itself into prosperity? No, you can't.

The sympathy in this country is never for those on whose shoulders the burden actually rests: the diligent middle class. The sympathy is directed at people like the woman who was killed last year after she fell asleep in a dumpster and was crushed by a garbage truck as it picked up the trash. The American people had that story thrown in their face for a week. They were told it was their fault that it happened! That the woman was so hopeless that she had to rummage around in dumpsters for food. Nobody put that woman in the dumpster, she climbed in herself. It later turned out she was not homeless but was just looking for a few bargains and she fell asleep. You sleep in a trash dumpster, you run the risk of being crushed by a dumpster truck. A sad and unfortunate story, to be sure, but not one aspect of it is the fault of the American economy or the American people.

Then there is the obligatory sympathy after the first freezing night of the winter when a homeless person is discovered dead on the sidewalk. The news reports are delivered solemnly and with deep feelings of sorrow. This happened, they say, because Reagan didn't care and because selfishness and greed now permeate American society. A couple of days later, after the autopsy, it is learned that the person was drinking a cheap brand of wine called Cool Breeze—referred to compassionately by reporters as "his beverage of choice"—and died from cirrhosis of the liver.

People are going to have to start accepting responsibility for their actions and stop bleeding the people in this country who accept their responsibilities and who see to it that the country works. This is still America, but increasingly many of us don't recognize it. Finally, I am weary and near my wits' end at having to listen to the complaint that the American safety net has holes in it and too many people are slipping through. Wrong. The problem is that too many people are using that safety net as a hammock.

                         Thank you and may God bless you.

The reaction of the audience was exceptional, which didn't surprise me. I'm used to that. Many said I should send it to the White House so that the President could use it in his State of the Union address.

ABORTION: OUR NEXT CIVIL WAR

IN WRITING ABOUT ABORTION, THE LAST THING I WANT TO DO IS TO rehash the old, standard arguments. We've all heard them, and we all have our own views on them. I'll touch on the arguments against abortion, but all I really want to do in this chapter is explain why I'm pro-life and proud of it. I'm not opposed to abortion because I want to force people to do things my way, or because I believe I possess the ultimate truth. I recognize that other people have wrestled with this issue and have sincere convictions that differ from mine. I just wish that more of the people who support abortion would see their way clear to recognizing that my views are sincere as well.

Suffice it to say that to me the issue is simple. I believe that life begins at conception and that killing that human life is justifiable only when it's necessary to save the mother's life.

But I am also pro-life because I am a human being who feels a sense of duty to civilization. I think it is incumbent upon us all to be concerned about the world we will leave behind. We also should be concerned about the values we transfer to succeeding generations. When we take actions that cheapen life, we are contributing to an overall decline in our society's moral values.

By allowing abortion (in situations other than where the mother's life is in jeopardy) we are indirectly promoting values that encourage crime, illegitimacy, the dissolution of the family, and callousness toward the living, especially the elderly. Abortion cheapens the sanctity of human life. We are now making decisions as to who lives and who dies on the basis of whether it is convenient for the LIVING. That's dangerous.

According to a recent survey of 1,900 women by the Alan Guttmacher Institute, a special research division of Planned Parenthood, just 7 percent of all abortions are motivated by "hard cases." Here is the breakdown: the mother's health (3 percent); when the baby has a possible health problem (3 percent); or when the pregnancy results from rape or incest (1 percent). The birth control, or social reasons (93 percent), break down as follows: 16 percent had abortions because they were concerned about how a child would change their life. Some 21 percent said they were not ready for the responsibility. 21 percent said they couldn't afford the baby, 12 percent blamed a relationship problem, 11 percent felt they weren't mature enough, 8 percent of the women said they had all the children they wanted. "Other reasons" accounted for another 4 percent. Again, only 1 percent said they were the victims of rape or incest.

This is staggering. Abortion proponents attempt to justify their views in several ways. The most common is that it is a woman's primary and fundamental right—in fact, her primary obligation, according to radicals—to choose. To choose. You see, it is her body and she has the right to do with it as she pleases. (Jane Fonda said recently that it is imperative to get the government out of women's wombs. Tsk-tsk. If she were honest she would admit that what she *really* wants is the government *in the womb*. That's what abortion on demand is all about, isn't it? That's why she and her radical feminist sisters insist that the government counsel pregnant women on their abortion options.) But have you thought about it? For instance, her right to choose what? Can a woman choose to steal, using her own body? Of course not. Can she choose to do drugs? Not according to the law. Can she legally choose to be a prostitute? Again, no, which establishes, as does the drug example, that there is precedent for society determining what a woman can and can't do with her body. Look at it in another, and admittedly provocative, way: What if a man claimed the right to rape, using the same principle found in the theory that it is his body and he has the right to choose?

The second most common argument advanced by pro-choice stalwarts relies on spurious compassion. Simply stated, the argument is that for a pregnant woman living in poverty to give birth to a child would be unfair to both. Bringing a child into the world under those kind of conditions isn't right, they say. You see, if the child is born, rather than aborted, it *might* suffer. An unwanted or poverty-stricken child won't suffer if it isn't born, therefore it's better that it not come into the world. The logic of that escapes me. We should kill a child in the womb so that it won't feel pain and suffering growing up? We should prevent suffering by killing? You figure it out.

ARGUING ON ABORTION

I try not to get involved in debates on abortion. They rarely change anyone's mind. But recently I went to a birthday party where I was seated next to a very intelligent professional woman who let me know she had a bone to pick with me. It involved abortion. She had me pegged as a stereotypical pro-life fanatic, which to her meant intolerant, insensitive, a macho pig consumed with imposing my will on her and every other woman. I had to defend myself when she claimed that the only reason I was pro-life was that restricting abortion would make it easier to deny women a prominent role in society. I told her that my views had nothing to do with that, and they really don't. In fact she has it backwards. The converse is true. Militant feminists are pro-choice because it is their ultimate avenue to power over men. And believe me, to them it is a question of power. It is their attempt to impose their will on the rest of society, particularly on men. Needless to say, she was not overly impressed with my arguments. She viewed abortion as so many feminists do.

Now, I don't know if the woman I had dinner with that night had ever had an abortion. That was definitely none of my business. If she had had one, I'm sure she couldn't possibly have thought she was committing any harm to society as a whole. But when you multiply one abortion by 1½ million and then multiply that figure by the twenty years we have had legal abortion in the United States, you get a stunning number: 30 million. It was the growing number of abortions, year in and year out, that convinced George Bush to change his stand on abortion in the late 1970s. He said he had become convinced that so many abortions were contributing to an overall decline in moral values in America.

Given all the rights and privileges people enjoy in America, how can they arbitrarily decide they are going to exempt themselves from such a basic responsibility as the preservation of life? We have to admit that some of our actions as humans have an impact on society and they have to be regulated. If they are not, our one individual action multiplied many times can corrode the entire moral fiber of the country.

Consider drug abuse. A lot of people say we should legalize cocaine and heroin. It would take the crime out of it and hopefully, as a result, some of the violence associated with it. Besides, the people who are inclined to use drugs are going to do so regardless of its illegality. But the fact that people are going to ignore and break laws is not a valid argument for decriminalization. The state would then be sanctioning, even promoting, conduct that is harmful to society. That is similar to today's trendy policies for the free distribution of condoms in our public schools and prisons. We are sending a message that such activity is okay, based on the specious argument that we know the activity is going to occur anyway. We might as well just carry this argument to its logical conclusion: The reason laws are broken is that there are laws. People are going to break the law. They are going to steal, rob, and kill. So what we need to do is eliminate laws and get rid of the police. That way there will be no crime. The point is that standards of right and wrong and basic decency must be established and maintained. We accomplish this through the establishment of limits on our behavior, which constitutes our law, which descends from the morality and values we deem important and necessary to an orderly and functioning society.

It's easy for people to say that if they shoot up on heroin the only people they're hurting are themselves. But that's not true. If someone becomes an irresponsible human being and a worthless citizen, he is directly or indirectly affecting everyone who is willing to live up to the responsibilities of citizenship. Drug abusers destroy their families, and the government-funded health clinics have to take care of them if no one else will. Many of them also become eligible for social security disability benefits.

If we legalize these vices, we erode the societal support for prohibitions against crimes such as murder. The erosion of the moral fabric of society is a gradual, insidious process. It happens, bit by bit, almost imperceptibly. Kids in inner cities used to play with plastic guns and knives. Now they pack real pistols to school at the age of eleven or twelve. Kids kill their fellow students for jostling them in the hall. Human life has become cheapened. Abortion has played a role in this, and that's another reason we have to reduce its influence on our society.

THE ABORTION AGENDA

Short of the caller abortions (described later) I performed on the radio, nothing I've said on the subject has gotten me in more trouble than when I said: "I am pro-choice. I just hope the choice is for life." I got all kinds of grief from the pro-choice camp. You can't be pro-life and pro-choice at the same time, they said. But I asked them, Doesn't choice mean having more than one option? I favor saving lives rather than destroying them. I was trying to point out to them that "pro-choice" isn't really an accurate description of the position. It means one thing: the promotion of abortion. Consider the way the pro-abortion crowd reacts when people try to counsel a woman against abortion.

Why should it matter to the pro-choice radicals if a woman is talked out of an abortion? Say a woman is on her way to Planned Parenthood to have an abortion. Outside their offices she's stopped by Operation Rescue and told that they have a shelter she can go to where she will be taken care of. She can have the baby, and it will be put up for adoption. But at least it will live. So why are the radical feminists so furious when that happens? What agenda is being harmed? Why get so mad when a woman who planned to have an abortion is talked out of it, if choice is really the objective?

One reason they get upset is that abortion is the fuel running their entire political agenda. It is the sacrament of their religion of feminism. Here then is the definition and real agenda of the feminazi: radical feminists whose objective is to see that there are as many abortions as possible. This is their primary mechanism of asserting their power. The second reason some abortion activists get upset is that there is money involved. Always follow the money on any public issue. Elsewhere in this book, I've said that the desire for money tells us a great deal about why people hold certain views. Abortion is a huge business in this country. Think about 1.5 million abortions a year at, say, $300 each. That's $450 million a year. There's a lot of money being made on abortions.

When the French RU-486 pill was developed in the early 1980s it wasn't just the pro-life people who initially opposed it. Many abortion activists also had qualms about it or even opposed it. Why? Because it took abortion out of the clinics where all the money was made and brought it into the privacy of a woman's bathroom. It was only when they realized that blocking the French pill would be contrary to their image that they switched sides.

WHEN DOES LIFE BEGIN?

Most people who favor abortion view it as a matter of a woman's individual rights. I, however, cannot escape viewing it as an issue of life. If the fetus is human life, that trumps any argument you can make about the individual freedom of the mother. I believe life begins at conception. It can begin nowhere else. Now some people call me up and say, Rush, if someone masturbates aren't they then killing some sperm, some potential life? Nonsense; you're not harming anything, because sperm have no potential to create life by themselves. But after conception, life begins. I know that abortion advocates say that isn't life. It's an unviable tissue mass. They dance around the issue, because once they concede that a fetus is life anytime before birth, they've lost the argument. I can understand some people's perplexity over the issue. But if there is doubt about something as all-important as the existence of life, isn't it morally imperative that we resolve that doubt on the side of life?

The Supreme Court averted the argument of when life begins when it set forth its trimester standard for life in *Roe v. Wade.* In the first three months no one can stop an abortion; or, in legal parlance, the woman's right to privacy supersedes the state's interest in regulating abortion. In the second trimester, the state has some right to regulate the practice. And in the last three months, an abortion can be stopped.

Roe v. Wade is bad constitutional law. Even liberals such as Michael Kinsley of the *New Republic* admit that. It's going to be replaced, and there will be a lot of confusion as a result. For years I've hoped we could avoid that. I've long been on record favoring a fair political fight on abortion. Rather than having abortion declared legal by the decision of nine guys in black robes back in 1973, I think it should be a moral choice, decided by the people in a democratic fashion. I've suggested this to countless feminists and they all recoil in shock. I agree with the view, best articulated by Judge Robert Bork, that there is no basis in the Constitution for the privacy right which was announced as the foundational basis for the constitutional right to abortion. He argues that because the Constitution is silent on the issue, so should be the Supreme Court, because when the Court begins inventing concepts such as this they are rewriting the Constitution. The framers were very specific as to the amendment process and there is definitely no provision for amendment by judicial fiat. Bork advocates judicial silence on the issue and says that the matter should be decided democratically, by the state legislatures.

I have asked the feminists who disagree with a democratic resolution of this issue what they are afraid of. If there is such massive support for the pro-choice point of view, pro-choicers should win in a breeze. They vehemently disagree. They know in their hearts that the majority of the American people are not in favor of unlimited abortion on demand. Liberals fear the democratic process because they don't think the people will agree with their agenda. They love an activist Supreme Court for that reason, because it gives them political victories they cannot gain in our democratic, accountable institutions. Even liberal commentator Hodding Carter, formerly with the Jimmy Carter administration, admitted that the Supreme Court was the only way liberals have been able to advance their agenda in modern times.

If the American people were so concerned with keeping abortion legal they would not have voted for Ronald Reagan twice and George Bush once. In those three elections combined, the pro-life presidential candidate won 133 states and the pro-choice candidate won 17 states. And Reagan and Bush did more than pay lip service to the pro-life cause. They made it a key element of their platforms and discussed it in speeches. They didn't cower from the issue as so many politicians do today. Feminists don't often put pro-abortion initiatives on state ballots, because they have lost more times than they have won. Take Washington State last year. They put a measure on the ballot that simply said that the voters supported legalized abortion regardless of what happened to *Roe v. Wade.* They were convinced they would win big, that they had it in the bag. But lo and behold, there were more votes against the proposition than for it. It was so close it took seven days to recount the votes. Only the absentees put it over the top, by the slimmest of margins.

Even in a state as liberal as Washington, which elects Tom Foley and voted for Michael Dukakis, there is no overwhelming majority of people in favor of unrestricted abortion, as the pro-choice crowd would have us all believe. By the way, on the same ballot voters rejected a so-called right-to-die measure that would have allowed the killing of elderly, infirm patients.

It's true the American people don't all agree with my position on abortion. Polls show the public is divided on the issue. But the vast majority of Americans do not want abortion used as a means of birth control. A lot of people are willing to allow abortions in the case of rape or incest, but those are an infinitesimal number of the ones taking place today—much less than 1 percent.

I would bet that almost as many abortions take place in this country because people don't want a certain kind of kid. One abortion doctor in Los Angeles who caters to women of Pakistani and Indian origin reported that 99 percent of the abortions he carries out involve female fetuses. The mothers come from cultures where the male child is prized and the female considered worthless. A lot of feminists are queasy about sex-selection abortions, but they are the inevitable result of a policy that makes abortion easy and cheapens life. As I've said before, the policy of unrestricted abortion coupled with advances in medical technology could present some incredibly complex dilemmas for this society in the future. Suppose in the not too distant future a doctor is able to tell the parents of a baby in the womb that it will have freckles and red hair and be prone to obesity. Then suppose the parents decide they do not want a child who would suffer from those characteristics and abort on this basis? We may be flirting with eugenics here, which I thought was Hitler's brainchild.

RAIN FORESTS AND ABORTION

Some people's priorities puzzle me. I get calls from nutso environmentalists who are filled with compassion for every snail darter that is threatened by some dam somewhere. Yet, they have no interest in the 1.5 million fetuses that are aborted every year in the United States. I love to argue with them and challenge their double standard. They'll call up and ask me if I believe the rain forests should be saved. I tell them that I don't think we're headed for a crisis on the rain forests, and that if Third World countries allowed people to own the rain forests there would be less incentive to chop them down. People who own private forests in the United States don't chop them down and leave stumps; they grow more trees on them. The parallels are irresistible, folks. As I point out in the Rodney King chapter, people don't burn down that which they own.

Well, the callers tell me I don't understand what we're losing by cutting down the rain forests. Every time we chop one tree down we could be ruining the chances for finding a cure for AIDS or a treatment for cancer. I then ask them if they support abortion, the killing of a million and a half babies in the womb every year. Well, it's a woman's right to choose, they say. I respond by pointing out that one of those babies that was aborted thirty years ago might have grown up to be a brilliant scientist and could have discovered the cure for AIDS. Well, they then mumble that there are too many people in the world. We don't want to bring people into the world who wouldn't have a happy home life.

That's when I pounce. I tell them the world is filled with people who've accomplished great things even though their parents didn't want them. Beethoven had a positively wretched childhood. Charles Dickens lived in indescribable poverty. Would you have wanted to abort them? I can't believe you are more concerned with the protection of leaves and fungi in some rain forest than with preserving human life. At that point, they usually lapse into clichés about the balance of nature. But I've made my point.

THE RIGHT TO KILL

It's not just abortion that is eroding our respect for human life. There's also death at the other end of the spectrum. Look at the right-to-die movement. They're not calling for a right to die, they're mostly talking about a right to kill. The advocates of euthanasia are asking the government and courts to step aside and allow people who are feeble and elderly to be snuffed out.

Now, I'm not opposed to people preparing a living will that sets out in advance what *they* want done if they are in a vegetative state or on life-support. But it is not proper for us to act unilaterally—even with the family's permission—to pull the plug on people. We all know of cases where people have recovered miraculously, and where people have been so depressed about their illnesses that they just wanted to end it all.

Look at the people who were "assisted" in ending their lives by

Dr. Jack Kevorkian, the Death Doctor in Michigan. Jack "The Dripper" wasn't killing terminally ill patients. They had Alzheimer's and were in a lot of pain, but they were alive and walking around. If his patients wanted to kill themselves, I wouldn't stand in their way. I don't endorse suicide but I do recognize that you can't prevent most people from taking their own lives if they really want to. But we shouldn't corrupt the medical profession in this country by allowing "assisted" suicide. Doctors are trained to save lives and prolong them. When you corrupt the medical profession, you might as well throw away the Hippocratic Oath. Its most basic tenet is: Do No Harm—and that means no harm to human life.

Doctors are no longer required to take the oath but they would do well to heed its words: "The regimen I adopt shall be for the benefit of my patients according to my ability and judgment, and not for their hurt or for any wrong. I will give no deadly drugs to any, though it be asked of me, nor will I counsel such." Allowing people like the creepy Dr. Kevorkian to hook people up to a death machine comes perilously close to murder.

Let me share a personal experience I had with a dying relative. A couple of years ago, my eighty-seven-year-old grandmother was very ill. She was feeble and finally had a stroke that put her in the hospital. The doctor called my mother and told her that her mother was on life-support and could not respond to people. "When you visit her, she probably won't know you're there," he said. "We would like your permission to turn off the feeding tubes and just let nature take its course."

My mother asked me what she should do. I asked her if she really wanted to take her mother off nourishment, even though she could be in a helpless state for a long time. She said no. I told her that that didn't surprise me. I just didn't think that she would have been able to live with herself if she had decided to let her mother starve, because that's what would have happened if they had taken the feeding tubes out. We both cried, and agreed that as a human being we couldn't treat her the way we would a stray cat that had been hit by a car.

The doctors probably knew my grandmother didn't have long to live. They were just trying to shift the painful decision to my mother. As it turned out, my grandmother died three days later.

I'm sure that some economist could total up the bill for the extra days she was under treatment, but I for one am glad that we didn't play a role in ending her life.

WHAT YOU CAN DO

Everyone should try in his own way to add to the respect that is accorded human life, rather than help to devalue it. I personally donate money to a group called The Greenwood Foundation. It provides a complete array of services to young people who decide not to abort their babies and instead carry them to term. They have homes all over the country where these young women can live while they are pregnant. Some even make it possible for them to study or train for a job.

After I'd been in New York for a while I was invited to an event sponsored by The Greenwood Foundation. It was a cruise around New York harbor on a crystal-clear weekday evening. It was one of the most memorable moments of my life. I met many fine people, from John Cardinal O'Connor to Wellington Mara, the owner of the New York Giants, to former New York Governor Hugh Carey, to former baseball commissioner Bowie Kuhn. The speeches that night were simple but stirring. I couldn't help but contrast them with the angry, bitter speeches I've heard at pro-abortion rallies and events. I thought to myself that the stereotypical image of people who are pro-life is completely wrong. These people wish only the best for others. Their goal is not to oppress anyone, it's simply not to allow harm to come to an innocent and defenseless party—the unborn child. I've had women call me on the show and say that they were almost aborted by their parents. You can't imagine the emotional wallop that packs. Think about your feelings if you were to shake the hand of someone who was almost sucked out of her mother's womb. Someone who almost didn't experience the joy and wonder of life, the thrill of being part of this great world.

That evening, as we circled New York harbor, I thought about those callers and I resolved that I will never retreat from my pro-life beliefs.

CALLER ABORTIONS

I have long thought that arguing with people about abortion doesn't have much of an impact, because people are so entrenched on the issue. So, I decided I somehow had to illustrate the moral tragedy of abortion. That's how I came up with the caller abortion, the most controversial thing I've ever done.

Its origins were on Valentine's Day, 1989. Some joker had decided that was a good time to declare National Condom Week. I had made a few comments about condoms that day, but nothing about abortion. But I got a call from a woman who insisted on commenting on abortion. It was out of place in the show, and I wanted to get rid of the call. But I was stuck.

You see, I've taken a pledge that I will never hang up on or abuse callers—for instance, telling them to "go gargle with razor blades," which the late Joe Pyne used to do. I don't insult callers, and I'm probably the most polite talk show host in America today. Only those who find my conservative opinions repugnant try to characterize me as rude. But I *really* didn't want to take this lady's call about abortion.

While I was sitting there listening to her go on about abortion, I casually made an off-mike comment to my call screener that I wished I could abort this call. Ta-da! A light went on. I suddenly had the idea for the caller abortion.

During a commercial break, I asked Phil Latzman, my gofer, to hunt up a vacuum-cleaner sound effect. "We're going to make broadcast history," I told Phil. "I'm going to abort calls. I can't get rid of the ones I don't want any other way. I promised the audience I wouldn't hang up on them." Phil came up with a twelve-second sound of a vacuum cleaner turning on, roaring away, and then switching off. We mixed that with a seven-second recording of a scream. He went to the management of the station and told them I was planning to abort calls. In their best blasé manner, they said that was okay. After all, we were in New York.

Now, as a technical matter, we were ready to start aborting callers. But I had some philosophical questions. The first thing I needed to know was: When does a call begin? After all, I needed to know at what point it was unsafe for me, the host, to abort the caller. I wasn't going to jeopardize my health or my life doing something like that.

So I called the phone company and finally got a scientist from New York Telephone on the line. I didn't want to talk with anyone who had an emotional interest in this matter. I asked the scientist, Sir, when does a call begin? Does it begin when I dial? Does it begin when I get a ring? Does it begin when somebody answers? And what does a busy signal mean? These are serious questions. When does that little, unviable electronic pulse actually become a call?

The scientist was a little confused by all this but told me that the phone company starts charging customers when someone picks up the phone. I told him that he had given me an answer: a call becomes a call when someone answers it. He said yes, but then he asked me why I wanted to know. I said that I was planning to start aborting callers. "Uh, okay," he said. After all, we were both in New York.

But I was still uncomfortable about all this because I personally don't answer the calls on my show. Bo Snerdley does. Sometimes he puts those calls on hold for minutes, gestating out there before they hit the air. I had to know how long it takes a call to gestate to full term. We arbitrarily decided on twenty minutes. If the call was on hold for twenty minutes, we couldn't abort it because it was then viable.

Someone on my staff was horrified at my plan. They told me that this wasn't like me. You shouldn't abort a call, Rush. Put it up for adoption. Put it on hold. Let the next host adopt that call, leave it for somebody else to take. But I told them I couldn't do that. Why, that poor call might be abused by the next host. I don't know what the adoptive host might do to it. It might languish out there for years before somebody takes it. I wasn't going to put the call up for adoption, not knowing what was going to happen to it.

No, I decided, I was going to abort the calls I didn't want. I even convinced myself that caller abortions weren't all that bad. Just think, we wouldn't have a homeless problem if we aborted more people.

One day I asked my audience if any of them wanted to volunteer to be the first aborted call in the history of radio. A lady called in and said she would be willing. Ladies and gentlemen, I said, I'm going to demonstrate what happens during a caller abortion. I asked the caller to start saying anything she wanted into the phone. She agreed, and began asking me my opinion on something. She was suddenly cut off by a loud *whoosh* with background sounds of a choked scream. And then there was silence. I paused for several seconds. Then I slowly leaned forward and asked the broadcast engineer, Jim McGuire, the critical question: "Jim, did we get it all?"

Well, they say the first time is the hardest. After that, every time I got a call I didn't like, I just hit that vacuum-cleaner button and sucked the caller off the air. I must have done about twenty caller abortions in two weeks. The reaction was incredible. Some people caught on to the message I was trying to send, and complimented me. But many others protested. They were outraged that I was doing this. I was getting hundreds of letters from people who normally would never have written or called in.

The pressure became so bad that we lost one station in Seattle, after people demanded the caller abortion be taken off the air. My syndicator told me that he was getting worried because of all the pressure other stations were getting.

After two weeks of this, I decided I had made my point. People were focusing on the few seconds of the caller abortion, to the exclusion of everything else I was doing on the show. I wanted my audience to know that they do have something to say about what happens on my program. Not much, mind you. But some.

So one day I announced that I was canceling the caller abortions. But I made clear to my listeners that there was a larger message involved in what I had done.

Ladies and gentlemen, for the past two weeks I have been performing what I have called caller abortions. Now, during those two weeks I have harmed no one, physically or emotionally. Who am I? I'm just a guy on the radio. What have I been doing? Just playing sounds. The recorded sounds of a vacuum cleaner, an ordinary household appliance, together with a common scream. I take those two sounds, mention the word *abortion,* and people go nuts. But the caller isn't really gone. No one suffered. Yet, I've been accused of insensitivity, cruelty, meanness, and a lack of decency. Some of my listeners have called me the worst things I've ever heard on the radio.

And what are you, my listeners, bothered by? Nothing. Nothing at all. Nobody was hurt. Some people even called up and wanted to record the historic moment when they were aborted by Rush Limbaugh so they could play it for friends. Given all this, what's the commotion about? None of what I did was real. Yet, in this country an abortion happens four thousand times a day. For real. The screams are real, the vacuum cleaner is real. There is real emotional distress. There is physical harm and there's death. And you are calling a guy on the radio and telling him that *he* poses a threat to society? You're telling *him* that *he* is cruel and heartless? He's harming no one. He's just telling you what's really going on in your neighborhood. He is forcing you to deal with the pain of thinking about the realities of real life abortion. We are so far removed from it that we don't think of it in graphic terms. Perhaps if more people did consider the horrors of ending life, they would be much less persuaded by their arguments of convenience. To the extent that I may have heightened awareness out there, I believe I have done a service, regardless of how distasteful it may have been to some.

Where is the outrage against those who do it for real just down the street from where they live? It's not there. They reserve it for calling a guy on the radio to complain about sounds he plays. I think some of them have their priorities mixed up. If you didn't know in your heart of hearts that abortion was a savage, violent act, what I did wouldn't have bugged you so much. I took you inside an abortion mill, and some of you couldn't take it. You can't handle it when it was only dramatized. Yet, you're not bothered by abortion when it happens for real. Is there not a contradiction here? Think about it.

Well, that kind of close was a real grabber for people. It got a lot of people thinking, and very few people then called up to argue with me. Since then, I've described how I did the caller abortions in my stage shows. It takes about thirty minutes to go through, and I can see people literally squirming in the audience. Many people get up and leave, and don't come back till I've gone on to something else. I know who they are—they're people who have had abortions or paid to have someone get one.

So, how should things be? How best to solve this issue that threatens to become this nation's next civil war? What is needed is a little responsibility. We have countless ways of preventing pregnancy, which, if utilized, would negate the need for so many abortions. Our society would be much better off if that responsibility were exercised, rather than abortion used as a selfish way of escaping what is, in truth, careless and reckless behavior.

IN DEFENSE OF THE EIGHTIES

THERE HAS NEVER BEEN A TIME IN HUMAN HISTORY WHEN HUMAN beings have not tried to improve their lives. But the 1980s were the first time that such behavior was characterized so widely as greed. But the 1980s were not the decade of greed. People tried to better themselves and for once there were fewer, and not more, obstacles in their way.

The prosperous eighties are attacked by liberals because that decade vindicates conservative economic policies, repudiates liberal economic policies, and thereby threatens the power base of the liberal left—which is dependent upon the perpetuation of the myth that confiscatory tax policies will bring prosperity to the majority of Americans. As a result, that glorious decade and its principal benefactor, Ronald Reagan, are ceaselessly maligned by the Democratic left.

Because they can't make their case against supply-side economics with empirical evidence, the liberals have reduced themselves to characterizing the eighties as the decade of greed. Even though the irrefutable evidence proves that all classes from poor to rich benefited from supply-side tax policies under Ronald Reagan, the left is unwilling to admit that. For the left to condemn these across-the-board improvements by labeling them as greed is tantamount to saying that they are opposed to prosperity for the poor and middle classes if the wealthy also happen to benefit. Only if the wealthy suffer will these demagogues be satisfied; but that will happen only by increasing marginal tax rates, which will inevitably punish the middle classes and the poor as well. Since when does prosperity become greed? Let's just cite one piece of the evidence which bears directly on the greed issue. As reported in *National Review,* "charitable donations by individuals rose from $64.7 billion (1990 dollars) in 1980 to $102 billion in 1989, an increase of 57.7 per cent. Moreover, after declining relative to national income during the Seventies, charitable donations rose from 2.1 per cent of income in 1979 to a record 2.7 per cent in 1989."

As Paul Craig Roberts observed in a column in *The Wall Street Journal* (Wait! Read this real carefully—it is crucial):

"All of the propagandistic claims of supply-side failure that dominated the economic news of the 80s have been laid to rest. We know for certain that the United States did not disinvest, the United States did not suffer declining productivity growth, did not become uncompetitive, did not create primarily dead-end, low-skill jobs and did not experience declining real family income in the 1980s.

"Prompted by criticism from economists that U.S. government statistics were failing to detect a weakening in the nation's industrial base, the Commerce Department undertook a two-and-a-half-year study of American manufacturing. The study, released earlier this year, shows the 1980s were years of an almost unbelievable revival by U.S. industry. In a front-page story that must have been galling for that paper's editorial writers, the New York Times reported on Feb. 5 that the rate of U.S. manufacturing productivity growth had tripled during the 1980s and was now on a par with Japan and Europe, and that manufacturing's share of gross national product had rebounded to the level of output achieved in the 1960s when American factories hummed at a feverish clip. Far from losing its competitiveness then, the report revealed the U.S. had experienced an unprecedented export boom.

"As far as jobs are concerned, the charge that Reaganomics had

created a nation of hamburger flippers was destroyed in 1988 when the Bureau of Labor Statistics reported that the percentage of new jobs in the higher skill categories was much larger in the 1980s than in the 1970s. The commissioner of the bureau testified before Congress in August 1988 that low-skilled jobs are not growing as fast as those that require a lot of training. The Reagan expansion created skilled jobs at a more rapid pace than our educational system could produce people to fill them.

"To paint a picture of the rich getting richer as the poor get poorer, the partisan Congressional Budget Office and a bevy of Democratic economists had to use unadjusted census data to construct a measure of average family income biased by rising divorce rates and the growth of single-parent households. What these critics discovered was the effects of the decline of the institution of marriage on family income, not Reagan economic policies."

Whoa! That is powerful stuff. Perhaps you should go back and read it again before continuing, because it certainly is not the picture painted by most economic prophets of doom and gloom. I'll wait right here until you get back.

Okay. Ready to resume? Here we go. We are constantly reminded by the media how people spent profligately and consumed obscenely—how the rich got richer and the poor got poorer—under Reagan. Don't you believe it. Don't let the liberals deceive you into believing that a decade of sustained growth without inflation in America resulted in a bigger gap between the haves and the have-nots. Figures compiled by the Congressional Budget Office dispel that myth.

A review of income and inflation figures during both the Carter and Reagan years reveals how much the American people prospered under Reagan, and how much they suffered financially under Carter. The report studies incomes from 1979 to 1983, the four-year period under Jimmy Carter and Ronald Reagan, and also the latter period of the Reagan administration.

How can anyone ever forget the Carter years, which gave new meaning to the phrase *misery index?* There was double-digit stagflation, gasoline lines, and interest rates were up 20 percent. The poorest fifth of the population had a drop of 17 percent in real family income during the Carter administration. (Now ask yourself: Why are these years never cited as dreadful, mediocre years? That's easy. Liberals love misery. It makes them feel necessary. And believe me, everyone was miserable. Such was not the case in the eighties and that, to them, was just too darned unfair.) Contrast this with the period from 1983 to 1989, the years of full-blown Reaganomics, during which the poorest 20 percent of the population saw their income rise 12 percent.

The richest fifth of the population also saw their income rise 12 percent. On a percentage basis, it is simply untrue that the poor got poorer under Reagan. In fact, family income levels rose across the board during the Reagan years.

The destitute became more destitute under Jimmy Carter. Many of you were probably destitute then and I'm sure you remember it well. I was and I do. The destitute always know who they are. You can tell by the way they vote the next chance they get. Hence, bye-bye, Jimmy. The quickest way to devalue anybody's cash holdings and earnings is inflation, and we all know that Carter's administration broke the mold in that category, catapulting it to new heights unequaled before or since. In fact, some scientists worried that inflation was soaring to such never-before-achieved altitudes that it posed a threat to the ozone layer. They later discovered that the threat was posed only by the gaseous emissions coming from the Carter administration itself. In contrast, we also know that Reagan brought inflation down. Way, way down. The inflation rate remained at 5 percent for most of the Reagan years despite the existence of sustained growth throughout that period.

This recent report further corroborates a report of the House Republican Conference in mid-1984. At that time the figures were just coming in from President Reagan's across-the-board tax rate cuts that went into effect in 1982. The Republican supply-siders, pioneered by Congressman Jack Kemp, had argued that "across-the-board rate reductions would increase tax revenues from the wealthy compared to the poor by liberating income from shelters and encouraging saving and investment. The reductions would shift the tax burden upward, toward the high earners, even though rates came down across the board."

The report of the House Republican Conference totally vindicated Reaganomics. Of course, you would expect that, but I believe them anyway. They are my soul buddies. It showed that the very rich—i.e., those making a million dollars or more—actually paid 41 percent more in taxes in 1982 under the tax rate cuts than they did in 1981. The lowest level of income earners—i.e., those making $25,000 and under—paid 12 percent less taxes in 1981 than in 1982. Thus, the rich paid more in tax revenues than they did under Jimmy Carter at much higher marginal tax rates. As Jack Kemp gleefully wrote about these results: "Not only did upper-income taxpayers contribute more in taxes absolutely, but they also shouldered a larger relative share of the entire income tax burden than before. The share of total tax revenues which was paid by those making $40,000 or more increased from 45.1 percent to 48 percent. The tax burden of those making less than $40,000 dropped by the equivalent percentage. This means that there was a substantial shift in the tax burden to upper income groups in the middle of one of the most severe business recessions on record. This result powerfully vindicates the incentive-enhancing argument for marginal tax rate reductions and demonstrates the base-broadening effects of lower rates."

Take your pick of the two reports, 1984 or the present. The results are the same. Each shows that Reaganomics did work, and that the gap between the rich and poor was narrowed rather than expanded during those years. The Democrats have to face the fact that by advocating increases in marginal tax rates, they are working for the benefit of the rich and to the detriment of the poor. The uncontroverted evidence demonstrates the folly of their belief that tax policy is a zero-sum phenomenon. This fundamental misapprehension is what fuels their belief that tax increases for the wealthy will result in redistribution of wealth from the rich to the poor. It is these demagogic promises of redistribution and other techniques of class alienation they use to get elected in their own districts year after year. They simply cannot comprehend the concept articulated by Mr. Kemp that "a rising tide lifts all boats."

Don't fall prey to the seductive emotional appeals of the Democrats as they attempt to pit one group of society against another with their politics of class envy. Let the facts speak for themselves. If a liberal president gets elected, he, like Jimmy Carter, will make sure "fairness" applies to all economic levels. There will be no discrimination against anyone. He will see to it that we all get poor again.

The decade of the 1980s is now history and the objective evidence is there for all to examine. The indisputable truth is that the decade was one of real economic growth without inflation. As a direct result of his tax cuts (and not as a coincidental occurrence or the result of a fortuitous positive business cycle while he was in office, as his detractors would have us believe), America became economically and militarily vibrant again. It was our strong economy spurred by these tax policies that allowed us to become strategically competitive with the Soviets again by providing sufficient wealth for us to enjoy guns and butter simultaneously. It was the Reagan years that squeezed the totalitarian lifeblood from the Eastern Bloc nations and the Soviet Union and brought the Marxist revolution to its knees.

Governor Mario Cuomo (pronounced COOMO on my show) is a master at blaming the 1980s for all of our problems. He appeared on *Meet the Press* a while back, and said that while Ronald Reagan was a nice man he had taught Americans that they didn't need to care about the poor anymore. Cuomo urges us to care more.

Liberals such as Cuomo love to demonstrate their compassion by throwing money—other people's money, that is—at problems. Liberals measure compassion by counting the number of people who receive some kind of government help. In attempting to solve society's problems by governmental transfer payments, they disregard human nature and the long-term effects of their programs. As stated by Senator Phil Gramm, liberals like to achieve fairness by spreading the misery. Conservatives seek to expand opportunity. By government giveaway programs, individuals are often hurt far more than they are helped. The recipients of these programs become dependent on the government and their dignity is destroyed. Is it compassionate to enslave more and more people by making them a part of the government dependency cycle? I think compassion should be measured by how many people no longer need it. Helping people to become self-sufficient is much more compassionate than drugging them with the narcotic of welfare.

Throwing money at problems has never solved anything. If it did we would have the most well-educated young people in the world. Instead, we will spend an average of $6,000 a year per student in this country in 1992 and one quarter of the students can't locate the United States on a world map. In fact, let's run the numbers on that $6,000. The average class size is what, 30 students? So 30 × $6,000 = $180,000 per classroom. The teacher probably earns around $30,000, so that leaves $150,000. Next we have books, chalk, utilities, building amortization, dead frogs (fewer and fewer, though, as many students wimp out at the thought of dissection, so they now use pictures, which are cheaper than dead frogs), spit ball remover, school buses, drivers, school board members, principals, condoms, abortion counseling, attendants to valet park students' cars, and computers. Remember, now, that we are spending $180,000 *per classroom*. How many classrooms are there in your neighborhood school? I'll bet you that we could do all of the above *plus* hire college professors and pay them $50,000 per year and limo students to and from school every day and still have money left over. So just where is all that money going? What are we getting for it other than a bunch of whiners who alternately demand and grovel for more every year? Think about that.

It didn't used to be this way. Previous generations were without many of the material riches that we enjoy today, but they knew how to read and write. Abraham Lincoln was probably educated in his day for the amount of money we spend on a school lunch for one student today.

LIBERALS LOVE MONEY TOO

We've all seen liberals who head foundations or Washington lobbies appear on television and condemn greed and selfishness. They like to pose as people with pure motives, who are completely uninterested in money. I help people, they say, I don't do this for myself. Well, come on.

I've talked with them at cocktail parties and such. Here's how the conversation goes:

LIBERAL DO-GOODER: I'm working with poor people in the inner city. Of course, I'm not doing it for the money.

RUSH: Are you getting paid?

LIBERAL: Yeah . . .

RUSH: Do you think you're getting paid enough?

LIBERAL: I could use more. But I'm satisfied with what I'm getting. Unlike greedy businessmen and others who are just out for themselves.

RUSH: Where do you get your money or operating funds?

LIBERAL: Well, from a government grant.

RUSH: I bet you're out there trying to get more money every year for your operation, aren't you? Money drives what you do. You couldn't do what you do without money, right?

LIBERAL: Well, I'm doing this from my heart.

RUSH: You may be, and everybody may be doing what they do from the heart, but you can't do it without money.

LIBERAL: Yes, but I'm doing good things with it.

RUSH: Well, so are other people. People who make money and build businesses create jobs for people. Those people pay the taxes that enable the government to afford giving you a grant.

LIBERAL: Those people will always be around.

RUSH: Not if you tell them it's immoral to want more, to strive for a higher standard of living.

LIBERAL: But . . .

RUSH: Just be quiet a minute. Not if you build disincentives to investment in the tax code under the pretense of fairness. To tell people it is immoral to want more money for themselves is the height of arrogance and will lead to less for everyone eventually.

LIBERAL: But . . .

RUSH: The reason you don't like the eighties is that you didn't get enough for your concerns. You're not against the accumulation of money, just that not enough of it comes your way.

The difference between my liberal do-gooder friend and people who work in the private sector is simple. The liberals who run these foundations and liberal lobbying groups aren't like the readers of this book. They don't work in the sense that most people do. They live off the contributions of others or government grants. They say they are doing their jobs because they care. But they need money just as much as anyone else. The difference is that they often go to greater lengths than you and I in hiding or denying it.

A survey of obscure government records found that of the 117 largest nonprofit organizations, more than 1 out of 4 pay their top executives $250,000 a year or more. You see, it isn't just evil corporate executives who get high salaries or keep them when the rest of their company is hurting. Many of these nonprofit groups don't even do charitable work. They are political agitators lobbying the government for money and regulations they can twist to their benefit. Unlike corporate executives, they don't create anything of value. All they do is raise money and trouble. What galls me is that these people would love to make you think they are pure philanthropists, that they are indifferent to money. They talk about their lives as if they are driven only by a sense of duty and social responsibility. But often they earn just as much money as do the people they criticize for being greedy. They don't want you to know that, but it's true.

People should know that the people on television berating them for wanting to keep more of their income probably make five times more than they do. Faye Wattleton of Planned Parenthood made $180,000 a year. She quit to earn even more money doing a television show. *Forbes* magazine found that Ralph Nader doesn't lead the monklike existence that he pretends to. He stays at his sister's place, a very fancy townhouse in a Washington neighborhood. Money motivates everyone. It's just that liberals deny it so they can make the rest of us feel guilty.

I'M NOT ASHAMED OF EARNING MONEY

As a conservative, I am sick and tired of being accused of being heartless and cruel because I don't believe compassion can be measured by throwing money at problems. I make no apologies for having money and earning it. I'm not a phony on that, and never will be.

Steve Kroft of *60 Minutes* asked me why I did my radio show. He said he had heard I did it for the money. I hesitated, and then plunged right in. "Sure, I do it for the money," I said. Then I asked Steve Kroft, "Are you doing your job for the fun of it?" They edited that part out. This exchange on *60 Minutes*, out of context, is somewhat misleading. True, I do my work for the money. I don't know about you, but I don't have anyone to support me if I chose not to work. But I also do it because I enjoy what I'm doing and I believe in what I say. To say that I do it for the money is not the same as saying that I can be bought, or that I will abandon my principles for money. I don't say things on the air that I don't believe in for the purpose of stirring controversy and ultimately making more money. I am sincere in what I say. I believe that my openness and sincerity is what enables me to be as successful as I am. I do not let considerations of money dictate the level or manner of my performance. I try to be the best (and generally accomplish it) I can be as a matter of personal pride. To the extent that I do a superb job—a great job, actually—the money follows. In fact, I am recognized by experts and laypeople alike as the best talk show host in the universe. And it shows.

The truth is, I have worked in radio for twenty-two years (long enough to retire in some professions) and made no money to speak of during the first seventeen. In 1983 I was earning $18,000 per year—less than I was making ten years earlier while in Pittsburgh. I have been fired seven times. I have been broke twice. Those years I was with the Kansas City Royals were awful financially. The house payment and the MasterCard bill were due during the same pay period, leaving me no cash for the period. That meant buying snacks at convenience stores because they, unlike supermarkets, accepted credit cards. I was overextended after buying a house I had no business buying, but I fell prey to the theory that everyone has to own a home. I would try to land extra jobs here and there. Back then, I felt lucky if I could earn a little extra doing a commercial.

I understand how difficult it is for working people to keep their heads above water. That's why I am so convinced that we must have a strong economy to enable as many people as possible to provide for themselves and their families. It's only people who have cushy jobs and don't work for a living who don't care if the economy is bad. That's how they can favor higher taxes and government spending that economists tell us can only slow down and cripple the private job-producing sector.

It's easy to talk about punishing wealthy people for their supposed greed. But when you talk about taxing the rich, you're talking about taxing capital. And taxing capital results in damage to more than just the wealthy. In other words, you can't punish the wealthy without also punishing the middle class. That's because the wealthy invest their capital to create new jobs, most of which accrue to those not wealthy. Many mistakenly view private-sector businesses as social institutions that spontaneously spring up to provide benefits and salaries to working people. But it is people, often upper middle class people, who start those businesses by investing their own risk capital. This risk capital must bring these entrepreneurs a reasonable return on their investment or they won't be willing to risk their money again. If they are unwilling to take those risks, then they won't invest their money and create new jobs and new products, and those potential employees and consumers of those products are the ones who will suffer.

A perfect example of that in our political system is the increase in the capital gains tax rates and the shortening of the allowable years of depreciation. Both of these "reform" measures were enacted by Congress for the ostensible purpose of taking away the unfair advantages of the wealthy. The result was to cripple the real estate market. I don't need to tell you that the negative impact of that affected all economic levels of our society, and arguably the middle class and the poor, more than the rich. Another example of a policy enacted in the spirit of class warfare (i.e., one that was designed to deprive the wealthy of unfair advantages) was the luxury tax on the yacht industry. By assessing a surtax on the buyers of luxury yachts in order to appear to be the champions of the lower and middle classes, Congress virtually ruined an industry as people simply stopped buying yachts. They went offshore for them. Tens of thousands of jobs for working people, not the wealthy, were lost in the name of compassion. Liberals refuse even to acknowledge this because it is such a textbook repudiation of their politics of class envy.

Whether you are a businessman or someone earning a salary, you should never apologize for trying to earn more money. Never feel guilty for wanting to keep more of it for you and your family. Do not accept the silly notion that there is poverty and suffering in America because you are greedy and aren't paying enough in taxes. Realize that regardless of the job you have, you are helping to create other jobs. The goods and services you consume help create employment for people who wouldn't otherwise have it. The confiscatory percentages in income and social security taxes you pay on any extra money you earn helps keep checks going to widows and orphans. If anything, you are morally SUPERIOR to those liberal compassion fascists who claim you are greedy. You have a real job; they just beg for a living.

AIDS—GOOD MONEY AND BAD: SOME HELP IS NOT DESIRED

EVER SINCE THE AIDS CRISIS BECAME POLITICIZED I HAVE BEEN LEERY of those who claimed that their primary purpose was to find a cure for the disease. My doubts were confirmed in January 1990. AIDS activists had begun to employ a strategy of confrontation, accusing various government agencies, elected officials, and "naïve" and "uncaring" people (everyone but themselves) for the spread of the disease. This, of course, was a transparent attempt to deflect attention away from drug abuse and unsafe sex, which are responsible for the spread of over 90 percent of all cases of AIDS, and focus blame for the disease on so-called homophobes who opposed sufficient funding for research and a cure. As a result of this formidable propaganda effort the notion evolved that money—and only money—could rid us of the horrors of the HIV virus.

In early 1990 I learned of the tragic story of Elizabeth and Paul Michael Glaser. CBS's *60 Minutes* did a feature explaining how Elizabeth had contracted the virus by way of tainted blood during a transfusion while in childbirth. Her baby contracted the virus and died. She and another child are HIV positive but at present are not suffering from the virus.

Unwilling to passively accept her fate without trying to help other families in the same plight, Elizabeth and a friend established the Pediatric AIDS Foundation to raise money to comfort people whose children had contracted AIDS. She was able to convince former President Ronald Reagan to record a thirty-second public service TV announcement for her foundation. The *60 Minutes* piece showed Reagan arriving at a studio, being thanked profusely and gratefully by the Glasers, and then recording the spot. Everyone was smiling and the Glasers' appreciation for the President's efforts was quite noticeable.

Then my rage and anger surfaced as *60 Minutes* ran an interview with a representative of an organization called Cure AIDS Now. The group was opposed to the Glasers' using Reagan in any way connected to AIDS research and funding. The group's leaders had written a letter excoriating the Glasers for using Reagan, because, claimed Cure AIDS Now, Reagan was himself responsible for the spread of the disease because he hadn't cared soon enough. Here is a portion of the letter:

February 7, 1990

Paul Michael and Elizabeth Glaser
Los Angeles Pediatric AIDS Foundation
1311 Colorado Avenue
Santa Monica, CA 90404

While I share in your grief of a loss of one child to AIDS, one child stricken with the virus and you, Elizabeth, also HIV infected, I note and understand your involvement and your pleas for help, as I have lost many people dear to me to this dreaded disease.

However, Ronald Reagan doing commercials for your organization, pleading for the understanding that HE lacked for 8 years and due to this costing more than one (1) million lives and a world wide plague of 20,000,000 infections that are out of control in 157 nations willing to admit it, this to me is intolerable. Allowing him to get off the hook with his lack of responsibility is tantamount to asking Adolph [sic] Hitler to do a commercial for the Jewish National Fund.

The Way Things Ought to Be

The REAGAN-BUSH legacy is a global holocaust. They were more focused on selling out this nation with the "Iran Contra" deceptions and claiming "executive privilege" to escape the laws of our country, while cost was no expense to save their skins. In our country and world wide, we "sinners," dealing with a dreaded disease of crisis proportion, were being ignored and treated as expendable by this Reagan/Bush Klan.

Now, out of office, Reagan comes to participate, so as to cover up his role in this crime against humanity and in the process slap each and everyone of us who have suffered the losses. What is the difference between him and Ceausescu of Romania?

CURE AIDS NOW believes that "life is terminal but AIDS is manageable" if detected early. Instead, Reagan/Bush have seen AIDS with a too little too late and "Why bother" attitude that has caused much pain to many, many people for no reasons . . .

The claims made in this letter are hysterical and nonsensical, not to mention threatening. During the *60 Minutes* piece the representative from Cure AIDS Now promised to contact the three network presidents and urge them not to run the Reagan spot. If they did, he warned, advertiser boycotts might ensue.

That did it for me. So there was good money and bad money in the fight against AIDS. This established that there were some things more important than a cure; that ideology mattered as well! If you were a conservative you had no place in the fight against AIDS. What was especially maddening was this: thirty seconds of Ronald Reagan broadcast to the nation would have raised far more money and understanding than all the gay rights marches you could sponsor. Yet, his involvement was unacceptable. My reaction was immediate. Here was a woman and her family devastated by a disease, and their efforts to help themselves and others in their situation were being challenged. The first thing I did was to make a point of all this on my program, to illustrate that the politics of AIDS was standing in the way of a cure, that those at greatest risk and in the greatest need of a solution were themselves opposing the very action they demanded because it was offered by a political enemy. I passionately read the Cure AIDS Now letter during my stage shows that spring and summer, trying both to arouse sympathy for the Glasers and to illustrate the disingenuousness of some in the AIDS activist community. In December of 1990 I sent a contribution to the Pediatric AIDS Foundation, with the following note enclosed:

The Pediatric AIDS Foundation
Mr. & Mrs. Paul Michael Glaser
2407 Wilshire Blvd. Suite 613
Santa Monica, CA 90403

Dear Paul and Elizabeth,

I am deeply touched by your plight and cheered by your courageous effort in dealing with it. May God bless you and your family.

My Best,
Rush H. Limbaugh III
Excellence in Broadcasting Network

But making a contribution wasn't enough for me. I decided to adopt the Pediatric AIDS Foundation as one of the "official" charities of the Excellence in Broadcasting Network and solicit donations from my audience for the foundation. I also wanted to record a public service announcement for Pediatric AIDS and play it during unsold commercial availabilities. I had no desire to be an official spokesman, nor did I want to be listed on the foundation's letterhead or invited to star-studded Hollywood fund-raisers as a means of meeting celebrities. I simply wanted to help an organization which had been maligned and, in my view, threatened by fringe extremists.

After conferring with Ed McLaughlin, the chairman of the board of EFM Media, parent organization of the EIB Network, and John Axten, the president, it was decided that our public relations director would first write, then call Elizabeth Glaser and inform her of our desire to help before we proceeded with any of our ideas. Our first contact was in January 1991. When the idea was not immediately accepted by the Pediatric AIDS Foundation, I sensed that the ultimate answer would be "no." And I felt I knew why: that I was politically incorrect and therefore would cause the foundation to be harassed by AIDS activists who would certainly object to any assistance I might offer, just as they had President Reagan's.

For three months we waited and responded to every request the foundation made. They wanted tapes of my radio program, which was odd, since all they had to do was turn on station KFI in Los Angeles to hear it three hours every day. They said that they wished to speak to me, then decided they didn't. Finally we got the word: Thanks, but no thanks. And don't have Mr. Limbaugh call us—our decision is final. We were never given a satisfactory explanation for why our offer was rejected.

During the entire three-month period I never spoke to anyone at the foundation, including Elizabeth Glaser, and on reflection I think this was my major mistake in the whole process. Had I made the first call and been able to speak directly to the directors of the foundation, I am confident that I could have allayed any fears and apprehensiveness they had about associating themselves and the foundation with me.

Needless to say, I was disappointed and a little perplexed. And a little mad. I had just been told that any assistance I might offer was unacceptable and would be summarily rejected. This is just more proof that there is good money and bad money in the fight against AIDS. I pondered my next move. Should I go public with this story? I decided not to because my intent from the beginning was only to help babies born with AIDS, and to flog the foundation in public would only detract from that. Besides, it would no doubt be interpreted and reported by some that I was simply seeking publicity. Should I ignore the wishes of the foundation and record and play a public service announcement anyway and force them to go public by demanding that I stop it? No, because that would embarrass and anger them and that, of course, was not my intent either. So I sulked, but remained silent—until an interview with Steve Kroft of *60 Minutes* some four months later. During the interview, which was part of a profile of me that aired in October 1991, Kroft hit me, as I knew he would, with the accusation "made by some" that I was heartless and insensitive toward people with AIDS. He said that some people viewed me as a bigot and hatemonger. What did I have to say about that? I tried again to suppress my anger at this distortion and told him the entire story of the Glasers and my efforts to help them. Afterwards I worried that I shouldn't have mentioned it, that I was defeating my own stated purpose in trying to help the foundation. As it turned out, the story was not included in the profile *60 Minutes* aired, probably because it took too much time. I felt greatly relieved.

I eventually did hear from Elizabeth Glaser, though. In January 1992, she called to tell me how angry she was at the way I had discussed Magic Johnson's first appearance at the President's Commission on AIDS. She said she wanted to go on my program to rebut some of what I had said. Needless to say, I was taken aback, given her earlier refusal of my offer to help. Here was a woman who had summarily discarded me now taking me to task for my opinion on how Magic was being used by certain AIDS activists. I remember thinking, "Wow, what gall she has."

I learned as she talked, however, that my original reaction to her from the *60 Minutes* piece was accurate. She was intelligent, thoughtful, and full of hope. Tireless, too. And I really believe she only does what she thinks best. This, if I may be bold here, is what really hurt my feelings when she rejected my help.

She said that Magic was the single greatest fund-raising hope they had since he was a high-profile athlete and hero to many, and that I was damaging the opportunity. She told me that I was intelligent and persuasive and had such a large audience that I needed to be turned around on this. Naturally I asked her why, if she felt this way about my audience and my persuasiveness, she had rejected my earlier offer to help, and had accepted Reagan's. She said they only look forward and that Reagan had changed his mind on some things, but that many people (not gays, she said) in the mainstream population she spoke to had felt that I was against gays. I pointed out that she had never spoken to me about that, so how could she be sure? I shared with her the details of my political opposition to much of the militant homosexual agenda but that I didn't care who sleeps with whom, that I harbored no bias per se against the lifestyle.

But even if I were, what would being antigay have to do with raising money for the Pediatric AIDS Foundation? How would that hurt my ability to raise contributions from my large audience, which didn't feel that way? Wasn't it one of her goals to broaden the base of contributors and understanding about the disease? I must admit I was flummoxed. And besides, I asked, what about this business of only looking forward? It seemed to me I was being rejected precisely because of what people's past impressions of me were.

THE DIET FOR PEACE

Since I am speaking of charities, let me share a great story that illustrates just how things eventually do work out. I was approached in mid-1989 by a diet company about advertising their method. You've seen this before: an overweight personality goes on the diet and shares the stupendous success he or she is having, which inspires others to do the diet.

Well, I wanted to do it differently, not like everyone else on radio did it. I thought this would be an excellent time to establish my own charitable foundation. My idea was The Diet for Peace. Heck, everything else was being done for peace then: kite flies for peace, Frisbees for peace, Grandmothers for Peace. Some lost souls were even lighting candles and floating them down rivers for peace. Others went to the mountaintops and chanted mantras for peace.

But my scheme was unique: Whereas all these loony ideas wouldn't do anything for peace (all they really accomplished was to make the screwballs who did this stuff feel better), mine would actually promote peace. How? By contributing the money raised to the Defense Department, which was being faced with mounting budget cuts. I wanted to lose enough weight that I could fit behind the stick of a B-1 bomber headed for Moscow.

We would raise money in two ways. People all across the Fruited Plain who didn't want or need to diet could nevertheless contribute so much per pound that I lost. Those who went on the Diet for Peace with me would pledge so much per pound that they lost and have their friends match their pledges. Now think of the loot we could have raised to start this foundation. It could have been astronomical.

In fact, the more I thought about it the more serious about it I became. I chucked the Defense Department as beneficiary because it was, as it turned out, illegal to contribute funds as you would to a charity. As the invasion of Panama wound down I got a different idea: we could donate our funds to the children of any servicemen and -women killed in action. We wouldn't be able to get our foundation funded in enough time to benefit the kids who lost parents in the Panama invasion, but surely there would be others. So I began in earnest to try to put this together.

It didn't work because the diet company which approached me wasn't interested in setting up what would be a huge organization to deal with this. They were interested in advertising their diet, not getting into a foundation business, which I understood. Still, I was disappointed. We pitched the idea to some other companies but none were interested. As it turns out, I didn't need one.

Through mutual friends in Sacramento I met a man in New York named Dick Torykian, who is a former Marine and works for the investment firm Lazard Frères. Torykian likes to feed people. He just sits there and watches people eat his food, whether at a restaurant or his home. He shoves it at you, won't take no for an answer.

The first night I was invited to his house he also invited a bunch of his old Marine buddies from the area. He knew nothing of the Diet for Peace, although you won't believe it after you read what's next. During the adult beverages these guys began telling old war stories, talking about their days in the Marines and the fun and sorrow they shared.

(I must say here that to hear people relive their war experiences is moving. Many people don't ever experience the camaraderie these people did, and the loyalty and love they have for one another is moving and profound. My father was a P-51 squadron leader in World War II and the happiest I believe I ever saw him was when his squadron got together for annual reunions. Those guys all went through something most of us fortunately will not and the bonds which united them are enviable.)

One of the men was a guy named Pete Haas, who now heads up the Marine Corps Scholarship Fund. You know what it does? The same exact thing I wanted to do with my foundation: It provides for the education of children whose fathers or mothers die as Marines in the line of duty. In fact, they expanded their contributions and aid to include the children of men and women in all branches of the service following the Gulf War.

The Marine Corps Scholarship Fund is amazing. Ninety-five percent of all dollars donated go to beneficiaries. Think of that. I know of no other charity with that kind of efficiency. The federal government, for example, is horrible. Only twenty-eight cents of every dollar of assistance actually gets to the beneficiary. Most other charities are lucky if 50 percent of what is donated actually gets paid out.

So, who needs my foundation? No one. It already exists as the Marine Corps Scholarship Fund, which is now one of my official charities. I have attended two awards banquets they've held, and believe me when I say I have rarely been so moved as when attending these functions.

If I had not learned what goodness, love, and compassion are when I met the people who run the Marine Corps Scholarship Foundation, I certainly would have learned then. They could patent it.

My decision to include this chapter comes after a great deal of agonizing and uncertainty. My sole purpose was to help, not hurt, the cause of the Pediatric AIDS Foundation, and when I was told that I would harm it by helping it I felt devastated. It was my first real exposure to just how politically incorrect I was considered by the left, and my first desire was to scream out all this on my radio program. My better judgment prevailed, however. Had I followed my initial reaction I would have ended up doing harm to the foundation and Elizabeth Glaser herself, which was the opposite of my intent.

I include these events now because I have spoken to Elizabeth Glaser about all this, and at that time she was amenable to new discussions on my original request to help. We have not had those discussions as the book goes to press. Regardless of their outcome, it is still my desire to be on the side which understands and helps AIDS charities of all kinds, including the Pediatric AIDS Foundation.

My respect and admiration, as well as empathy and compassion, for Elizabeth Glaser and her family remain the same. I intend to pursue this when the time is right and see if it can't be done again with a different outcome. In the meantime, do me a favor. Should you find it within yourself to contribute to a charity, and should you have the means, please seriously consider the Pediatric AIDS Foundation.

We are talking about the essence of innocence: babies and young children who, along with their families, will benefit greatly from any help they receive. True, there are many misunderstandings and much anger about AIDS, but don't let those emotions prevent you from offering what these people need most: your support and love. It may be all they have.

THE IMPERIAL CONGRESS

A SATIRICAL AD I PLAYED ON MY SHOW DURING THE TIME OF THE House Banking scandal says it all:

ANNOUNCER: And now, another Capitol Hill Bank moment.

HOUSE BANK EMPLOYEE: I'm working behind the counter at the bank, when in comes another freshman congressman. He puts $500 into his new checking account. Boy, you should've seen the look on his face when I told him that $500 in a Capitol Hill checking account is unheard of. Congressmen never keep that kind of money in the bank.

CONGRESSMAN: So, this kindly teller tells me my $500 is worth $60,000 to $100,000 in check writing privileges. Until that moment, I never realized how much I was going to love living in Washington. Heh, heh, heh.

ANNOUNCER: Capitol Hill Bank, for personal service.

HOUSE BANK EMPLOYEE: I like to really get involved with my customers. Why, once a congressman called me from this big drinking party he was throwing. Said he needed some more checks, so I went to this party with a box of checks. Why, he even paid for that party with one of those checks. I felt like I really made a difference.

CONGRESSMAN: I don't remember much about that party, but I do remember my Capitol Hill Bank associate. He really saved me. You know, people like Ted Kennedy can rack up a big bar tab. Capitol Hill Bank made me look like I had money and influence. You don't get that kind of treatment from a bank very often. Capitol Hill Bank.

ANNOUNCER: Capitol Hill Bank, for worry-free checking.

CONGRESSMAN: If I get named, that kid's going down with me.

ANNOUNCER: Capitol Hill Bank, member FLEECE, a special privilege lender.

The banking scandal in the U.S. House of Representatives is proof positive that something is terribly wrong with our government. In a three-year period, 355 members of Congress wrote 20,000 bad checks, according to the General Accounting Office. Two hundred legislators kited checks in excess of their next month's paychecks, which are estimated at about $5,000, at least once during a three-year period. Ninety-nine legislators wrote bad checks in excess of their next month's paychecks at least twice during the three-year period. These ninety-nine members of Congress bounced checks worth at least $11 million. Fifty-five major abusers were overdrawn so consistently as to make it clear that they were deliberately availing themselves of their ability to obtain a permanent no-interest loan.

The Wall Street Journal has dubbed the check-kiting scandal the Kiting 55, a takeoff on the Charles Keating savings and loan scandal. This was a hideous and scandalous story. And for the longest time it received only slight coverage in the mainstream press. The Speaker of the House, Tom Foley, originally said it wouldn't be "useful" to list all the offenders. To do so, he said, would be to compromise the independence of the House. Not useful? Not only was it useful, it was imperative. Anybody in their right mind, concerned about public trust and confidence, would have felt obligated to list the offenders. The House Ethics Committee earlier announced plans to list only twenty-four of the offenders as scapegoats, but to withhold the names of the other three-hundred-plus violators. Of the twenty-four who were to be named, five were not then in office.

Most of us have written a bad check at some point in our lives. I have, and I've always been greatly embarrassed by it. I've also been penalized for it. Many people have actually served time behind bars for doing it far less than does the average congressman.

The difference between you and me and many congressmen is that most of them don't feel any shame for having written dozens or even hundreds of bad checks. I was on the *MacNeil/Lehrer News Hour* during the early days of this sordid and lurid period, debating Representative Vic Fazio, whom I know well since he represents Sacramento. Fazio lived up to his nickname as the "Prince of Perks" when he said that criticism of the House Bank was merely an effort by conservatives "to avoid the subjects that we really need to be talking about, the scandal in health care, the prolonged recession, the high rates of unemployment, the things we were elected to do." I passionately pointed out that he and his gang in Congress hadn't been doing anything for twelve years, ever since Reagan was elected. They were the reason there was government gridlock. Their only concern was to deny Reagan as many legislative victories as possible. Why now, in March 1992, in the midst of perhaps the largest House scandal in history, were they all of a sudden so concerned about the things people sent them to Washington to do? And what a joke that is, by itself. Plus, those arguments don't seem to deter Democrats every time they smell a Republican scandal. For instance, Foley plans to push ahead with a ridiculous investigation of the so-called October Surprise, where sinister agents of the Reagan/Bush campaign were supposed to have had clandestine meetings in France with Iranian representatives to cement a deal whereby the Iranians would not release the fifty-four hostages held in the American embassy before the 1980 election. Foley actually said that there was no evidence to support the allegations and it was precisely for this reason they needed to investigate! "We need to put this deeply disturbing period behind us," said the deeply disturbed speaker. Disturbing to whom? Talk about a waste of time. This is nothing more than a political witch hunt fueled by the Democrats' realization that the only hope they have of winning the White House is to shame the Republicans out of it via scandal. But wait! What about the scandal in health care, the prolonged recession, the high rates of unemployment, the things the people elected Congress to deal with?

The bank scandal highlights the arrogance and condescension of members of Congress. Some of the excuses and rationalizations they offered were at the same time hilarious and disgraceful. Some said they didn't know this was happening because the bank did not keep records. It didn't? How can this be? How is it that we know who the offenders are? Besides, should that have exempted the congressmen depositors from keeping records themselves? The rest of us have to keep records or neglect to do so at our own peril. We do not depend on the bank to keep records for us. We can't avoid keeping records, knowing that our bank will cover us for whatever amount we want to write checks above our bank balances. None of us can write a check for money we don't have.

It's an outrage when members of Congress set up a system whereby they can spend money they don't have. I've had members call me up and say, "Rush, there isn't anything to this bank thing. It was a cooperative." Excuse me, there is no other group of people in this country who can do that for very long and get away with it. You and I can't. John Gotti can't. Al Capone couldn't. Yet, members of Congress had been doing this for over a hundred years.

There are lots of people serving time in jails in this country for what some members of Congress did with their House checking accounts. Recently, a judge in Macomb, Mississippi, released a woman from prison who had written bad checks because "what's good for elected officials is good for the common folks." The judge declared that until Congress pays a price for its bad checks he wasn't going to sentence people to prison for writing bad checks unless they were repeat offenders.

As much as I admire the judge's nerve, the solution isn't to let check kiters go free, but to prosecute the ones in Congress who are guilty of serious crimes. Joseph DeGenova, the former federal prosecutor for Washington, D.C., called me and told me that some members will probably face charges under the same statute that was used to convict people in the Iran-Contra scandal. It's called "Conspiracy to Defraud the U.S. Government."

Now I know some of you believe the stories about how no taxpayer money was at risk in the House Bank, so the only people the check kiters harmed were other members. But that simply won't wash. It was *all* taxpayer money. We pay them. They work for us. Courts have twice ruled that the money in the House Bank belongs to the U.S. government until it is physically removed by members. That's why all change errors were made up with taxpayer funds. Three times in American history, the latest being in 1947, Congress has bailed out the losses of people who have embezzled from the House Bank. The only reason taxpayers didn't lose any money this time was that members shifted money from their campaign accounts to cover their shortages at the House Bank, also a move of dubious legality.

There are criminal possibilities and tax consequences that exist here. It is wrong when members can be overdrawn to the tune of $100,000 or $200,000 a year and not have it reported or have any penalty imposed—even if they were not directly using taxpayers' moneys to cover the float. Although taxpayer money wasn't used to subsidize the overdrafts, it was used to operate the bank. Apparently some $1 million of taxpayer money was used to operate the bank, which made it possible for members to use one another's funds to cover their overdrafts. In normal commercial banking, the bank must pay its own administrative costs, including supplies, equipment, personnel, etc. It pays for these costs through the time value of money it is able to capitalize on, in part through deposits in the checking accounts of its customers. So it is inaccurate to say that taxpayer money was not used to enable these members of Congress to accord themselves advantages unavailable to other citizens. It clearly was. With taxpayer moneys being used to subsidize the operational costs of the bank, members' funds were freed up for use as float by other members.

Of course, this scandal and the cocaine dealing in the House Post Office are merely symptomatic of a much greater problem, which is the overall institutional corruption of the Democrat-controlled Congress. This is a Congress which has exempted itself from its own laws; and which has generated a $400 billion annual budget deficit and a nearly $4 trillion national debt by refusing to treat the taxpayers' money as a sacred commodity, over which Congress is merely the custodian, not the owner. For members to argue that their excess spending is due to the overwhelming needs of the people is an outrage; it is a demonstration of their unbridled arrogance. In fact, this excess spending occurs precisely for the benefit of incumbents in several ways. First, a great amount of funds is casually allocated to building up massive staffs for members for the ostensible purpose of better enabling them to serve their constituencies, but for the actual purpose of public relations for the benefit of the incumbents. They use their staffs to ingratiate themselves with the voters in their districts—thereby helping to perpetuate their terms in office. Second, congressmen fight for pork-barreling funds for their constituencies in exchange for votes to keep them in office.

THE MEMBERS BITE BACK

My criticism of the House Bank last spring did not go unnoticed.

Representative Donald Pease, an Ohio Democrat, complained on C-SPAN that his office had been flooded with calls, almost all of them generated by that "bombthrower, Rush Limbaugh." I only throw bombs if I have the right ammunition, Congressman. The media also went after me. Jon Margolis wrote a column in the *Chicago Tribune* called *House Members Convicted in the Court of Talk Radio.* He claimed that I had lowered talk radio into the "pit of undiscriminating disdain toward all elected officials." He wrote that there were "far worse" things than congressional arrogance. Tell that to John Sununu, who was pilloried for his arrogance in using government planes by the very members of Congress who are now running for cover in the House Bank scandal.

With his explanations of the House Bank, Speaker Tom Foley has acted as if the American people are idiots. He was warned about the massive overdrafts at the bank in 1989 and yet did nothing about it. He says the bank wasn't really a bank, even though members were able to get their magnetically encoded House Bank checks to be accepted by the Federal Reserve, something only a bank can do. He says no crimes were committed using the bank, ignoring the loans that some members made to their campaigns, the money laundering some of them probably engaged in, and the failure of many members to report their interest-free loans on their tax returns. I think Speaker Foley suffers from the Pinocchio disease, but instead of his nose getting bigger when he doesn't tell the truth, his ears do. Foley's ears are positively enormous these days.

CONGRESSIONAL ARROGANCE

The people in Congress have insulated themselves from the American people. Because they've gotten away with so much for so long, many of them must believe the American people are stupid. But it's not entirely the fault of the voters. The media has covered up Congress' sins for a long time. Many journalists are lazy and they live off the snacks of information passed out by congressional staffers. They love prepackaged stories they don't have to work at uncovering themselves. In return, reporters only rarely bite the congressional hand that feeds them.

The congressional scandals that go unreported in the media, until recently, are stunning. Some of them are only irritating, such as the fact that Congress had ten parking garage attendants in 1959 and today it has over one hundred. There are 1,227 policemen for the Capitol, about seven for every acre of the Capitol grounds, yet the one time they tried to investigate a cocaine scandal at the House Post Office they were removed from the case by Speaker Foley's aides. This is as good a time as any to explain the House Post Office scandal. Once again, a commercial which aired on my show:

ANNOUNCER: The Capitol Hill Post Office. Over a hundred years of service.

RETIRED, WALTER BRENNAN–SOUNDING POST OFFICE WORKER: Yeah, I remember my first day behind the counter of the Capitol Hill Post Office. It's something I'll never forget.
(FLASHBACK)

(YOUNG) POST OFFICE WORKER: Well, hello there, Mr. Congressman, is there anything I can help you with there?

CONGRESSMAN: Well, yes, son, I need a couple of them there first–class stamps.

POST OFFICE WORKER: Is that all, sir?

CONGRESSMAN: Now, can you cash this check for a thousand dollars?

POST OFFICE WORKER: Boy, sir, I don't know, I don't think so.

CONGRESSMAN: Trust me son, you can. It's just the way we do things up here on the Hill.
(RETURN TO PRESENT)

RETIRED, WALTER BRENNAN–SOUNDING POST OFFICE WORKER: Oh, sure the congressmen have come and gone and retired, but some things remain the same.

POST OFFICE WORKER: Well, hello there, Mr. Congressman, is there anything I can help you with there?

CONGRESSMAN: Yeah, check my mailbox.

POST OFFICE WORKER: Okay, just a check statement from your bank, sir.

CONGRESSMAN: What check statement?

POST OFFICE WORKER: Oh, yes, sir, I'll just tear this up right away.

CONGRESSMAN: Good kid, good kid. Hey, I need some postage stamps, just one.

POST OFFICE WORKER: Okay, that'll be twenty–nine cents.

CONGRESSMAN: Here's a constituent's check for five thousand.

POST OFFICE WORKER: And here's your change. Thanks, Congressman.

CONGRESSMAN: And kid, you keep that stamp.

POST OFFICE WORKER: Hey, thanks.

CONGRESSMAN: (Thinking) That way, if I'm indicted, he's my accomplice, ha ha ha.

CONGRESSMAN: (Speaking) Bye–bye.
(PRESENT)

The Way Things Ought to Be

RETIRED, WALTER BRENNAN–SOUNDING POST OFFICE WORKER: Yes, sir, I guess it's true what they say about congressmen and the Capitol Hill Post Office. Neither inquiry, nor bribes, nor abuses of power should keep our appointed leaders from making their rounds.

ANNOUNCER: The Capitol Hill Post Office, another special-privilege institution.

The biggest scandal on Capitol Hill is the list of laws that Congress routinely exempts itself from. Every other American has to obey them, but not Congress. Senator Charles Grassley of Iowa sent me a list of them. They include:

The Social Security Act of 1935
The National Labor Relations Act of 1935
The Equal Pay Act of 1963
The Civil Rights Act of 1964
The Freedom of Information Act of 1966
The Occupational Safety and Health Act of 1970
The Privacy Act of 1974
The Ethics in Government Act of 1978 (no surprise there)

And the list goes on and on. If any person running a business were to run afoul of any of the above laws you can bet he would be hauled into court pronto. But the authors of those laws have nothing to worry about. No government lawyers sue them; no bureaucrats harass them; no media harasses them. There is nothing anyone can do about a congressional violation of those laws, save for taking it to the lapdog Ethics Committee. This only breeds contempt for Congress among the public. It says to the average person in this country that Congress considers itself above the law.

But Congress' hypocrisy may have finally caught up with it this year. Reporters weren't able to contain the bank story, even though many of them originally thought it was a minor issue. The public was so outraged about it that they finally had to report it. Polls show the bank story may be the straw that breaks the camel's back for a lot of voters this year. *The Wall Street Journal* reported that for the first time in history less than 50 percent of voters are willing to reelect their own congressman. We may see a complete housecleaning this November.

TERM LIMITATIONS

For a long time I resisted the arguments of my conservative friends who support term limits on Congress. I didn't like the fact that they limit democracy. But 80 percent of the American people, according to a *Wall Street Journal* poll, now favor term limits. They are democratically deciding that the only way to clean up Congress is to make sure that fresh blood is pumped through it on a regular basis.

I've also found that the Constitution is filled with limitations on democracy. You can't serve in the Senate unless you are thirty years old. You have to be a native-born citizen to be president. States are allowed to set residency requirements for voting. Felons can't vote. And, of course, the president is limited to two terms in office, and I don't see that any great damage is done there. I find it ironic that the same people in Congress who oppose term limits so vociferously are doing nothing to remove the term limit on the presidency.

I've concluded that term limits are necessary because while most people go to Congress with good intentions, they are eventually corrupted by the aphrodisiac of power they imbibe in Washington. Our founding fathers never intended that Congress be a career. Until the New Deal, we had a citizen legislature, with most members serving only four or six years and then returning to their districts to live under the laws they had written.

In the meantime, we have a lot of members of Congress who deserve bouncing this November. Nothing has quite captured my attitude toward Congress and the House Bank scandal as well as the "Vote 'Em Out Rap" I play on my show:

So you got caught with your hand in the till,
Living high and mighty up on Capitol Hill.

I bet it felt nice to have money at will,
Then next thing you know, you're spending half a mil.
Chorus: Vote 'em out! Vote 'em out! Without a doubt!
Well, here's a mighty fine-smelling kettle of fish,
You buy anytime you want and anything you wish.
When you get caught, you can't take the heat,
You're a squirmin'-and-a-squeamin' on your Capitol seat.
So you blame it on your wife, you blame it on your mother.
You blame it on your father, and your sister and your brother.
You blame it on the banker, the butcher, the baker,
The Speaker of the House says, "I'm no lawbreaker."
Chorus.
You've been living like a king, and that's what we've expected,
But you need the common man to get you reelected.
We're no longer content to be playing your fool,
If you're going to make the laws, you gotta play by the rules.
If this story suffers from overexposure,
Then give us what we want—full disclosure!

WHY WE HAVE GOVERNMENT GRIDLOCK

The major political problem in this country is that there is a disconnect between the results of presidential and congressional elections. The real debate about where this country should be headed takes place every four years when we vote for president. In the last three elections, the people of this country have indicated in landslides that they want conservative leadership in Washington.

But Congress is not elected on that basis. Congressional elections don't concern ideology or the nation as a whole, but are about issues in individual districts. Members of Congress try to steer their elections away from national issues and focus instead on their individual talents and their ability to bring pork back to the home district. Most people elect a congressman because he or she will be good in hunting down Aunt Millie's social security check or bringing a water project home. Congressmen have become so good at dragging goodies home that most members have convinced voters that they have to return them to office or the goodies will stop.

Members of Congress are elected primarily on the basis of local concerns, but when they get to Washington they experience a mad power rush and you see things like Jim Wright acting like another secretary of State as he negotiates with the Sandinistas. In 1985, Jim Wright, David Bonior, the current House Democratic whip, and several other members signed a "Dear Comandante" letter to Daniel Ortega in which they practically begged him to make some gesture towards peace that they could use to block the Reagan administration's policy of arming the Contras. That's not what the Constitution intended when it made the President the commander-in-chief.

Congress isn't supposed to set day-to-day policy in our system of government—especially not in the area of foreign policy. It is supposed to write laws that have broad application and that set down the parameters within which the President can carry out his policies. Instead, Congress has done its level best to impede the actions of every President we've elected since 1980. They have ignored the people's will on countless occasions and dismissed the fact that the voters have endorsed conservative policies in three presidential elections. People are not fools when it comes to electing a President. People know that election is a defining one. They study the candidates and they care about their decisions. They don't do that very often with elections for Congress. That is because people's loyalties are torn between their concern for their districts and their concern for the national interest. The best illustration of this is a phone call I received from a guy in Pensacola, Florida, who was faced with a huge dilemma in his 1990 congressional election. The incumbent was a liberal Democrat, well placed on several key committees. The conservative challenger represented the values and morality the caller believed in and wanted to see more of in Washington. But there was a slight problem. Pensacola has a huge naval base and there was a big battle raging over where a large aircraft carrier was to be based. Would it remain in Pensacola or be transferred to a port in Texas? An aircraft carrier based in your port means a terrific economic boost for your community. The caller feared that the conservative challenger, as a freshman Republican, would not have the clout of the incumbent liberal and would therefore lose the aircraft carrier to the more experienced representatives from Texas, who also would have more seniority than a newly elected Republican. This is a classic explanation of why people elect a President of one party and a congressman from another. And why gridlock then ensues.

ANIMALS HAVE NO RIGHTS—GO AHEAD AND LICK THAT FROG

RIGHTS VERSUS PROTECTION

I HAVE SPOKEN EXTENSIVELY IN THIS BOOK ABOUT THE VARIOUS fringe movements and the spiritual tie that binds them: radical liberalism. Two groups that are particularly close, to the point of being nearly indistinguishable, are the environmentalists and the animal rights activists. Because I devoted a chapter to the environmentalists I thought it only fair to include one about animal rights activism. I certainly do not want to be accused of discrimination. Every wacko movement must have its day in my book.

I'm a very controversial figure to the animal rights movement. They no doubt view me with some measure of hostility because I am constantly challenging their fundamental premise that animals are superior to human beings. They may deny holding that belief, but the truth is inescapable when you examine the policies they advocate and their invariable preference for the well-being of animals, and their disregard for humans and their livelihoods. It especially bothers them when I state my belief that animals have no fundamental rights. In fact, this statement has bothered more than just animal rights wackos. Many fellow animal-loving members of my audience misunderstand my point on this as well. But before you jump to the conclusion that I am callous, insensitive, and a heartless animal-hater, hear me out. Before beginning the discussion of rights, let me make it perfectly clear that my belief that animals don't have rights is not equivalent to saying that human beings have no moral obligation to protect animals when they can. I am not saying that at all. But this is more, my friends, than a semantical distinction. The animal rights movement knew what it was doing when it deliberately adopted the label "animal rights." The concept of "rights" is very powerful in the American political lexicon. It carries with it no small amount of clout. If the movement can succeed in drilling into the American psyche the concept that animals have rights, then there will be far less outrage at the antibusiness policies the animal rights people foist onto the public. If animals have rights, which is after all what we humans have, then what legal or moral basis do we have to protect ourselves in this war for dominance of the planet? Let me try to explain the concept of "rights" and why animals have none.

Rights are either God-given or evolve out of the democratic process. Most rights are based on the ability of people to agree on a social contract, the ability to make and keep agreements. Animals cannot possibly reach such an agreement with other creatures. They cannot respect anyone else's rights. Therefore they cannot be said to have rights.

Thomas Jefferson, in drafting the Declaration of Independence, did not begin by saying, "We hold these truths to be self-evident: that all *animals* are created equal; that they are endowed by their creator with certain unalienable rights; that among these are life, liberty and the pursuit of happiness."

Webster's defines a "right" as "something to which one has a just claim. The power or privilege to which one is justly entitled. A power, privilege or condition of existence to which one has a natural claim of enjoyment or possession. A power or privilege vested in a person by the law to demand action or forbearance at the hands of another. A legally enforceable claim against another that the other will do or will not do a given act. A capacity or privilege the enjoyment of which is secured to a person by law. A

103

claim recognized and delimited by law for the purpose of securing it."

Notice the words *one, person,* a claim against *another.* All of these words denote human beings, not animals or any other creatures. Inherent in the concept of "rights" is the ability to assert a claim to those rights. Implicit in all of these dictionary definitions is that in order to have rights one must know that he has a just claim to them; one must be able to assert them. Only a moron would argue that an animal has the capacity to assert a claim to any rights. An animal cannot avail himself of legal protection through our judicial system or otherwise. Only if humans intervene on its behalf will it have any protection at all.

In my opinion, at the root of the assertion that animals have rights is the belief that animals and men are equal in creation, that man evolved from apes, and that creation is an allegorical myth contained in that wonderful piece of literature known as the Bible. There is no escaping the connection between secular humanism and animal rights activism.

The Bible teaches that God created man in His own image and that He placed him on this earth in a position superior to all other creatures, and gave him dominion over animals and nature. God did not create other animals in His own image.

Even if you reject the Bible as the Word of God—even if you believe in evolution and disbelieve in creation—you must still admit that man is the only earthly creature capable of rational thought.

Mortimer Adler, associate editor of the Great Books of the Western World—part of the classics, for those of you in Rio Linda—explains that in the great tradition of Western thought, from Plato right down to the nineteenth century, it was almost universally held that man and man alone is a rational animal. He says that only since the time of Darwin has the opposite view gained any acceptance; and it's mostly among scientists and the educated classes. This relatively new view holds that the difference between man and other mammals is one of degree, not kind. All animals have intelligence, man just has more of it. Adler then goes on to articulate his belief that the traditional view (that man is essentially different from other animals) is undeniable. In support of his belief he cites man's unique ability to make things. Sure, he concedes, bees make hives, birds make nests, and beavers make dams, but those productions are purely instinctive. Man's creations involve reason and free will. "In making houses, bridges, or any other of their artifacts, men invent and select. They are truly artists, as animals are not."

Adler also points out that men build machines which are themselves productive. Animals solve problems when they are confronted with a biological urgency of finding a way of getting what they need. But no animals sit down and ponder things and think through problems as man does. Human thinking, he notes, is discursive and involves language. Animals make sounds and communicate; but they do not communicate thought. No animal ever utters a sentence which asserts something to be true or false. Sorry to offend you porpoise and dolphin worshipers out there.

Finally, Adler posits that man is the only animal with an historical development. Men transmit ideas and institutions, a whole tradition of culture, from one generation to another, and it is this which accounts for the history of the human race. In that regard I should like to pose the question to animal rights purveyors: Who is it that writes books about the history and development of animals? Maybe there is dolphin literature in the depths of the ocean, but I'm not going to enroll in the Kennedy Scuba School to find out.

One woman called my show to protest that animals do at least have one right: to kindness. I told her she was mistaken. Look at what they do to each other. They tear each other limb from limb. Humans do that too, but it is not the accepted norm. We accord ourselves redress for such wrongs. Animals don't think about right and wrong. They exist in the anarchical state of nature: survival of the fittest. When I suggested to my dog that animals had rights, he laughed out loud. To this day I don't think he respects me the way he did before I had that conversation with him.

Human beings are the primary species on this planet. Animals and everything else are subspecies whose position on the planet is subordinate to that of humans. Humans have a responsibility toward lower species and must treat them humanely. *Humanely,* now that's an interesting term. Doesn't that mean as a human would like to be treated? Why not treat them animally? Because that would mean killing them. Can't you see? That's my point exactly. Animals often treat each other with no respect, and they have no redress, absent human intervention on their behalf.

RESPONSIBILITY VERSUS HYSTERIA

Regardless of that, I believe that if people use animals to achieve their goals, they must do so responsibly, so that we don't eliminate any species from the planet. That would be wantonly stupid and selfish. We should not allow elephants to become extinct just so a few people can have ivory carvings. There is no reason to trap animals just so we can make coats out of them. But if we raise minks and other creatures for the express purpose of making coats, that is a different matter.

Please note that none of the animals mankind raises for its own benefit are on any endangered species list. The African elephant is in danger of extinction everywhere but in Zimbabwe, Malawi, Zambia, Botswana, and South Africa, where elephant herds are increasing by 5 percent a year. Elephants thrive in those countries for the same reason that cows are so numerous in America: it is legal to sell elephant products. At the Kruger National Park in South Africa about 350 elephants are culled from the herd each year. The $3 million they raise from selling tusks and hides supports park management and pays for antipoaching efforts. In Zimbabwe, the wildlife industry is worth up to $200 million a year to the local population. They make a lot of money from selling a set number of hunting permits for elephants every year, so they have an incentive to make sure the herds survive.

It's a different story in Kenya, where the number of elephants has fallen from 140,000 in the 1970s, when a hunting ban went into effect, to about 20,000 today. Poachers, who obviously have no incentive to nurture the herds, bribe game wardens and shoot as many as they can.

The local population encourages the slaughter. Since they can't make money off the elephants, they see them merely as beasts that knock over trees and consume scarce grass and water supplies.

The way to save endangered species is to give someone a stake in preserving them. By allowing legitimate ranches to privatize them, we can make sure others don't pulverize them.

As you can see, I'm not opposed to the protection of animals. But the best way to do that is to make sure some human being *owns* them. On their own, animals have no chance to make it in this world.

I don't ever want to give the impression that I have no concern for animals. I melt around little dogs, for example. One of the things I miss most in life are the two little dogs I lost as a result of my divorce. I've never killed an animal, I never intend to kill one. But I am not going to let my concern for animals blind me to the ways they are being exploited for political purposes. I will not stand for having animals assigned rights and privileges that many human beings don't yet enjoy.

The animal rights movement, like so many others in this country, is being used by leftists as another way to attack the American way of life. They have adopted two constituencies who cannot speak and complain about the political uses to which they are put. One of them is trees and other plant life; the other is the animal kingdom.

People for the Ethical Treatment of Animals (PETA) takes in over $10 million every year by preying on people's concern for animals. Most of its contributors think most of the money goes to making sure animals are treated kindly. But the *Detroit Free Press* reports that 80 percent of all animal-related charities give less than half of their income to animal programs. The rest is eaten up by administrative overhead, political activism, and direct-mail expenses. PETA is among the worst of these "charities," using only about 15 percent to 20 percent of its income for animal welfare.

PETA's real mission is destroying capitalism, not saving animals. It recently ran full-page ads comparing mass murderer Jeffrey Dahmer's behavior to that of the meat industry. Don Matthews of PETA explained the ads by saying: "We are at war. We'll do what we need to win. If we got rid of the slave trade, we can get rid of the beef industry." PETA members have often violated the law in their efforts to destroy the fur industry by, for example, throwing blood at people wearing fur coats. Ingrid Newkirk, the cofounder of PETA, claims she doesn't sanction such actions, but she won't condemn them either.

The easiest way for the left to exploit animals politically is to try to play upon this notion that the difference between animals and man is only one of degree. They seem to go even farther by forwarding the notion that the only difference between us and other mammals is that we have the capacity to subjugate other species. An entire myth has evolved that animals have special abilities and deserve to become a new protected class in society. If you don't believe me, here are some examples I've collected showing just how far the movement to accord animals rights that equal, or even exceed, those of humans, has gone. All of these items are completely true.

The New York Times science section recently carried a piece on what it seemed to be saying was the most intelligent being roaming the planet today, our good friend, the dolphin. Many people are convinced that human beings would be infinitely better off if they were only smart enough to understand the dolphin. You see, man is the dunce of the planet, according to animal-rights enviro-wackos. The dolphin is a noble, pure creature.

This twaddle has even crept into science reporting. *The New York Times* reported, "As much as puppies, or pandas or even children, dolphins are universally beloved. They seem to cavort and frolic at the least provocation, their mouths fixed in what looks like a state of perpetual merriment, and their behavior and enormous brains suggest an intelligence approaching that of human beings or even, some might argue, surpassing it."

I was offended by that. Could somebody please show me one hospital built by a dolphin? Could somebody show me one highway built by a dolphin? Could someone show me one automobile invented by a dolphin?

But vengeance was mine. The *Times* article went on to say that researchers off the coast of Australia have come across male dolphins that engage in very chauvinistic behavior toward female dolphins. This activity is called "herding." "The males will chase after her, bite her, slap her, hit her with their fins, slam into her with their bodies." In other words, Mike Tyson behavioral rules dominate the male dolphin population.

Despite the dolphin's poor dating manners, it's clear that people had better be careful in how *they* approach this noble creature. Consider Allen Cooper, a hapless fellow from Sunderland, England, who last year was accused of "indecent behavior with a dolphin." Animal rights activists on a pleasure boat testified that they had seen Cooper fondling a dolphin's penis. Cooper was totally humiliated by the resulting publicity, but a court finally cleared him of indecent-assault charges after expert witnesses testified that dolphins often extend their penises to swimmers as a "finger of friendship."

Apparently not all animals are created equal, according to some animal rights activists. Some animals that have been happily owned by humans turn out to be politically incorrect and presumably have to be curbed. Take the poor cow. The May 1992 edition of *Countryside* magazine has a story called "The Last Roundup for Beef?" In it, liberal eco-pest Jeremy Rifkin argues that without cattle, the world would be green, well fed, and peaceful. He claims that 1.28 billion cattle are now taking up 24 percent of the world's land mass, a ridiculous figure that few in the media will ever challenge.

Rifkin is bent out of shape because he says the cattle consume enough grain to feed hundreds of millions of people. The reason the cattle are eating the grain is so they can be fattened and slaughtered, after which they will feed people, who need a high-protein diet. The combined weight of the cattle exceeds that of the world's human population. I presume Rifkin somehow supports curbing the cow population to limit the damage they are inflicting on mankind.

You may recall that Martin Sheen, the actor, once declared Malibu, California, a sanctuary for the homeless when he was honorary mayor. Well, the Malibu City Council recently went him one better by passing a resolution declaring that Malibu was a "human/dolphin shared environment," and urging "warmer relationships between humans and animals." Francis Jeffrey, the cofounder of the Great Whales Foundation, hailed the resolution: "This is a new concept, to say that dolphins are citizens of the community." Mary Frampton, the head of the local Save Our

Coast group, told the council that "the dolphins thank you." I wonder how Frampton knows when any dolphins are thanking anyone. Why can't the little talking geniuses communicate this message themselves? After all, Frampton may be lying about what the dolphins told her. We need to hear it from the dolphin's mouth—that is, if we are smart enough to understand what they are trying to tell us. This whole episode just proves what happens when rich people in trendy coastal communities have too much free time on their hands.

Many ski boots are lined with dog fur, and the New York City ASPCA wants to outlaw such boots. Once again, animal rights activists are lunging for the law rather than examining the facts. Technica US, a ski-boot maker in New Hampshire, says all of its boots are made using dog skin from China, where dogs have been raised for food for thousands of years. At least they aren't using cat hair to line their boots. Then Technica's products would be called "Puss in Boots."

Damon and Pythias are two Burmese cats who lived in a Fifth Avenue co-op until their owner, a widow named Terri Crumholt, died. They had been pampered to the point that they had a therapist who treated them for "intercat hostility." When Ms. Crumholt died she left a large portion of her estate to the cats along with her Fifth Avenue home. The co-op board protested, claiming their rules do not allow cat owners. The cat therapist whom the felines had been seeing insisted that the cats had to remain in the co-op until they died because making them leave would "create a tumult in their lives." Yah, right.

The town of Colburn, Idaho, population 20, is going to be wiped off the map because the state wants to build a five-lane highway right through the town. It's too bad these people don't have some 20 endangered beetles or bugs in their town because then they could stop the highway. There is far more concern for animals today than for people.

Folks in Hegins, Pennsylvania, hold an annual pigeon shoot in order to control the pigeon population and to raise money for the town. This year, the pigeon shoot was disrupted by animal rights activists who tried to release the pigeons from their cages. I can't help but think these animal rights activists are the same people who believe in controlling the human population through the use of abortion. Yet, they recoil at a similar means of controlling pigeons. What rank hypocrisy.

Then I got a call one day from Tom, the owner of Pets Unlimited, in Carlisle, Pennsylvania. He told me that the local nursery school decided not to bring its class through his store anymore because he listens to the Rush Limbaugh program. Apparently, the class stopped by one afternoon and one of the teachers decided they should leave after she heard my show being piped through the store. She told Tom that I had a poor attitude on animal rights, and she couldn't understand how he could run a pet store and listen to my show. I commended Tom for sticking to his guns and fighting Political Correctness. Today, Tom plays a Rush video in his store and even his animals seem to like it.

Have you heard of frog licking? Now I know you all lead busy lives, so you probably missed it when it showed up in the papers. But I was amazed when I read that frog licking has become a major preoccupation in Colorado. How could this possibly get started? It had to be this way. An environmentalist is out in the woods communing with nature. Probably some overgrown Boy Scout in little green shorts, a backpack filled with wheat nut mix. He's wearing his Walkman, skipping along some nature trail listening to Madonna music, probably the *Don't Bungle the Jungle* album.

So he's communing with the Nature Goddess and maybe even humming. Ommmmmm-Ommmmmmm-Ommmmmmmm. He looks at a tree and maybe he says, "Hi, Greg." Maybe he hugs the tree. "Oh, I am at one with this tree." Then he spies a frog and suddenly stops. "Oh, look at that frog. Maybe I should pick it up and lick it." And gets high as a result. You see, the Colorado spotted toad secretes a hallucinogenic substance that can get you high if you lick it near the back of its head. Well, I'm sorry, but most people I know wouldn't lick a frog even if it did give them a buzz. Can you imagine doing that? Well, somebody did it. Somebody had to—otherwise we wouldn't know of this enlightened and marvelous way of turning on. But the amazing thing is that the first person who did it had to tell someone else he did it, who then passed it on for posterity's sake.

Tell me, who would do that kind of thing? I don't know, but

they couldn't be considered normal. There may even be a conflict here between environmentalism and animal rights types. Isn't it a violation of the frog's rights if he is licked?

Frogs aren't the only creatures we have to worry about, of course. You know, the sea turtle is an endangered species too. How so, you ask? Well, evil shrimpers happen to nab a couple of sea turtles now and then while murdering zillions of shrimp. Anyway, a guy in Florida was hauled into court for stealing some sea turtle eggs. The judge found him guilty and fined him $106,000. He said, "Wait a minute, these are not sea turtles, these are sea turtle eggs, and there's no law saying I can't steal them." "Sir," the judge replied, "they're going to be sea turtles. Guilty." The guy was stuck with a $106,000 fine. All this makes me wonder about our priorities. When does a sea turtle's life begin? At conception or when it's laid?

By the way, did you ever wonder why people always worry about sea turtles but ignore the lives of the shrimp? Flipper, the dolphin, is high on everybody's protection list. We kill maybe 2 dolphins for every 1 million tuna, and yet nobody is expressing any concern for the tuna. They're just a bunch of useless creatures. But dolphins are another matter. They're smart and they're cute. They even have a smile on their face! And they try to talk to us. Too bad we're not intelligent enough to understand them.

CONCLUSION

The point is that animals do not have rights but are accorded protection by human beings. When we establish laws against cruelty to animals, some mistake the laws to be the same as rights. They are not, however.

I received a letter on this subject from a listener, Chris Huson, of Champaign, Illinois. He agreed with the premise that animals have no rights but are instead accorded protection by humans. He then illustrated the difference by observing that the "right to privacy" is not a right, but rather a protection granted by the government. The "right to privacy" does not allow you take drugs in your car or home with impunity. The privacy is protected but does not therefore allow you to break the law.

He further stated in his letter that the basic right to life of an animal—which is the source of energy for many animal rights wackos—must be inferred from the anticruelty laws humans have written, not from any divine source. Our laws do not prevent us from killing animals for food or sport, so the right to life of an animal is nonexistent.

He is right and I don't think it can be stated much better. Yet, we are confronted daily by people who wish to obstruct human progress and individual economic choices by virtue of elevating the importance of animal existence to that of human existence. The only way this can happen is for the force of law to be used to devalue human life.

Well, it is time some of us began to speak up for the sanctity of *human* life and the glories of humankind, which was created in God's image. If the wackos prefer to live in caves, let's provide them with free transportation there. As for the rest of us and our posterity, let's do what we can to treat ourselves with the respect and dignity that God intended.

THE SAGA OF ANITA HILL

INTRODUCTION

THE CLARENCE THOMAS CONFIRMATION HEARINGS WERE LARGELY uneventful until the last-minute testimony of Anita Hill. All of a sudden, the focus of the inquiry shifted from Judge Thomas's position on various constitutional questions to his moral turpitude. The odious congressional leaks of FBI reports leading to the testimony of Anita Hill, her testimony itself, the testimony of her witnesses, the media's treatment of the event, and the feminists' reaction to it speak volumes about the feminist movement today. As such, I decided to devote a separate chapter to a discussion of the issues because so much of our societal future will be determined by who wins the battle of ideas on which this episode turned. For example, a bevy of female candidates for public office based their campaigns on righting the wrongs exacted on Anita Hill. They said they were humiliated watching the "way she was treated." Well, what were certain senators supposed to do, just accept Anita Hill's testimony despite the fact that she had no evidence to support her charges? She and her allies, many of them silent Senate Judiciary Committee staff members, were the aggressors in this attempt to destroy Clarence Thomas. Besides, that committee hearing room is the big time. They play for keeps there and if you enter you can't demand to be treated as though you've checked into a resort. Just ask Robert Bork.

To me, this is just a bunch of feminists wanting it both ways: to be treated gently, softly, as feminine women, but to be allowed to play as rough as they need to win. An examination of the episode reveals the extent to which feminists and their political allies are willing to go to advance their proabortion, militant leftist, antimale agenda.

ANITA HILL AND THE SEXUAL HARASSMENT ISSUE

Right after the Anita Hill and Clarence Thomas fiasco was over, I got a fax from some twelve women employees of the Sullivan Glove Company in Oregon. They sent me a copy of a letter they had delivered to their management. It actually authorized certain conduct by the managers of the company. Now, this is conduct that today could be considered sexual harassment, and the women wanted to make sure their bosses didn't walk around in fear of their jobs. The authorized conduct included hugging, touching nonprivate parts, displaying posters of the opposite sex, telling off-color jokes, and a number of other things. Of course, the female employees informed their managers that they would have reciprocal rights to do the same things in dealing with them. Hey, you've got to give these women a hand.

To me, this illustrates what the polls have conclusively shown. The vast majority of American women, 63 percent according to the polls, didn't believe Anita Hill and don't think sexual harassment is the most important issue of our time. Plus, they also think they can handle the situation themselves.

115

RUSH H. LIMBAUGH, III

THE EFFORT TO DESTROY CLARENCE THOMAS

The rumor-mongering against Judge Thomas was an eleventh-hour attempt to ruin his life, and I have never witnessed anything so despicable. Irrespective of the truth of the allegations that Clarence Thomas sexually harassed a female employee, his reputation and career have been incurably degraded and his life has been dramatically affected.

These allegations were lodged by people who stopped at nothing to defeat his nomination, including destroying his character with unsubstantiated innuendo. To them the end justified the means. Certain people feared Thomas's confirmation because it threatened their very political existence. In order for them to survive as a minority with preferred treatment, they believed it necessary to thwart his bid by whatever means necessary.

The civil rights coalition in this country has had its way with the Democratic party since 1957. That was the last time the coalition, as a liberal constituency, was defeated. The coalition includes the ACLU and the leaders of such civil rights organizations as People for the American Way and the National Association for the Advancement of (Liberal) Colored People.

How have the leaders of these civil rights organizations become so empowered? They do not have normal jobs. Benjamin Hooks of the NAACP, for example, raises money and keeps a percentage of it for himself as head of the organization. The same is true for the head of People for the American Way. They do not have real jobs, yet they have power. They derive that power by utilizing the tools of class envy and hatred.

These people enjoy power for only one reason. Their sole source of strength is their monolithic constituency—which determines the number of liberal votes they can deliver to Democrats on election day. This monolithic constituency delivers up to 90 percent of the minority vote to the Democratic candidate for president every presidential election year. The ability of all these civil rights groups to deliver the vote for Democrats has invested them with power. This vote, in turn, has invested the Democrats with power. It's a win-win situation.

Then along comes Clarence Thomas, who, by contrast, has held many fine jobs. He works and earns money for a living. He does not head an organization that begs people to contribute money to it. He is a man who has escaped the bonds of poverty by methods other than those prescribed by these civil rights organizations. He has succeeded by relying on himself, rather than prostituting himself into the dependency cycle. As a result of eschewing their prescription, he has risen to levels far above what would have been possible for him had he relied on the black leadership's formula for achievement.

The elevation of Judge Thomas to the Supreme Court represents the greatest threat to the civil rights constituency since 1957. Clarence Thomas, a man of conservative moral values, as an associate justice of the highest court of the land, will set an example for members of the minority community in America who will want to follow his successful lead. The message is that there is another way for blacks to achieve vertical mobility. As a result, blacks inevitably will be drawn away from the traditional civil rights leaders.

Once that happens, a certain percentage of minority votes will likely abandon the Democratic party. Such a scenario threatens the careers of the civil rights leaders, because their only ticket to power is their guaranteed delivery of minority votes to the Democratic ticket. With this probable exodus, the power of the civil rights leadership would be permanently eroded. In addition, the Democrats' lock on Congress would be jeopardized.

It is neither farfetched nor unfair to draw an analogy between the civil rights leadership and the Soviet Communist leadership, insofar as exploitation of their people is concerned. The leaders of both enjoy the privileges of class at the expense of the masses, who do all the work and whom the leaders purport to serve. They may consider themselves hard workers by virtue of the amount of time they spend on the phone asking people for money or playing politics, but they certainly do not subscribe to the basic work ethic common to this country. Their efforts produce no goods or services to be contributed to the economy, but in fact have just the opposite effect. They discourage achievement by merit, which is tantamount to discouraging the production of wealth.

Clarence Thomas will no doubt siphon much of the civil rights rank and file away from this monolithic constituency. There was only one way to avoid that—to undermine and destroy him—thereby saving the civil rights leadership and perhaps the Democratic majority in Congress. Hours before the Senate confirmation vote, senators were receiving anonymous telephone calls urging them not to confirm Thomas. These calls were phony and orchestrated by those desperate to defeat Thomas in order to preserve their own thrones of exploitation. Unfortunately, many senators were unnerved because the calls were coming from their own constituencies.

The objective of Thomas's opponents was, and still is, to ruin him as a man and as a judge.

This was one of the most heinous, malevolent attempts at character assassination that has occurred in decades. Judge Thomas has categorically denied the allegations leveled against him. But it does not matter. The allegations succeeded in surfacing and will never be forgotten. No matter how great and decent a man Clarence Thomas is, a part of his life will be forever ruined.

THE UNRAVELING OF ANITA HILL

Emma Jordan, one of Anita Hill's attorneys, went ballistic on how offended she was by Senator Alan Simpson's threat to reveal the contents of letters and faxes on Anita Hill's character which arrived unsolicited from all over the country. Those were unsubstantiated allegations, hearsay evidence, she complained.

Well, excuse me. Isn't that precisely what the angelic and virtuous Anita Hill was doing? Tossing around unsubstantiated allegations? Ten-year-old allegations at that. She made her first claim of sexual harassment against someone when she was working at a Washington law firm in the spring of 1981. That was before she had even met Clarence Thomas. It was only later that she changed her testimony to say that the sexual harassment occurred in the fall of 1981.

Oh, sure, she had four "corroborating" witnesses. Three of

them said she spoke of being harassed by an unnamed "supervisor," a curious term for someone who is chairman of a large federal agency. The fourth, Judge Susan Hoerchner, said Anita Hill told her about the harassment in the early spring of 1981. But, again: Anita Hill did not go to work for Clarence Thomas, did not even meet him, until September 1981! This timely bit of information, and a lot more, can be found in the yeoman research effort by Washington investigative reporter David Brock in a cover story in the March 1992 issue of *The American Spectator.*

Clarence Thomas denied all of Anita Hill's allegations. But now that she was on the national stage she not only did not back down, but began adding details that she had never before mentioned, even to the FBI agents who took her affidavit.

The left screams about Senator Simpson's efforts on behalf of Clarence Thomas because they were defeated by someone using their own tactics. Senator Simpson and Clarence Thomas's other defenders on that committee shouldn't apologize. They should be applauded for resisting an orchestrated effort not to seek the truth but to destroy Clarence Thomas's life.

THE AFTERMATH OF THE THOMAS HEARINGS

The feminists haven't given up. Let's look at some of the things that happened after the Senate hearings. When the Thomas hearings were over, three professional women who were to testify before Congress on job discrimination refused to appear because of how Anita Hill had been treated. Senator Paul Simon, of Illinois, allowed as how he "hoped that in the future we are going to be able to assure witnesses they will be treated well." These people are acting as though Anita Hill's scurrilous testimony about a man with impeccable credentials and an unblemished record should have been accepted without question or cross-examination by the body whose job it was to determine Judge Thomas's fitness as a Supreme Court justice.

Now, I can see through that like a shower curtain at the Mustang Ranch. The three women said they were afraid their careers might be jeopardized. You mean like Anita Hill, who is now being wined and dined all over the country and showered with awards? I wouldn't be surprised if the next Democratic president rewards her by appointing her a federal judge.

Anita Hill recently came to New York to address a seminar on sexual harassment titled "Women Tell the Truth." The feminists don't understand that their credibility is undermined when they have a keynote speaker on truth who happens to not tell the truth. The vast majority of the American people DID NOT believe Anita Hill. I'll tell you this: the truth about this whole sordid attempt to destroy a man's life will eventually find its way into the mainstream press—several respected and accomplished journalists and scholars are already discovering and reporting information that is devastating to Anita Hill—and when it does, you who have supported and believed her will be embarrassed and shocked. Mark my words. In fact, go ahead and mark this place in the book so you can instantly refer to it when the time comes. Go ahead—do it.

NOT WOMEN, BUT LIBERAL WOMEN

After the hearings, Ted Koppel featured the Anita Hill topic in a town hall meeting on ABC. Congresswoman Maxine Waters argued that if only there had been more women on the committee the outcome would have been different. This is insulting to all women. Was she implying that women would have been more prone to accept a lie? That women would have been willing to rely on false testimony to advance another woman's agenda?

Several senators on the show agreed with Maxine Waters that there should be more women in the Senate. Paul Simon clucked about the inequity. So did Bill Bradley. Well, guess what? Both of those senators defeated women in their last elections. If Bill Bradley wants more women in the Senate, why doesn't he give up his seat to Christine Todd Whitman, who almost beat him? The same with Paul Simon, who ran against Lynn Martin, now the Secretary of Labor.

The reason is that they were Republican women. It's not *women* that the feminists want in the Senate. It's *liberal feminists* they want, as long as they are not in their district. The women's groups supported Bradley and Simon for election, not their female opponents. You must admit that that is revealing.

The reason we don't have more women in the Senate is simple. It's because the democratic process works. Most of the women who run as Democrats represent the NOW position on issues. NOW does not represent the mainstream of American thought, or even of women. It represents maybe 1 percent or 2 percent of the population. The feminists are fairly represented in the Senate. They have Barbara Mikulski from Maryland, a radical feminist. But she's the only one who has been able to win. The other female senator is a Republican, Nancy Kassebaum of Kansas. What are we supposed to do, create a feminist quota for the United States Senate just to make things fair?

SEXUAL HARASSMENT: A DOUBLE STANDARD

Ron Woodson, a black neighborhood leader, also appeared on the Ted Koppel show on Anita Hill. He said there is a double standard on who in politics is charged with sexual harassment. If the man involved is liberal, there is sudden silence. Take Gus Savage, the congressman from Illinois. He fondled a Peace Corps worker in Zaire for a couple of hours in his limo. Yet, there was no effort to punish him beyond a wrist-slap from the Ethics Committee. There was certainly no hue and cry from the feminists, who are not about to condemn a man so in line with their political views, regardless of whether he abuses women. So you see, the issue is not sexual harassment, but liberalism. To the extent that conservatives can be discredited by charges of sexual harassment, then sexual harassment acquires full-blown significance for radical feminists. Otherwise, it does not.

Another example of this double standard is the feminists' treatment of Ted Kennedy. Here's a man who could write books on sexual harassment and how to get away with it. He even has a room named after him at the La Brasserie restaurant in Washington, because he and Senator Chris Dodd once sandwiched a waitress between them one night by throwing her onto Senator

Kennedy's lap. How do feminist leaders respond? They look the other way, and talk about how he is a great leader of liberal causes.

Just look at how the rape trial of William Kennedy Smith was handled in order to protect the Kennedy family. Patty Bowman made much more serious charges against him than Anita Hill leveled against Clarence Thomas. Even Anita Hill never said that she was touched in any way. In fact, this tough woman said nary a word for ten years after the alleged incident.

Feminists not only did not come forward to defend Patty Bowman, but some of them remained silent when *The New York Times* delved into her sexual history and wrote a negative psychological profile of her. Are we really gullible enough to believe it is women's rights these feminists are asserting?

THE TYSON TRIAL

After Anita Hill failed to destroy Clarence Thomas, the feminists predicted there would be a backlash against women. They said that if a woman now comes forward with evidence of sexual harassment, she won't be believed and men will be free to mistreat her. Yet, look at how Mike Tyson's rape trial turned out. This Miss Black American pageant contestant came forward and said that Tyson had assaulted her. Did the feminists rush to her aid? No, not for a second. Maybe it was because she was a beauty contestant. Feminists don't like those types of contests because they "degrade" women.

Well, the young woman brought forward compelling testimony on what happened. Tyson was convicted. On my show, I was incredulous. I said, How can this be? The feminists have said that no woman would ever get a fair hearing again after Anita Hill had gotten the shaft from the Senate. I told my listeners, Wait a minute, there's a big difference here, folks. Anita Hill had no evidence. Anita Hill had no credibility. Her testimony was riddled with inconsistencies. Her witnesses weren't compelling. Mike Tyson's accuser was easily more credible. The difference is that since there was nothing political about the trial, the feminists weren't interested. This is just more proof that feminists aren't concerned about all women, but with liberal women, or, more accurately, liberal causes. The American judicial system worked exactly the way it was supposed to. It certainly didn't need feminists pushing it to make it work. All that was required for a victim to get justice was some real evidence. Something Anita Hill didn't have. It might also be fair to mention that Tyson's accuser didn't wait ten years after the incident to make her complaint. But maybe that's because Tyson's victim couldn't be sure that Iron Mike would be nominated for the Supreme Court in ten years, where she would get a chance to get even better revenge.

Anita Hill could have gone to court. She chose to not to do so, because she didn't have any evidence. So she and her allies gambled on a Senate hearing (where the rules of evidence are considerably relaxed), and they lost big. They just don't get it. The vast majority of the American people didn't buy their agenda, and they certainly didn't like the character assassination of Clarence Thomas.

THE MEDIA AND ANITA HILL

The media will continue to use Anita Hill as a symbol of the oppressed woman, which proves once again how far out of touch they are. *The New York Times* had a headline and a story following the Anita Hill hearings. It read: "IMAGE MORE THAN REALITY BECAME ISSUE—LOSERS SAY." But imagery was not the real issue in the hearings. Liberals always attribute their defeats to losing the image game. They simply cannot own up to being defeated on substantive issues. According to them, Reagan defeated them only because he had a great image and the right marketing and packaging. Liberals devoutly believe his substance wasn't a factor, couldn't have been. Same with the hearings on Anita Hill. They believe that if people had only listened to her and the substance of her remarks she would have been believed. Wrong. It *was* the substance of those hearings that defeated Anita Hill, pure and simple—not to mention the fact that she wasn't called to testify during the regular hearings and was only called at the final hour, when all other efforts failed to block the confirmation of the would-be death knell for *Roe v. Wade*. The American people listened carefully and drew their own conclusions. They knew that some special-interest groups had formed an alliance with the liberal media and leaked what amounted to an FBI report on Anita Hill's accusations. They knew the Senate had weighed the hearsay evidence and dismissed the report. They chose to believe Clarence Thomas.

After Clarence Thomas was confirmed, the media rushed to take pity on Anita Hill. *USA Today* ran a headline: "NORMALCY IS THE BEST ANITA HILL CAN HOPE FOR." Oh? Why was there no sympathy for Judge Thomas in *USA Today*'s story? He was the man whose life had nearly been ruined. Why all this sympathy for Anita Hill? Certainly the public wasn't that sympathetic toward Ms. Hill. Stephen Hess, a scholar at the liberal Brookings Institution in Washington, wrote, "When only 24 percent of the American people believe you, that has to hurt." Well, it should hurt. If you're lying, and only 24 percent of the people believe your lies, you should be worried. Instead, Anita Hill has become the latest poster child of the gullible, infantile left.

LESSONS FROM ANITA HILL

One of the most disturbing aspects of Anita Hill's charges was that it didn't matter to many feminists if she was telling the truth. The automatic assumption was that she was, and Thomas wasn't. The feminists rejoiced at the mere airing of her charges without even pausing to consider their validity. Anita Hill was nothing more than a football to be kicked around to score points for feminism. The feminists wanted a referendum on their definition of sexual harassment. They just aren't happy with the results.

Judge Susan Hoerchner, the witness for Anita Hill, exposed the real agenda. She said that this whole incident was about the inequities of power. Feminist leaders view men as evil, sitting in positions of power and unwilling to share any of it with women. Radical feminists want to use issues like sexual harassment to

---

The Way Things Ought to Be

intimidate and terrorize people and secure power for themselves. The Anita Hill caper exposed the lengths to which feminists and liberals will go in their quest for that power.

Despite losing this battle, they fight on. One of the "expert" commentators for the networks during the televised hearings was Catharine MacKinnon, a law professor at the University of Michigan. She was just a fringe feminist before the hearings, but being presented as an analyst by the networks accorded her "expert" status. Ms. MacKinnon teaches, and I assume therefore believes, that all sex is rape, even the sex in marriage. Women just don't know it because they are in love and unaware of the power and denigration being heaped upon them. You laugh or you disbelieve, but I assure you this is true. I don't make things up.

Ms. MacKinnon represents a growing number of radical fanatics who believe that all men, in their natural state, are potential rapists, that all rape and sexual harassment are natural components of 1990s' masculinity, that our society today has been reduced to a sexual men-vs.-women existence (it hasn't yet, but if it does it will be due to the ridiculous notions of feminists like the lovely and gracious Ms. MacKinnon). Now don't just consign this to the weirdo pile and forget it. This was the concept that fueled an entire one-hour prime-time special in the spring of 1992 on ABC called *Men, Sex and Rape*, hosted by Peter Jennings. These oddballs are now represented by the mainstream press as the spokeswomen for all American women. They grumble and growl about the fact that there are only two women in the Senate. Well, those in the Senate were elected. Who elected Catharine MacKinnon to speak for them?

THERE WAS HUMOR TOO

I must admit that Anita Hill's testimony provided endless opportunities for humor, not about sexual harassment, mind you, but about the ridiculous charges she made. As I am prone to do on many subjects, I suggested a movie be made of the hearings and the whole sordid episode. Some possible titles for the movie were:

My Left Foot in My Mouth
Driving Miss Sleazy
I Wish I Had Three Men and a Baby
A Pack of Lies—Now
Desperately Seeking Clarence
From Smear to Eternity

But the hearings also provided some sobering lessons in how far America is being dragged into the cloud-cuckoo-land of feminism. After the hearings, the Sunday *Times* of London ran a column titled: "A NATION BEING STRIPPED OF ITS SEXUALITY." The woman who wrote it, Barbara Amiel, noted, "The charges of sexual harassment are getting too far out of hand in America." She responded to the claim an attorney made on CNN during the hearings that "sexual harassment must be judged by the responsible woman, not the responsible man." Ms. Amiel noted that what this lawyer really meant was that "the response of the pathologically neurotic woman has become the standard for judging sexual harassment, and extreme feminism has become the state religion in America." She concluded that Anita Hill had only one valid argument on her side in her effort to derail Clarence Thomas. It was that anyone crazy enough to ask Anita Hill out wasn't fit to be a Supreme Court justice.

CONDOMS: THE NEW DIPLOMA

BUNGEE CONDOM COMMERCIAL I

ANNOUNCER: This is a Bungee jumper. He's about to jump off a cliff with only a band of rubber to protect him from instant death on the rocky beach below. He leaps off the precipice. The rubber stretches to the limit and he will live to jump again. But, take another look. That Bungee Condom is no ordinary band of rubber.

JUMPER: Hi, I love to Bungee jump, but whether I'm doing something dangerous like jumping off a cliff or jumping into a strange bed, I always depend on the strongest, most reliable rubber products available. That's why I always use Bungee Condoms.

ANNOUNCER: Bungee Condoms, made of pure four-ply industrial-grade rubber for safety and durability. And this patented inner tread means Bungee Condoms hug the surface to prevent dangerous slips and slides.

JUMPER: And no matter what size you buy, it always has "extra-large" stamped right on the side. I like that.

ANNOUNCER: Bungee Condoms, now available in the handy eighteen-pack "Kennedy Saturday Night Special." Or, pick up your free Bungee Sampler Pack at a high school near you. Bungee Condoms.

JUMPER: 'Cause whether it's love or Bungee jumping, when you fall hard, you want to be able to bounce back, ready to go again.

BUNGEE CONDOM COMMERCIAL II

ANNOUNCER: The 1950s.

STUDENT: You wanted to see me, Principal Smith?
PRINCIPAL: Jimmy, take out your wallet.
STUDENT: My wallet?
PRINCIPAL: What is that circle imprinted on the side?
STUDENT: Nothing, sir.
PRINCIPAL: Don't give me that. It's one of those c things.
STUDENT: A condom?
PRINCIPAL: Don't take it out right now. I certainly hope you weren't planning to use the thing.
STUDENT: No, sir.
PRINCIPAL: You won't, now. I'm taking that c thing and destroying it.
STUDENT: Yes, sir, but just one thing—don't tell my parents.

ANNOUNCER: The 1990s.

STUDENT: You wanted to see me, Principal Smith?
PRINCIPAL: Yes, Jimmy, take out your wallet.
STUDENT: My wallet?
PRINCIPAL: What is that circle imprinted on the side?
STUDENT: I don't have a circle.

PRINCIPAL: Just as I thought. Put this in your wallet right now.

STUDENT: This *c* thing?

PRINCIPAL: It's a condom, Jimmy, and you better make plans right now to use it.

STUDENT: Yes, sir, I won't destroy your faith in me.

PRINCIPAL: Good, Jimmy, but just one thing, don't tell your parents.

ANNOUNCER: This message has been brought to you by Bungee Condoms. Celebrating forty years of progress from being hidden in your dad's wallet to be handed out in your schools. Bungee Condoms—where quality is more than just a word, it's a slogan.

BUNGEE CONDOM COMMERCIAL III

FATHER: Princess, it's time you and I had a little father-to-daughter talk.

DAUGHTER: Sure, Daddy, what about?

FATHER: Well, you're how old now?

DAUGHTER: Fifteen.

FATHER: Then I guess it's time you know. I don't suppose you know what this is?

DAUGHTER: Sure, Daddy, that's a Bungee Condom. It's the Bungee Double Grip, no slip ultrathin with extra spermicide and reservoir tip, stock number 37794B. Available in seven designer colors.

FATHER: Then you know how to get these?

DAUGHTER: Well, I can get you plenty at school if you really need them, Daddy.

FATHER: No, I . . .

DAUGHTER: Although I personally prefer the Bungee X27 model him-hugger with extra torque capability. They come in a Kennedy Weekend dozen or the Wilt Chamberlain carry-home crate. For you, Daddy, I'd recommend the Bungee

Senior Reusable model T400. Let me see if I have a few of those in my purse.

ANNOUNCER: Bungee Condoms. We're a bigger part of your child's education than you are, and we're damn proud of it.

As is flawlessly illustrated by the above three mock commercials which run from time to time on my radio program, the logic and motivation behind this country's mad dash to distribute free condoms in our public schools is ridiculous and misguided. Worse, the message conveyed by mass condom distribution is a disservice and borders on being lethal. Condom distribution sanctions, even encourages, sexual activity, which in teen years tends to be promiscuous and relegates to secondary status the most important lesson to be taught: abstinence. An analysis of the entire condom distribution logic also provides a glimpse into just what is wrong with public education today.

First things first. Advocates of condom distribution say that kids are going to have sex, that try as we might we can't stop them. Therefore they need protection. Hence, condoms. Well, hold on a minute. Just whose notion is it that "kids are going to do it anyway, you can't stop them"? Why limit the application of that brilliant logic to sexual activity? Let's just admit that kids are going to do drugs and distribute safe, untainted drugs every morning in homeroom. Kids are going to smoke, too, we can't stop them, so let's provide packs of low-tar cigarettes to the students for their after-sex smoke. Kids are going to get guns and shoot them, you can't stop them, so let's make sure that teachers have bulletproof vests. I mean, come on! If we are really concerned about safe sex, why stop at condoms? Let's convert study halls to Safe Sex Centers where students can go to actually have sex on nice double beds with clean sheets under the watchful and approving eye of the school nurse, who will be on hand to demonstrate, along with the principal, just how to use a condom. Or even better: If kids are going to have sex, let's put disease-free hookers in these Safe Sex Centers. Hey, if safe sex is the objective, why compromise our standards?

There is something else very disturbing about all this. Let's say that Johnnie and Susie are on a date in Johnny's family sedan. Johnny pulls in to his town's designated Teen Parking Location hoping to score a little affection from Susie. They move to the backseat and it isn't long before Johnny, on the verge of bliss, whips out his trusty high school–distributed condom and urges Susie not to resist him. She is hesitant, being a nice girl and all, and says she doesn't think the time is right.

"Hey, everything is okay. Nothing will go wrong. Heck, the *school gave me this condom,* they know what they're doing. You'll be fine," coos the artful and suave Johnny.

Aside from what is obviously wrong here, there is something you probably haven't thought of which to me is profound. Not that long ago, school policy, including that on many college campuses, was designed to protect the girls from the natural and instinctive aggressive pursuit of young men. Chaperones, for example, were around to make sure the girls were not in any jeopardy. So much for that thinking now. The schools may just as well endorse and promote these backseat affairs. The kids are going to do it anyway.

Well, here's what's wrong. There have always been consequences to having sex. Always. Now, however, some of these consequences are severe: debilitating venereal diseases and AIDS. You can now die from having sex. It is that simple. If you look, the vast majority of adults in America have made adjustments in their sexual behavior in order to protect themselves from some of the dire consequences floating around out there. For the most part, the sexual revolution of the sixties is over, a miserable failure. Free love and rampant one-night stands are tougher to come by because people are aware of the risks. In short, we have modified our behavior. Now, would someone tell me what is so difficult about sharing this knowledge and experience with kids? The same stakes are involved. Isn't that our responsibility, for crying out loud, to teach them what's best for them? If we adults aren't responding to these new dangers by having condom-protected sex anytime, anywhere, why should such folly be taught to our kids?

Let me try the Magic Johnson example for you who remain unconvinced. Imagine that you are in the Los Angeles Lakers locker room after a game and you and Magic are getting ready to go hit the town. Outside the locker room are a bunch of young women, as there always are, and as Magic had freely admitted there always were, and that you know that the woman Magic is going to pick up and take back to the hotel has AIDS. You approach Magic and say, "Hey, Magic! Hold on! That girl you're going to take back to the hotel with you has AIDS. Here, don't worry about it. Take these condoms, you'll be fine."

Do you think Magic would have sex with that woman? Ask yourself: Would you knowingly have sex with *anyone* who has AIDS with only a condom to protect you from getting the disease? It doesn't take Einstein to answer that question. So, why do you think it's okay to send kids out into the world to do just that? Who is to know who carries the HIV virus, and on the chance your kid runs into someone who does have it, are you confident that a condom will provide all the protection he or she needs?

Doesn't it make sense to be honest with kids and tell them the best thing they can do to avoid AIDS or any of the other undesirable consequences is to abstain from sexual intercourse? It is the best way—in fact, it is the only surefire way—to guard against sexual transmission of AIDS, pregnancy, and venereal diseases. What's so terrible about saying so?

Yet, there are those who steadfastly oppose the teaching of abstinence, and I think they should be removed from any position of authority where educating children is concerned. In New York, the City Board of Education *narrowly won* (4–3) the passage of a resolution requiring the inclusion of teaching abstinence in the AIDS education program in the spring of 1992. No one was trying to eliminate anything from the program, such as condom distribution or anal sex education (which does occur in New York public school sex education classes). All they wanted was that abstinence also be taught. Yet, the Schools Chancellor, Joseph Fernandez, vigorously fought the idea, saying it would do great damage to their existing program! Well, just how is that? The fact is that abstinence works every time it is tried. As this book went to press, the New York Civil Liberties Union was considering filing a lawsuit to stop this dangerous new addition to the curriculum. Now what in the name of God is going on here? This is tantamount to opposing a drug education program which instructs students not to use drugs because it would not be useful.

The Jacksonville, Florida, school board also decided that abstinence should be the centerpiece of their sexual education curriculum, and the liberals there were also outraged about this. What is so wrong with this? Whose agenda is being denied by teaching abstinence and just what is that agenda?

Jacksonville teachers are telling seventh-graders that "the only safe sex is no sex at all." Sex education classes provide some information about birth control and sexually transmitted diseases, but these areas are not the primary focus of the classes. Nancy Corwin, a member of the school board, admits the paradox when she says that the schools send a nonsensical message when they teach kids not to have sex but then give them condoms.

Instead of this twaddle, the Jacksonville school board has decided to teach real safe sex, which is abstinence. However, six families, along with Planned Parenthood and the ACLU, are suing the schools over this program. This bunch of curious citizens says that teaching abstinence puts the children at a greater risk of catching AIDS or other sexually transmitted diseases. Greater risk? !£#$£@! How can that be? What kind of contaminated thinking is this? The suit alleges that the schools are providing a "fear-based program that gives children incomplete, inaccurate, biased, and sectarian information." You want more? Try this: Linda Lanier of Planned Parenthood says, "It's not right to try to trick our students." Trick the students? #£&@£!? If anyone is trying to trick students, it's Planned Parenthood and this band of hedonists who try to tell kids that a condom will protect them from any consequences of sex.

Folks, here you have perhaps the best example of the culture war being waged in our country today. To say that "teaching abstinence is a trick" is absurd. Is Ms. Lanier having sex every night of the week? What adjustments has she made in her sex life because of AIDS? Does she think that a little sheath of latex will be enough to protect her?

This is terribly wrong. The Jacksonville public school system is attempting to teach right from wrong, as opposed to teaching that sex does not have any consequences, which I believe is the selfish agenda these people hold dear. I have stated elsewhere in this book, and I state it again here, that there are many people who wish to go through life guilt-free and engage in behavior they know to be wrong and morally vacant. In order to assuage their guilt they attempt to construct and impose policies which not only allow them to engage in their chosen activities but encourage others to do so as well. There is, after all, strength in numbers.

Promiscuous and self-gratifying, of-the-moment sex is but one of these chosen lifestyles. Abortions on demand and condom distribution are but two of the policies and programs which, as far as these people are concerned, ensure there are no consequences. As one disgusted member of the Jacksonville school board said, "Every yahoo out there has a social program that they want to run through the school system. We are here for academic reasons and we cannot cure the social evils of the world."

The worst of all of this is the lie that condoms really protect against AIDS. The condom failure rate can be as high as 20 percent. Would you get on a plane—or put your children on a plane—if one in five passengers would be killed on the flight? Well, the statistic holds for condoms, folks.

Ah, but there is even more lunacy haunting the sacred halls of academe. According to the *Los Angeles Times*, administrators in the Los Angeles public schools have regretfully acknowledged that the sex education courses undertaken in the early 1970s "might" have a correlation to the rising teen pregnancy rates in their schools which can be traced to the same years. They have devised an enlightened and marvelous new approach to modernize and correct the sex education curriculum. It is called Outercourse. I am not making this up. Outercourse is, in essence, instruction in creative methods of masturbation.

"Hi, class, and welcome to Outercourse 101. I am your instructor, Mr. Reubens, from Florida, and I want to remind you that this is a hands-on course." We will know the graduates of Outercourse 101 in about forty years. They will be the people walking around with seeing-eye dogs.

SAFE TALK

I became infuriated with the media-hyped twaddle that implied that the use of condoms absolved people from taking responsibility for their sex lives. I started the "Condom Update" on my radio program, and introduced it with a song from the Fifth Dimension: "Up, Up and Away (In My Beautiful Balloon)." Then, on Valentine's Day, 1989, I had an inspiration. It was the first day of National Condom Week, and all I was hearing was that condoms were the way to ensure safe sex. I thought about how I could demonstrate to my audience that this was preposterous. Then it hit me. The Excellence in Broadcasting Network would guarantee that my radio program would only engage in Safe Talk. I sent my staff out to buy an assortment of condoms. After we went on the air, I very carefully stretched one out and put it on the golden EIB microphone, making as much noise with the latex as I could. After it was on, I carefully popped the reservoir chamber a couple of times for effect and certified that the mike was safe.

"Ladies and gentlemen, you are now fully protected," I told my listeners. "If I utter anything offensive, you will not be offended because the condom will screen it out. If I happen to utter a profanity today you will never hear it. It will allow me to curse and you will be safeguarded against any irresponsibility on my part. This is the best thing I can do for the cause of Safe Talk in America." For this I was called reckless and fear-based.

Of course, I then pointed out that the reason my show practiced Safe Talk had nothing to do with the condom stretched over my studio mike. It was because I had chosen not to say anything offensive or profane. The only way to ensure Safe Talk was for me and others in the radio business to practice prudent behavior. To exercise self-restraint. Using a condom for Safe Talk or Safe Sex was an evasion of moral responsibility.

Since then, the Condom Update has been one of the most popular features of my live performances. People in the audience sometimes throw condoms on stage as a greeting. I've also learned remarkable things about condoms. Did you know there is a glow-in-the-dark condom? It's called the Glow Worm, and it gives off a greenish shine in the dark. My question has always been: who's going to see it, and if you need a Glow Worm condom, what exactly are you doing?

A fellow in Florida wrote in to me to tell me there are *flavored* condoms on the market. He worked in a state requisition office and had processed a thirty-nine-dollar order for three flavored condoms. One was strawberry, another was sugar-coated. I told my audiences that I never knew there were taste buds down there. Heh, heh, heh. That one really frosted them.

It would be easy to understate the significance of society's recent infatuation with condoms by saying that it is just symptomatic of the larger moral decline in our societal values. But that would miss the vital point that free condom distribution in public schools can be a matter of life and death. Yet, the myths continue, and in the name of protecting our youth, the condom pushers are putting their lives at risk. In light of all this outright stupidity, is it any wonder that the parents and middle-class citizens of this country are ready to explode with rage over the moral and ethical directions in which their kids are being taken?

TO OGLE OR NOT TO OGLE

THE PHILANDERER

(Sung by a Ted Kennedy sound-alike to the tune of "The
Wanderer")

Oh, well I'm the type of guy who would never settle down
Where pretty girls are, well you know that I'm around
I kiss 'em and I love 'em 'cause to me they're all the same
I get so gosh darned hammered, I don't even know their
   names
'Cause I'm a philanderer, yes a philanderer
I sleep around, around, around, around, around

Well my views are on the left, got a bimbo on the right
Only God will know where I'll be passing out tonight
And if you want to ask me which girl I love the best
I'll tear open my shirt, got mother Rosie on my chest
'Cause I'm a philanderer, yes a philanderer
I sleep around, around, around, around, around

Oh yeah, I'm the type of guy, he likes to roam around
I'm never in one place, I wake from town to town
But when I find myself falling for some girl
I walk right in that car of mine and I take her for a whirl
Because I'm a Kennedy, yes I'm a Kennedy
The car skids round and round and round and round and
    round

KENNA-DAY-O

(Sung by Harry Belafonte sound-alike to the tune of "The
Banana Boat Song (Day-O)"

Kenna-day, Kenna-day, Kenna-day, Kenna-day-ay-o
Kennedy clan is in trouble once more
Say Mr. Kennedy put back your banana
Kennedy clan is in trouble once more
Uncle Ted is naked out on the veranda
Kennedy clan is in trouble once more
Late one night down in Palm Beach town
Kennedy clan is in trouble once more
Brought young girl back to the big compound
Kennedy clan is in trouble once more
Hormones. Hormones.
Kennedy clan is in trouble once more
Kenna-day-o, Kenna-day-ay-o
Kennedy clan is in trouble once more
Up in Chappaquiddick Teddy looked for romance
Kennedy clan is in trouble once more
JFK couldn't keep it in his own pants
Kennedy clan is in trouble once more
Kenna-day-o, Kenna-day-o
Kennedy clan is in trouble once more
Kenna-day-o, Kenna-day-o
Hormones are raging, they won't leave us alone

Here are some reports from the sexual harassment battlefront.
Read these carefully. Some are humorous, but they make a point

about how far this issue has poisoned relations between the sexes. Sexual harassment is a legitimate issue, but its exploitation by feminists who seek to advance their political agenda has resulted in total confusion and chaos. What are we men supposed to be anymore? How are we supposed to act?

• In 1991 the Canadian subsidiary of Sears was attacked by feminists for selling boxer shorts, that, during daylight or bright light, said NO, NO, NO all over them. But when the lights went out, or when darkness descended, the NO, NO, NO magically and wonderfully became YES, YES, YES through the use of fluorescent paint. The feminists became hysterical and claimed that this encouraged date rape. Sears caved and pulled the shorts off its shelves. I'll tell you, folks, this is crazy. Absurd. Rape? Now think: By the time a man sees those boxer shorts, the question of NO or YES has no doubt been settled. I'd say consent is manifest in this situation, wouldn't you? If not, what rapist would be stopped by the word NO plastered all over the shorts?

• A recent study by three management professors found that men who work in a predominantly male workplace are more loyal and more likely to stay on the job than if they work with a lot of women. Men are more comfortable around other men at the workplace, especially with the constant threat of lawsuits. If that cloud was lifted, I think there would be a lot less tension at the workplace. Men can no longer enjoy themselves or tell jokes with a lot of women around, because anything they say within the earshot of women can be construed as sexual harassment. Many men say they feel they can't even be friendly in the office now because you never know when a woman, for whatever reason, will accuse you of sexual harassment. You don't believe me? Well, Claudia Weathers of the NOW Legal Defense Fund says that sexual "harassment can be almost anything that the employee finds offensive." Sorry, but that is not a beautiful thing. It is wacky and bizarre, not to mention preposterous. One cannot write open-ended laws like that. Allison Weatherfield, a crony of Ms. Weathers at the NOW gang, says a man can ask a woman out only once and then very carefully. If she says no, he should never ask her out again. And these women think they are representing the mainstream? It's getting to the point where a man who naturally expresses any interest in a woman whatsoever can be accused of lecherous behavior. My friends, if this isn't men vs. women, at least as far as these freak feminists are concerned, then what is it? I, for one, have had it with this creeping philosophy which says that men, in their natural state, are all rapists, molesters, and reprobates. That's what these dimwits really believe and I resent it.

• Almost any kind of attention paid to women can now run afoul of the New Fascists. Consider the case of Richard Hummel, a University of Toronto professor. Last year, he was banned from a campus swimming pool and ordered to take sensitivity counseling. What had he done? "They" said he was ogling female swimmers. One woman said he had "leered" at her through his swim mask and used his flippers to catch up with her in the pool. Another stated he regularly swam to the bottom of the pool and ogled women swimming above him near the surface. He was found to have violated the university's harassment regulations. So, just *looking* is harassment? Good grief, that's what men are supposed to do. That's how the old ball gets rolling. Heck, most can't help it. It's built in, biologically, from the factory. Blame it on a defect in the womb. You know something else? They wouldn't have minded one bit if it were Warren Beatty ogling them. They would have probably shoved each other out of the way so he could get a better angle.

Well, a petition was posted in the men's locker room defending Mr. Hummel. It stated: "Looking, by any name, in itself does not constitute sexual harassment in the free environment of recreational activity." If Professor Hummel can be found guilty of harassing women by merely looking at them, what will be next?

• Helen Gurley Brown, the editor of *Cosmopolitan* magazine, wrote an op-ed piece for *The Wall Street Journal* at the height of the Anita Hill frenzy. She made some very valid points about how sexual harassment must be clearly defined for there to be a legal problem. Otherwise, a lot of creative energy at the office would be stifled. She described a game called Scuttle, which was played at a radio station she had worked at forty-odd years ago. The object of the game was to chase a woman, catch her, and pull her panties off. Brown claimed the game was enjoyed by all concerned. Folks, it's obvious that times have changed. The only time I see panties being thrown around at radio stations is when some long-haired, maggot-infested FM-type rock star shows up to mumble his way through an interview. But I believe Helen Gurley Brown when she says it happened. Feminists were outraged that she would tell that story. She was unrepentant, though.

• Have you heard of Mrithi, the gorilla? He was the star of the movie *Gorillas in the Mist,* and he used to live in Rwanda. He doesn't live there anymore because he died, the victim of a bloody civil war in Rwanda. I learned of Mrithi's sudden and shocking death one afternoon near the conclusion of my show. An assistant stormed into the studio with the bulletin: Mrithi was dead. It was not a beautiful thing. It was a sad thing. I read further and came across a quote attributed to a woman named McKeenen, who was involved with some animal defense fund. Choking back tears, she had said, "He was the first gorilla who ever touched me." The first gorilla who ever touched her? Again: the first gorilla who ever touched her! Be still my beating heart. All we men have to do today is *look* at a woman the wrong way and we find ourselves accused of sexual harassment, lechery, and molestation. Yet, here is this woman sobbing because she was never again going to be *touched by a gorilla?* This settles it for me. I'm going to dress as a gorilla from now on at every Halloween party I attend.

I KNOW SEXUAL HARASSMENT WHEN I SEE IT

One of the assertions made in the Anita Hill fiasco was that only women are truly qualified to recognize sexual harassment. Men don't understand what it is. This, of course, is more stupidity. It is based on the fallacious premise that you must experience something in order to be qualified to understand and comment on it. I resent that very much. I'm a decent person, and I think a decent person knows when there is sexual harassment. If I had a sister or a wife and I saw her being harassed, I would know it. I would try to stop it.

But men are now being told they have to shut up and have harassment defined for them by someone else with an ax to grind. I'm convinced that there are women today who simply

141

want to punish men for being themselves. If someone asks a woman out to dinner after work and uses the word *baby*, that can now be construed as sexual harassment. I don't condone groping or sidling up to someone, but a joke or the raising of an eyebrow at work is in another league.

Even feminists are divided on the issue of sexual harassment. Camille Paglia, a self-described "renegade feminist," is a professor at the University of the Arts in Philadelphia. She says that harassment of women is one of the risks women have to take into account when they have any dealings with men. She believes women's studies programs that attack men are "junk" and are destroying a whole generation of women. As for the William Kennedy Smith rape trial, she felt that if a woman drinks with a man until 3:00 A.M. and then goes home with him, she should realize the risks she is taking. I don't agree with all of Paglia's conclusions, but she proves that there is no monolithic view of sexual harassment, even in the feminist community.

PRIVATE CLUBS

Sexual harassment has become such a vague, all-encompassing term that we now see feminists who have invaded previously all-male preserves complaining about the behavior they see there. They charge harassment. This shows the need for both sexes to have some private space to themselves that is free from contact with the other sex. Before feminism infested American life, there were clear rules between the sexes. Men had to honor and respect women. Now that women are forcing themselves into locker rooms and private clubs, they are finding out what men are really like. Men use crude language among themselves all the time. They act grossly sometimes. Yet, women who want to invade these male preserves turn around and demand that this kind of normal male behavior stop. They can't have it both ways.

And they have no sense of humor about any of this. One of my fabulous routines from the Rush to Excellence concerts concerns a San Francisco men's club which lost its battle to exclude women from membership. The courts ruled that they had to admit women on the basis that businesswomen were being unfairly denied opportunities to do business. This is specious. If some businessman wanted to discuss a deal with a woman, all he had to do was invite her to lunch or dinner with him. How much business did women think they were going to get as a result of forcing their way in? Anyway, after one year, the female members demanded their own exercise room. They were probably tired of being ogled by a bunch of slobbering men while they pumped iron and rode LifeCycles clad in leotards and spandex. The men agreed and, with grace and humanity, offered to install the first three exercise machines in the women's new workout room. The ladies were thrilled.

When they arrived on that first exciting day they found, to their stunned amazement, a washing machine, an ironing board, and a vacuum cleaner. Heh, heh, heh.

Well. When I guested on the CBS *Morning News,* this wonderful segment from my *Rush to Excellence II* video was aired to promote my upcoming interview. Paula Zahn said to her co-host, Harry Smith, "If he says that on this show, he won't get out of this studio alive. Who thinks that is funny?"

SEXUAL DIFFERENCES

Harassment really can be in the eye of the beholder. There are those who will tell you there are no basic, natural differences in the ways that men and women look at a given situation. Baloney. Evidence of these differences is all around us. Examples of such are called in to my show every day.

An acquaintance of mine from Sacramento, Fred Hayward, has an organization called Men's Rights, Inc. Fred opposes discrimination against men in the media. Every year he gave out awards that showed media items that men could take offense at if they chose to view them the same way that feminists view everything in the media.

One year the award went to a jeans commercial. The ad showed a man and woman wearing jeans and walking through what looked like New York's Central Park. What was unusual was that she had her hand full of his butt. Now, Fred became mad as hell at this and told me about it. Imagine if the roles had been reversed, and the man had been shown with his hand on *her* butt. You would have heard such feminist carping that the ad would have been taken off the air.

I told Fred to calm down. You see, I said, you're missing the point. The difference is that every man looking at that ad wishes he were in it. Every man in the world would like to have a gorgeous woman like that coming on to him. Especially today, when women are supposed to be aggressive and taking things into their own hands—so to speak—men would view that prospect with pleasure. But women would understandably find an ad with a man holding a woman's rear threatening. Most women would find that too forward an act. Most men wouldn't. Just another one of those natural differences that feminists find offensive and bothersome—because, try as they might, they know they will never be able to change it.

Earlier this year, another example came up on my show. I had a bad sore throat and my voice was somewhat weak. This woman called and said she had the *perfect* cure. I said, "Hmm, what is it?" She said: "A throat massage. With my tongue." I was stunned and incredulous, totally taken aback. But—and this is the important thing—I was not offended. I laughed and told her I found her idea intriguing. (I had never tried it.) "Is your tongue long enough to do that?" I asked. "Oh, yes," she said. "No problem whatsoever." I confess, I liked that exchange. I was smiling and all the people watching the show were in tears. It was a hoot.

Well, I got a prof note (electronic mail) on my computer from a guy who asked me to imagine how much outrage there would have been if a female talk show host had been told that by a male caller. The guy was right. Think about it. There would have been hysterical accusations of sexism, vulgarity, and obscenity. Shouts of "It's Daryl Gates's fault" would have echoed through the streets of America. Someone would have called the ACLU, the NAACP, Interpol, the EEOC, the NAB, *A Current Affair*, the NOW gang, and any other agency to which they could complain. A massive search by land and air would be launched to find this beast, this rat, and bring him to justice. Anita Hill would make a speech offering solutions to the crisis. Emergency aid would be allocated by Congress to counsel the poor hostette on dealing with such terror.

Yet, my good friends, I didn't feel at all sexually harassed by the call. I liked it. It just proves how men and women instinctively and naturally look at events differently. And this is nothing new. It's always been this way. It's a beautiful thing.

I'd like to say to any women who have read this chapter and been offended or outraged that I apologize. It was not the purpose of the chapter to offend. Anyone, without any talent at all, can do that. I have simply tried to be as honest as I can be about my feelings on this sensitive and touchy subject. Yes, it is a tender subject, too, and I have been tender and gentle in discussing it. I want people to get along with one another, without making a legal case out of everything. I deeply resent the politicization of social relationships. It bothers me no end, especially when so many people think the government should intervene to solve these things.

Let me leave you with a thought that most honestly summarizes my sentiments: I love the women's movement . . . especially when I am walking behind it.

WE NEED A NEW NATIONAL SYMBOL

I HAVE COME UP WITH A NEW NATIONAL SYMBOL FOR THE UNITED States. I think we need to junk the eagle and come up with a symbol that is more appropriate for the kind of government we have today. We need to replace the eagle with a huge sow that has a lot of nipples and a bunch of fat little piglets hanging on them, all trying to suckle as much nourishment from them as possible.

Of course, the problem is that while the sow is large she is near death. She's not fat and flourishing, she's emaciated. A lot of the piglets have dropped off and are running around lost because they can't get any more nourishment.

This symbol would have many uses. Can't you just see it painted on *Air Force One?* Imagine that every time a congressman speaks, that symbol would be on the podium in front of him. Truth in advertising.

We should also change the national motto. Now that God has been exiled from our classrooms, it's clear that "In God We Trust" won't do anymore. Our motto will now be one taken from that immortal cartoon character, Porky Pig. "Bedep, bedep,

bedep . . . Th . . . Th . . . That's All Folks!" Thanks for the mammaries.

The reason I suggest a sow for the national symbol is that too many Americans now automatically think the government should help them when they have a problem. We have witnessed an explosion in entitlement spending in the last thirty years. Warren Rudman, the retiring senator from New Hampshire, says that 60 percent to 65 percent of the federal budget by the year 2000 will be entitlement spending.

Well, God help us, there's no way this country is going to survive if that happens.

Our inner cities are now collapsing, our children are going uneducated, crime is running rampant, and yet all the money we've poured into those problems hasn't helped. The reason is that we are trying to use dollars to remedy a breakdown in societal values. The money not only doesn't help, it exacerbates the problem. The federal government has assumed the role of the wage-earning father for a lot of kids, and the results are obvious. In the last thirty years, the illegitimacy rate has gone from 5 percent to 26 percent. It's 63 percent in the black community.

Well, it's time someone stood up and said enough is enough. Someone's got to say, Folks, a majority of Americans are going to be hooked on entitlements if we don't change things. We can't afford that. We're going to have to wean people away from entitlements; wean them off the sow.

I'M ENTITLED . . .

The people we need to wean off government aren't all poor. Many are middle-class people who've been suckered into believing that social security is an insurance program and that the money they get comes from a trust fund where their contributions have been deposited. It's not true. The social security check someone gets tomorrow is paid for by the payroll taxes someone kicks into the system today. Everyone is going to have to tighten their belts or the whole system will collapse in about forty years.

A lot of people refer to these entitlement programs as welfare. I

RUSH H. LIMBAUGH, III

don't like calling them welfare. People think I'm engaging in poor bashing when I attack government spending. I'm not. We have to worry about cutting back on subsidies to everyone. Plus, who can seriously say it is compassionate to bankrupt the country by robbing from our future generations?

The government just gives too much money away. Economist Steven Schindler once wrote that a country cannot remain free for long if the government takes over 50 percent of its economy's output in taxes. Our government spends 25 percent of the nation's income. Add in the cost of state and local governments, and about two out of every five dollars in this country is consumed by government. Every group looks to government as a source of funding. All those who have yet to partake of the government pie want a piece of it; those who already have, want a bigger piece. All of them claim their need is more important than anyone else's. One group wants more funding for AIDS research. Another for underprivileged kids. This is the United States of America, not The United Way.

It's the people who have never looked to the government as a charitable foundation that are most angry now. They are paying more in taxes every year and are getting less and less in return. Most people in America don't think that prosperity is created in Washington. They are relying on themselves for their success. In fact, they view Washington's main role not as creating but as destroying their opportunities for prosperity. The main ideological battle in this country is between those who think the government should be the primary allocator of benefits in society and those who believe the private sector should have that function. I myself have never looked to a government agency for a solution to any problem I've encountered. Now, I know people will say that even Rush Limbaugh benefits from government.

Sure, I use the public streets and the post office, and if I get a disease someday I may benefit from the government's medical research. I also benefit from the byproducts of our defense spending. But the streets cost twice as much as they should and always seem to have potholes. The mail service is twice as slow as it should be. With some diseases the Food and Drug Administration keeps as many lifesaving drugs off the market as it approves. Even the government services all of us use don't always have to be run by the government. Private companies could pave and maintain the highways. Many states are building private toll roads that people use without ever having to stop and pay a toll. They buy a road-use card with an electronic bar code on it that allows them to zip through toll stations. United Parcel Service already delivers a lot of mail and packages more efficiently and at a cheaper price than the post office.

But most government spending today doesn't go for services most people use. They are transfers of income from one person to another. In short, massive redistributions of wealth. A bunch of liberals have convinced people that disadvantaged people can't make it on their own without some social workers helping them. Some people are raised to believe they are incapable of achieving anything unless government helps them, either through welfare programs, which destroy self-reliance, or affirmative action, which insults their intelligence and resourcefulness.

Of course, wealthy people also abuse the system. The halls of Congress are filled with people seeking special government subsidies and tax breaks. The Rural Electrification program has expanded its functions way beyond providing electricity to poor farmers. Now it pays for things like installing ski lifts at resorts in Colorado. I'm just as opposed to rich people getting subsidies from the government as poor people. Even Ross Perot made his millions largely by processing Medicare claim forms for the government, and in the 1980s he used Jim Wright to land him a $34 million grant to develop a private airport he was building near Dallas.

TEACHING THE RIGHT STUFF

Government programs may help some people, but the damage they do to the character of the recipients far outweighs any good they do. My mom and dad provided for me, but they made sure I learned the value of making my own way in the world. They deprived me of some things. Smart parents do that. They don't want to destroy initiative by giving their kids too much. The reason is that parents want us to realize our potential, and they know we won't do that unless we work at it ourselves.

I can think of no single action that would better help us do that than letting someone back into our schools that liberals would probably call a dead white man. I'm talking about God.

Think about it. We now teach kids how to use condoms, we instruct them in multiculturalism, we tell them lies about American history, and yet we can't teach them the Ten Commandments. We can't teach, "Thou Shalt Not Steal," "Thou Shalt Not Kill." This is nothing less than depriving children of their moral and mental nutrients during their formative years. Now, I know the arguments about separation of church and state, and I certainly don't want to force a Hindu kid into reading the Bible every day, but in no way can it reasonably be argued that the government is endorsing or establishing a religion when it merely permits students the time to pray if they so choose. But isn't the government's denial of that right an encroachment on the free exercise rights of students? In their secular fervor, the left is unable to concede these distinctions, which gives rise to the question of whether it is the students' rights they are protecting or a secular humanist agenda.

But a school voucher system would go a long way toward making those problems moot. The average family pays thousands of dollars a year into the public school system. Parents should be able to take that money and spend it on a school, public or private, that teaches the values they believe are important for their kids.

It's time liberals had some compassion for parents who are trying to raise their kids in the moral vacuum that liberal policies have created. Liberals ask that we trust them to make sure the money we give government is spent properly. Well, people are tired of that con game. We can no longer expect people to pay taxes for government programs without giving them any voice in how the money is spent. When I give money to a charity, I can pick an organization with a good track record that I know does good work. I can't do the same with the government. I know their track record is lousy.

Moreover, it has been argued that the reason why liberals are so adamant about busing and forced integration, and against choice in secondary education, is that the public schools are the only remaining breeding ground for liberal ideas. It's where new little liberals are shaped and formed amid an avalanche of liberal propaganda that has made its way into the curriculum. I won't go so far as to say that there is a conspiracy at work here, but there can be no question that history revision, sex education, free condom distribution, and the like are outgrowths of the left. As such, the left has a vested interest in preserving public funds to support schools with those programs. They are smart enough to realize that if a voucher system was invoked, there would be a mass exodus from those institutions they call schools and I call war zones.

People are going to have to learn to depend less on government. We are going to have to separate them from the federal budget sow. But we can also make their lives better by giving them more choice in how the tax money they do pay is spent. We should cut social security taxes so people can invest in their own IRAs. People need more options in health care. Poor parents can receive scholarships for their children if they can't afford private schools; it would still be cheaper than the money we now waste on inner city public schools.

Conservatives today want to give people value for their tax dollars and open up real opportunities for poor people to better themselves. That's real compassion, not the fake kind liberals peddle when they throw money at problems so they can add to the power they have over other people.

SORRY, BUT THE EARTH IS NOT FRAGILE

AND THE LORD CREATED . . .

MY VIEWS ON THE ENVIRONMENT ARE ROOTED IN MY BELIEF IN Creation. I don't believe that life on earth began spontaneously or as a result of some haphazard, random selection process; nor do I believe that nature is oh-so-precariously balanced. I don't believe that the earth and her ecosystem are fragile, as many radical environmentalists do. They think man can come along, all by himself, and change everything for the worse; that after hundreds of millions of years, the last two generations of human existence are going to destroy the planet. Who do they think we are?

I resent that presumptuous view of man and his works. I refuse to believe that people, who are themselves the result of Creation, can destroy the most magnificent creation of the entire universe. We cannot comprehend many of the wonders of the universe. The human mind, or that small percentage of it that we use, is incapable of imagining the size of the universe, its origins, or even *where it is*. Although some incredibly arrogant scientists believe that they are capable of scientifically unlocking every

152

mystery of the universe and of understanding everything in purely material terms, I believe there are certain things that the mind of man simply cannot discover or ascertain. There are certain things we were not meant to understand, cannot understand, and must accept on faith.

I am in awe of the perfection of the earth. This one small planet has the conditions necessary for life and is ideally situated in our solar system. If it were a little farther away from the sun the entire planet would be one gigantic Antarctica; if it were a little closer, it would be one continuous Sahara Desert. Earth's placement is precise; and that, my friends, is not a result of chance. It is astonishing that life flourishes on this small sphere, located in this small solar system, located in this small galaxy, located in this endless universe.

The more I learn about the interaction of all life-forms on the planet and the more I witness, with my own five senses, the beauty and magnificence of nature, the more awestricken I become. We humans had nothing to do with the earth's creation, its placement, or its functioning. We are only a part of it, which is not to downplay our role or significance in this world. We are as much a part of it as any of its other inhabitants, both animate and inanimate; as much as a redwood tree or a spotted owl, as much a part of it as a glacier. But environmentalists paint humans almost as an aberration; as the natural enemy of nature. According to them, we are capable of destroying this wondrous planet merely by being ourselves. That is true vanity, or what I call humanity vanity.

I don't understand how the same people who say we are powerful enough to destroy the earth, just by acting according to our natures, also say we are no better and no more worthy of respect than a frog. This is the great paradox of the environmentalist.

The animal rights crowd, which is largely sympathetic toward much of the environmental fringe movement, believes there is a continuum from a mosquito to a rat to a boy. They seem to think that all life-forms on the planet, other than human beings, peacefully coexist. But humans destroy, they say. That is such a foolish notion, not only because most animals and insects depend for their very existence on consuming each other, but because humans are the only creatures capable of cleaning up the messes made by themselves and all other creatures. I cannot deny that we have made a mess of parts of our world, but when I hear that fifty years of driving automobiles, fifty years of fluorocarbons and air-conditioners are going to destroy us, I want to cringe.

The fact is, we couldn't destroy the earth if we wanted to. *(Warning! Common sense is found in the next eight sentences. Skip them if you can't cope with it.)* The earth is over 4 billion years old. The archenemy of nature, man, has been on the planet no more than 200,000 years. Man cannot even come close to creating the powerful forces of nature—many of them damaging and destructive—yet these forces have been around for the same 4 billion years the earth has. And the earth is still here! Imagine that! It is a beautiful thing. Even if we dedicated all of our mental and physical resources to destroying the planet, even if we put Daryl Gates in charge of the effort, we couldn't do it. Not even Mikhail Gorbachev, who can do anything, could destroy the planet.

Consider this hypothetical: Environmental Enemy Number 1, Ronald Reagan, decides in a Cabinet meeting that he wants all Democrats to get skin cancer. Knowing that ultraviolet radiation in sunlight can cause skin cancer, Reagan must therefore see to it that the protective ozone layer in the upper atmosphere is destroyed so that all of that mean ultraviolet radiation can reach the Earth's surface and make cancerous all that Democrat skin.

So he orders the head of NASA to destroy all stratospheric ozone by the end of the year. The head of NASA would quickly come to grips with his impotence, realizing that he couldn't do it unless he had the power to destroy the sun. Why, you ask? Because ozone is *created* by the sun, particularly ultraviolet sunlight. And yet these dunderhead alarmists and prophets of doom want us to believe that because there are occasional reduced levels of ozone over Antarctica (which, incidentally, always rebound to normal levels), our own activity, based purely on our natural behavior and technological advancement, is responsible for what they predict will be the destruction of the ozone layer. Poppycock. Balderdash.

Mount Pinatubo in the Philippines spewed forth more than a

thousand times the amount of ozone-depleting chemicals in *one* eruption than all the fluorocarbons manufactured by wicked, diabolical, and insensitive corporations in history. So much so that respected scientists now say that a 4 percent to 6 percent ozone loss could—*could*, but may not—occur over the Northern Hemisphere in the next two or three years. Now, wait—before you think I have just destroyed my own argument, remember this: volcanoes have been doing this for 4 billion years. And guess what? We still have a healthy ozone layer! Isn't it wonderful? Aren't you thrilled? Hmmm. You still don't get it? Read it again, folks. One eruption, in 4 billion years of eruptions—a thousand times as destructive as all man-made CFCs—and a temporary maximum loss of 6 percent of the ozone. Conclusion: mankind can't possibly equal the output of even one eruption from Pinatubo, much less 4 billion years' worth of them, so how can we destroy ozone? In other words, Mother Nature has been attacking her own stratospheric ozone for millions of years and yet the ozone is still there, and in sufficient quantities to protect Democrats and environmentalist wackos alike from skin cancer.

If you tell environmental wackos this they say, "That makes it even more imperative that we cut back on whatever amount of fluorocarbons we do create." But what they really want to do is attack our way of life. Their primary enemy: capitalism. We are supposed to feel guilty about our lifestyles. Well, let's look at the facts. We have been measuring ozone only since 1956. That's A.D., my friends. Yet, these scientists think they know enough to justify telling us to change our way of life.

In just *one day* in January, NASA measured the amount of chlorine and another gas in the atmosphere of the Northern Hemisphere and found an unusually high level compared to normal. They didn't wait to properly analyze the data; they didn't wait two or three months to take further measurements; they just released them in the alarmist fashion that has become the signature of the environmentally obsessed. There were headlines for days about an ozone hole in the atmosphere above North America. In fact, Senator Al Gore, who had just published an alarmist book on how we are in the process of destroying our ecosystem, predicted that President Bush would soon come around on all this because of the "ozone hole over

Kennebunkport," despite the fact there was no such thing—nor had the NASA data indicated any such occurrence. In fact, there was no ozone depletion, just the unusually high levels of chlorine. Within a few weeks, it was learned that most of the unusual measurements could be attributed to Mount Pinatubo's eruption, a fact the agenda-oriented scientific community attempted to ignore. Want to know something else? Similar discoveries were made in 1989, with the same apocalyptic predictions made about a Northern Hemisphere ozone hole opening up. One never did.

What drives some scientists to go wacky over this stuff? Well, you can't divorce science from politics. Scientists say they have no agenda, but they do. They always want more funding, and today that means government funding. What could be more natural than for NASA, with the space program winding down, to say that because we have this unusual amount of chlorine in the atmosphere we need funding? Obviously, we have to research this. But first we have to "inform" the public. What a scam.

Now, I want to make clear that when there is damage to the environment, there is no one who wants to fix it more than I do. However, I refuse to believe it is necessary to attack the American way of life or to punish the American people for simply being themselves. We don't have to punish progress in order to fix the environment. Take the Cuyahoga River, which caught fire about twenty years ago because it was filled with so much junk and sludge. We set out to clean it up, we rolled up our sleeves, and we did it. I'm sure some regulation was used, but the major factor was good old American know-how. If you go to Cleveland today you'll see nonpolluting businesses operating all along that river. The key to cleaning up our environment is unfettered free enterprise, our system of reward. The more economic growth we have, the more a prosperous people will demand a cleaner environment. The poor have other things to worry about, such as feeding their families.

For a study in contrasts, look at the level of man-made pollution in countries with totalitarian regimes. Pollution in Eastern Europe and the former Soviet Union is horrendous. If you go there you will see dead, not dying, forests. You will see three-eyed fish in the streams. When no one owns private property, there is no incentive to keep it clean and pure because no one has a stake in keeping up its value. No environmental reporting was allowed by those in power in those countries. They didn't want the truth to come out, so they covered it up for years. We Americans, on the other hand, learn every time a spotted owl is accidentally toppled by some logger in Oregon.

When you compare the environmental situation in America with that of other countries, we win hands down. We have the cleanest country in the world. Well, maybe Switzerland is cleaner, but it is merely a tourist museum. The world has never seen anything like the United States of America. In higher education, economics, lifestyle, prosperity, form of government, and personal freedom, we are blessed with more and better than any other country. Yet, the environmentalist wackos go out of their way to find fault with everything in America. They criticize our profit motive, even though it's given us the most sophisticated pollution-control technology in the world.

Why do these people do this? I think they just don't like our way of life. They are bitter; they're not happy unless this country becomes Sweden or Nicaragua—as it was under the Sandinistas. Our prosperity has created a leisure class that has too much time on its hands, so they use it to complain about America. In the process they also enhance their self-esteem. If they agree that things are wrong and need to be fixed, they also believe they are the ones to fix them. They believe that they are the ones who should have the power in society, not some business owner or civic leader.

These people Care. They care so much that caring becomes a crutch that makes them feel special and more noble than the rest of us. Whether their caring accomplishes anything is irrelevant, as simply caring makes them feel better.

Recently, I appeared as a guest on a show called *New York at Night.* The host asked me a bunch of questions on homelessness, the environment, and all the other issues people purport to Care about. They were completely unprepared for my responses. I told them, "Hey, we've got problems, but we can deal with them." Sexual harassment is a problem, but we don't need to misdefine or exaggerate it. Homelessness isn't an epidemic. The environment is cleaner than ever. The host and the other guests became terribly upset. One of the guests was a twenty-two-year-old guy named by *US* magazine as one of the sexiest bachelors in America. He was totally blown away by my remarks. He's an actor, a member in good standing with the Hollywood Left, and caught up in all this trendy caring. Here I was saying that his caring was misspent energy. He and the other guests got mad. I wasn't giving them the satisfaction they wanted. I wasn't telling them that because they cared they were automatically good people. It was almost as if I had attacked their religion.

In a sense, I had. Many of these people have replaced religion with secular environmentalism. Some of them even worship the earth goddess Gaia. When they get together, their gatherings take on the air of a religious revival meeting. There were 750,000 people in New York's Central Park recently for Earth Day. They were throwing Frisbees, flying kites, and listening to Tom Cruise talk about how we have to recycle *everything* and stop corporations from polluting. Excuse me.

Didn't Tom Cruise make a stock-car movie in which he destroyed thirty-five cars, burned thousands of gallons of gasoline, and wasted dozens of tires? If I were given the opportunity, I'd say to Tom Cruise, "Tom, most people don't own thirty-five cars in their *life*, and you just trashed thirty-five cars for a movie. Now you're telling other people not to pollute the planet? Shut up, sir."

And how about this incident which occurred during the filming of the same movie: Cruise speeds along the beach at dawn in his stock car while seagulls and other birds are feeding. As Cruise's car approaches, the birds majestically fly away to avoid death as he roars past them with the wind blowing through his Hollywood hair. To accomplish this magnificent scene, bird feed was scattered all along the beach to ensure that the birds would land on the beach. It worked. The seagulls began feeding and Cruise started his engine and sped down the beach. Only one thing went wrong: the birds did not majestically fly away— there were run over by Cruise and his stock car. Mass bird murder at Daytona Beach. Oh well, at least they had good intentions.

There are countless other examples of such hypocrisy. Take

Paul Ehrlich, the doomsayer of the population-control crowd. In 1968 he wrote a book called *The Population Bomb.* Almost nothing he predicted came to pass. The book bombed, so to speak, in terms of accuracy. But because it played to the fears of the day, everyone embraced it.

Ehrlich has come out now with another book to cover up the inaccuracies of his first. It has just as flawed a thesis: The average American baby will pollute the planet a thousand times more than the average Ethiopian baby. Well, why don't we just pack up all our kids and move to Ethiopia and raise them there.

The point Ehrlich is making is that American free enterprise is evil. This blows my mind. In an age when communism has been irrefutably repudiated as an economic and political system and we have all the people of Eastern Europe and the former Soviet Union now trying to emulate us, Americans like Ehrlich are trying to tear our system down. We've got to stop listening to people who earn their money by writing books, based on misinformation, that predict our doom.

MINDLESS MUSH FROM HOLLYWOOD

Who are the carriers of all this environmental twaddle? It isn't Paul Ehrlich who goes on *The Tonight Show* to tell us how the world is going to end. Rather, it is actors whose skulls have been filled with this drivel. Ted Danson of *Cheers* actually said, in 1990, "We only have ten years left to save this planet." That was totally irresponsible. But nobody challenges him. Talk show hosts just grin and nod in agreement at such statements.

Why do actors engage in propaganda for the environmentalist wackos? Well, you've got people who have earned a lot of money, and many of them feel guilty about it; they feel that they don't deserve it. Also, they make their money portraying people they are not. You can only do so much of that before you want to be known for something you do yourself. Ted Danson wants to be taken seriously, not just as the guy who plays the bartender in *Cheers.* People have gotten hold of Ted and filled him with all this tripe about oceans, so he goes on TV and proclaims that we have only ten years left.

Shows like *Entertainment Tonight* feed into this nonsensical frenzy. They get their ratings by showing the glamour of Hollywood, not by challenging the most asinine statements ever made. You'll never hear their talking heads say, "Ted, cite your sources for your belief the world will end in ten years. Do you really think mankind can destroy the Earth?"

SPOTTED OWLS

We've got the spotted owl living up in Oregon and Washington. I don't happen to believe it is an endangered species. The controversy is only about one subspecies of owl that differs only slightly from many others. But that point doesn't matter a whit to the nature crowd. They call it an endangered species, so we have to deal with it on that level.

I once asked a long-haired maggot-infested FM-type environmentalist wacko who he thought was threatening the owl. He said, Man, the enemy of nature. Everything in nature is fine without man. "Okay," I said. "Would you then say that the human species is far superior to any other species?" "Well, man, let me think about that." You see, they don't want to admit that, but it's true.

Then I closed in for the conversational kill. "Would you say the owl has evolved to a superior position over the mouse?" I asked. "Oh, yeah, man, an owl can fly, he sees at night, man." Precisely—the owl can swoop down at night and gobble up that mouse. The poor mouse has no chance. You've seen it on animal shows. That's what they show: animals eating each other. The mouse gets eaten by an owl headfirst, with its little legs dangling out, and all you can say is, "Oh, God, why am I watching this?" That's how nature really is; these animals don't even cook their own food out there. At least we do that.

So I have the environmentalist in a corner. "So, is it not the responsibility of the mouse to adapt to the potential threat of the owl?" "Oh yeah, man, but that's nature, that's nature." Well, there you have it, I told him. If the owl can't adapt to the superiority of humans, screw it. He went catatonic.

Now, I know that sounded heartless. But my argument follows

simple, pure logic. If a spotted owl can't adapt, does the earth really need that particular species so much that hardship to human beings is worth enduring in the process of saving it? Thousands of species that roamed the earth are now extinct. Do you hear anyone making the case that the earth would be better off if dinosaurs were still roaming the planet? Why, we could even survive without any owls. So what if they are no longer around to kill the mice. We'll just build more traps. Either that or we'll breed more cats.

Of course, we are human beings and we do care about owls. We have an obligation to act responsibly toward those creatures that are less developed than we. There's no reason that we should adopt a survival-of-the-fittest policy. Why isn't it possible for both of us to coexist in harmony? There's no reason to put the timber business out of commission just because of twenty-two hundred pairs of one kind of owl. Yet, people think that's the humane solution—i. e., to be less humane to humans than we are to other species. Who cares if thirty thousand jobs are lost, so long as we are saving the owl. That's the wrong set of priorities, my friends.

JUNK SCIENTISTS VS. RUSH

Whenever I counter the latest environmentalist fad or fantasy, I invariably receive irate calls and letters. "How dare you dispute the existence of global warming," they'll say. "You prove your ignorance. You ought not to discuss such things, because you can't know anything about science."

Well, these are the tactics that are always used to shut people up on environmental hoaxes. It happens all the time.

The Alar scandal was over a chemical additive that made apples more desirable-looking and palatable. The environmentalist wackos said it was carcinogenic. They were led by actress Meryl Streep, who, hellbent on impressing someone from Hollywood, in reference to Alar wailed before a Senate committee, "What are we doing to our children! What are we doing to our children!" This is nonsense. But they ridicule anyone who challenges their pseudoscience as either unqualified or in the hip pocket of business.

We closed down a whole town—Times Beach, Missouri—over the threat of dioxin. We now know there was no reason to do that. Dioxin at those levels isn't harmful, yet we were bombarded by TV reports showing people in spacesuits walking through the empty town.

Steve Kroft of *60 Minutes* finally tracked down the acid rain story. A government commission spent $500 million and ten years studying the problem and concluded that the problem was minor and correctable. Kroft confronted one of the acid rain fanatics with the evidence. The guy refused to admit he was wrong and mumbled that we still needed funding for further research.

The environmentalist wackos have also tried to criminalize much of the food we eat, in an effort to change our eating habits on the basis of very flimsy evidence. Remember when they said that oat bran would reduce cholesterol? Although that was disproven, people who were skeptical about those claims at the time, such as myself, were derided for daring to question the dogma.

How many years have you believed, as I have, that there was a link between coffee consumption and heart disease? Now the latest research shows there is no such link.

Junk scientists are popping up everywhere. A couple of years ago, anthropologists announced that the mother of civilization was a black woman who lived in southern Africa about 250,000 years ago. This was supposed to give great self-esteem to the black community. They went around saying to whites and others, "You came from our mother. We are responsible for your being around. We are smarter than you. You came from us." Well, now we're told that there were genealogical roots and trees the anthropologists failed to explore, so this woman might not be so seminally important after all.

The point I want to make here is that you must think for yourselves. Do not automatically think you are an idiot or unqualified to express an opinion merely because you don't have a Ph.D. in science. A few very vocal, ideological, agenda-armed scientists are trying to buffalo the American people into accepting their view of the world. More-reasoned scientists are either too scared to speak up, for fear of losing funding, or are pushed into the background by the media. The fingerprints of junk science are all over the environmental movement. It is their lifeblood.

Many scientists don't know nearly as much as they pretend to about the environmental issues they address. They may be credible scientists in their respective disciplines, but they often talk on subjects outside their fields. Paul Ehrlich claims to be an expert in areas where the most respected scientists scoff at him. Carl Sagan is a very gifted astrophysicist, but he comments on things about which he has very little expertise, such as global warming and nuclear winter. Remember his prediction, and that of others, that should Saddam Hussein ignite all the Kuwaiti oil wells there would be catastrophic global climate changes from which it would take years to recover? (Among the most hysterical and apocalyptic predictions were that soot from the smoke would lower global temperatures by blocking sunlight and that sulfur in the smoke would combine with rain and destroy crops as far away as Russia.) And that it would take five years to extinguish those fires? Well, he was wrong on both counts, embarrassingly wrong. And the proof is in. *The Wall Street Journal* of May 15, 1992, reported that scientists from the University of Washington, Seattle, and the National Center for Atmospheric Research in Boulder, Colorado, took measurements in the region from two aircraft between May 16 and June 12, 1991. They found that global environmental damage was insignificant, although there was significant local damage for a while in the Persian Gulf region.

Here are some interesting details about the soot from the fires. The amount was thirteen times the soot emitted daily from all combustion sources in the United States, yet there was no significant global damage. The reason? Smoke must rise high enough in the atmosphere and stay there so strong winds can circulate it in order for there to be any chance for global impact. But—and I love this—the Kuwaiti smoke was not in the atmosphere long enough to rise very high. Why? It was dissipated by rain and clouds! Rain! It just came along and just cleaned it right up!

Now, my friends. Do you realize how fundamentally and profoundly wrong the experts were on this? What else are they wrong about? I think it would be wise to hold all else they predict to serious scrutiny, because it is obvious from this example that they haven't the slightest idea what they are talking about, yet they are never challenged. Their credibility should be what is catastrophically damaged, but it isn't because the doom and gloom they predict is not only politically correct, it is desired by those who believe them. I don't claim to be an expert on any science, but I do know enough to ask commonsense questions and not to swallow everything that's presented to me.

I'm not saying that the people who send me scientific refutations of my positions are never right. But I'm right far more often than they admit. I refuse to let scientific elitism prevent me from asking commonsense questions that are skeptical of their "findings." You shouldn't let them stop you from challenging their conclusions either. The minute you are intimidated into believing that you have no right to comment on scientific assertions, you have surrendered your First Amendment rights.

The best way you can arm yourself against the junk scientists is to read a book by Dixy Lee Ray, the former governor of Washington State and the former chairman of the Atomic Energy Commission. Her book, *Trashing the Planet*, was published by Regnery Gateway in Washington, D.C., and I used it for much of my source material on ozone in this chapter. It is the most footnoted, documented book I have ever read. She proves that this whole doomsday campaign has become an entire industry unto itself. People are making money from the doom and gloom trade. I urge all readers to get her book if you want to understand the con job the environmentalists are trying to pull on us.

DECENT FRIENDS OF THE EARTH

I want to make it clear that there are some decent environmentalists. My comments are directed at the doomsday fanatics who want to sharply change the American way of life. The Sierra Club wants to limit the number of kids you can have to two. They are trying to limit the way you drive your car. They are trying to stop people from preserving food by irradiating it. They are into power and controlling people's lives. They go way beyond their nominal environmental agenda.

Decent environmentalists are those such as the Audubon Society. Did you know they have a wildlife refuge in Louisiana that has oil rigs on it? Audubon members carefully monitor the rigs so that there is no damage, and the revenue the oil companies turn over to them helps pay for additional efforts they make to preserve wildlife.

One of Rush's Unalterable Laws is that man and the environment can live together in harmony. Capitalism is good for people AND for other living things. Take trees, for example. We keep hearing that trees are being chopped down and that we have fewer trees than ever before. But look at the numbers. We have more trees in this country today than when the Declaration of Independence was written. The wackos will tell you that's impossible. Haven't they ever heard of fires started by lightning that no one could put out? Today, we put out a lot of fires that used to burn areas the size of Connecticut.

Groups like Earth First say that a fire caused by lightning is natural, so we should let it burn. It is only man-made fires that are evil. Well, if Earth First had its way we probably would have FEWER trees today than ever before because they wouldn't want to put out the fires caused by lightning. Their position is absurd. Trees are a valuable commodity, and companies have an incentive not to overcut them if they have clear ownership rights to them. Today, private companies are planting millions of trees on their own land and carefully harvesting them.

Environmentalists always appeal to memories of a simpler, more natural time. They are regressing, wanting to go backward in time. Well, let's look at some of the consequences of that. In 1900, the life expectancy in this country was 54.9 years. Today it's 76 years, and the improvement is not totally attributable to medicine. It is due in part to the fact that there is less pollution, our food is cleaner, by and large, and our sanitary standards are more advanced. Consider that cities in 1900 were filled with some of the most unsafe, foul-smelling pollutants you can imagine. Take horse manure, for example. It was everywhere and was a major carrier of disease. The invention of the automobile enabled us to no longer depend on fly-attracting horses for transportation.

THE ENVIRONMENTAL MINDSET

I used to think that environmentalists were a bunch of political liberals who were just using a different angle to advance their cause. Some of that goes on. But it goes beyond merely advancing liberalism. There are two groups of people that have made environmentalism their new home: socialists and enviro-religious fanatics. And they have chosen two new constituencies which cannot speak or disagree and therefore cannot refuse their "help and assistance": animals and trees.

With the collapse of Marxism, environmentalism has become the new refuge of socialist thinking. The environment is a great way to advance a political agenda that favors central planning and an intrusive government. What better way to control someone's property than to subordinate one's private property rights to environmental concerns.

The second group that has latched on to the environmental movement are people who believe it is a religion; that God is the earth and that God is nothing more than the earth. Actually, it is a modern form of pantheism, where nature is divine. This group wants to preserve the earth at all costs, even if it means that much of the Third World will be forever condemned to poverty. Rather than elevate the Third World, they want to move us closer to Third World conditions. That's somehow cleaner, and purer. It's the way things were before Western white people came along and terrorized the earth by inventing things. They want to roll us back, maybe not to the Stone Age, but at least to the horse-and-buggy era.

Both of these groups are consumed with egocentricity. They behave as though they believe the world began the day they were born and that it's going to end the day they die.

Now, I've spoken about the leaders of the radical environmental movement. The followers are also interesting. They are the people who just want to feel good; the people who want to receive accolades for their perceived care and concern for the environment. Then we have the media who willingly serve as conduits for all of these predictions, studies, prophecies, and tall tales that the environmentalist wackos disseminate.

But there are also many average Americans who consider themselves environmentalists. It is quite natural to want a clean planet, with clean water and air for ourselves and our children. It is quite commendable to not want to destroy that which enables us to live. So, if some scientist comes along and is given credibility by the media, it is not surprising that a lot of people believe him. That is how hundreds of thousands of people are mobilized for the cause and end up on the Mall in Washington and in Central Park in New York.

What these decent people have to realize is that regardless of what perspective they have—socialist, religious, or whatever—a common characteristic of those in the radical environmental movement is the belief that private property rights will have to be severely curbed in this country. That's what is behind the move to take private land out of circulation to preserve wetlands, and the efforts to save the spotted owl. If it rains in your backyard one day and you have an inch of water there, all of a sudden your yard becomes a wetland and you can't build anything there.

This hostility to private property, my friends, is based on the belief that human beings can't be trusted to own very much of the land; that we are selfish and cursed with the desire to change nature. We are 4 percent of the world's population here in America and we use 25 percent of the world's resources. How dare we be so selfish. Never mind the fact that our country feeds the world. Never mind the fact that our technology has improved life everywhere on this planet.

I believe that many environmental leaders are quite sincere, but that they all operate from a fundamentally different viewpoint than most other people. You and I and the vast majority of other people work for a living. We hold jobs in which we produce something or perform a service. We create commerce.

Most of the people running environmental groups don't work. What they do is persuade other people to donate to their cause. They live well, with a fair amount being siphoned off for expenses, conferences, and high salaries. They've become dependent on the income from donations. These people want to improve their standard of living and so they have to build up their donations. There are only so many people who will give to create bird sanctuaries in this country. That's why some environmentalists have gone into crisis mongering to increase the level of their donations. Their appeals and their scare tactics are designed to transform people into foot soldiers in the army of doomsday environmentalism.

It's interesting to note which environmental hazards these people really worry about. It is those that are caused by business or man-made things. Consider the danger of radon gas. If there is one environmental problem that is real, it is radon. Some Easterners have homes where radon seeps in from under the ground and reaches levels many times beyond what is considered safe. But there is no hysteria over radon. Why? Because it's natural, man didn't put it there. There are no dramatic calls for radon studies, nor any calls for evacuations. Everything that happens in their deified nature is somehow acceptable. Things will work themselves out. Well, man-made disasters can also work themselves out. Take the *Exxon Valdez* spill. We were told that the cleanup would take hundreds of years. Now we see that through natural processes and the incredibly resilient powers of the planet, the tide has taken care of much of the damage that man didn't clean up. And, would you believe that more fish were caught last year than ever before in Prince William Sound.

My friends, the earth is a remarkable creation and is capable of great rejuvenation. We can't destroy it. It can fix itself. We shouldn't go out of our way to do damage, but neither should we buy into the hysteria and monomania which preaches, in essence, that we don't belong here. We have a right to use the earth to make our lives better.

NOW WE THANK PEOPLE FOR
OBEYING THE LAW?

WHEN YOU THINK ABOUT IT, THE AMOUNT OF CRIME WE TOLERATE IN this society is unbelievable. The way we approach the rights of accused criminals has changed so much over the past twenty-five years that if the same changes had taken place drastically, overnight, I am convinced the people wouldn't have put up with it. But it took place gradually. Every so often the Supreme Court rules and society grants all kinds of new rights to criminals, and with each ruling there is increasingly less concern for crime victims, victims' families, and potential victims.

Liberal activists, with the American Civil Liberties Union in the forefront, care so little about the rights of victims (unless the victim is a minority beaten by the police) that they believe the relatives of a murder victim should not be able to appear at the murderer's sentencing and talk about the pain they have suffered or about the kind of person the victim was. They say this would inflame emotions and be prejudicial to the criminal. The defense lawyers can talk about the criminal's background and how it mitigates his guilt, but the prosecution cannot talk about the value of the victim's life and what he meant to other people.

We are becoming desensitized to violent crime. We now seem to simply accept that certain people are going to be criminals and there's nothing we can do about it—we just have to learn to tolerate it and live with it, rather than deal with crime and stop it. It's almost as if being a criminal were just another alternative lifestyle. But even worse is the liberal attitude that criminals are products of the discriminating and inequitable nature of capitalistic society. In many cases the criminals are no longer seen as the actors who commit crimes and who are responsible for their own behavior. They are viewed as victims of society who are driven to behave in ways society has "chosen" to define as criminal.

Rather than punish criminals appropriately and effectively, we rationalize and excuse their lawless behavior. Sometimes, when we are feeling especially kind, we thank them for obeying the law. You laugh? Well. David Dinkins, esteemed and venerated mayor of New York, known to his supporters as "the healer," was hailed last spring for his great effort in preventing rioting in New York following the burning of Los Angeles. He took to the air and begged people not to burn the city. Nothing burned, but a few storefronts were destroyed and a little disturbance took place when a loving mob roared into Madison Square Garden during a New York Rangers hockey game. Aside from that, it was just the usual number of robberies, muggings, purse snatchings, and so on. What did Dinkins do? He took to the air the following day and *thanked—yes, thanked!*—people for obeying the law! Good grief, what have we come to when we gush with gratitude and practically slobber with relief and thankfulness that our criminals didn't burn the city? Hell, next time let's throw them an appreciation party.

Just recently, in Vernon, Connecticut, a woman shot her fiancé in the chest with a .38 revolver because he told her, a week before their scheduled wedding, that he didn't want to marry her. So she snapped and shot him. At the trial, the judge threw the case out, saying that she acted that way because of emotional shock, that it was understandable. The judge felt confident that she would never do anything like that again and disposed of the case by putting her on probation on very lenient terms. Perhaps that should be established as the legal doctrine that "Hell hath no fury like a woman scorned"—an absolute defense to murder by a scorned woman.

Now, stop to think about this. You shoot someone and, because you did so under emotional distress, you are not required to spend one day in prison. Another recent twist is that we are urged to feel sympathy for a criminal because he was an abused child, or because he went to a bad school, or because he has shown remorse. We're supposed to look for goodness in everyone, to treat everyone with compassion. Our religions certainly teach us forgiveness toward wrongdoers, but that is an altogether different matter from excusing them from the penalties of the criminal system. The latter is at best a prescription for anarchy.

Our "revolutionary" ideas are being exported. Australia, for example, is picking up our notions of how to handle criminals. An Australian man named Richard Dickinson, who trampled his own mother to death to the sounds of the Bob Dylan song "One More Cup of Coffee," was let out of prison for one night to see Bob Dylan in concert. This is straight out of the Michael Dukakis–Willie Horton story. Dickinson, who is now twenty-five years old, killed his fifty-nine-year-old mother five years ago when she complained because he was playing Dylan's album *Desire* at four o'clock in the morning.

He told police that he thought his mother was an evil character from the album and that the music had given him the strength to kill her. He sprinkled instant coffee over her body afterwards. He was found not guilty by reason of insanity. And this guy was allowed to attend a Bob Dylan concert because his doctors said it would help him get in touch with his feelings! Psychobabble at its finest. And now they're importing that, too.

I mentioned Willie Horton. There's a classic example of everything that's wrong with our thinking about crime and criminals. All we ever hear about Willie Horton is how George Bush's campaign used Willie Horton to pander to racism—or to say it in the fashionable vernacular, to engage in race baiting. It's almost as if Willie Horton were a victim—of the media, of the Republicans, and so on. We don't hear about what Willie Horton actually did.

Often the charge of racism is used to shift our focus from the criminal to society's inequities. The media, the liberals, and the black leadership have created a climate of censorship with respect to any issues involving race, other than their prescribed views on the subject. They have been successful in labeling many events as racist when clearly they were not. The Willie Horton issue is a classic example of this. The Willie Horton ads are now unquestioningly accepted as a sordid, racist blemish on the Republican party. But this description is infinitely more than the facts allow. The truth is that the Willie Horton political advertisement had nothing whatever to do with race. The issue was crime and the message was Michael Dukakis's softness of approach with criminals. Willie Horton was one of eleven convicted killers permitted to leave prison to visit their families as part of a furlough program under then Massachusetts Governor Dukakis. Horton was in prison for murdering a man after castrating him and stuffing his genitals in his mouth. During his furlough in 1987, Horton tied up a man and made him watch while Horton raped the man's wife. After the incident, the state legislature tried to stop killers from getting furloughs, but Dukakis fought against it because he said the program was 99 percent effective. The Republicans thought that it might be appropriate to communicate that truth to the American people. Apparently, so did the *Eagle Tribune*, a Massachusetts newspaper that won a Pulitzer Prize for exposing the flaws in Dukakis's furlough program. Of course, when this publication ran the story long before the ad was even contemplated by the Bush campaign, no one called that liberal publication racist.

The Horton ad was an excellent illustration of the tangible consequences of the liberals' general approach to the criminal justice system. Their sympathy is almost always reserved for the criminal rather than for the victim of the crime. The Willie Horton incident brought that point home with lurid realism. The fact that Willie Horton was black was downright irrelevant, and for Democrats to suggest otherwise is patent intellectual dishonesty. Are we to be so afraid of putting any black person in a bad light that we cannot even tell the truth about an incident involving a black without being labeled racists? Liberals may dominate the airwaves of the media so as to choke off any legitimate discussion of these issues, but they certainly have failed to capture the hearts and minds of the voters. Most voters know that the liberals' deliberate mischaracterization of the Willie Horton ad as racist was a ruse designed to divert attention from an egregious error of their presidential hopeful, Michael Dukakis.

I find it hard to believe that in the 1988 presidential elections, the press actually went around asking Willie Horton who he would vote for. Who cares? What difference does it make what Willie Horton does, as long as he's in jail? If he gets out of jail, then you can be sure I care about what he's going to do. This transformation of Willie Horton into a victim is a snapshot of what is happening throughout the criminal justice system.

We're making victims of people who commit crimes. And we make ordinary law-abiding citizens feel guilty about being afraid of crime or wondering why we have so much crime in America. Why is it that, at Thomas Jefferson High School in Brooklyn, New York, a kid merely gets mad at another kid and pulls a gun and shoots him? When you and I were in school, of course we got mad at some kids, but it never even occurred to us that we could kill them. In Providence, Rhode Island, a teenager was arrested for murder after he wrote an essay, just for an ordinary school assignment, describing, in detail, how he killed someone. It probably has to do with the overall decay of values in this society, a cheapening of human life to the point where there is no more concern or respect for the sanctity of life. I have stated elsewhere in this volume my belief that legalized abortion is one of the reasons for that, and the increasing acceptance of euthanasia at the other end of life is another.

The point is, we have an increasing number of people in this society who want to go through life without facing the consequences of their actions, who want to do everything for their own convenience, regardless of how it affects anyone else. I don't want my grandmother around, she's a hassle, she doesn't even know who I am anymore, so let's get rid of her. Total selfishness. Recently, the *Entertainment Tonight* show asked me to talk about a series of assassin cards that had been in the news. These are regular trading cards, except that instead of baseball players, they feature notorious assassins and serial killers, such as Lee Harvey Oswald and Ted Bundy. When the producer of the show came up, I didn't want to say something totally predictable, so I said, "These cards are admittedly tough to deal with, but there is a good side. You see, the way history is being taught in this country, we don't know what our kids are learning—what's fiction and what's true. But these cards—they're a hundred percent historically accurate."

This guy was completely humor-impaired, and he was taken aback. "Do you mean to tell me there's absolutely nothing wrong with it?" "No," I said, "I think these things are absolutely fine." "You can't be serious!" Finally, I had to talk about it in an entirely different way. I said, "You know, this amazes me. You sound like you're really upset about these cards. Well, for crying out loud, here you are, *Entertainment Tonight*—you routinely make stars and heroes out of Freddy Krueger and all the other stars of the slasher movies, all these damn Halloween and Friday the 13th movies where kids get mauled and killed and sliced and diced, and you think 2 Live Crew is great. It's censorship if we try to shut them up. Well, now you sound like you want to censor these cards."

This is the market at work. People want these cards, so they buy them. Our society is preoccupied with death, from movies to books and now to trading cards. Do I think this is bad? Of course I do, but the cards are the symptoms of our declining moral base, not the cause of it. The simple fact of the matter is that these kids have been desensitized to such things, for a variety of reasons. If you want to improve this situation, you've got to start in their homes, you've got to make them understand that law is not about preventing people from enjoying life or oppressing them, but the establishment of limits on behavior. Laws are the tools we use to build an orderly society. An orderly society cannot be achieved or maintained if we allow people to do whatever they want to do, with no regard for anything but their own pleasure.

First, we make excuses for hedonism and antisocial behavior. Then we end up making excuses for violent crime. We excuse people from all personal responsibility for their actions.

CAPITAL PUNISHMENT

Look at the case of Robert Alton Harris, the convicted murderer who was recently executed in California. Fourteen years ago, Harris stole two teenagers' car with the teenagers in it, from a fast-food joint, because he needed a car to rob a bank. One boy was sixteen, the other fourteen. He shot them both. When one of the boys pleaded for his life, he told him to "stop crying and die like a man." After he killed them, he ate their hamburgers—which I really don't think is very relevant, but somehow captured the fascination of the media and the public. I suppose the fact that he was able to eat immediately after his brutal acts shows how wantonly and cold-bloodedly he murdered those boys. But to many people, it was almost as if eating the hamburgers were a bigger sin than killing the kids. Maybe this reaction is representative of the wrong-headed way we look at these things.

But let's get back to Robert Alton Harris. He kills the two boys and then gets caught. Next follow the endless years of trials and appeals. Harris was found guilty and was sentenced to die in the gas chamber, six years after the people of California voted overwhelmingly, in a statewide referendum ballot initiative, to reinstate capital punishment.

For twenty years since that vote, the will of the people had been thwarted at every possible turn. California State Supreme Court Chief Justice Rose Bird never once voted to uphold a death sentence. The State Supreme Court was packed with liberals, and in most capital cases either the death sentence or the conviction itself was reversed on some technicality. In one case, the prosecution had obtained a death sentence by arguing that the murder was especially cruel because the victim had been stabbed numerous times. But the court decided that this argument was inadmissible: the multiple stabs, you see, were not inflicted with the intent to make the victim suffer, which nevertheless occurred because the victim took a very long time to die. The court held that since this was not the intent of the killer, he could not be executed simply because the victim had a quirky resistance to death. And we expect the public to have respect for our criminal judicial system?

175

When the people were given a chance to expel the officials who were thwarting their will, they did just that. In California, State Supreme Court justices have to be reconfirmed from time to time by a popular vote. The voters threw out Chief Justice Rose Bird and several other like-minded judges. But the liberals still didn't get it.

Remember this about liberals: They survive and thrive on a fundamental belief that the average American is an idiot—stupid, ignorant, uninformed, unintelligent, incapable of knowing what's good for him, what's good for society, what's right and what's wrong. Liberals believe their mission is to save people from themselves; not to help them become the best they can be, but to keep them from degenerating to the point that their naturally helpless condition would lead them without the liberals' intervention. So they impose affirmative action, quotas, welfare.

Capital punishment is wrong, they say. We have no right to take a human life. You must understand that Mr. Harris was not himself. We must be a compassionate society. If you want him to die for his crime, you're no better than he is. You are nothing but a bunch of bloodthirsty hawks, nothing but a bunch of savages with no compassion. But we'll make up for your deficiencies. And so, in this democratic country they continually thwart the will of the people by the instrument of the undemocratic judiciary. And the anger of the people in California builds up and continues to seethe.

Finally, changes that were made in the structure of the court system in California allowed a definite execution date to be set for Robert Alton Harris. The liberals' favorite trick of having jury decisions overturned on technicalities doesn't work anymore, because California now has a state supreme court sympathetic to the rights of victims rather than those of criminals.

And yet in the days leading up to Harris's execution, there was a series of new appeals made on the basis of supposedly new evidence. Much of it was not really new but was dredged up again to appeal to people's sympathy. One of the arguments was that Harris had been the victim of fetal alcohol syndrome, of an alcoholic mother who drank while she was pregnant with him. Now, wait a minute here. Who do you think made this argument? The ACLU. And who was it that argued before the U.S. Supreme Court that the standards of *Roe v. Wade* should not be changed to accommodate the Pennsylvania law restricting abortion? The ACLU. Their position is that the fetus in the womb is not a human life at all, just an inanimate mass of tissue. But in the case of Robert Alton Harris, the same people say that when he was in the womb, he was a person with a brain that was damaged by his mother's drinking. That's right—a foolish consistency is the hobgoblin of little minds.

The purpose of invoking the fetal alcohol syndrome, of course, was to suggest that Harris really wasn't responsible for the murders he committed. His attorneys claimed that because of brain damage, he was so retarded he couldn't understand the concept of right and wrong. This negates the requisite criminal intent, or *mens rea*, as lawyers call it. Yet, the same Robert Alton Harris was on TV explaining quite coherently why he thought it was wrong for the state to take a human life.

Another excuse proffered to absolve Harris from responsibility for his heinous acts was that his father had kicked him when he was a baby, so whatever he did wasn't his fault.

There was a clemency hearing before California Governor Pete Wilson. As much as I have been disappointed in many of his other policies—on taxes, environmental regulation, and abortion—Wilson was brilliant in that clemency hearing. His reasoning, his compassion for the victims, and his understanding of the basic issues were absolutely flawless. Governor Wilson's announcement of his refusal to grant clemency to Harris had exactly the right tone.

Victimized [by Fetal Alcohol Syndrome] though he may have been, Harris was not deprived of the capacity to premeditate, to plan or to understand the consequences of his actions. Society must hold accountable . . . Robert Harris and all members of society— excepting only those who have been clearly shown to lack the capacity to meet a minimum level of responsibility.

I do not agree that Harris was deprived of his capacity to understand his act, or that he was deprived of the capacity to resist doing it. We must do everything possible to avoid the victimization of children by preventing Fetal Alcohol Syndrome and by

177

preventing child abuse and domestic violence. We must also do what is necessary to protect the innocent members of society from becoming the victims of heinous crimes.

It is not an indiscriminate application of the death penalty to apply it to those who, whatever their own victimization, take life, having the capacity to understand and to resist the performance of their homicide. We must insist on the exercise of personal responsibility and restraint by those capable of exercising it.

Robert Harris, the child, had no choice. Robert Harris, the man, did have a choice. He chose to take a life. I cannot excuse or forgive the choice made by Robert Harris the man. Clemency is denied.

Then came, in my opinion, the most bizarre challenge of all: the argument that the use of the gas chamber as the method of execution itself constituted cruel and unusual punishment, because the condemned man may take a few minutes to die. The obvious question is: Why wasn't this taken up a month before, two months before, or fourteen years ago? These last-minute appeals were designed to keep delaying the execution by bringing up new issues. And liberal opponents of capital punishment glibly argue that the death penalty provides no deterrent to the commission of capital crimes. Well, how on earth would we ever know? Only if we have swift and certain justice will we ever have an opportunity to test the deterrent effect of the death penalty.

The U.S. Ninth Circuit Court of Appeals issued a stay of execution each time it was requested—a total of four times—on various grounds. Here, I'd like to digress and take a look at what sort of court it is and some of the wacko things it has done before. The Earth Island Institute went before this court and asked for an injunction banning the import of canned tuna from countries where dolphins are killed in the process of catching tuna. It seems to me that this is a clear violation of the democratic process, telling other countries what to do by way of judicial sanction. You guessed it: The court granted the injunction.

Finally, after reversing the four stays of execution that came from the U.S. Ninth Circuit Court, the Supreme Court said: That's enough. This is ridiculous. We are not going to allow any more of this. There will be no further stays of execution unless granted by the Supreme Court itself. After six hours of delay—on top of the previous fourteen years—Robert Alton Harris was put to death in the gas chamber.

Now, let's talk about cruel and unusual punishment. The opponents of the death penalty who always try to obtain these last-minute stays of execution will probably say: Hey, we're just trying to save this guy's life. But what happened as a result was that in a period of six hours, this guy was led into the gas chamber and strapped into the chair twice. Each time, it was called off because a stay had been granted. Once, the telephone call came one minute before he was to die; the other time, five or ten minutes before he was to die. He had six hours to ponder all this. He was in and out of there. The witnesses were brought in and out. It was an absolute circus. And on the subject of compassion toward the condemned man, you could hardly think of anything more cruel to do if you deliberately wanted to torture him.

But there's another very important point. What was it that finally allowed the will of the people of California to be carried out? Conservative judges on the state supreme court and conservative justices on the U.S. Supreme Court. The justices were willing to stay up all night to deal with those appeals and to bring this process to its conclusion.

And some people think it doesn't matter whom we elect as President. Well, conservative judges, or more accurately, those who believe in judicial restraint, are appointed by conservative elected leaders. If Ronald Reagan and George Bush had not been presidents of the United States and their liberal opponents had won and were making the judicial appointments, the will of the people of California would have continued to be thwarted to this day.

Think about that when you contemplate for which presidential candidate you are going to vote. People ask me: "Rush, who are you going to vote for in the election?" I don't know, but let me tell you one thing. I don't want the next President calling Ted Kennedy, Barney Frank, or Jesse Jackson and asking them whom to put on the Supreme Court. Activist liberal judges have one main goal: to thwart the will of the people by judicially legislating the liberal policy agenda. We need conservative judges on the courts of appeals and conservative justices on the Supreme Court. I'm not talking about activist conservatives who will impose their conservative beliefs on the population, but men and women who will interpret the law. We don't know how any of the justices on the Rehnquist court personally feel about the death penalty. That never came up. It had nothing to do with how they ruled. They simply and properly upheld the law of the land in California, which allows capital punishment for convicted murderers.

Of course, capital punishment is not the only answer to crime. I don't want to hear anyone say, "So what are we going to do, build more prisons?" Yes, exactly. If we have too many criminals, build more prisons. We are told that it's too expensive. But it doesn't have to be. The state of Texas, for example, forces incarcerated criminals to work and pay off some of the expenses. That's a constructive idea. Another solution is to cut down on all the luxuries criminals have in prisons that a lot of honest working folks can't afford. It's not only expensive, it's an outrage. A lot of neighborhoods in New York still aren't wired for cable TV, but the criminals in the Riker's Island jail have cable. If you send someone to jail, it's not supposed to be pleasant. It is supposed to be hard. That's why it's called punishment.

Most Americans agree with what I'm saying. But we have to fight liberal officials and liberal activists who think criminals are entitled to more rights than victims. We have to fight people like Mario Cuomo, who has vetoed every bill reinstating the death penalty in New York even though most people in the state support it. We have to fight people like Michael Dukakis who think convicted murderers deserve weekend furloughs.

LAW ENFORCEMENT

Ordinary people in our cities—white, black, Hispanic, Asian— live in fear. They put bars on their windows and double locks on their doors. They don't go out late at night. They put No Radio signs in the windshields of their cars. Yet, as a society we have come to tolerate this. Instead of getting to the bottom of the problem, we come up with all sorts of gimmicky socialist solutions that are supposed to help prevent crime.

For example, now that we're downsizing defense and bringing troops home from Europe, there's talk of what to do with the soldiers who are going to be out of work. Some people are saying: Let's put them on the streets to fight crime, to push the war on drugs. What rubbish. We already have police forces. If we would just let the cops do their job, and let the criminal justice system do its job properly, we wouldn't need any soldiers patrolling the streets.

Last year, Mayor David Dinkins was making his annual speech at the swearing in of the graduating class of the police academy in New York. And what was his message? Do you think it was, All right, guys, the streets are tough out there, innocent people are being victimized every day, you must go out and fight crime and keep our streets safe? No. His message was: Do not be brutal. Do not embarrass your mayor. Do not embarrass the city. Do not be cruel. Do not go out there and use excessive force. This happened shortly after the incident in Los Angeles in which Rodney King's beating by the police was videotaped. It goes without saying that no decent person is in favor of police brutality. But this kind of advice, in my view, is a classic example of how misplaced our priorities are. We put cops on the defensive. We're telling them what not to do. We have them more concerned about not doing something wrong than about doing what's right—and about doing the job they are hired to do, which is essentially to maintain order for the benefit of all of us. Pretty soon they'll decide that the best thing is to play it safe: When in doubt, don't do anything. Perhaps that explains in part the delayed response of the police in the L.A. riots following the Rodney King verdict.

Of course this cautious attitude is not exclusive to police departments. If you examine businesses having difficulty in the private sector you will often discover a defensive mentality on the part of management. Their primary concerns center not on how they should attack problems, but on what they shouldn't do. It's a defensive mentality, if you will.

It is society's concern when we saddle police officers with this

defensive mentality and shackle them with unnecessary re-
straints designed to protect the rights of the criminals. These are
people whom we ask to go out and deal with some of the most
hardened thugs in the inner cities, in neighborhoods where
drugs are bought and sold on every corner. We ask them to put
their lives in jeopardy—and they do, especially in the big cities.
Their lives are on the line every day.

The inefficiency of the court system compounds the dangers to
which they are exposed. They'll go and make an arrest, and three
hours later the perpetrator is back on the streets. And if there's
vengeance in his heart, there's nothing to stop him from going
after the cop. So why should the cops even care about their jobs?
When citizens destroy neighborhoods because of rage and we are
asked to "understand" and "sympathize," what we are being
asked is to have compassion for rage. Well, what about the rage of
cops who see their efforts thwarted daily by a system which
returns an endless parade of human debris to the streets to
commit more crime? What about the rage of cops who have to
track deadly drug dealers who earn millions violating the law
while they, the cops, earn a comparative pittance trying to
enforce it? How about a little "understanding" and "sympathy"
for them and what they face every day?

There's a lot of anger about crime and it's boiling over. When
Robert Alton Harris was about to be executed in California, I got
a call from a guy who said, "You know, Rush, I'm a conservative
and I listen to you all the time, but I'm alarmed. People just can't
wait for this guy to die. I hear them screaming for blood, like a
mob, and they're just too excited, too happy about it."

And I said, "Under normal circumstances, sir, I would agree
with you. But these days, I don't agree with you. Why? Because
you must understand what's happening to people in California.
They are being terrorized. Some of the most heinous serial killers
in our nation's history have operated there. And the people have
done everything in their power to prevent that and to punish the
guilty. Yet, the people's will is continually thwarted.

"So they've had it with demands that they be tolerant and
understanding. These are people who don't feel safe in their
homes, people whose five- and six-year-old kids are being killed
by random gunfire in certain Los Angeles neighborhoods. Their

streets have literally been stolen from them. There is no sanctuary for them in their own communities. Gang warfare there is at an all-time high. There are shootings on freeways, drive-by shootings, and nothing is being done about it, so people are scared to death and they are fed up. They can't believe this is being tolerated. They never imagined that they would lose control of their society—that they would have their right to live in peace taken from them in the name of compassion, by bleeding heart do-gooders. They can't believe the people who continually come forward to offer excuses for people who commit these crimes. You can be sure that these people intervening on behalf of the hardened criminal have not themselves been victimized by the terror they seek to protect. So it's understandable that ordinary people want some action taken. I understand it completely.

"It doesn't mean that these are bloodthirsty people. I'll give you an analogy. When I get on my radio show and talk about a strong defense, people call up and say: You love war, don't you? You love people dying, just so long as it's not you or your kids, right? And I say, 'Wrong. We hate war. We despise it. It's our last option. We have no desire for war. But the surest way to avoid war is to be prepared for it. A strong military militates against being attacked. Or, as the Ronald Reagan sloganeers pithily put it: Peace through strength.'

"It's the same thing, sir, with crime in the streets—in California or anywhere else in this country. The criminals in our society are no longer intimidated by our criminal justice system. They're not frightened by it. They're not frightened at the sight of a cop. They're not afraid of going to court. They don't think they're going to go to jail, and they know that if they do, it's not going to be for very long. So they're not deterred at all, sir. And the people know this. And the people are mad."

At present, there is less than one chance out of a hundred that a criminal who commits a serious crime will serve time in jail. Law-abiding people are fed up with this. They want their homes back. They want their neighborhoods back. And they want to send a message. Not because they want to see someone die. Not because they want to see blood. But because they want to be able to live in peace. Bill Bennett tells a story that happened when he was Drug Czar. He was headed to Memphis to meet with a black neighborhood group and he was warned that the guy he was scheduled to meet was a real tough character, a no-nonsense guy who refused to be patronized. So Bennett shows up for the meeting, ready for battle, ready to get hit hard and all that. Which he was. Do you know what the neighborhood guy told him? He said he and the folks in the neighborhood were tired of seeing convicted criminals being returned to the neighborhood long before they had served appropriate time in jail. He said to Bennett: "Look, if you want to conduct some new social experiment with the criminal element, go ahead, but don't release them to our neighborhood, for crying out loud! Let 'em come to your neighborhood, but keep them away from here." See? People want society to protect their rights to life, liberty, and the pursuit of happiness. And this requires peace, justice, and order in their communities.

FEMINISM AND THE CULTURE WAR

INTRODUCTION

FEMINISM, AS DISTINGUISHED FROM FEMININITY, IS A TOPIC I FRE-quently discuss on my radio talk show. It is one of the many topics I feature in the form of an Update, where I relate a current newsworthy item pertaining to a particular topic, which serves to illustrate, by real life example, my view about a particular issue and why I hold that view.

This is also, in my opinion, the topic about which I am most often misunderstood. Feminism is another of those issues which has established itself in the political correctness hall of fame. As such, it is not fashionable to take issue with or poke fun at the philosophy which underlies this movement. Those who have the courage to do so are quickly impugned as women-haters, bigots, chauvinists, sexists, and a host of other epithets. Name-calling becomes a substitute for meaningful debate of the issues and it works quite well in the political arena. That is unfortunate, because the name-calling, while it may have a chilling effect on the genuine discussion of issues, does nothing to satisfy the millions of people who share the views of those who are the targets of those insults.

Ordinary people are discriminating enough to understand that pundits and politicians can oppose the excesses, the antics, and the obvious political agenda of a certain group without hating that group or believing it is somehow inferior. A commentator who criticizes Israel's particular policies at the moment is not anti-Semitic for so doing. A columnist who challenges the inequities of racial quotas is not a racist for so doing. A radio talk show host who challenges the scientifically unsubstantiated doomsday alarmism and hysteria of certain environmental extremists is not an enemy of planet earth for so doing. A television commentator who disputes the fraudulent statistics promulgated by homeless advocates is not lacking compassion for so doing. A politician who advocates across-the-board reductions in marginal income tax rates coupled with spending cuts is not at war with the poor for so doing. An analyst who points out the militant agenda of today's feminist movement is not a person who hates women.

I make no apologies for taking issue with those in the forefront of the feminist movement, such as the National Organization for Women (NOW). I love and respect women and find it repugnant that I cannot utter even the most innocuous criticism of the militant feminists without being accused of harboring some heinous sexist mentality. The truth is that although those in the leadership of the movement do not speak for anything close to the majority of women, they presumptuously purport to represent their interests. "Their" interests are not the interests of the American female, but rather the political agenda of the feminist leadership, which is decidedly leftist.

So, before launching into a substantive discussion of the feminist issue, I want to make clear my perspective and attempt to establish a level playing field in the discussion. May I be so bold as to assert that most of my views are not out of step with those of the mainstream female in this country. My disagreements are only with the feminist leadership. Despite their claims to the contrary, they do not represent the average woman. Their worldview is radical and completely out of touch with the majority of women.

Unfortunately, feminism is another of those vehicles which attempt to transport unpopular liberalism into mainstream society. Leftist extremists have finally recognized the fact that they are unable to sell their inimical ideas to society as a whole. Cleverly, they have decided to repackage those ideas in more politically palatable gift wrapping, and feminism is one of those packages. After all, who can be opposed to equality for women, which is the way the feminist leadership chooses to phrase the question. Admittedly, the phenomenon of the feminist movement is far too complex to describe it simply as a group of liberal women who have donned a disguise for the purpose of attacking American values, capitalism, and our form of government—although that is certainly part of it. The movement is also driven by women who are angry—very angry, for a number of reasons —with their particular lot in life. Many of the women who have risen to leadership ranks in the movement are man-haters. They are not seeking equal pay for equal work on behalf of their so-called women constituency. They are on a mission to change the fundamental relationship between the sexes. They are at war with traditional American values and fundamental institutions such as marriage and the American family.

Recall the controversy surrounding the 1992 season finale of the CBS sitcom *Murphy Brown*. Murphy, a popular TV anchorwoman who is divorced, gave birth to a child out of wedlock, which, to some, glorified illegitimacy and promoted single motherhood. A day later, Vice President Dan Quayle denounced the episode, saying it sent the wrong message to a culture racked by value decay and family disintegration. Naturally, he was savaged by the dominant media culture, most comedians, Democrats, and the Hollywood community, who complained that it was only a TV show with fictional characters and therefore had no message. Well, how can that be? Aren't these the same people who admit using their TV shows to get their message across, like Linda Bloodworth-Thomason and her *Designing Women* episode, which was her version of the truth in the Anita Hill/Clarence Thomas hearings (and for which she won an award from her peers)? Aren't they the same people who think it makes sense for actors and actresses to give "expert" testimony before congressional committees just because they played a role in a movie or TV show? Aren't they the same people who complain about the portrayal of upwardly mobile blacks on TV, such as those in *The Cosby Show,* because such a portrayal sends the wrong message about the black condition in America today? How, if there is no influence?

No, Quayle was right on the money, although I think there was one aspect overlooked. That is that militant feminists are, in truth, searching for power, and the absolute best way they can exercise it is in the area of reproduction. The real message of that *Murphy Brown* episode was that women don't need men, shouldn't desire them, and that total fulfillment and happiness can be achieved without men or husbands. Many feminist leaders are humorless, militant, pugnacious, and very unhappy people who do not want to equalize the status of women, but instead want to irreversibly alienate women from men and vice versa. Does this sound extreme? Before you jump to the conclusion that I am the one being extreme, consider these quotes from Sheila Cronen, one of the feminist movement's most "respected" leaders and spokeswomen: "Since marriage constitutes slavery for women, it is clear that the women's movement must concentrate on attacking marriage. Freedom for women cannot be without the abolition of marriage." And from the *National Organization for Women Times,* January 1988, "The simple fact is, every woman must be willing to be recognized as a lesbian to be fully feminine."

It is from this perspective that I want to share with you the following thoughts on feminism.

MY EARLY EXPERIENCES WITH FEMINISM

My first experience with feminists came when I was seventeen years old, in the late 1960s. I was a disc jockey in my hometown of Cape Girardeau, Missouri, doing an afternoon drive-time show. Every Saturday morning, I was at Sears doing a live broadcast. The show drew crowds, and we played records and sometimes interviewed students. One student was named Donna, and she started talking about the women's liberation movement. She was only a junior in high school, and attractive. Oops! Sorry for including that. Forgive me for noticing *and* reporting it. I remember immediately getting into an argument with her. I told her to lighten up. I've always been good at that. It seemed so unnatural for her to be so worked up at just sixteen years of age—to be hellbent on joining a cause to deal with what she believed were extreme disadvantages in her life because of male discrimination. She and her buddies started running around with what seemed like chips on their shoulders. They were mad that they had to play with Barbie and the guys got G.I. Joe. She was upset that people expected her to be a nurse and us guys to be doctors. You know, the usual rigmarole about institutional and environment-oriented discrimination. I was confused by what she said, but I knew enough to recognize that the alligators were in the swamp and that it was time to circle the wagons.

The issue of feminism was then dormant in my life for a while. I moved from Missouri to Pittsburgh, Pennsylvania, a major media market. I remember doing a morning radio show at WIXZ in McKeesport. By then, women's lib was a full-blown movement and its leaders were no longer pleasant people like Donna. They were bitter and angry women. I made some jokes about the excesses of the local National Organization for Women gang and they complained to the station. The program director took me aside and told me that I had to stop making fun of them. You see, they were a serious ISSUES GROUP. That was when I realized I was going to be locking horns frequently with them.

I believe the women's movement started out as a genuine and sincere effort to improve conditions. The original concerns of feminists, such as equal pay for equal work, were laudable and justifiable. People had a right to be upset at the treatment some women received, and some of their activism and protests were understandable.

Then gradually there was a shift in their approach and in the type of women who were attracted to groups like NOW. The profile of the NOW woman came to be that of a loud, militant person whose views were based on a belief that women no longer needed men. They seemed to believe that to love and need men would somehow compromise women and set them back. They set out to avoid and attack the traditional role for women because they believed it was responsible for making them subservient to men.

Soon I was encountering feminism when I would go out on dates. You may laugh, but this mess got so bad that it became sexist to compliment a woman on her appearance. "What about my brain, you pig?" sneered one woman when I greeted her at the beginning of an evening. I'm serious. To this day I am a little queasy about complimenting a woman on her appearance because to do so meant you were probably a lecher, interested only in cheap sex, and that was wrong. I could afford more.

These women had been conditioned to accept the whole feminist ideology, which went way beyond equal opportunity. The roles defined by nature for men and women had become clouded in their minds. This led to all kinds of confusion, suspicion, and distrust between the sexes.

Men and women eventually just didn't know how to function around each other. It degenerated to the point that men would wonder if they should open a car door for a woman. Men weren't sure if they should still walk on the outside of a woman as they went down a street. The confusion was running rampant. Chivalry had become synonymous with male chauvinism. Roles, defined by nature, were now obliterated and everybody was running around trying to be what they thought they should be, which was certainly everything *but* themselves. For a while it became sensitive to cry. It was a beautiful thing. After a few years of that, women started complaining that there were no real men anymore, so men stopped crying. It wasn't pretty. The feminist leadership vowed revenge and retreated to plot a new destructive and divisive strategy.

You must understand that I was experiencing this transformation in male/female relationships in my early twenties, which were very formative years. These experiences had a profound effect on me. I admit I am still confused about how I should view women, because it is hard to keep up with the current gender protocol. Women seem to be told different things every year. Even to this day, I will sometimes say, "Pardon me, I don't mean to offend you, but you look really nice today." That will often evoke looks of surprise because women have no idea why they should possibly be offended by such compliments. Fortunately, many young women today have little in common with the militants of the 1970s, many of whom are now the embittered feminazis.

It's almost as if America went through its own Cultural Revolution in the 1970s and early 1980s. Everything went mad for about ten years, and only now are we seeing young people who now view those years as somewhat bizarre. But, of course, things aren't yet completely rational or back to normal. There are plenty of people who want to resurrect and supercharge the feminist Cultural Revolution.

After Pittsburgh, I moved to Kansas City. I got into a knock-down-drag-out fight with the NOW gang there. The head of Kansas City NOW made repeated efforts to get me censored. The feminazis would call the station management and demand a meeting. The management would cringe and say, "Oh gosh, the women are after us." Those were the days when controversy on the radio was to be avoided at all costs. The feminists came in to meet with the management, and they rolled over without a peep. I was told to cool it.

Well, the next time the feminists came to call at the radio station they had the federal government with them. Remember that radio stations were then very much regulated by the federal government. The liberal establishment got the FCC to push quotas for women in broadcasting. Management at radio and TV stations began hiring women just to get them on the payroll for the sake of complying with the regulations. It didn't matter if they were qualified to be on-air talent. Any deficiencies could be remedied through on-the-job training. Such free rides were not available to men. Men were expected to work their way up the ladder of success by first starting in very small markets. But these women were treated differently, and in some places qualified men were let go. Owners often had to fill quotas just to make sure they stayed out of court. Though I personally was not affected by these quotas, I knew a lot of men who were. This turned many of those who had previously been sympathetic to the women's movement against it. It was the insinuation of raw politics into a job situation.

Men have not reconciled themselves to all of this. There's a lot of resentment out there against feminism. It's being forced on people. Changes that might happen naturally are being shoved down people's throats. It's not what most men want. It's not what most women want. *Time* magazine reports that 63 percent of American women reject the feminist label. Increasingly, feminist groups are viewed as a fringe element who, because they are incapable of assimilating into mainstream society, are exacting their revenge on it. They are trying to change society to make it conform to them, rather than accepting the fact that they are not the mainstream.

I don't want to make too much of this, but when Patricia Ireland, the head of NOW, admitted to living with another woman, apart from her husband, it made people wonder about the women's movement. *The New York Times* estimated that 30 percent to 40 percent of NOW's membership is lesbian or bisexual. I know that if a man in charge of an organization in Washington had confessed to having a homosexual lover—or a heterosexual one, for that matter—and to living away from his wife, he would be ridiculed unmercifully in the media. But NOW is allowed to get away with having Patricia Ireland as president. She's called a visionary for having the courage and bravery to fight convention and thumb her nose and other body parts at the Establishment, to be herself. It is a beautiful thing. I feel confident that she will one day soon win the annual Kennedy family award, the prestigious and much sought after Profile in Courage Award (the 1992 recipient was Lowell Weicker, the enlightened governor of Connecticut, for his daring, dauntless, and fearless decision to establish an income tax for the state). Given NOW's membership and proclivities, it's no wonder that people now view the NOW gang as being obsessed with only two issues: abortion rights and lesbian rights.

FEMINISM'S SLIDE

This obsession with abortion and lesbian rights became entrenched in the women's movement in about 1978. That's
approximately the time when feminism became separated from
its original concerns and veered into strange new territory. I date
it from the 1978 conference in Houston that was chaired by
Congresswoman Bella Abzug of New York. Jimmy Carter had
caved in and caused the federal government to pay for this
women's conference, and it was taken over by the radical left.
Gone were concerns about equal pay, assertiveness, and expressing one's individuality. In their place were women ensconced in
bitterness, hatred, and resentment. The NOW gang became a
fringe movement, and lost a lot of women who no longer wanted
to call themselves feminists. The women's movement was taken
over by radical leftists and became an adjunct of the Democratic
party.

I prefer to call the most obnoxious feminists what they really
are: feminazis. Tom Hazlett, a good friend who is an esteemed
and highly regarded professor of economics at the University of
California at Davis, coined the term to describe any female who is
intolerant of any point of view that challenges militant feminism.
I often use it to describe women who are obsessed with perpetuating a modern-day holocaust: abortion. There are 1.5 million
abortions a year, and some feminists almost seem to celebrate
that figure. There are not many of them, but they deserve to be
called feminazis.

A feminazi is a woman to whom the most important thing in
life is seeing to it that as many abortions as possible are
performed. Their unspoken reasoning is quite simple. Abortion is
the single greatest avenue for militant women to exercise their
quest for power and advance their belief that men aren't necessary. They don't need men in order to be happy. They certainly
don't want males to be able to exercise any control over them.
Abortion is the ultimate symbol of women's emancipation from
the power and influence of men. With men being precluded from
the ultimate decision-making process regarding the future of life
in the womb, they are reduced to their proper, inferior role.
Nothing matters but me, says the feminazi. My concerns prevail

over all else. The fetus doesn't matter, it's an unviable tissue mass.

Feminazis have adopted abortion as a kind of sacrament for their religion/politics of alienation and bitterness.

WOMEN'S NATURE

I believe that nature has defined behavioral roles for men and women. These roles are ordained in large part and are not easily altered. You want a superb example of this theory? Try this: A woman walks into a bar, or library, or art gallery, or museum, or church, or a pro-choice march, or an animal liberation protest—whatever least offends you. She encounters two equally attractive men and strikes up a conversation with each of them separately. The beginnings of the mating dance, so to speak. As always happens in these situations, she gets around to asking them what they want out of life, what things are important to them. This is because she is interested in what a future with either of them would be like. (As my father said: "Women always marry up." Which is true, despite your obvious emotional objection. Even Gloria Steinem dates men who earn more money and are more powerful than she. You can look it up.) One of these Romeos tells her that he has the ambition to be the best he can be at whatever he does and to be as educated as he can be. He describes the material things he hopes to own (if they live in New York, it is imperative that he mention at this point that he intends to have a summer house on the island), that he hopes for a family, a nice home, and a prosperous future. All the normal, usual stuff.

The other Don Juan, however, presents different options. He figures she is a liberated woman of the eighties and nineties and he wants to get on base now. He launches into a sensitive and magnificent description of how he loves children and is tired of the rat race and all the cutthroat competition "out there." Too much insincerity, he tells her. Too many phonies—you can't trust anyone anymore. Just a bunch of hedonists who want some fast action, then move on. None of that for him, he assures her. No, what he wants is children. He loves them and wants to raise them. That's how you get in touch with your real self, he says. He respects and admires career women and totally supports them. He thinks it would be terrific for society if more women worked full-time and men stayed home and raised the kids. That's what he wants to do, he tells her. A beautiful thing. Now, which of these two guys do you think she will be more inclined to respect and pursue and marry? Yeah, I know. Case closed.

For the past few decades we have been browbeaten into pretending that the differences between men and women are the product of our collective imagination; that the very concept of such differences was formulated by men in order to subjugate women. Can you believe that we have been so conditioned to believe that men and women are identical except for a few technical details that *Time* magazine, presumably with a straight face, came out with a cover story announcing (as if it were a discovery on the order of electricity) that men and women are born with different natures?

In the early 1980s, the conservative social critic George Gilder wrote a fascinating book called *Men and Marriage.* It has influenced many people, including Ronald Reagan. Gilder's theory is that civilization would not have developed unless the natural tendencies of men were subordinated to the natural tendencies of women. Women, he explained, are by nature more nurturing and caring. Men, if left to their predisposition, are prone to roam, and to avoid taking responsibility for anything but their own desires. But when a man and a woman mated and the woman gave birth, the man was forced to assume responsibility and subordinate his natural tendencies.

Ronald Reagan told a joke about this early in his first term. I'm sure he meant to compliment women, but some didn't take it that way. He told a women's group that men would still be a bunch of cavemen if it weren't for women. The women were feminists and they went nuts. All they heard was that their role was to exist solely to make men responsible and civilized—that they were not to have an individual life of their own. They took that to mean that women were consigned to the cave so that when John Q. Stud came back they would still be there, always ready to serve his needs. This was intended as a great compliment, but the feminists misinterpreted it as an insult.

Women have played a very powerful role in civilizing men. This realization is not a slight to women. It is not to say that this has been their only role or that they should not have an identity apart from men. But look at what has happened in cities as the welfare dependency cycle has grown. In 1960, a generation ago, the illegitimacy rate was barely 5 percent. Today it is 26 percent, up five times. In the black inner cities, it is now 62 percent. Illegitimacy is not linked to race, it's linked to the welfare state. The Swedes have an illegitimacy rate of 52 percent, and they are desperately trying to cut back their welfare state in order to reduce that number.

In many cities the federal government has replaced the wage-earning husband and father with a welfare check. The man is no longer essential for financial support. Welfare is given with good intentions, but it has emasculated John Q. Stud. He has reverted to irresponsibility.

This pattern is now showing up in the middle classes too. Feminism has had a profound impact there by convincing women that they don't need men and will be just as well off as single mothers. Because it has become societally acceptable to have an illegitimate child with the government being substituted as the family's breadwinner in lower and lower-middle classes, the fathers of these children are, in their own minds, free to shirk the responsibility and consequences of their actions. Bye-bye family.

THE FEMINIST MISTAKE

Feminists love to attack the United States for being unfair to women. Yet, when millions of women decided they wanted to enter the workplace and have careers, the economy found places for them. Then their complaints switched from not being able to get jobs to not being able to get powerful jobs. "When do I get to be president of General Motors?" and all that. They seemed to be demanding that power be handed to them on a silver platter as payment for its having been denied to them since the Garden of Eden. Well, nobody just gets what they want. You have to earn it—unless you are a Trust Fund Kid, born into wealth, where your only challenge is to reach the age of twenty-one so it can be transferred to your name. (Many of these people end up as United States senators.) You have to spend long, grueling years climbing the corporate ladder.

One of the reasons why women aren't climbing the ladder as fast as men is simple: it's spelled C-H-I-L-D-R-E-N. Career women in droves delayed childbirth so they could climb that ladder. So many women did what they thought they should be doing, following the new pop culture of having it all *now*. They tried to be just like men, to act just like men—to pretend that there were no fundamental differences in our natures.

Well, after a while reality slapped many of them in the face. As these career women who had yet to have children confronted their biological clocks in their mid-thirties, they began to change their minds. They started to have children. At first they went back to work with the help of daycare. But then many of them grew to miss their children and the joys of full-time motherhood. They became worried that people they didn't even know were raising their kids during those precious days of their formative years.

But part of the feminist credo was that it was a good thing for the government to raise kids. They wanted them to be raised with liberal values. So many liberals today believe that the problem with kids is their politically incorrect parents. They aren't being raised with the proper "progressive" values.

A lot of women who had kids in their mid-thirties were able to get parental leave to stay home with them for a while. Then many of them decided to give up their outside jobs altogether so that they could stay home and raise their kids. I am gratified to see this trend occurring, not because I have any problem with women in the workplace. I simply believe that children are better raised, and that the family unit is more sound, when a mother stays home with her children during their formative years. More and more women are making that choice, and it is driving the feminists nuts.

This is one reason why women aren't climbing the corporate ladder as fast as men. A certain number of women get off the ladder, and it's understandable that businesses have to consider that fact when they make promotion decisions.

I'm all for making adjustments at work to allow women the

flexibility to handle their role as parents. Take Kiki de la Garza, my broadcast engineer. She went on maternity leave for ten months early in 1992 after giving birth to a beautiful boy. During her pregnancy it was no problem if she had to go to the doctor or come in thirty minutes late because of her child-rearing duties. That was fine and we were all happy for her and encouraged her to do whatever she thought necessary. We covered for her and had someone else do the show. But imagine if a male had tried that. Imagine if a man said, "I can't do the show. I have to take the kids to nursery school." I guarantee that he would be viewed differently from other men, especially by management. Eyebrows would be raised. Society accepts certain differences between the sexes. It is not that men are not capable of child-rearing. We just accept the fact that women have it in their nature to nurture children, and we strive to accommodate that. Feminists are inconsistent in so many areas. Although they insist on perpetuating the myth that men and women are identical (other than the fact that men are jerks), they want even more allowances to be given to women. If they had their way, our entire business structure would be overhauled to accommodate the special needs of women. But how can women have special needs when they aren't different from men? This leaves many of us men just a bit confused.

THE CHILD COMES LAST

Let me illustrate where the priorities of radical feminists are.

A man and a woman were living together in Oakland, California. Both were unmarried, both about twenty-eight years old. She was seven and a half months pregnant when she suddenly had a brain hemorrhage. She slipped into a coma and was pronounced brain dead at the hospital. But her fetus was just fine. Every part of her body except her brain could be kept functional on life support. She was never going to recover, but the fetus could survive if the mother could be kept on life support for at least one month.

The problem was that since the couple wasn't married, the decision-making authority was held by the parents of the comatose woman. They asked the doctors to disconnect the life support because they didn't want the child around to remind them of their lost daughter. The father stepped forward then and said that he wanted the child to be born. "I was in love with the mother of my child, and that child is a product of our love. I want to raise him as the only link to one of the happiest moments of my life," he said.

Well, it soon seemed that every feminist in the Bay Area was bound and determined that the child not be born and that the father's wishes be disregarded. You see, they were afraid that the case would go to court. If the court ruled in favor of the father, it would establish a father's legal right to be part of the decision of whether an abortion should be performed. Recall that *Roe v. Wade* gave women the exclusive right, subject to the state's right to regulate in the second and third trimesters, to determine what would happen to their bodies. Fathers were relegated to the status of mere onlookers.

Well, the father refused to back down, and the hospital was besieged by protestors. To keep from going to court, the parents negotiated with the father. He offered to have his sister help raise the child and promised to provide for it in all ways. The parents relented, and the baby was born healthy using a C-section delivery. He's doing well.

The feminists were still upset, though. They didn't want a man to have a say in the future of a fetus, even if he was the father. Consider another example. A couple in Tennessee couldn't get pregnant and were going to use artificial insemination. They had seven frozen embryos, or zygotes, in a dish and were waiting to attempt the procedure. While they were waiting they began to have problems with their marriage and filed for divorce. The embryos became part of the divorce battle. It was up to the judge to decide who owned them. He said he would have to consider them as children, rather than as property, for purposes of his decision. The feminists again went ballistic, afraid that a legal precedent would be set should the dreaded would-be father end up with control over the zygotes. The would-be dreaded father didn't want his ex-wife to end up as the mother of his children, nor did he want to pay child support sometime down the line for any of the embryos that became children.

You can see how absurd this whole thing was, but it exposed the feminist agenda. Here you had seven frozen embryos outside the womb that were considered children by the court. But if they had been inside the womb they would have been nonviable tissue mass. They wouldn't have existed. This contradiction is one more reason why *Roe v. Wade* cannot stand up to legitimate constitutional scrutiny.

ANOTHER OFFSHOOT OF FEMINISM: THE ISSUE OF WOMEN IN COMBAT

Congresswoman Pat Schroeder of Colorado is leading the charge to have women in the military be given the choice of entering combat. I would point out that if she were seeking *total* equality, she wouldn't speak in terms of giving women a choice. Men aren't given any choice about going into combat. They have to go.

Pat Schroeder's claim is that unless women are allowed to serve in combat roles, they won't get to climb the career ladder of the military and become generals. Consider her theory on how an army is to operate. I'm sure she would run it so as to ensure that just as many women as men are riding around in chauffeured limousines and being saluted by everyone. Her philosophy illustrates precisely why we have to keep the ideology of feminism out of the military. What will feminists seek in the military, first and foremost? Equality. Fairness. Gender quotas. Well, the military's chief goal is excellence. We shouldn't emasculate (pun unintended) the military by shackling it with the demands of every silly social movement that is currently fashionable in society. The military has a job to do. Its primary purpose is to kill people and break things—or at least to be prepared to do so in the event the need arises. Its success will always be measured by its ability to destroy and decimate; not by whether it has a requisite percentage of women in foxholes, in daycare centers, or flying F-16s. I know this sounds harsh, but that's the way war is. Frankly, I don't believe that women should be in combat roles even if they can do the job. Why? you ask. Simple. Women have a civilizing role in society. War is that cruel last option in human relations. It isn't about career opportunities.

Women have definite societal roles that are crucial to the continuation of mankind. They establish enduring values that are handed down from generation to generation. Women are the ones who give birth, without which the propagation of the species would not be perpetuated.

I just don't believe that we have to subject women to the horrors and rigors of war. During the Persian Gulf war, two women soldiers were captured by the Iraqis and sexually tortured. Can you doubt that this goes a long way toward weakening our resolve, because no one wants to see American women treated that way? It's bad enough that men come home in body bags. Why do we need to put women in them as well?

EXCEPTION: THOSE WOMEN WHO DO BELONG IN COMBAT

I know that by now many of my readers will think I have an old-fashioned, romantic notion of women—that I put them on a pedestal and think of them as special. Well, I do believe there are plenty of roles for women in the military other than combat. However, I realize that my position is in the minority in some quarters in the Pentagon. So, I am willing to concede that I may have to compromise on this. After all, compromise is an essential part of politics and many other aspects of life.

Upon deep reflection I have recently softened my position somewhat. I think there is a way we can allow women into combat after all. We are all aware of certain basic facts about women. We know that when women are grouped together in an office, a dormitory, or a barracks, their menstrual cycles mysteriously become synchronized. It just happens. We also know that women get PMS. Even some courts seem to have taken judicial notice of the fact that women with PMS can become the most vicious, potentially violent animals walking the face of this earth. Their behavior is inexplicable. Women have been acquitted of murder by explaining that they had PMS and didn't know what they were doing or couldn't control their behavior at the time of the crime.

Now, folks, I have a compromise proposal to allow certain

women into combat. I propose the formation of the All American First Cavalry Amazon Battalions. We will have fifty-two battalions, one for every week of the year. That way we can guarantee we will have a combat-ready battalion of Amazons with PMS who will always be available to do battle with the enemy.

Imagine you are Manuel Noriega, or Saddam Hussein. Take your pick. You're in your presidential bunker, under attack by the Americans. But you're holding out okay—somehow you have even managed to elude the new highly touted American "smart weapons." The only hassle you've got is that some American GIs are playing rock-and-roll music at about 800 decibels right outside your bunker. Sometimes you want to commit suicide, because you're convinced they are sending subliminal messages as part of the music. But you're coping with it and you certainly aren't threatened with any physical harm.

Then, suddenly, outside your window you hear a bloodcurdling cry: "I AM OUTRAGED BY IT! OUTRAGED, I TELL YOU!" Sure enough, you look outside and it's Sergeant Major Molly Yard leading the first battalion of Amazons with PMS over the hill, coming right at your bunker. The sight would be enough to scare the pants off of anybody, and there's only one thing you could do: surrender. Voilà! The good guys win again.

Now that's the way to integrate women into combat roles— and the most militant ones, at that. But something tells me the feminists won't like my idea. Or this one:

FEMINAZI TRADING CARDS

FEMALE: I'll give you two Gloria Steinems for one Anita Hill.

ANNOUNCER: Trading cards have always been for males only, it's just not fair, it's not right.

FEMALE: Damn, I spilled nail polish on my Betty Friedan!

ANNOUNCER: Well. EIB is proud to introduce "Feminazi Trading Cards." For you to save, to collect, to trade. Feminazi Trading Cards are designed with the woman in mind. On the front, an action shot of a leading feminist burning a bra, dominating a TV show, picketing an all-men's club, protesting a Rush Limbaugh concert, charging into a men's locker room. Denouncing Ronald Reagan.

FEMALE: I'd do anything for Pat Schroeder.

ANNOUNCER: On the back, all the vital statistics: waist, hips, the documented age, the number of abortions, and, where applicable, the alimony payments and divorce settlements. Each file has at least one profound thought and a beauty secret. Get them all! Each set includes not only today's feminazi superstars like Molly Yard and Eleanor Smeal, but yesterday's heroes like Bella Abzug and Gloria Steinem. Plus, outstanding rookies like Anita Hill and Judge Susan Hoerchner. Don't get left out. Start collecting Feminazi Trading Cards today!

MULTICULTURALISM

A FEW YEARS AGO, RADICAL STUDENTS AT STANFORD UNIVERSITY
protested against a required course in the great texts of Western
civilization. They organized a march, led by the Reverend Jesse
Jackson, with a chant, "Hey, hey, ho, ho, Western culture's gotta
go." And Stanford capitulated and abolished the Western civilization requirement. It was replaced with watered-down courses
in which books were supposed to be examined from the perspective of "race, class, and gender," and readings from St. Augustine
and John Locke were interspersed with such works as the
autobiography of Guatemalan Marxist guerrilla fighter Rigoberta
Menchu and a documentary on Navajo Indians entitled "Our
Cosmos, Our Sheep, Our Bodies, Ourselves."

Multiculturalism is billed as a way to make Americans more
sensitive to the diverse cultural backgrounds of people in this
country. It's time we blew the whistle on that. What is being
taught under the guise of multiculturalism is worse than historical revisionism; it's more than a distortion of facts; it's an
elimination of facts. In some schools, kids are being taught that
the ideas of the Constitution were really borrowed from the
Iroquois Indians, and that Africans discovered America by

crossing the Atlantic on rafts hundreds of years before Columbus and made all sorts of other scientific discoveries and inventions that were later stolen from them. They are told that the ancient Greeks and Romans stole all of their ideas from the Egyptians and that the Egyptians were black Africans.

In fact, most historians and anthropologists will tell you that while there was a lot of cultural exchange in the ancient world and the Greeks and Romans absorbed some of the Egyptian ideas, it was only one of many influences. And the ancient Egyptians were dark-skinned but not black, even though many scholars have been so intimidated that they will only say this off the record. My purpose here is not to be critical of Africans or African culture, but simply to point out that not one syllable of any of our founding documents can be traced to the roots of tribal Africa—and that neither I nor anyone else is going to improve racial relations by pretending otherwise.

There is a fallacious premise out there that black kids have low self-esteem because they don't have any roots. They don't have anything to relate to in their past except slavery and degradation, and to elevate their self-esteem we must teach them about the great cultures of their ancestors. I think the multiculturalists are perpetrating a tremendous and harmful fraud when they take young black kids in public schools and teach them things that are irrelevant or even counterproductive to their future as Americans. They teach that street slang is just as good as grammatical English, that whites are cold and logical but blacks are warm and intuitive, and that Africans have a different approach to numbers that doesn't emphasize precision. Well, if you want to get a job with IBM you've got to have the skills that will help you get that job. And that involves a lot of things. Not just the skills, such as logical thinking and mathematics, but language, appearance, showing up on time. And if the kids have been taught that learning these things means compromising themselves and conforming to white values, how on earth can they be expected to succeed? If you want to prosper in America, if you want access to opportunity in America, you must be able to assimilate: to become part of the American culture. Just as in any other country of the world—if an American moved there, he would have to adapt to its culture if he wanted to succeed. The so-called minorities in this country are not being done any favors when the multiculturalist crowd forces their attitudinal segregation from mainstream society. The politics of cultural pride are actually the politics of alienation, in a different uniform.

Americans have always seemed to pride themselves in describing theirs as a melting-pot culture, where everyone is welcome and all will be treated equally. There is no question that this country has severe blemishes in its past (slavery) with respect to equality of treatment and access to opportunity. But the way for us to overcome that, in my opinion, is to strive toward racial color-blindness, rather than to encourage members of different cultures, especially their youth during their formative years, to dwell on their native cultures. I believe I have a consistent position here because I certainly do not advocate the schools' focusing on a historical review of my ancestry either. For America to truly arrive as an integrated society, we have to begin behaving as though we are all Americans; that we have a culture ourselves, and that all of the various cultures that compose our great nation should work toward blending into a harmonious society. It can be argued that such a position is easy for a white man in this country. To that I can only respond that I admit that racism continues to exist in every imaginable direction among all races. But we are certainly more likely to make inroads against those attitudes and make progress toward actual equality if we learn to view one another as human beings; not as blacks, African-Americans, WASPS, Jews, Native Americans, Asians, or Latinos.

What is this American culture toward which we should all aspire? American culture is defined primarily by the idea of self-reliance. That's how this country was built: people of every background fending for themselves and for their families. And it's something we are losing. If you tell someone to get a job, you are using dirty words now; you are being insensitive. Now you are told to define yourself by your place within a tribe or a group. People have accused me of racism or insensitivity when I challenge the multiculturalist view on history and education. But far from being a racist, far from being a bigot, I have a great deal of compassion and love for people of all backgrounds, and I also love my country. I want this to be a great country, and a great country needs as many great individuals as there can be. These young black kids in public schools in America are Americans. Not Africans, not Jamaicans, but Americans. And we have to treat them as such. It is in our nation's best interest, and in their best interest too, for them to grow up as good Americans, to know American culture, to learn to prosper in America. And I have that hope. I want everyone to be taught the things that are necessary for them to prosper as Americans, not black something or brown something or red something, but as Americans.

Of course there are people in the multiculturalist movement who have the best of intentions, who think the movement is dedicated to helping members of minority cultures become more well rounded. And I don't want to castigate all advocates of multiculturalism. In fact, if people want to teach ancient African history, or Third World cultures, or women's studies, that's fine—as long as it doesn't become the primary perspective and doesn't supplant the things that all American kids need to know—and as long as it is not coupled with the fraudulent message that the minorities' best opportunity of succeeding in this society is to jealously cling to their past.

The historian Arthur Schlesinger, whose book *The Disuniting of America* was published recently, writes that if ethnic subcultures have genuine vitality, they will be instilled in children by families, churches, and communities. The children will not need encouragement from the schools to learn about their ethnicity and their heritage, to learn their language, and so forth. If the communities do not instill these things in their children, then it's obviously not a very important part of their lives to begin with. So, there must be some other motives behind the drive for multiculturalism than making children aware of their heritage.

Multiculturalism is primarily—though not exclusively—a tool of black educators and of those sympathetic to the injustices blacks have suffered and continue to suffer in America. There is a feeling that blacks will never be able to make it if they have to play by the same rules, because America is so flawed and American culture is so racist and prejudiced. But there's something I'd like to know. How is it that boatloads of Vietnamese people, without any prior exposure to American culture or any knowledge of the English language, can arrive on the West Coast and, seven years later or less, speak the language fluently, run prosperous businesses, and have their kids scoring near the top in our schools? In California, the Asians are outperforming everyone else on college entrance exams—so much so that the University of California actually has instituted quotas on admissions of Asian-Americans, because otherwise many whites and blacks wouldn't get in. I'm sure many blacks and whites are embarrassed by this. And the fact is that I don't see these Asian-Americans getting any special Asian-studies courses in high school or grade school to boost their self-esteem. No one is setting up Vietnamese-history courses for these kids—and they seem to be doing just fine anyway.

Why is that? In my opinion, it is primarily because their families came here, intact, to escape oppression in their own countries and to take advantage of the opportunities that America offers. They are not told that they should be bitter about America and that they should dwell on the study of their own cultures. They come here to join in the culture and to succeed within the rules, not to change the rules. And it's not just the Vietnamese but people from other Asian countries and blacks from the West Indies and from Africa who are seeking to come here. On the other hand, many people who were born here have the attitude that they shouldn't be required to make an effort to educate themselves and get themselves out of poverty—society owes it to them, as compensation for the injustices perpetrated against their grandparents. For the black leadership to continue to encourage their people to absorb themselves in the past, instead of helping them get beyond the bitterness, is doing them a great disservice.

Of course, the argument is that black Americans are different from all other groups. They didn't choose to come here; their ancestors were brought here in slave ships. I won't deny that, nor will I defend this country's original sin. But there's nothing we can do about it now. It may not be fair, but we can't change the past. Black Americans are here. The only solution, as I said, is for blacks to be treated as Americans, to be taught the things they need to know as Americans, and to be held to the same standards as other Americans. I realize that my suggestion that we encourage assimilation rather than alienation is easier said than done. But an overhauling of our attitudes toward one another, so as to de-emphasize rather than to emphasize our cultural differences, will do far more in the long run to advance the plight of minorities, than will the artificial remedy of reverse discrimination.

Now let's talk about fairness for a moment. I get frustrated listening to all this talk about fairness. And it's not restricted to multiculturalism. We demand a fair and level playing field in foreign trade, for example. But are we going to get it just because we demand it? You have to deal with things as they are; that's one of the earliest lessons kids need to be taught.

Things in life are not always going to be fair. Even John Kennedy said life isn't fair. Yes, the Japanese won't import our products, but that has nothing to do with why Americans don't buy American-made goods. The Japanese aren't playing fair but that's not why some of our products are inferior. There is no causal relationship there. So in formulating our solutions to this problem we shouldn't allow our emotions to interfere with our good judgment.

Here's another example: After I was on *The Phil Donahue Show*, my rabid fans, God love them all, started calling and saying, "Rush, you were great but gee, we felt sorry for you. He wasn't fair to you. He didn't let you finish your sentences, he tried to misrepresent what you said, he took you out of context. He was so mean." And I said, "What did you expect? It's Phil Donahue. He's a liberal, I'm a conservative. Were you surprised by anything he did? Well, neither was I." When they invited me to be on, do you think I said, "All right, but only if he's nice, only if he's fair?" No, I went into the arena knowing the ground rules and fully anticipating the treatment I was to receive. I had seen *The Phil Donahue Show*, I knew what it was like. If I had had an affair with my wife's mother and sister, or if I were castrated and still afraid of the bicycle bar, I would have been occupying the moral high ground on Donahue's turf. But I went in there as a conservative, and I knew I would be persona non grata; I knew it was going to be rough. And I think I handled it superbly. I didn't let Donahue get away with distorting my views, although he did a masterful job trying. The point I am trying to make is that if you insist on fairness before you do anything, you're never going to get anything done.

Multiculturalism is based upon the premise that there is such terrible unfairness out there that minority cultures can't triumph over it. All of us are constantly exposed to a barrage of negative news. We are told that misery has finally taken over in America, that the American dream is dead. And what I find especially appalling is that so many people seem to be happy that misery persists, because it enables them to say, "I told you so." If you agree that misery is everywhere and you wallow in it, then you are caring and compassionate. If you encourage people to extricate themselves from it, you are told that you are uncaring. If a minority member succeeds in bettering himself, he is resented by those who haven't. Clarence Thomas and Michael Jordan are among those who are sometimes accused of abandoning their roots to succeed in the white man's world. Because Clarence Thomas worked hard and was able to rise from an impoverished background, to play by the rules of American society and succeed, he was accused of being uncaring and insensitive toward his fellow blacks who had not escaped poverty. Success means an automatic inability to relate. How ironic it is that the black leadership purports to stand for the betterment of its people, but when its people do succeed they are immediately outcast. Here, try this: Soon after the final episode of *The Cosby Show*, a group of black sociologists released the results of a "study" they had conducted of the show. Their conclusion: *The Cosby Show*, by portraying blacks as successful, upwardly mobile residents of the middle class, sent the wrong message to both blacks and whites. What message? Why, the nonsense that blacks can make it in America if only they try. So there you have it—again. Black success is to be denied, is not even to be portrayed, because it does not happen. Well, it does happen, and often. As I point out in the following chapter, which deals with the Rodney King affair and its aftermath, the largest percentage of the 29 million black people in America—67 percent—are middle and upper-middle class.

It is my conviction that the people who concocted multiculturalism and are now trying to institute a multicultural curriculum in New York are basically miserable. And rather than look at their own responsibility in this, or try to find solutions that involve a change in attitudes, they simply blame institutions. They blame

America. So multiculturalism, which portrays American history and even all of Western civilization as nothing but misery and racist, sexist, capitalist oppression, is the tool of revenge of many who have failed to assimilate and fit into mainstream American life. And the primary targets of their revenge are our children. They are taking it out on our kids by filling their minds with mush and teaching them how horrible America is.

Look at all the attacks on Christopher Columbus in this quincentennial year of 1992. There's no question that Christopher Columbus was a major historical figure. You can say what you want about some of the things he did, but he certainly changed the course of history. The tribes that populated America when he arrived did not change the course of history. The Vikings who sailed to America did not change the course of history. Columbus did.

Now, five hundred years later, in history classes where multiculturalism has reared its ugly head, and also in books, in the media, and let's not forget Hollywood, Christopher Columbus is being portrayed as a mean, vicious, cruel monster. He was probably a racist, a sexist, a homophobe, and a bigot.

He chopped off the hands of natives in the West Indies and in the Caribbean, he took slaves, he originated the plundering of the environment—he did all kinds of horrible, evil things. People are saying, "Columbus! White male Europeans, they're the cause of the problems we're having today."

What I really love to see is the propagandists of multiculturalism getting caught in their own trap. Recently, some historians were speculating that Columbus might not deserve credit for discovering the New World after all, because it may have been Columbus's wife who told him which course to take. The new theory was that he was going to sail in the other direction, but his wife (her name was probably Hillary) said, "No, go that way." So, you see, it was his wife, obviously one of the pioneering feminists in America, telling her husband what to do and which way to go, who is responsible for America's discovery by the Europeans. This is bizarre. Feminists are in league with multiculturalists, saying that white European males are the problem, and now we learn that perhaps the first feminist in the world sent Columbus here! So the feminists are responsible for

211

the advent of Western civilization in this land, and all its attendant evils. Now, that's justice.

But let's get back to Columbus. All right, just for the sake of argument, let's say that the Columbus-bashers are right. Let's say he was as evil as they make him out to be and that he committed all those horrible things of which they accuse him, and more. Let's even stipulate that he is related to Daryl Gates. Would somebody please tell me where, in the founding documents of the United States of America, there is anything based on Christopher Columbus's beliefs, or his actions, or his philosophy? It just isn't there. The American system of government did not come from Columbus.

But that's not the way the multiculturalists see it. To them, it's the single best way to get at easily influenced young minds and tear the country down. If the man who discovered America is flawed, if he's a bad guy, then everything that followed from that discovery has to be immoral—the fruit of the poisonous tree. In the same way, we are told that because George Washington and Thomas Jefferson held slaves, and because Jefferson supposedly had a sexual relationship with one of his female slaves—which is a lie to begin with—the constitutional system of government that they created is tainted. But it's not just the kids who are being spoon-fed these lies. So are we adults. And we're not challenging it. What happened to our backbone?

No one can convince me that the point of all this is not to discredit all that America stands for—and the ultimate goal, I firmly believe, is the destruction of the capitalist way of life, the destruction of free enterprise, and the establishment of socialism, because socialism to these people equals fairness. De Tocqueville observed, "Democracy and socialism have nothing in common but one word: equality. But notice the difference: while democracy seeks equality in liberty, socialism seeks equality in restraint and servitude."

When you look at what's being taught in the schools today, as Dr. Schlesinger has shown, the primary culture of America is being ripped apart, criticized, denigrated, and people are being told to look to their ancient ethnic roots for salvation and goodness.

If you think about it, multiculturalism flies in the face of what this country is all about. This country was built by people who were fleeing the oppression of the societies in which they were born. You know, there is something to those old clichés about America being a beacon of hope and prosperity. These may be clichés but they really are true. When there's a food shortage anywhere in the world, where do those suffering go for help? The United States. When somebody needs technology, where do they go? The United States. When somebody needs a donation, a handout, a loan, they come to the United States. And when somebody wants to escape oppression, where do they go? The United States. The people fleeing Haiti did not go to St. Thomas or to Cuba. They tried to come to the United States.

The reason all those people from different countries have been coming to America is that America is different from the countries they left. America offers individual freedom and the opportunity to make something of yourself. But multiculturalism is the exact opposite of that. We are now supposed to teach these people the values and the alleged virtues of the oppressive societies which they fled, rather than the values and virtues of the free society they sought. Please cogitate on that for a moment. We're even trying to teach it to the kids who never lived in those oppressive societies—we're supposed to teach them to champion the very things their parents escaped, many of them risking their lives in the process.

Let me say it again: Ethnic communities that are committed to preserving some of their cultural values and their heritage should be free to instill these values in their children—at home, at church, in the neighborhood. Surely it is not the office of public schools to promote separatism and heighten ethnic tensions. The bonds of national cohesion in the republic are fragile enough as it is. Public education's aim should be to strengthen, not weaken, them.

19

THE RODNEY KING AFFAIR

I COULD HARDLY WRITE A BOOK INVOLVING MY VIEWS ON CURRENT political issues without including a chapter on the Rodney King affair. The Rodney King verdict and its aftermath were among the hottest news items in the United States in the past several years. I think it is important to consider the verdict itself separately from the wave of violence that occurred in its wake. Also worthy of separate consideration are the solutions being offered to address the problems with our inner cities, for which the Rodney King riots have now become a symbol.

THE VERDICT

We all witnessed that videotape of four Los Angeles police officers beating Rodney King repeatedly. Most of us assumed that the jury would return a guilty verdict for several of the officers involved. In fact, we were so confident that most of us paid no attention to the trial. After all, this was a slam dunk if there ever was one. However, the night before the verdict was rendered, I, talking to my brother while we watched the latest news report on the jury deliberations, predicted an acquittal. This was just taking too long. When the jury's deliberations continued day after day, it became apparent that they were having "reasonable doubts" about the state meeting its burden of proof. Despite having predicted an acquittal, I admit that I was still stunned when I first heard the news of the verdict. It just didn't seem right in view of the video that we all watched.

Like many people, I wondered what evidence was presented to the jury which negated the effect of the video. At no time did I suspect white racism of playing a role in the verdict. Yet, there they were, the media and the all too common alliance of liberal politicians and civil rights leaders unanimously denouncing the verdict and attributing it to pure racism. In the first place, remember that the jury did *not* acquit the officer who struck Rodney King more than any other. The jury deadlocked with respect to Officer Powell, and a mistrial was declared. There will be a retrial of the man who has the greatest chance of being convicted. This is a crucial point, yet it was overlooked and ignored. If the jurors had been so eaten up with prejudice toward blacks, doesn't it stand to reason that they would have acquitted this officer as well? A sufficient answer is not that he swung his stick more times than the other officers so an acquittal for him was harder for the jury to justify. If racism had been their motive, it wouldn't have mattered how many times that officer hit Rodney King. If these jurors are as filled with hate for blacks as so many commentators seem to believe, then they would have rewarded the man who hit Rodney King the most times. But the truth is that this verdict was not motivated by racism. None of us were on that panel, nor did we witness a significant part of the trial. Like I said, we hardly paid it any attention, so sure were we of the cops' guilt.

On the other hand, Los Angeles City Councilman Mark Ridley-Thomas, after the riots, complained that the jurors were responsible because they should have known an acquittal would cause riots. Wasn't Mr. Ridley-Thomas, in effect, insisting that the jury should have had racist, stereotypical expectations of the ghetto blacks as rioters and looters? Wouldn't it have required racism on the part of the jurors to believe that these blacks would destroy their own neighborhoods if the verdict was not to their liking?

The reaction of the black leadership has been riddled with inconsistencies. Daryl Gates, on the Saturday prior to the verdict, predicted riots in the event of a not-guilty verdict. He was denounced as racist and bigoted. Alas, he was right. Yet, wasn't his attitude exactly that which Ridley-Thomas was demanding of the jury?

It is alarming to me how so many people can second-guess the motives of people they don't even know just because of an eighty-one-second videotape that they watched, which didn't even have an audible sound track to accompany it.

Jury verdicts of acquittal can sometimes be frustrating and seemingly unfair to alleged victims, because our system is designed to afford special constitutional protection to the accused. (In fact, in this case the system worked exactly as liberal activist groups such as the ACLU and People for the American Way have intended. Unfortunately for them, in this case they were done in by the very constitutional safeguards they helped create in their quest for justice.) Here's how it works: The defendant is presumed innocent, the state has the burden of proof, the defendant's guilt must be proved beyond a reasonable doubt, etc. All of this is to ensure that a person isn't convicted by the state of a crime he or she did not commit. This system often protects blacks (as defendants) just as it does whites. This case is a bit unusual in that the accused (the defendants) in the Rodney King case were the state or at least officers of the state. So here, instead of having *state v. individual* we have *state v. state*. So in this case the shoe is on the other foot because the accused are agents of the state and that seems inequitable to people because it is the state against whom people are supposed to be protected with our system of jurisprudence. But we cannot deny private-citizenship status to officers and suspend their constitutional rights and protections just because they are agents of the state. Because our system accords special protection to the accused, the guilty sometimes go free in a close case, and that's the way the system was designed.

But it is fair to note that when the state is on trial, the alleged victim has additional avenues for relief. Here he can and has filed civil-rights suits seeking $83 million in damages against the city of L.A. and the officers individually under Title 42, Section 1983, of the United States Code. Also the FBI has started its own civil rights investigation. In addition, there is still pending an internal disciplinary proceeding against some of these officers. And finally, one of the defendants, as mentioned, faces retrial because of a mistrial declared as a result of a hung jury.

In this case, the jury was exposed to the totality of the evidence, including three months of testimony and evidence, not just the eighty-one seconds of the video shown over and over again for a full year on TV. The jury watched the very first frames of the video, which clearly show King lunging at one of the officers as he got out of the car. During the trial they learned that Rodney King, a recent parolee and not a saint, started this episode by committing a crime (for which, by the way, he has never even been charged). He then led the police on a high-speed chase, deliberately risking the lives of innocent citizens. The jury also learned that the other two people with King were black, they didn't resist arrest, and they were not beaten one iota (by these same alleged racially possessed officers). Rodney King was thought by the officers to be on PCP because his behavior was erratic and unpredictable; he continued to resist, as is abundantly clear on the video; the officers didn't know whether he was armed; and he would not submit to the arrest. And we mustn't forget that Rodney King, for whatever reason, chose not to testify. This had an impact on the jurors, as some of them stated after the verdict.

Now, about that video. The video was actually about four minutes long, not eighty-one seconds. And what the public was exposed to day after day was not even the full eighty-one-second segment, but a deliberate and continuous replay of the ten to fifteen seconds that were the most damaging to the officers. If everyone is so confident that the video speaks for itself, why did the media not play the entire segment, part of which showed Rodney King in a bad light?

A jury verdict of not guilty doesn't mean the accused officers were totally innocent; just that the state didn't meet its burden of proof beyond a reasonable doubt. And with regard to that, another fact that has been conspicuously omitted from most commentaries on the verdict: the charge that the prosecution chose to file required proof that the officers assaulted Rodney King with a deadly weapon and intended to inflict on him serious bodily harm rather than to simply subdue him. If the state had chosen the lesser charge of simple assault, for example, it wouldn't have had near the burden and would have been far more likely to gain a guilty verdict, according to several judicial scholars. One judge in Oregon made the point that in his state, the equivalent charge to the one leveled at the four Los Angeles cops would have been attempted murder.

It was apparently easy for the defense to convince the jury that the officers were not using deadly force, which is indeed where the case turned. Just ask yourselves: After watching the eighty-one-second video, did you think the cops were using deadly force—that they were trying to kill Rodney King? In watching that video, how can we ascertain the state of mind of those officers beyond a reasonable doubt? We cannot. Yet, that is what so many around the country are doing, in effect, when they are willing to convict the officers without a trial. Remember, the cops did not know they were being videotaped. If they had wanted to kill King they would have done so. It is just that simple. If there was overkill here, it was on the part of the prosecution, which thought they had a guarantee of a guilty verdict because of the videotape alone. They went for the whole nine yards in a display of judicial greed.

It is important that whites as well as blacks acknowledge that, based on the video, it appeared that the officers may have used excessive force. But under our system, guilt and innocence is not determined through the lens of a video camera, but rather through the eyes of the defendants. That is to say, the jury was charged by the judge to look at the evidence from the eyes of the defendants, to determine what the officers were seeing from their perspective, and, from such a vantage point, whether they were acting reasonably under all the circumstances. The fact that racial epithets were tossed back and forth between officers in squad cars unrelated to this incident is disgusting, but totally irrelevant.

We must respect the system if the integrity of the system is to be preserved. I remember several people asking me a couple of days after the verdict why I didn't seem so outraged over the outcome. The answer is that I accept the system and its workings. I have been disappointed and angry countless times with jury verdicts I didn't understand or with judicial activism I thought wrong and unfair, such as that used to create quotas, affirmative action, forced busing, and other left-wing nonsense, but not once have I thought we should throw the system away and resort to emotion-based solutions. The selective indignation displayed by the soft-on-crime crowd when cops are acquitted is especially maddening to me, particularly when you consider that they seem to abhor the enforcement of law and order against truly dangerous convicts such as Willie Horton and Robert Alton Harris. Mark my words, when the dust has settled on this and the judicial scholars and experts have had their say, the consensus will be that the Los Angeles police trial verdict was correct, given the legal circumstances.

THE L.A. RIOTS

Almost as if they were poised to begin rioting, the thugs and hoodlums—criminals, to be blunt—took to the streets immediately upon the public announcement of the verdict. We were all horrified as we watched the mayhem on television proceeding unchecked. People were being killed and beaten before our very eyes.

An attorney for one of the defendants gave a reasonable analysis of the violent aftermath of this verdict. He said that it is hardly surprising that we have this kind of violent reaction when the President of the United States and the mayor of Los Angeles both announce their prejudgment of guilt in this case based on their viewing of a video, and then the mayor again announces his disagreement with the verdict after it is rendered. The President's postverdict announcement also literally added fuel to the fire. He said, "We are left with a deep sense of frustration and anguish by this [verdict] but we must abide by the system and the rule of the law." (The defense attorney remarked that in China, they would have lynched the defendants in advance without a trial.)

Regardless of how unfair some may think the verdict was, can't we concede that the mayhem and violence in response to it were abhorrently disproportionate? Rodney King, at most, was beaten badly. He was not killed. He lives and breathes, walks and talks today. The dead, mostly innocent victims, will never take another breath on this beautiful planet. They won't have any opportunity for redress, a damage suit or otherwise. Their crime was being at the wrong place at the wrong time.

PROPOSED SOLUTIONS

In my opinion, the reaction of many in the media, many in the black leadership, and many politicians has been outrageous. There has been no expression of outrage toward the rioters on the part of these people. They seem to accept the violence as a justified and even necessary reaction to "years of racial oppression." Where is their sympathy for the innocent victims and their families who lost their lives and their businesses? Where is their anger at the perpetrators? Who is saying, "If this happens again, it will not be tolerated. If this happens again we will move immediately to stop it, taking whatever steps necessary to enforce the law."? No one is saying it. There is no rationalization that can explain away this barbarism.

The biggest problem with the reaction of these people is that they are viewing these riots as a social rather than a criminal problem. To say that these murders, arsons, robberies, and assaults were caused by societal inequities, rather than say they were committed by criminals, is inexcusable. Civilized people don't behave the way these rioters, looters, and murderers did. When I watched the riots on TV I didn't see the faces of rage. I saw glee on the faces of hoodlums who were kicking and beating people to death, burning properties, and looting businesses. People appeared to be enjoying the opportunity to wreak havoc on society, without fear of reprisal by law enforcement, which was noticeably absent.

What we have here is liberal pandering at its most disgusting level. In true form, they refuse to place blame on those who are responsible. In fact, Congress is at this moment debating an Aid to the Cities bill, which actually rewards the rioters by responding to their demands and threats that more of the same will follow unless more money is transferred from Washington to the neighborhood. Individuals are always given an excuse to avoid responsibility for their behavior. Usually, they claim that society, primarily the last twelve years of Republicans, caused them to do it. But if liberals think the American public is going to take the blame for this one, they've got another think coming. Reasonable people know better.

The blame must be placed on those who committed the crimes. And they must be viewed not as victims but as criminals. My view, friends, is *not* in the minority. If it seems that way, that's just because the media doesn't give you both sides. It just continues to fan the flames of hatred by showing you the other extreme viewpoint.

I cannot believe how tolerant of crime we have become. We are encouraged to no longer even view it as crime but as economic determinism. The poor have no choice but to engage in criminal behavior to compensate for society's mistreatment of them. It is fine for us to seek solutions for poverty and to work on improving the inner cities, but to condone this kind of violence for any reason is engaging in subhuman thinking.

Let's not talk about the conditions and circumstances we are told caused this violence (because they did not); let's talk about the *solutions* to the problems of our inner cities: educational inferiority, illegitimacy, declining values, economic hardship, criminality, and the explosion of youthful street gangs.

The liberal reaction: To blame this on the last twelve years of Republican administrations—is predictable but nonetheless absurd. Some part of the blame for our inner-city problems must be placed on the liberal solutions. The rallying cry has now become, "The inner cities have been ignored by an uncaring government, so we must give them more federal moneys." Ignored? Since the Great Society began in the midsixties we have pumped some $3 trillion into these cities and the problems have not been eliminated; they've grown worse. Some of the blame must also be placed on the shoulders of those who mislead, misrepresent, wrongly motivate, and otherwise let down. Most of the established minority leadership certainly falls within that category. Liberals have created, and the minority leadership has exploited, a community of dependent people, unaware of the true route to prosperity and happiness: self-reliance and self-investment. Instead, people are told that America is unjust, unfair, and full of disadvantages. They are told that their only hope is for government to fix their problems. What has happened is that generations of people have bought into this nonsense and as a result have remained hopelessly mired in poverty and despair— because the promised solutions don't work. And, they will *never* work—they never have.

The problem is attitudinal as much as it is systemic. While it may be a stretch to blame the unrest and unhappiness on specific programs of Lyndon Johnson's Great Society of 1964, it certainly can be said that an attitude of dependence was created by the whole idea of the Great Society. Only four years earlier, remember, John F. Kennedy got his loudest applause when he said, "Ask not what your country can do for you. Ask what you can do for your country." Here's how bad it's gotten: A poll taken in early May reported that 75 percent of blacks in America feel the government doesn't care about them. (Doesn't care about them! They should feel lucky. Heck, I wish the government didn't even know I existed.) But there you have the illustration of the problem. Seventy-five percent of black Americans have been conditioned to derive their self-esteem, self-worth and self-respect from their perception of how much their government cares about them. How many of you derive any of your happiness from your thoughts about what the government thinks of you or your situation? How many of you are made to feel confident by what you hear politicians and elected officials say they are going to do for you? Isn't it a fact that you are the most motivated, the most upbeat and positive about the future when some candidate or elected official describes for you how he intends to get as much government as possible out of your life? Remember Reagan? Believe it or not, there are some reasons for optimism among blacks.

America's largest 100 black-owned companies reported a 10.4 percent increase in sales last year, despite the recession. This is a dramatic change from the previous year's rise of only 5 percent, and their total revenues were $87.2 billion. Earl Graves, publisher of *Black Enterprise* magazine, says that this increase indicates that the recession is ending and that black-owned businesses are getting more sophisticated. Graves, and people like him, are the ones who need to go into Los Angeles and teach blacks that they can succeed. The media tries to portray all blacks as being one with those who looted and rioted. The Rodney King verdict is not the most important thing on people's minds, yet liberals try to create the impression that black America is accurately reflected in the L.A. riots. It is "maddening" that so many people are either refusing to recognize or are unable to recognize the difference between blacks who riot, and the majority of blacks in the American middle class. According to University of Chicago sociologist William Julius Wilson, of the 29 million blacks in America, the largest percentage—35 percent—are upper middle class, both professional (lawyer, doctor) and white collar; 32 percent are middle class, and 33 percent are considered poor. I wish people would realize this, and not lump all blacks together under the stereotype of "poor, welfare-collecting ghetto blacks." Why, for example, isn't Clarence Thomas, one of the most powerful black men in America, a role model?

So how in the world have we arrived at this point? The honest answer is that those who find themselves in leadership positions, by accident or by design, have performed one of the greatest disservices in the history of this country by knowingly misleading as many people as they could. Jesse Jackson, for example, "cautions" us that it is not "useful" to "call names"—to refer to the rioters, looters, and murderers as thugs and hoodlums. Well, why not? That's what they are. What, are they going to get mad at us and be even meaner, so we are supposed to be "nice" to them in the hopes they won't riot and kill again? This from the man who called New York "Hymietown"? Jesse Jackson complains that Rodney King was not given a jury of his peers. Think about that. Rodney King was not the one on trial. Or doesn't that matter, Reverend Jackson? Tom Snyder, on his radio program one night during the rioting, said to Ted Koppel that Jesse Jackson should just stay off TV for a while and instead march into the neighborhood and demand that the rioting and looting stop. Koppel suggested that such action probably wouldn't make any difference. Bill Bennett suggested to me that if Reverend Jackson would march into South Central L.A. and tell those black men to

223

marry the mothers of their children and legitimize them and start raising their families responsibly, he would vote for him. Will this happen? Sadly, no. Anytime the illegitimacy rate in black America is raised, Reverend Jackson and other black "leaders" immediately change the subject. Too bad, because the real problem can be *traced* to this fact: 62 percent of all black babies born in America today are born to single mothers. Do you realize the impact this has on families and neighborhoods? Here you have the true destruction wrought by the Great Society and liberalism in general. The federal government has assumed the role of the wage-earning father in too much of black America and as a result there are no male role models for young blacks growing up in these communities. Have you ever wondered why boatloads of Asians, knowing not even one syllable of the English language, manage nevertheless to prosper and acculturate in American in just five to seven years? It is because they arrive with families intact, with parents intent on teaching the difference between right and wrong, good and bad, and the importance and merits of hard work. Things we never hear from Jesse Jackson and other "responsible" black leaders. Instead, we hear how gang leaders, rap artists who advocate the killing of white people, and rioters, looters, and murderers must be understood. And if they are not understood, then, we are warned, it will happen again. "No justice, no peace."

It is also irresponsible and dangerous for so many politicians and civil rights leaders to run around shouting on national TV as often as they can get on (which is as often as they like) slogans like, "No justice, no peace!" Maxine Waters, congresswoman from South Central Los Angeles, did just that in the aftermath of the rioting, which for her was many months. She even shouted this in mid-May during an angry diatribe at the Save Our Cities, Save Our Children rally at the foot of the Washington Monument. Think about that: A member of Congress, sworn to uphold the Constitution while establishing the law of the land, actually giving voice to a threat which in essence promised more of the same type of behavior we saw in Los Angeles if she (they) didn't get what she (they) wanted—more and more goodies from the Washington Christmas Tree. It is my honest opinion that Ms. Waters is herself consumed with rage and hate and actually welcomed her self-appointed role as chief spokeswoman for all angry blacks in the country.

Liberals and the black leadership, instead of condoning this violence and blaming it on society, should be trying to build hope for the poor people in our inner cities. They should be seeking ways to wean them off the government dependency cycle and, quite frankly, from dependence on the self-serving black leadership.

Blacks complain that most of them were outraged by the violence. I am sure that is true. Why, then, did the media show us only one side: those who condone the violence? Why does Bryant Gumbel proclaim rap artist Sister Souljah as a visionary black community leader, when she announces that more whites should be killed? She says that too many blacks were killed in the riots. Are whites too good to die? she asks. Are we to assume that Bryant Gumbel shares her view, or that he believes she speaks for the majority of blacks? May God help us if the answer to either of those questions is yes. Either the black leadership speaks for the majority of blacks or it doesn't. If it doesn't, then why haven't we heard from the other side—those blacks who detest the violence? This should tell you something about the media and its willingness to stoop to any level to increase ratings. Get the extremists on the television shows; it doesn't matter if they are representative, as long as it builds ratings.

The black leadership tells us that these were *multiracial*, "rainbow" riots. How can this be, if, as they say, the riots were caused by *white* racism against blacks. Note that no one has said that they rioted because of white racism against Latinos, Asians, Mexicans, or Jews. Yet, when Peter Ueberroth was appointed to lead the commission to rebuild the war zone, black leaders said that this was wrong and threatened again to blow up the neighborhood if only white businesses were used in the rebuilding effort. The gall of demanding the terms under which the neighborhood they destroyed will be rebuilt! They should feel lucky that people who had no part in the destruction of the neighborhood would even consider joining the effort to rebuild it, particularly when there are threats on the table to burn it again and again and again.

Our problem in the inner cities is not just economic poverty. It is a poverty of values. As such, the socialistic solutions of liberals won't work. Simply pouring money into these cities may improve the plight of the politicians who do it, but it won't address the poverty of values rampant in those areas. One black leader warned that if the government rebuilds this area, "we'll just burn it down again."

We must realize that the liberal approach of equalizing outcomes or wealth simply cannot and will not work. What we need to work on is equalizing opportunity. Values are principally learned at home. That's why any sensible approach to our declining value base must start with the family. We must do something to bring families together. One way to do that is to reform the welfare system so as to remove the disincentives to upward mobility. We must quit rewarding fathers for leaving their families and mothers for having more kids out of wedlock. We must remove government as the father figure support base in these inner-city families and provide incentives for the real fathers to stay home.

I also believe that Jack Kemp's solutions will help. His ideas of Enterprise Zones, HOPE, and ownership replacing tenant status are promising. His point that people do not burn down that which they own is irrefutable. Therefore, his idea that we must invest people with ownership is on the right track. If it takes money, so be it. But at least the money won't just be thrown at the problems. It will be used to help people help themselves out of poverty and the government-dependency cycle.

Lest I be accused of hard-heartedness, or worse, of racism, let me make one point very clear. I am not denying that poverty is rampant in our inner cities or suggesting that we do not need to address the problem. What I am saying is that there is no nexus between the conditions of poverty and the violence that occurred. That is why I chose to talk about each of these very important subjects separately.

CONCLUSION

We must be very careful not to send the wrong messages in response to the riots. If we pump large amounts of money into the stricken areas, we will be sending the message that crime pays. By rewarding those who tore down their own neighborhoods, we send the message that their violence was society's fault, and that we are not only not mad about it but feel responsible for their criminal behavior. We must resist the temptation to denounce the jury verdict as racist. Our entire judicial system is at stake here and we should be aware of the consequences of our irresponsible analyses of the verdict. We must not allow this sordid episode in our nation's history to propel us even further into the mire of socialism and the massive redistribution of wealth. Wealth redistribution does not equalize peoples. It destroys wealth. This ugly part of history does not teach us that capitalism will not work. Quite the contrary: It teaches us that socialism does not work; that liberalism is a failed ideology; and that it's time we invested in the individual rather than Big Brother to solve our problems.

All of this causes me much pain and gut-wrenching. I cringe at the sight of poverty and indigence and I long for solutions. They seem so readily available to me, at a fraction of the cost we have spent so far. For example, take drug education. How much extra does it cost to have a teacher instruct students not to get involved with drugs? What else is there to say? How can there be any debate about that? How do we teach right and wrong in our homes? Discipline, which is born of love. We simply tell our kids what they should and should not do, for their own good, because we love them and want the best for them. And how much extra family income does it take to teach a kid not to steal or kill? How often have you heard a mother or father complaining that they need a raise so they can teach their kids to avoid drugs? Never. It doesn't take money, it requires values and the confidence to teach them.

The same philosophy applies to poverty and opportunity. When I hear the same old conventional wisdom about solving poverty—more and more money—I am filled with rage because the conventional wisdom doesn't work. What is so threatening about teaching young poor Americans that the way out is by investing in themselves? What is the risk?

GORBASMS: ALWAYS FAKE

December 7, 1987. A cold, overcast day. Windswept Andrews Air Force Base outside Washington. Gathered on the tarmac are some two thousand people, invited guests of the President, the White House, and the State Department, and members of the media. All are filled with anticipation, bubbling over with enthusiasm. All are ready to explode with sheer joy and happiness. Because he is coming.

Suddenly a shout goes up from somewhere in the crowd: "There it is!" An Ilyushin 62 jetliner (the technology to build that Ilyushin no doubt stolen from Boeing at some point) is on final approach.

As the plane lands, thunderous applause erupts from the huge gathering at Andrews, and as it taxies in, the anticipation and excitement are almost too much for the crowd to bear. Because he has come. He is the one man who can save the planet from annihilation, the one man who can save the animals, the one man who can save the earth from environmental catastrophe, the one man who, if just given the chance, can save the world from every evil known to man (and those still unknown).

The plane taxies to a stop. Heavy breathing can be heard

228

among the crowd. The steps are rolled up to the front door. The door opens. Moments pass as there is movement but no discernible face.

Then, finally—when the crowd can wait no longer—he appears. Mikhail Sergeyevich Gorbachev, with that birthmark on his forehead, which looks more and more like the continental United States because it is growing. I've noticed this ever since 1987; it is expanding, in typical Soviet expansionist fashion, and right now it looks like you can see Florida, a little bit of the Gulf of Mexico, the tip of Texas, you see Chappaquiddick up there, a little bit of Maine—Kennebunkport maybe? As more and more people fall prey to the myth that he is the answer to everything, that birthmark begins to look more and more like the continental United States.

The man who, single-handedly, is going to nullify the dangers posed by Ronald Reagan, descends the steps and, walking on a red carpet, approaches the microphones. A giant scream and another burst of applause erupt from the crowd. The Beatles never had it so good. And then the very first Gorbasm in the history of mankind occurs, as the people can no longer contain their euphoria, their excitement, their hopes, their thrills, and they scream, *Aaaaargh!* The first standing Gorbasm. It is almost a Gorgy.

A Gorbasm, ladies and gentlemen, is fake. A Gorbasm is a phony feeling of bliss and euphoria. Mikhail Gorbachev was credited by the media, and by many liberals in this country, with preserving the peace and security of the planet threatened by that warmongering Ronald Reagan and with bringing freedom to Eastern Europe and what used to be the Soviet Union.

In fact, I believe, things have happened in the past three years that were beyond Gorbachev's ability to control—things which he was given credit for accomplishing but for which credit was really due to no one other than Ronald Reagan.

On his visit to the United States in May 1992, Gorbachev first lectured and encountered his first Gorbasm at Stanford University, which has offered him a full professorship. His speech at Stanford was a big hit and much less expensive than speeches elsewhere on the fleece. They didn't need any translators there.

Next, he gave a speech at Westminster College in Fulton, Missouri, in which he said that the Cold War is over but it is not an affirmation of anybody's particular values and it shouldn't be considered a victory for the West. And we invited him in to say that? When will we ever learn? Well, he's dead wrong. The end of the Cold War and the defeat of communism in the Soviet Union was a clear victory for American values, for the American way of life, for the republican, democratic, free-market ideals of the United States of America.

Gorbachev's continued refusal to admit this makes me suspicious of his ultimate long-range goals. He's not an old man yet. I have yet to hear him denounce communism. And he wrote in the last year, in a *New York Times* op-ed, that he still believes in socialism. He's still devoted to both, and is of the opinion that they just haven't been given a fair chance yet.

Gorbachev is not the only one who refuses to admit it, or get it. Another of the Gorbasms which occurred on his 1992 Spring Fleece was a speech before several hundred doting droolers at the Kennedy School of Government at Harvard University. Seated there, all composed and respectful, was Senator Ted Kennedy (who was giving Gorbachev far more respect than he ever gave Reagan) and other members of the Kennedy family along with a few specially invited Super Droolers from academia, all longing for the good old days when the great social experiment of communism was in its heyday.

After his uneventful and boring speech, in which he again sought to downplay the Soviet Union's and his eventual incompetence, Gorbachev submitted to a few minutes of Gorbasms. Questions from the droolers, in other words. The first was from someone who asked some esoteric question about dialectical materialism and its functional relationship to the economics of John Kenneth Galbraith. Gorbachev dealt with it masterfully, answering it as boringly as it was asked. The next question, though, came from a spy. It had to be someone who sneaked in. "Mr. Gorbachev, would you please explain the role of President Reagan's deployment of Pershing II missiles in Germany and his promise to develop the Strategic Defense Initiative in bringing about the end of the Cold War? I am primarily interested in your assessment of his threatened use of force in bringing about peace."

Oooohh! There were muted hisses. Gorbachev strode back to the microphone and said something to the effect that he didn't feel comfortable answering the question just then . . . but that basically, it is always wrong to use force to accomplish one's goals and that the threat to do so is never justified. Massive Gorbasms could be heard and seen throughout the lecture hall. Another standing Gorbasm, as the droolers and Super Droolers thanked Gorbachev for standing firmly behind them, even though they and Gorbachev were standing there in the ignominy of defeat; granted, they were probably too conceited to understand it. As discussed later in more detail, it was precisely Reagan's threats of SDI deployment (which the Soviets knew we could do) and his unwillingness to allow the Soviet expansion to continue unchecked (remember that they were driven out of Afghanistan with massive U.S. aid and arms) which brought about Moscow's fall. It would have happened whether Gorbachev was around or not, although Gorbachev should be given credit for not resisting it at the end with military force. He did mismanage it terribly, from his own political and personal historical point of view, but who cares about that? Only the droolers and Super Droolers.

All you have to do is ask yourself: Would the Berlin Wall have come down if we had had Jimmy Carter, Walter Mondale, and Michael Dukakis for President in the 1980s? Would the Soviet Union have collapsed without Ronald Reagan in the White House? The answer to both of these questions is, No. To me, it is obvious that President Reagan's no-nonsense attitude toward the Soviets scared them for the first time. Before that, they had had American presidents wrapped around their little finger— remember Jimmy Carter smooching with Brezhnev? But when Reagan began making jokes about starting the bombing in five minutes, and calling the Soviets an Evil Empire and the focus of evil in the modern world, that scared the living daylights out of them. KGB files prove it, folks. Sorry.

With the Reagan defense buildup, we showed that we could maintain a world-class defense and a first-class economy. And we showed that the Soviets could not. They crumbled trying to keep up. They couldn't feed their people. Here was a country that could build state-of-the-art tanks but could not build a washing machine to last five days—or deliver it to the buyer earlier than ten years from the purchase date. That's what you get with a command economy.

Remember how everyone—the concerned scientists, the politicians, the peace activists—kept saying that the Strategic Defense Initiative would never work? Rubbish. It worked before it was even deployed. The very idea of SDI, which could nullify a nuclear first-strike capability, was a powerful deterrent. And that's exactly what nuclear arms control has always been about.

People also complained about defense spending and asked why we needed so many nuclear weapons. Phil Donahue and his ilk kept lamenting the fact that we already had enough nuclear weapons to blow the world up forty-five thousand times over. But that's not the point. In these situations, the aggressor makes the rules. If the aggressor fires on you, you have to be able to withstand that and have enough left to fire back. So the numbers are irrelevant. What matters is parity.

This is something that I think many people never understood. We weren't driving the arms race; the Soviets were. They were the ones who continued to modernize and build up. Then came Ronald Reagan, who proposed the SDI, which would nullify their first-strike capability. Even if it didn't get every missile, even if it only got one. The point was that we were going to build a defense against a first strike, and they knew that we could do it. And with that came their defeat. (Remember, the Soviet Union was but a Third World nation without its military might. Reduce that and what were they?) Throughout history, whenever the American people set their minds to something, they have been able to do it. It's important to remember also that the SDI was a defense initiative. That's what the *d* and *i* stood for. Yet, the liberal media, in their effort to prevent the project from getting off the ground—pun unintended—successfully characterized the project as an offensive, war-making machine. They purposely called it Star Wars, to attach a pejorative connotation to the entire effort.

The Soviets knew that Reagan was going to be in office for

years, and they knew he was serious about it. And this is one of the great accomplishments for which Ronald Reagan will never get his due—except, perhaps, from the former Soviets themselves. In the fall of 1990, at a conference organized in Moscow by a Washington think tank, one of the American speakers denounced the Reagan defense buildup and the U.S. military as a parasite draining the life out of the poor American taxpayer. Imagine the surprise of the Americans when the next speaker, Russian economist Boris Pinsker, got up to the podium and said, "Ladies and gentlemen, if it had not been for the Reagan defense buildup, if the United States had not demonstrated that it is willing not only to stand up for freedom but to devote considerable sums of money to defending it, we probably would not be sitting here today having a free discussion between Russians and Americans." My friends, this is a point that is impossible to overemphasize. It wasn't just Ronald Reagan's talking tough that brought the Soviets to their knees. His was not merely empty rhetoric. More than any other President in recent memory, he followed his words with action. It cannot be denied that the resurrection of our national defenses at the direction of Ronald Reagan, including the promise of the SDI, coupled with our strong economy dramatically accelerated the collapse of the Soviet empire.

This has happened again and again. Remember how all the liberal media were horrified when President Reagan called the Soviet Union an Evil Empire and said that communism was destined for the ash heap of history? They thought it was ridiculous. They blasted him as a Cold Warrior. But as soon as people in the Soviet Union got the freedom to say what they really thought, many of them began to say openly that their government was, in fact, an Evil Empire. (What else do you say about a system that murdered at least 40 million of its own people?) And often they quoted Reagan's actual words, because, of course, Reagan's "Evil Empire" speech had been widely publicized in the Soviet Union as evidence of the nefarious designs of American imperialists. It is interesting how the liberal media in this country and the Soviet propagandists were almost in perfect agreement on this matter.

And the media still just don't get it. Right after the defeat of the

Soviet coup, Sam Donaldson interviewed Boris Yeltsin's foreign minister, Andrei Kozyrev, on ABC. And Kozyrev said, "Yes, we are very happy that the coup failed because we have now really destroyed the communist empire, the Soviet state, and of course, as Ronald Reagan said, it was indeed an evil empire and we are glad that it is gone from the earth." And Donaldson was speechless. It was his worst nightmare. The Russian foreign minister celebrating the collapse of the Evil Empire and giving Ronald Reagan credit for calling it that.

But it's Gorbachev who ends up being on the cover of *Time* not just as Man of the Year but as Man of the Decade. (Why not Man of the Millennium while they're at it?) It's Gorbachev who ends up receiving the Nobel Peace Prize—right after he sent the tanks and the "black berets" to crush peaceful protesters in Lithuania. By the way, when they gave the Peace Prize to Gorby, Yelena Bonner, the widow of the great human rights activist Andrei Sakharov, who received the same prize in 1976, said that she wanted to return it on her late husband's behalf, because she knew he would not want to share an award with a dictator. However, it seems that the Nobel Committee has a no-returns policy.

Isn't it curious that while so many gullible Americans (and people in other Western countries) were having one Gorbasm after another, the people in the Soviet Union were completely dissatisfied with him? There was a magazine photo of a huge protest rally in Moscow, and some of the demonstrators were carrying a huge poster that showed Gorby getting booted in the behind—and it said, FROM RUSSIA WITH LOVE.

Our liberal media kept telling us that Gorbachev was unpopular in Russia because he was too good—he was trying to change the communist system and the Russian people didn't like that. Nice try. The fact of the matter is, the Russian people hated communism. They wanted communism to go. And they knew that Gorbachev only wanted to tinker with the system a little, make it more efficient, do what he had to do to preserve it; not get rid of it altogether. When Yeltsin came and told them he wanted to get rid of communism, the Russian people voted for him.

In May 1992, Mikhail Gorbachev toured the United States on

what I like to call a nationwide fleece, making speeches around the country at the rate of a hundred thousand dollars per speech and attending fund-raising dinners. He was flown around in the Forbes jet. The security arrangements alone must have cost a fortune. True, there were no big public Gorbasms this time— maybe it's just not as sexy when the man is no longer the head of a superpower that has missiles pointed at you—but everywhere he went, he was greeted and feted with the utmost enthusiasm. He was cheered by the traders at the Chicago Commodity Exchange and the New York Stock Exchange. He gave a commencement address at Emory University, calling on the students to work for the good of mankind and the environment rather than their own selfish ambitions. He was given a freedom award at Yeshiva University in New York, which is akin to rewarding Pharaoh for freeing the Israelites.

This is the same man who, less than a year ago, was sending his tanks to roll over people in Lithuania—and trying to muzzle the Russian press to stop it from reporting what was going on. This is the man who covered up the meltdown at the Chernobyl nuclear plant, and he's lecturing us about the environment. The same man who cut off Sakharov's microphone in the Soviet Congress when Sakharov tried to demand that the Communist party's constitutional monopoly on power be abolished. But it seems no one holds that against him anymore.

Just as they have done with Ronald Reagan and the decade of the eighties, the liberals are revising history to glorify Gorbachev and his accomplishments, rather than admitting that the system he tried to preserve is a failure. In every case, the reason for the revision is the same: Liberals can't afford to have history accurately recorded and interpreted, because it would constitute a total repudiation of everything they have stood for. Instead of admitting that they choose the easier route of distorting facts, an art they could easily have learned from their bedfellow, Mikhail Sergeyevich Gorbachev.

It will always amaze me that Americans were so smitten with Gorbachev when his own people were not. Even though it is clear the Soviet people prefer Boris Yeltsin, these smitten Americans refuse to let go of Gorbachev as their hero. The droolers and Super Droolers are still trying to give him credit for engineering the fall of communism in the Soviet empire.

In truth, the Soviet people rejected communism in spite of Gorbachev. He could not do anything about it. Lest anyone doubt that Gorbachev was more a communist and an opportunist than a reformer, consider these facts: (1) He publicly reaffirmed his loyalty to the Communist party immediately upon resuming power after the failed coup—it was only when Boris Yeltsin demanded he do so that he abandoned his allegiance to the party. (2) During the coup, Gorbachev was portrayed as a victim of communist hardliners. But the people who orchestrated the so-called coup were handpicked by and confidants of Mikhail Gorbachev. No one has ever accused Gorbachev of being stupid. He was more than intimately aware of the politics of those eight thugs when he deliberately surrounded himself with them. He had to know that they were extreme hardliners and yet chose them as his principal advisers and personally elevated most of them to their leadership positions. Don't forget that Gorbachev brought troops into Moscow six months before the coup to prevent peaceful pro-Yeltsin demonstrations. (3) The true believers in reform, such as Eduard Shevardnadze, resigned and publicly disassociated themselves with the hardline elements of the Soviet leadership under the direction of Gorbachev. When push came to shove, Gorbachev demonstrated his true colors by siding with his inner circle of hardliners rather than Shevardnadze, the democratic reformers, and the suffering people of the Soviet Union themselves. (4) When the republics asserted their independence, he squashed them with unadulterated military terrorism. (5)The liberals' darling prince of peace never once decelerated his production of nuclear and conventional weapons throughout this so-called period of perestroika and glasnost—in fact, the Soviets' level of buildup was exponentially greater than ours, even during Ronald Reagan's years of buildup. But you won't ever hear that from most of the media. Here are the facts (from a column by Mona Charen): During the Gorbachev years alone the Soviets increased their number of ICBMs by 715, compared to the United States' 70—a ratio of 10 to 1 in favor of the Soviets; during that period they added 270 long-range bombers compared to our 103; they built 490 submarine-based ballistic missiles while we built 200; they built 54 nuclear submarines compared to our 24; and they produced 13,100 multiple rocket launchers compared to our 1,635. (6) Despite the fact that Gorbachev had announced nominal political changes in the past few years, absolutely no substantive economic reform took place while his people were starving. (7) The fact that Gorbachev did not implement these true economic reforms and disavow the Communist party prior to his attempted ouster is proof positive that he wasn't going to make any more changes than he absolutely had to. The argument that he couldn't have made those changes given the hardline opposition among his own Cabinet is disprovable on its face by mere reference to the fact that Yeltsin made those changes without even being in control of the central government. In other words, the fact that Yeltsin, with the aid of a few tanks and a few thousand rebellious people, was able to break down the will of these hapless Stalinists proves that Gorbachev could have done it anytime he wanted to. He had infinitely more power at his disposal than Yeltsin had ever thought about having at the time. The inescapable fact is that Gorbachev's heart was not in it. And he was certainly not converted even after the attempted coup and his temporary return to power. The misguided fellow still believes in communism; he was raised on it. His wife was a university professor of Marxism. He is apparently incapable of understanding a market economy; like all Marxist/Leninists, he has been brainwashed for so long that he has a learning deficiency when it comes to political freedom and capitalism. It devastated Gorbachev to have to acquiesce to Yeltsin's demands, but he had no choice. Moreover, Gorbachev did not voluntarily implement true reforms precisely because he knew what would happen to his power base. Dictatorial power is only compatible with a totalitarian government. No leader can enjoy such unfettered authority under a democratic system, including Boris Yeltsin— which I am sure is perfectly fine with him.

The hardliners apparently weren't completely satisfied with Gorbachev either, otherwise they probably wouldn't have attempted his ouster. They weren't satisfied with him because in their view he was yielding too much to the reform forces as evidenced by the proposed Union Agreement. The truth is that Gorbachev wanted to have it both ways—while being a committed communist, his major concern was his own power. In trying to please everyone, he pleased no one (except the droolers and Super Droolers of this country).

Everybody thinks we Gorbachev critics are disappointed because we won't have Gorbachev around to criticize anymore. That is utter nonsense. We are happier rejoicing for the people of the Commonwealth of Independent States, who are the true winners here, than we are in criticizing the failed ideology of communism and those who have stubbornly adhered to it. It is the left which has disappointment and disillusionment in store. After praising socialism, collectivism, and, yes, even communism (to wit: liberal economic guru, Harvard professor John Kenneth Galbraith) for all of these decades, they are going to be lost. Before they might have argued that the Soviet system, in terms of its production and distribution of economic resources, was not inferior to ours, but that such an opinion was a propagandized and fabricated version of the right wing, which in their view was simply paranoid about communism. Now that the empirical evidence is in, they can no longer hide behind such inane analysis. This is a victory for the people, for their freedom and independence and thus for political conservatism, which champions every one of those things.

The time for worldwide jubilation and celebration was the day the Soviet Union disintegrated. Gorbachev's ouster has given the best reason in the world to have that one final, but sincere, Gorbasm. For now that the communist regime, one of the most murderous in the history of the world, has imploded, there truly is a chance for lasting peace.

THE FRAUD OF HOMELESSNESS
ADVOCACY

Ronald Reagan and his policies created America's homeless.
That's the message homeless advocates and the liberal media
have been pumping out for the last decade. The very word
homeless hardly existed before Ronald Reagan became President.
It became a household word—excuse the pun—because some
way had to be found to discredit Reagan's policies and shift
attention from the economic recovery he helped bring about.

Until 1985, I was unaware of the extent to which the homeless
were being exploited for propaganda purposes. I was living in
Sacramento then, and was at home one Thanksgiving quietly
watching the half-time show of a football game on television.
Suddenly, some local reporterette interrupted the show with a
report on how the homeless were spending Thanksgiving in the
shelters. She interviewed an unshaven, unkempt, bedraggled
homeless guy stuffing food into his mouth as if he hadn't eaten
for years and might never again. The implied message of her
report was that while the television audience might be prosperous and warm at home, they dare not enjoy it as long as there
were people living in conditions of such squalor.

That burned me up. The homeless man on my TV screen

wasn't in that condition because of anything I had done or because I didn't care. I hadn't done anything to cause his homelessness. The fact that I had a home and a turkey wasn't the reason he was in a shelter, any more than cleaning my dinner plate as a child would feed the starving Chinese. But why was this homeless man in that shelter? Could he perhaps have been even partially responsible for his plight? It would have been totally unthinkable to this reporterette to pose that question.

Now, you people should understand that I am not some bastion of noncompassion, without any concern for my fellow man. But what galls me is something many people have learned when trying to help the homeless, even though such experiences are never reported in the media. When you try to help them, they often refuse. I've been accosted on the streets of New York City by homeless people asking for money. I sometimes have offered to take them to a diner and buy them a cheeseburger. They've refused. Why? Because many of these "starving" people have other plans for the money they want from me and you.

My next encounter with Homeless Hype came on an abnormally cold day in Sacramento. A giant rally organized to protest homeless policies was ruined when none of the homeless showed up. They weren't idiots; they didn't want to come out in the cold. But the local television crews did, and they had to salvage some kind of story. They panned the empty plaza in front of City Hall and mournfully explained that the homeless would soon show up at the plaza to protest for their rights. As in Tom Wolfe's brilliant novel *The Bonfire of the Vanities*, the television cameras were there to tell the story the media wanted to tell rather than what actually happened.

It was at about this time that I first realized the hidden agenda behind much of the homeless advocacy efforts. Homeless advocates enjoyed having a problem that provided them a platform to point the finger of blame at Ronald Reagan, the achievers of America, and the free enterprise system. And at the same time, they could peddle the guilt generated by their activities to get federal funding to set up their own version of the "poverty Pentagon" that black conservative Robert Woodson talks about.

Oh, how they relished blaming Reagan administration policies, including the mythical reductions in HUD's budget for public housing, for creating all of the homeless! Budget cuts? There were no budget cuts! The budget figures show that actual construction of public housing INCREASED during the Reagan years. The only reductions in HUD's budget occurred under Jimmy Carter's administration, despite his grandiose plans to pour yet more money into failed housing projects.

But there is a deeper motive at work in the constant attention focused on the homeless and the plethora of misinformation disseminated about them. The homeless are being used as a prop by liberals for the resurrection of class envy in America. The media folks have fallen for this completely. It fits in with their desire to always display their good intentions and their genuine concern for the downtrodden. So long as something makes them look good and imbued with an empty well of compassion, to hell with the facts—and with anyone who dares to defy them by exposing those facts.

When I left Sacramento to move to New York for my national show, I resolved to do a bit on how the homeless were being exploited in furtherance of a liberal agenda. What I needed was a song—an appropriately hokey yet thematically correct song which itself would define the purpose of the Homeless Update. My first idea was "The Boll Weevil Song" because of the chorus: "I'm lookin' for a home . . . lookin' for a home." I wasn't thrilled and said so on the air. I just causally mentioned that I couldn't start the Update until I found just the right theme.

A couple of days later I received in the mail a pristine 45 RPM copy of a 1950s recording by one Clarence "Frogman" Henry, titled, "Ain't Got No Home." I said, "What's this?" I'd never heard of it. As a DJ I had played everything from the grooveyard of forgotten favorites that even came close to being a hit and I had never heard of this song. So I stashed it in the back of my mailbox and forgot about it. Two weeks went by and still no satisfactory theme was found.

Meanwhile my mailbox was beginning to look like a trash compactor so I started throwing stuff out. In the process I almost tossed that 45 in the garbage. But something, I don't know what, made me do a double take. I stared at it, figured it was a long shot, and asked Frank D'Elia, a supervising engineer, to listen to it and tell me what he thought. He took it and I continued emptying my mailbox. About five minutes later he came racing around the corner, laughing, telling me I should hear it. I did. The rest is history. We had found our Homeless Update theme.

It was perfect, and ever since then Frogman's song has served as the official theme song for my now famous Homeless Updates. During the Rush to Excellence Tour of 1990 I was honored to have the Frogman appear on stage with me in Sacramento, where we performed the song in front of seventy-five hundred people. It was a hoot.

In my Homeless Updates I have pounded home three themes, which I'd like to share with you. The first is that most of what you hear about the homeless is fraudulent. Second, the so-called solutions to the homeless problem advanced by liberals usually involve nothing more than the liberals' age-old solution for all problems: throw federal money at it. Their proposed solutions do not remotely alleviate the problem, but are offered by liberals simply to assuage their unbounded feelings of guilt and to build support for their big-government agenda. Third, we must examine why people end up on the streets. Real solutions to the homelessness problem can only be found by understanding its root causes, most of which are tied to a lack of personal responsibility and a generation-long decline in respect for the traditional American values of hard work, self-reliance, and respect for the law. We should strive to help these people put their lives back together, to begin to take responsibility for their actions, and to assimilate into society. But we must also recognize that there are different types of homeless people. Some of them are mentally ill. These people are best helped by getting them into an institution.

FRAUD, LIES, AND DECEIT

One of the main targets of my Homeless Updates over the years was Mitch Snyder, the nation's premier homeless advocate. You remember Mitch. He's the guy who went on a hunger strike until President Reagan coughed up several million dollars for his shelter so he wouldn't die on network news. He finally assumed room temperature in the spring of 1990, by means that only Dr.

Jack "Jack the Dripper" Kevorkian would endorse. But during his last years Mitch committed more mischief, spread more outrageous propaganda, and simply *made up* more "facts" than almost anyone else I know in America.

What really frosts and frustrates me—a condition I call frostrating—is the ease with which the media will believe almost any "fact" about the homeless. Mitch Snyder claimed early in the Reagan years that there were three million homeless in America. This figure was accepted on faith by almost everyone in the media. You heard that number bandied about everywhere. "This country can't be doing well. We have three million homeless." All of our homeless policies were supposed to be based on this number drawn from Mitch Snyder's fevered imagination.

But in 1990 the Census Bureau decided to settle the controversy by a special census with which they planned to count the number of homeless on a given night. You would have thought that Mitch and company would have welcomed this effort. But noooo. They told the homeless not to participate. They told them that the government was only going to use the information to harass them and that they dare not participate. Who knows how many people chose not to cooperate with the Census Bureau because of that.

When the night of the Homeless Census rolled around, it took only hours for the media and others to declare it a failure. Television reporters would stand in out-of-the way corners where a few homeless were hiding and report that no Census worker had visited them.

The final Census Bureau count of the homeless was 272,000 people. In fairness, I believe the number of homeless is actually higher—closer to the Urban Institute's estimate of 600,000—but the Census Bureau's effort was helpful in dispelling the grossly exaggerated numbers of Snyder and his disciples. The reaction of the homeless advocates who had counseled the homeless not to cooperate was sputtering rage. They couldn't deal with it. They ranted and complained about the inaccuracy of the count. Just for the sake of it, let's give them that. Let's say the number was grossly undercounted . . . say by 100 percent. If we missed 100 percent of the number of homeless and arrived at 272,000, then the actual number would be 544,000. Still less than the Urban

Institute number and far less than the 3 million claimed. Still not satisfied? Okay, let's say the census missed 500 percent. We are still below 1.5 million. The point is that there is absolutely no way we have, or ever did have, 3 million homeless people in this country.

Now wouldn't you think a bunch of people who claim to want to end homelessness, who claim to really care about these people and their plight, would be ecstatic about the fact that there were far fewer homeless than was thought? Uh-uh. The truth threatened their power base. Not having 3 million homeless would mean less funding for their programs and would expose as fraudulent their claims that America would have 15 million homeless by the end of the century. They didn't want to hear any good news about the homeless, or anything to the effect that the problem wasn't as bad as they claimed. After all, if it wasn't that bad, their own meal ticket was in jeopardy.

There is nothing the homeless advocates won't say to make Americans feel guilty. Before he assumed room temperature, Mitch Snyder gave a speech at Lehigh University in Pennsylvania in which he stated—and I'm not making this up—that 45 homeless people die every second. When I saw this report, I couldn't believe it. I ran the numbers and found that for that to be true, some 23 million homeless people would die in America every year. This is a classic example of how the media doesn't check the statements of the "good intentions" crowd. Mitch Snyder was trying to "help" people, so why embarrass him with the facts. Why point out his checkered past: that he ran out on his wife and kids and was prone to telling outrageous lies about almost everything.

But distortions about the homeless aren't limited to homeless advocates such as Mitch Snyder. Some members of the New York clergy recently took out ads in *The New York Times* warning people that not doing everything possible for the homeless was the equivalent of denying Mary and Joseph a room at the inn. What unmitigated gall! Imagine comparing the Virgin Mary and Joseph, a gainfully employed carpenter, with some street people. Let's not forget why Mary and Joseph were traveling that night. They were going to register to pay their taxes. They were taxpayers!

The Way Things Ought to Be

Homeless advocates aren't satisfied with comparing the homeless to the Virgin Mary. They want to use them as vehicles in their effort to portray America as an uncaring society. When it was announced that the Democratic convention would be held in New York in the summer of 1992, there were newspaper reports that Mayor David Dinkins—I call him General Dinkins—would make sure that the streets were cleaned and the homeless encouraged not to congregate near the convention site.

As you might expect, the homeless advocates went ballistic. They not only demanded that the homeless not be kept off the streets, but that the news media be encouraged to show them in their squalor and beam the images across the nation! It would be another opportunity to blame the Republicans for the plight of our inner cities.

The homeless-rights crowd is even trying to indoctrinate America's young people with homeless propaganda. The Smithsonian Institution, the nation's premier taxpayer-supported museum, is sponsoring a new exhibit on the homeless. Visitors become "performers" in the exhibit. They can lie in a morgue and pretend to be a dead homeless person. They can fight off an attacker and get arrested. They can even listen to a prostitute having sex in a box next to them! How charming. What a beautiful thing. No doubt teachers will delight in taking their classes through this exhibit and educating them about the homeless and prostitution.

Teachers in classrooms all over America are bombarding young skulls full of mush with homeless propaganda. A caller told me that when his six-year-old daughter came home from school one day and he asked her what she had learned, she replied piteously, "I learned that if Daddy gets fired, we'll all be homeless soon!" Kids are being told that all Americans are only a paycheck away from homelessness. Nonsense! We will never have a greater percentage of homeless than we have now, as long as the Democrats don't get into the White House or unless more cities pass rent control.

The tide is finally starting to turn against homeless hysteria. In the 1980s, many public parks were turned over to the homeless so they could sleep in them. The homeless have turned them into such pigsties that the public is demanding they be reclaimed.

Tompkins Square Park in New York City had become a center for drug dealers who were helping to spread AIDS by passing out dirty needles. The homeless were finally evicted after a riot. O'Hare International Airport in Chicago used to let the homeless sleep in the terminals. Now, only those with tickets can enter them after ten o'clock at night. The American people are fed up with the constant barrage of homeless stories that have nothing to do with the real causes of homelessness. They are saying enough is enough.

LIBERAL FEEL-GOOD SOLUTIONS

Liberals delight in proposing solutions to problems such as homelessness that make them look good, but they do *nothing* to solve the problem. Take the actor Martin Sheen. His portrayal of Mitch Snyder in a TV movie about the homeless inspired him to sleep on a sewer grate one night to show his solidarity with their plight.

What good did that do? It merely attracted attention to Martin Sheen. Liberals think the solution for anything is simply caring. I'm here to tell you that caring alone doesn't mean diddly squat. Caring is the first step, but for it to be more than empty rhetoric, action must follow. Sleeping on a sewer grate for one night amounts to nothing more than histrionics and publicity seeking. Martin Sheen got up off that sewer grate the next morning and went back to his luxurious home in swanky Malibu.

We didn't hear from Mr. Sheen again until he became the honorary mayor of Malibu in the spring of 1989. He promptly declared Malibu a haven for all displaced species, whether they be animals, birds, or the homeless. He declared that all would be welcome in Malibu.

Well, I like to illustrate the absurd by being absurd. I decided to test Mayor Sheen's sincerity, so I announced on the air that I was organizing a caravan of buses to take the homeless to Malibu. I made arrangements with our affiliate in Santa Barbara, for example, to bus the homeless down to Malibu for a day. This drew national attention, including an article in *The New York Times* in which I was accused of pulling a stunt. It bothered me that my actions were so misunderstood. I was simply trying to illustrate a point. Liberals like Mayor Sheen don't really want to have the homeless live in their town. They just want to demonstrate that they care, through such empty gestures as declaring Malibu a homeless haven. When the residents of Malibu learned what Comandante Sheen had done, they naturally went crazy. Johnny Carson, who lives in Malibu, questioned whether Mr. Sheen had it all together upstairs. I had made my point.

Mr. Sheen has plenty of company in promoting false, feel-good solutions to the homeless crisis. Take Project Dignity, a community organization in Orange County, California. The homeless in Orange County like to drag all their worldly possessions with them in shopping carts, which they "liberate" from supermarket parking lots. Now, supermarket owners are naturally unhappy about losing their carts, which cost an average of $120 apiece.

Every so often they would ask the police to round up shopping carts that had been stolen from them. The folks at Project Dignity were outraged. How dare the police take away their residence of choice! "That's all they have," they bleated. "How insensitive and callous!" Project Dignity set out to end this injustice. They raised money to buy the homeless their own shopping carts. They spared no effort in this project. Once the shopping carts were purchased they were color-coded so that each homeless person would know which cart was his.

The carts were, however, different in one respect. The homeless, you see, don't always understand the principle of leverage. They would roll their carts along until they reached a curb. Then, instead of putting their foot on the rear axle to lift the cart up, they would jam the cart against the curb harder and harder until it cleared the curb. So, Project Dignity considerately put extra rubber on the wheels of their carts to enable the homeless to abuse their carts with impunity.

This whole affair boggled my mind. How is it, I asked, that it is compassionate for one human being to say to another, "I love you, I really care for you, so here's a shopping cart"? What kind of compassion is that? The solution is to find some way to address the problems that made this person homeless, help him clean up his life, and teach him to access opportunity. It is a total insult to think that giving a homeless person a shopping cart is contributing to the solution to the problem.

But I guess once you have a worthless concept of help and assistance, most of your ideas will be skewed. Again, Project Dignity. Early in 1992, *Newsweek* reported that Project Dignity had produced a video they dubbed "Dumpster Dining." This video is shown at homeless shelters because most homeless people do not have VCRs hooked up in their shopping carts (unless they live in South Central Los Angeles). It actually demonstrates what should and should not be eaten out of trash dumpsters! Do you get that, folks? A group which claims to have more compassion than you do produces a video on dumpster nutrition. And with typical liberal logic: they advise the homeless not to get food from dumpsters—"but if you must, here's what not to eat."

Well, heck, why bother telling them not to do it? It's the same as saying, "Don't steal a shopping cart from the supermarket. But if you do, make sure nobody sees you." The next thing you know Project Dignity will be demanding that we install incline ramps and handlebars so that the disabled homeless will have easier access to dumpsters. How else are they going to get in and out of the things? Oh, and there should be a flag or some other warning device on dumpsters so that the guys in the garbage trucks will know a homeless person is rummaging around in the dumpster. Otherwise the homeless will be dumped and compacted. This of course would not be a hazard had they not designed auto dumping during the Reagan years.

But you see, the liberals don't want the homeless to hold a job that has any real promise. They prefer to accommodate and humor them by making it easier for them to stay in their present condition. That's why they vigorously advocate a constitutional right to beg. And Judge Leonard Sand so ruled when he declared that the homeless should be allowed to accost subway riders as a First Amendment right of free speech. I simply refuse to believe that this nation's Founding Fathers, who were all achievers and believed in encouraging rather than deterring the achievements of others, meant to write into that sacred document that bums have a right to invade public property and harass people for money.

When he was mayor of New York, Ed Koch would sometimes try to offer the homeless a life outside of begging. His aides would go down to City Hall Park and offer them jobs, bus them to interviews, hold jobs open for them. All to no avail. The simple fact is that some—not all—of the homeless consciously choose their plight. They don't want to work. It's a hard fact to swallow, but some fellow members of our species just refuse to accept the responsibility of being human beings. Why should we romanticize what they are doing?

ANTIHOMELESS LIBERALS

I want to make clear my belief that many of the homeless can and do want to pull themselves out of their misery. They just are getting all the wrong messages from their self-appointed advocates and the media. Consider the months-long strike of the New York *Daily News* last year. The *Daily News* was desperate to keep its circulation up in order to retain its advertisers. But many obstacles were placed in their way. They couldn't sell from newsstands because the unions had pressured the owners not to carry the paper. So management hired the homeless to distribute the paper and let them keep all the money they took in from selling it on street corners. Well, the homeless welcomed this opportunity and some of them even became mini-entrepreneurs by selling chewing gum and pencils along with the papers. What was the reaction of the homeless advocates? Why, this was exploitation! The homeless aren't prepared, they said, to handle this kind of activity and it is unconscionable not to give them a real, permanent job. This reaction showed the twisted logic of the liberal mindset. Here people were learning valuable lessons by selling papers. They were taught that hard work is rewarded, they were earning income without having to beg for it, and they were learning that there were opportunities to sell other products on the street. But this was viewed as dangerous by liberals. They don't want people becoming self-sufficient. Liberals can't stay in power if people become self-sufficient. The Poverty Industry would have fewer clients, and the meal ticket of a lot of social workers would no longer be punched.

We now know that the liberals don't like the homeless selling papers on the streets. So what do they want them to do? Picking up cans and bottles for recycling is acceptable. The homeless in New York and other cities fill their shopping carts with cans and bottles and drag them into local supermarkets. But that's not all they do. They loiter around, wander through the aisles, and block the checkout stands as they sort their junk. The markets are required by law to take in products for recycling, but they shouldn't have to put up with people who disrupt their businesses. Besides, picking up cans is no way to earn a living, and is unlikely to provide a homeless person with enough money to get a real apartment. But that's fine with the liberals. Liberals will let the homeless have pocket money, but nothing that gives them a real chance to get out of their condition.

THE REAL HOMELESS AGENDA

I want you to pay attention. This section is important, if you are to understand the mindset behind all of these outrageous stories. Notice that in all of them the so-called homeless crisis is used by the left to drag down the American way of life. That is the common theme in all of them. The message is that the American people are at fault, and the downtrodden—whether they are drug abusers or homeless people—can't be at fault. You're never supposed to blame the downtrodden. Who, then, should we blame? It's true that some of the homeless have lost their homes. But the government's disastrous policies of urban renewal are responsible for destroying many of the single-room-occupancy hotels they used to live in. And many of the homeless have only themselves to blame. They either aren't willing to assume the responsibilities that go with being a citizen or they are mentally ill or abusing drugs or alcohol. Of course, we have to find some way to help them, but is it necessary to lie to them or ourselves about their own contribution to their condition? Their actions often are responsible for their problems. Unless we recognize and are honest about that, we aren't going to be able to clean up our streets and help repair these wrecked lives.

SOLUTIONS

I sometimes get callers who say, "So, Rush, you have all these complaints about the homeless advocates, but what's your solution?" They obviously haven't been listening. The solutions to the homeless problem are rooted in common sense, which is why the liberals will never accept them.

Here is my Five-Point Program to deal with the homeless.

One, we must first have an *honest* count of how many people we're talking about. It's more than the Census Bureau's 272,000 counted in 1990, but it's certainly nowhere near the 3 million figure drawn from Mitch Snyder's fevered imagination. Let's find out, once and for all.

Two, we need to make a cold-eyed assessment of the reasons why people are homeless, realize that there are different categories of homeless people, and fashion separate solutions for the various categories. Analyst Peter Rossi estimates that some 40 percent of the homeless are alcohol or drug abusers. Another 25 percent or so are people with serious mental problems. Others, and this will be controversial, *CHOOSE* to be homeless. Mark my words, people would be surprised how many people choose to be on the streets and won't go into shelters or other places of refuge regardless of how much people beg them. We're told that "no one would choose that lifestyle." Well, I'm here to tell you that some do.

You don't believe me that some homeless people choose to live that way? Take the case of Richard Kreimer, a homeless man in Morristown, New Jersey, who liked to frequent the public library there. He would stare at patrons, and many had to leave the library because of the strong stench he gave off. He refused to bathe, and would wander about the library as if it were his living room. The library passed a rule barring the homeless from disrupting its activities. Mr. Kreimer sued, and won not only the right to permanently reside in the library during open hours but a $150,000 settlement! It is an outrageous decline in civil standards when a library has to kowtow to the likes of Mr. Kreimer, but library officials must have at least expected that $150,000 would rid them of his presence. After all, he could now afford an apartment! But no, Mr. Kreimer is still haunting the streets of

251

Morristown and still visiting the library. He says the money isn't enough to let him buy a house, and he has a right to live any way he chooses. I rest my case.

Three, for those who are drug or alcohol abusers, we have to find some way to get them into rehabilitation clinics. I'm talking about using tough love here. Telling the homeless they are responsible for at least part of their plight and that they can't forever blame the rest of society might be a start at forcing them to confront the misery caused largely by their own behavior.

Four, those that are mentally unbalanced or ill should be institutionalized. People say we don't have enough beds for them. Well, we could. There are a lot of military bases and hospitals that will be closing down and they could be used to house some of the homeless. Some of the mentally ill homeless can function in society if they take their medication. But many don't, and the ACLU blocks those who would force them, as a condition of their being allowed to remain in society, to take the medicine that separates them from paranoia, schizophrenia, or deep depression.

Five, the able-bodied homeless who are not mentally ill must be educated in how to access the boundless opportunities in the American economy. I'm convinced that a lot of people simply don't know what's available out there and how it is possible to find a job and work your way up if you are willing to accept responsibility for your life. I know what it's like to be on the bottom. I've been broke. I've been fired seven times from jobs. And I don't even have a college degree. But I didn't blame anyone else for my problems. I knew that if I didn't try to solve them on my own or with the help of friends or family members, no one else was going to take care of me.

My solutions to the homeless problem are no panacea, but they are realistic. They do not emanate from a misguided obsession with blaming the American way of life, mythical Reagan budget cuts, or the inherent unfairness of our free enterprise system. Real problems deserve real solutions, not name-calling.

What is our greatest obstacle to solving the homeless problem? It is simple, but it will shock you. Simply put, the liberals don't want the problem solved. They are interested in power, and the way they maintain their power is to build up a giant network of government programs that employ their friends; a welfare state that constantly lobbies for its own expansion. The Poverty Pimps don't want solutions to these problems.

If you don't believe me, look at how they've treated HUD Secretary Jack Kemp's ideas to replace failed public-housing policies with the politics of hope. Jack Kemp has visited the ghettos and barrios of this country. He has talked with public-housing tenants, and his proposals are based on what *they* told him would improve their lives. He has asked Congress to approve tenant ownership or management of housing projects, enterprise zones for the inner cities, and vouchers to enable the poor to find their own private housing outside of the projects. The Democratic Congress has rejected and blocked every one of these initiatives, although following the L.A. riots, some Democrats opportunistically talked—*talked*—about a bipartisan plan to do what Kemp has been advocating for years.

Remember the reaction to the New York *Daily News* offering the homeless jobs selling papers, jobs which allowed them to keep 100 percent of the money they took in? The screams of the liberals and homeless advocates were deafening. *The homeless were being exploited. Some of them might even be in danger of overcoming their homeless status!*

The leaders of the alms race and the hate-America left will continue to focus their homeless efforts on blame rather than solutions. Their primary scapegoats are, of course, capitalism, the decade of greed (the 1980s), and the wealthy. Topping their list of villains will always be Ronald Reagan. But the truth is that many of the homeless are responsible for their own plight. That doesn't mean we should abandon them; real efforts aimed at helping them clean up their lives will do a lot more than false compassion. But if homeless advocates are so intent on assessing blame and if they really want to know who is most guilty of prolonging the suffering of the homeless, they need do no more than look in the mirror.

WHAT HAPPENED TO HOLLYWOOD?

When I was growing up, Hollywood was a magical land which could transport you to places you had never imagined. Its movies made you laugh, cry, and sometimes even think. Walt Disney, John Ford, Alfred Hitchcock, and others had an instinctive grasp of what middle-class America wanted to see. Movies also became America's most successful export, carrying American values and perspectives all around the world.

Today, Hollywood is in trouble. Box office sales are way down. The reason isn't so much the recession. It's that Hollywood has forgotten who its audience is. It now makes a lot of movies that disparage American institutions and traditions or which promote wacko leftism. Hollywood has become part of the dominant media culture. They love to make fun of what people like you and I hold dear. They make fun of people who believe in God. They ridicule the traditional family, heterosexuality, and monogamy. They disparage American heroes. Ben Stein, a writer in Hollywood, says that whenever businessmen are portrayed on TV they are usually villains—greedy crooks like Ivan Boesky or egomaniacs like Michael Milken.

The irony is that Hollywood loves to rail against capitalism, greed, and the profit motive, but many of their problems can be traced to the greed of people in Hollywood itself. The Steven Spielberg movie *Hook* grossed some $180 million, yet it probably lost money because of the huge salaries that Robin Williams and other stars collected. Orion Pictures had three huge hits recently, including the Academy Award winner *The Silence of the Lambs.* Yet, the studio is losing money because the stars and directors are taking huge fees in their deals. As Billy Crystal quipped during the last Academy Award ceremonies, "My God, they can't afford another hit."

Still, I can't shed any tears for the producers of those films. They wanted those stars and they agreed to their demands. That's their business. But for people in Hollywood to then turn around and criticize the rest of America for being "greedy" is the height of hypocrisy. These Hollywood moguls sit around and criticize people who make money, and they are out there doing exactly the same thing. And the deals they cut dwarf what people in Hollywood used to make, including their number one enemy, Ronald Reagan.

HOLLYWOOD GOES POLITICAL

It's not enough that Hollywood has to attack the traditions and institutions that have made this country great. Now stars are suddenly instant experts on everything. They try to tell us how to vote, and, of course, increasing numbers of them go to Washington to testify before Congress on this or that liberal cause. Who can forget the sight of Jessica Lange, Sally Field, and Sissy Spacek testifying on farm problems? Their qualifications? Why, they had just played farm gals in movies about the injustices on the farm. Meryl Streep showed up to wail, "What are we doing to our children!" as she joined forces with misguided new-agers who were trying to get the chemical Alar off the market. Apple growers use Alar to maintain a red robust color on apples and it has been proven harmless. Still, the expert Ms. Streep and her band of paternalistic whiners nearly destroyed the apple industry. Next we'll have Willie Nelson testifying on IRS reform, Arnold Schwarzenegger explaining the feasibility of manned

255

space flights to Mars, and Anthony Hopkins giving expert analysis on why Jeffrey Dahmer did it.

Carroll O'Connor and Rob Reiner did a commercial for Jerry Brown. Jim Garner made a horrendous commercial against an initiative in California that would have required that political districts be drawn fairly. He showed pictures of the *Exxon Valdez* disaster and oily seals and said the plan could lead to an environmental disaster. This was absolute misinformation designed to preserve the current power base which is friendly to Hollywood's causes. It was nothing but pure scaremongering, but it worked because the other side didn't have any money. The initiative for fair districts lost. Martin Sheen, as honorary mayor of Malibu, proclaimed his community a haven for the homeless (and dolphins), then promptly refused to admit any of the homeless onto his property, which is typical of the left. They devise these utopian schemes, then exempt themselves from them because they wouldn't be caught dead actually doing any of the things they recommend. Sort of like the House of Representatives.

The list of Hollywood propagandists for leftist causes is a long one. You've got Ted Danson running around saying the planet will be destroyed by pollution in ten years. Bob Barker of *The Price Is Right* is an animal rights activist. Mike Farrell and Ed Asner flack for the communist rebels in El Salvador—or wherever they can find any these days. In fact this is not all bad. I think we should preserve at least two communists as instructors at each major university in the country so we never forget what those people were about. But that's another story. For this chapter, we'll have to settle for the bearded, Castro-type commies like Daniel Ortega of Nicaragua Sandinista fame. Peter, Paul, and Mary loved him and his wife. They had him up to their New York apartment (I never knew they lived together) back in the mid-eighties, when Reagan was poised to nuke the world, and sang peace songs while eager attendees sipped white wine and croissants laced with baked brie smothered in almonds (gee, all that fat). Then they all went shopping for sunglasses. Ortega spent two thousand dollars, while his people were eating cockroaches marinated in mud. But he was a good little commie, opposed to Reagan and all, so he was okay. Then, of course, there is Hanoi Jane Fonda on every leftist cause you can name. Most recently she was savagely attacked by jealous feminists for daring to have had breast implants. Jane's main thrust these days is the pro-choice movement. Her battle cry is, "Keep the government out of our wombs!" Sounds like another tasteless Kennedy joke to me.

Oliver Stone is in a class by himself. His films, whether it's *Salvador*, or *Wall Street*, *Platoon*, or *JFK*, are all anti-American creeds. Now I hear from Ollie North that Stone is secretly trying to buy the rights to his story. I can just imagine what kind of a psychopath they would paint North as. There are three—count them, three—big actors in Hollywood who will admit to being conservatives: Charlton Heston, Arnold Schwarzenegger, and Tom Selleck. And Selleck gave money to Paul Tsongas and Jerry Brown, so I would be hard pressed to consider him a conservative, notwithstanding his promo for the conservative periodical *National Review*.

What bugs me is that when Ted Danson talks about the environment or Meryl Streep hypes organic foods, no one ever questions their motives, their knowledge, or their qualifications to speak out on these subjects. There are reasons for this.

Today, there is a whole slew of TV shows based on interviews and profiles of celebrities. They can survive only if the stars cooperate with them. *Entertainment Tonight* would be Entertainment Canceled if it didn't treat the stars with kid gloves. If they were not catered to and fawned over, the stars wouldn't show up. I'm sure Mary Hart and John Tesh consider themselves real journalists and they take what they do very seriously. But in reality they are nothing but a bunch of obsequious powderpuffs for the celebrities. Aggressive journalism? Hardly. The stars can do no wrong.

Unlike politicians, who do get challenged on their political views, celebrities get a free ride. No one ever asks them how much money they make, what percentage of the gross they got for their last film, or what their sources were for some of their outrageous social, political, and environmental claims. They care, you see, and their intentions are good, so what difference does it make that they haven't the slightest idea what they're talking about? Don't misunderstand me here. These fine Americans have every right to be wrong, just as much as anyone else does. And they have the right to openly proclaim their inaccuracies because they are Americans and as such have access to the First Amendment. (For those of you in Rio Linda, that is the one that grants us freedom of speech.) The problem ensues when a fawning entertainment press refuses to challenge their claims and thereby grants them expert status on whatever cause they choose to speak.

Why do people like Ted Danson want so desperately to be involved in social causes? It's not hard to fathom. They want to express themselves, not just memorize and parrot lines from a script. Most people want to be taken seriously as human beings. They work and derive their sense of self-esteem from interacting with people as themselves, and being known for what they think and can do. Actors have a very fulfilling career on some levels, but their jobs are limited. They portray people whom they aren't. It may take great talent to do that well, but in terms of psychological health, it's often not satisfying. Some actors get enough inner satisfaction from their families or other aspects of their lives that being known for playing someone they are not doesn't bother them.

But as for others, I am convinced they are unhappy with the limitations of acting. Take Ted Danson. His job requires him to portray a rehabilitated alcoholic owner of a bar on *Cheers*. He doesn't want to be known as that kind of person. He wants to be valued for his own beliefs and opinions. That's why he and others similarly situated are such easy prey for radical leftists who enlist them to raise money and make publicity for their causes. The leftists tell the actors that they will be taken seriously as individuals if they get on the bandwagon against global warming or animal research, or some other fashionable cause.

I'm not saying that actors adopt causes they don't believe in. But they do become walking robots for them. They aren't experts on any of these issues. They only know the words that people put in their mouths. In the mid-1980s, Jane Fonda ran a mountain training academy for the Hollywood Brat Pack on how to be politically correct on the issues of the day. Can you imagine the cries of "mind control" that would come from the left if a rightist organization engaged in such activities?

This insertion of actors, America's royalty, into politics is dangerous. These people are attacking the system that helped them achieve success. Yet, they are dissatisfied with themselves and feel guilty about their success. Many of them feel they don't really deserve all those riches, so they transfer their guilt by indicting American institutions and America itself. You've heard all this mumbo-jumbo: How can America let people live in homeless shelters? How dare we bomb people in El Salvador? What gives us the right to destroy the ozone? Why, if we would just develop an understanding with the Russian people, maybe they would realize we don't want to bomb them back to the Stone Age. (Actually, the Stone Age would be a giant leap forward for most Russians.)

But these actors and the rest of the Hollywood Left still like to live the good life. Even when they are trying to relate to the world's problems they show how pampered and elitist they are. A couple of years ago there was an environmental dinner held in Los Angeles. The limos pulled up outside and many of them were left idling for an hour, spewing carbon monoxide into the air. Inside, people were served different kinds of meals. A few people got a gourmet feast to represent the small number of people in the world with middle-class lifestyles. A large number got a basic, no-frills meal. And the rest, a majority, were given a handful of rice and a small piece of fish to represent the world's poor. Well, that was a fine story for the media who were present. And again, very typical. Just how do you think the world's poor felt knowing that Hollywood stars were eating the same slop they eat every day? Rather than send Wolfgang Puck and a gazillion of his pizzas to the world's poor and treat them to an improved food situation, the stars sit around and eat slop—for a couple of minutes, anyway. If you were eating slop every day, what would you rather have, Wolfgang Puck pizzas or a bunch of Hollywood stars eating slop with you? If you were homeless, what would you rather have? A nice heated home or Martin Sheen kicking you off your sewer grate for the night so he can demonstrate how sensitive he is to your plight? In both examples, which actually happened, they accomplished nothing in terms of solving world hunger or homelessness. But for them, the concerned, the endeavors were still a splendid success. They appeared to be concerned and caring and, of course, all the cameras were there to record their compassion. That's what the Hollywood left cares most about. But remember this: Not one poor, hungry soul was made prosperous and sated. Not one homeless individual found shelter. And it is *your* fault, because you don't care enough like the Hollywood Left does.

THE SOCIALIST UTOPIANS

Now that communism has collapsed, and communist leaders like Mikhail Gorbachev are fleecing six-figure honoraria (fees, for those of you in Rio Linda) for speeches devoted to the ridiculous idea that we did not win the Cold War, it's time we reidentify today's biggest threat to the American way of life. I'm convinced it's what I call the Socialist Utopians. Despite what it sounds like, they are not a rock group from MTV or a new-age religious cult from Southern California. They are a great many people who come in a variety of shapes and sizes and who belong to this or that activist group. There is a common bond which spiritually unites these people, which is that attitude of cultural radicalism carried over from the 1960s. Theirs is an anti-American credo, which abhors American political and governmental institutions and this nation's capitalistic economy. Their value system is at war with the Judeo-Christian tradition upon which this country was founded and is centered in secular humanism and moral relativism. Theirs is the me generation, which seeks immediate gratification, presumably because there is no spiritual tomorrow. Their God is not spiritual or personal. Their God is in every fiber of nature and is impersonal. He is just as much a part of the plant

RUSH H. LIMBAUGH, III

and animal kingdom as He is a part of the human soul; thus, their pantheistic devotion to animals and the environment. Their God did not give them dominion over nature and the animal kingdom, positioning them at the top rung on the hierarchy of creation, as did the Judeo-Christian God who inspired Genesis. As their emphasis is on this world, they cling to the belief that man is morally perfectible and that Utopia on earth is achievable.

If you look at popular culture and TV shows or go to any major university you will find that the ideals of the 1960s generation are alive and well. They march under different labels now: political correctness, gender politics, peace studies. But they are all based on the same misguided premise held by the '60s radicals: that Utopia is possible. They think that a centralized governmental authority can bring us Utopia. I say that's bunk. I think it is Utopian to expect that every citizen will eat equally well on every day of the year. I think it is Utopian to expect that every citizen will be provided health care in whatever amount and to whatever degree he wants every day of the year.

I think it is Utopian to believe that we can eliminate suffering of all kinds. It is certainly an honorable goal to attempt to reduce hunger, provide health care, and diminish suffering. But it is simply not realistic to expect that every citizen will have what he considers enough good food and fine health care. It's not even possible to guarantee everyone an adequate supply of those things, because the definition of *adequate* always changes with rising affluence. The poor in America today are incredibly rich compared with the much higher percentage of poor people at the turn of the century. Why, in America, over half of those classified as poor own a dishwasher, most have a car, and nearly all have a television set. Most have enough to eat, but now we hear complaints about the quality of their food. We hear that too many fast-food joints operate in poor neighborhoods and therefore the poor aren't getting a nutritious enough diet. You can never wipe out the poor because the standard for being poor keeps rising.

Equalizing outcomes and ensuring everyone a mediocre minimum was what communism tried to accomplish. That's what the socialists tried to accomplish. They tried to produce a Utopia and failed miserably.

They failed because Utopia is impossible. Every human being

has different abilities, talents, desires, and characteristics. There is no way those differences can be equalized, other than through the use of force. I don't mean military force, but laws backed up by force, if necessary, which redistribute wealth and penalize achievement.

The Utopians believe that it's unfair that some have so much and others have so little by comparison. But that only stirs up envy and bitterness among people and doesn't create any new wealth. The way you help the poor improve their lot in life is to empower them to do it themselves. Self-reliance and achievement develop pride and breed self-reliance, respect, and motivation. It is a cliché, but it nonetheless must be said: When someone earns something by virtue of his own effort, as opposed to its being given to him, he has infinitely greater appreciation for it. We at present aren't doing enough to help people access the opportunity this country has to offer. In fact, we are in the business of punishing achievement and criticizing those who succeed for doing so. However, our current system is riddled with disincentives for people to extricate themselves from poverty status. If welfare recipients begin to earn income on their own, they risk disqualifying themselves from government assistance. Thankfully, there is a widespread movement under way to bring about welfare reform to correct some of these problems.

Regardless of what the naysayers and enemies of capitalism would have you believe, opportunity still exists in abundance. Emmanuel Modu is a young MBA from Wharton. He has written a book called *The Lemonade Stand: A Guide to Encouraging the Entrepreneur in Your Children.* He tells inspiring stories about how kids as young as ten set up their own small businesses and made something of themselves. Some sixteen-year-olds are supporting their parents on their earnings. It's easy to say that these are a few exceptional kids, but how many kids have we encouraged even to take that step? It's easy to blame Washington, Daryl Gates, Ronald Reagan, George Bush, or the system for the fact that certain people haven't succeeded in this country. Liberals say that the poor have no control over their lives, that they have no way of reaching a decent standard of living by themselves. I say we must instill in them the same spirit that lifted millions of immigrants to America out of poverty in a single generation. We have to do this not just to help the poor but to save the middle class. The middle class is being taxed to death and if it doesn't get relief soon it will no longer have the strength to support the government and keep this country afloat.

The latest Utopian scheme is called national health care. It's true our present health care system is out of control, but that should not be viewed as an indictment of the private sector. In reality, it's not at all a private system. The government pays half the bills, micromanages the rest, and stifles innovation. Does anyone really believe that we can improve our medical system by turning all of it over to the government? It would be run with the efficiency of the Post Office and the bedside manner of the IRS. This is not a criticism of the people working in government. They no doubt would like to help build Utopia. But so long as they remain in government they face the wrong incentives. They are not subject to the same pressures as are private businessmen. There is so little accountability that the primary concern of the bureaucrat is not being economically efficient or profitable— because it's not his money anyway—but self-preservation and continued employment. There's no market signal if they do something wrong. The bureaucracy is stifling and little of the money reaches the intended recipients. The administrative cost of many welfare programs in this country is 72 cents per case. For every dollar in taxes set aside for welfare recipients, only 28 cents winds up in their pockets. Yet, the Utopians still believe we have to create more government entitlements.

It is one of Limbaugh's Undeniable Truths that the more entitlement programs that are created by the Utopia industry, the poorer this country is going to get. Because trying to eliminate poverty and create Utopia by transferring wealth is an impossible quest. It is led by a group of blind, well-intentioned people whose worth in life is wrapped up in doing what they consider good works but which solve nothing. At the heart of the Utopian philosophy is the belief that man lacks the intelligence to solve his own problems. The Utopian has no faith in human ingenuity or man's ability to triumph over the odds in life. That is their justification for big government. Man must be forced into doing what is good for him by the liberal repositories of truth. The liberal Utopian will help man, in spite of himself. In truth, if the

Utopians would just redirect their focus a little bit they could feel just as worthwhile. If they would only help people help themselves, this business of trying to create Utopia might actually have a future.

The point is that we cannot merely write off the efforts of these well-wishers as innocuous exercises in goodwill, because there is a heavy societal cost to their frivolous pursuits. Their belief that absolute economic equality can be achieved entirely ignores the realities of human nature. Their attempt to equalize incomes is not philanthropic because it involves coercion. If the government confiscates the wealth of the middle class and spreads it among the poor, there is nothing compassionate flowing from the middle class. The middle class have no choice in the matter. In the process of trying to achieve Utopia the idealists cause harm to the very people they seek to help. You cannot overburden the middle and upper classes with taxes without negative consequences. Although the Utopians' foolish prejudices won't allow them to admit the obvious, it takes the investment of capital to create jobs and wealth. When nothing but disincentives haunt the entrepreneurial risk-taker at every turn, he will respond by not investing. There will be less wealth for all economic classes.

It's important that people in this country who still hold sacred our American traditions be made aware of the constant assault that is being waged on this society by its Utopian enemies. It is important that they see these people for who they are and what their goals are, and that they not be deceived by the harmless disguises they wear. Who, for instance, can be for impoverishment? No one, but the Socialist Utopians don't tell you that their agenda to end it merely spreads the misery to include more people. That is the warped thinking of the activists today. And so far they are getting away with it. The frightening thing about these people is their insidious nature. They would present much less of a threat to this society if they would simply be honest and open about their agendas. Instead, they disarm us with such harmless platitudes as "we are in favor of clean air" or "we are against poverty." People should be aware of the extent to which our way of life is under siege by an increasing number of groups with candy-coated causes, but poisonous agendas.

265

WHO NEEDS THE MEDIA WHEN THEY'VE GOT ME?

ACCOUNTABILITY, RESPONSIBILITY, AND ATTITUDE

THE PROBLEM IN WRITING A SPECIFIC CHAPTER ABOUT THE MEDIA IS that it is difficult to avoid redundancy. The Media is referenced throughout this book, although not always by name. For example, in "The State of the Union" chapter I wrote pointedly about how I am tired of hearing about how the problems of homelessness, drugs, AIDS, and the economy are the fault of the middle class. How did I hear about all those things? The Media, obviously. In the Rodney King chapter I expressed my anger and frustration with the message that seemed to dominate The Media: that we should try to understand the rioters and looters. In other chapters I wrote about the "dominant media culture," a term coined in the mid-1980s by TV critic John Corry, which ridicules and impugns the things I believe in and hold dear, and how it permeates not just the news, but books, newspapers, television shows, and Hollywood. Still, there are things I have not said which I believe are appropriate and necessary.

The problems of The Media lie in the areas of accountability, responsibility, and attitude. First, accountability and responsibility. Because of the First Amendment, government regulation of the media is impossible, as it should be. Yet, it should be noted here that many highfalutin reporters relish the idea of regulating Big Business and its executives because of their inherent belief that anything to do with Big Business is dishonest. Many in The Media are the first to demand government regulation of other businesses to protect the public from cheats and dishonest practitioners, yet they feign total surprise and incredulity when asked about regulating those same abuses and characteristics in The Media business.

This means that The Media must be accountable and responsible to and for itself, which we all know is a fallacious premise at best. "No, let's let Congress investigate itself. That is the only way to get to the bottom of this check business," or words to that effect, were uttered by countless congressional leaders and we all laughed. The problem here is that members of The Media will not even admit that they have an impact on the outcome of events, so why should the subject of accountability and responsibility even come up?

Attitude is another problem. One of the things that has always bothered me about people in the media is that they pretend they aren't in a business. They think they work for a public service. That is why so many of them don't care if the customers are happy or not. When market realities force the networks to cut back on their news divisions, journalists act as if life as we know it is ending. Theirs, you see, is a higher calling. They demand exemption from bottom-line concerns and openly criticize the owners (risk-takers and investors) of the very companies which employ them when those people make decisions to keep the business running profitably. Journalists, you see, are the sacred guarantors of the First Amendment.

Well, excuse me, but who do they think they are? They are working stiffs in a business that is supposed to supply information and sometimes entertainment. They have a responsibility to their customers, but in reality they seldom accept that. Journalists will not admit that they change the outcome of events, that their presence often dictates what happens. Protestors often time their events for the evening news, and reporters often coach crowds on

267

how to act and what to say. No other business in the world that I'm aware of is filled with people who hold their customers in such disdain.

But beyond their denial that they are involved in a business, even more appalling is The Media's attitude of self-importance. They have adopted a religious zeal regarding The Media, not the institution of The Media but themselves, as sacrosanct. They behave as if they consider their jobs more important than life itself. There is no higher allegiance fathomable than their allegiance to their First Amendment God.

Let me give you an illustration. During the Gulf war, CNN correspondents Bernard Shaw and John Holliman were bravely occupying their post at the Al Rasheed Hotel in Baghdad. They got a lot of kudos for their bravery and courage, but we now know the U.S. planes had been very careful to avoid their hotel. They didn't make a big deal of it, so Bernard Shaw and John Holliman were viewed as big heroes for being so courageous.

Well, after Shaw came back to the United States, the government asked to debrief him, so that he might share with them any valuable information he might have gleaned while reporting courageously and bravely from inside a hotel which was never targeted for destruction. He refused. He said doing that would compromise his integrity and neutrality as a journalist. CNN is a global network, he said. We can't take sides.

Can't take sides? — — —! These were American journalists and they can't take sides? That attitude illustrates the haughty arrogance of people in the news business. If they don't realize that their freedom lies in the United States of America and that therefore they should defend this nation, they are hopelessly misguided and, may I suggest, flirting with megalomania. Keep in mind that the military was not requesting that the correspondents distort their reporting, merely that they share with our side any intelligence they may have incidentally acquired while in enemy territory.

This is why, my good friends, that the profound anger and distrust of our political institutions felt by so many Americans now includes The Media as well. When people say they feel betrayed and sold out by the old-line political institutions of the country, they include The Media in the mix. The Media is now considered just another part of the arrogant, condescending, elite, and out-of-touch political structure which has ignored the people and their concerns and interests. People are beginning to view the media not as a watchdog against governmental abuses of power but as an institution which is itself engaging in the abuse of power.

We are living in momentous times. Institutions and traditions are changing—in some cases dying—right before our eyes. Jeff Greenfield of ABC News made the point to me that it is no longer the Big Three automakers, the Big Three networks, and possibly not even the Big Two political parties anymore. These institutions are being fractured and are falling apart and are being replaced by enterprises with new approaches and ideals. Talk Radio, for example, is to The Media what Ross Perot is to the two political parties. And The Media reacts the same way to Talk Radio as staid, entrenched politicians of both parties reacted to Perot.

As an example: There were stories in Los Angeles and Atlanta during the late spring and early summer of 1992 which examined the "threat to an informed public" posed by Talk Radio and its "irresponsible" hosts. This is obligatory and generally occurs soon after Talk Radio is thought to have influenced some event, such as the House Bank scandal or congressional pay-raise issue. The Media, with blatant audacity, skewers this branch of The Media, saying that its audience is composed of ignorant, easily misguided suckers who are constantly worked up into a lather by reactionary, uninformed hosts. The folly is astounding. The arrogance and condescension—two prime characteristics of liberals—are undeniable. Here we have a bunch of sniveling, hypocritical journalists all bent out of shape because people are being influenced? Perhaps what we have is a case of jealousy and envy. In all other cases, they would champion the involvement of other branches of The Media. Why? Because they control those branches, and the people themselves have far less interactive involvement. With Talk Radio, there is a greater degree of audience participation. And don't forget, the people don't know what's good for them. To the extent that Talk Radio allows them a voice, that is detrimental to the public good. So there we have it. We need The Major Media in order to protect people not only from government but from themselves. Because Talk Radio allows these self-destructive, ignorant people to participate, it is harmful to the nation. Go figure.

MEDIA LIBERALISM

Just as much as the Hollywood left, elements of The Media have jumped on the bandwagon of leftist causes. The cynical journalist of the past has been replaced in many cases by an enthusiastic cheerleader for causes. This has happened for two reasons.

If you go to a journalism school today and ask the students why they are studying journalism, you'll get a standard answer: They want to make the world a better place. I would ask them, What, then, are you doing studying journalism? The job of a journalist is to chronicle events, not to stand up and cheer for one side or the other. Well, today's budding reporters and reporterettes will tell you the world is facing threats that are too dangerous to ignore. There is too much injustice and unfairness out there and this story must be told so that changes can be made.

The way this attitude and goal manifests itself is especially noteworthy. I have been amazed, for example, at how so many ridiculous claims are allowed to become conventional wisdom. Mitch Snyder used the figure of 3 million for years to denote the number of homeless people in America. It was never questioned, nor did The Media demand that he cite his source. Yet, when I announce the size of my radio audience and point out the fact that it is the largest on earth, The Media demands sources and surveys which prove it. Even after being furnished with the information, they still report that "Limbaugh *claims* to be" the most-listened-to talk show host in the country, rather than confirming it as fact. And it gets worse. Some pseudoscientist from the Doom and Gloom crowd will announce that if we don't do something about the ozone hole, 400,000 new cases of skin cancer will develop this year alone. Really? No one in The Media challenges the number. Other assorted "facts" mysteriously appear: Some lamebrain member of the Apocalyptic Elite actually said we are destroying 50 to 100 species a day—a day, folks!—by burning and clear-cutting rain forests all over the world. Not one challenge could I find from The Media. They just ran with it and blasted it all over the front pages and in editorials on the Earth Summit.

How about the myth of heterosexual AIDS? Despite endless predictions of an epidemic, it has not happened, yet each year we are hit by The Media with alarming new predictions. Why is it that whenever a corporation fires workers it is never speculated that the workers might have deserved it? Nah, all workers are flawless and all management is evil. The answer was provided by Bernard Goldberg, a reporter for CBS News' *48 Hours.* He wrote a piece in *The New York Times* which was critical of many in his own profession and which shed some light on it. He said that too many in The Media are compromised by focusing on "the good intentions" of those they cover. So what if Mitch Snyder is a little off when he says that 45 homeless people die every second (23 million per year if you run the numbers)? His intentions are good; he's only trying to help people. Well, doesn't this "good intentions" theory sort of substantiate a certain bias on the part of some in The Media? Besides, I thought it was truth, not sensitivity, they purport to safeguard.

Why does this happen?

Many journalists have gone beyond the idealism of "good intentions." Many are Utopians, trying to alter the world to fit an impossible vision. Others are just part of a liberal brat pack that thinks alike and reports the news with the same spin. During the New Hampshire primary, Hendrik Hertzberg of the *New Republic* reported that of forty-seven reporters he talked to there, every single one supported Bill Clinton. Even he, a liberal, thought that was unhealthy.

Journalists are very gullible today, and yes, even uninquiring, when it comes to their pet causes. They certainly don't exhibit the same amount of skepticism with them that they pride themselves in bringing to other stories and their sources. Journalists understand issues a little better than the Hollywood left, but too many of them are robotically hyping left-wing causes and giving credence to crisis scenarios on most of the stories on which they report. I'm not saying they shouldn't deal with such issues, but I wish we could get their views served up with just a little more humility. You would think that a fraternity that holds itself out as intellectually inclined would tend to be a bit more discriminating and a great deal less predictable and monolithic.

However, not all is lost. There are signs that some in The Media are beginning to question, if not change, some of their long-held doctrines. In the print media, *Time* magazine has suffered two giant circulation drops. One came after they made Gorbachev the Man of the Decade, one of the silliest moves I've ever seen. An award for Chump of the Decade would have been more like it, given Gorbachev's refusal to part with the fantasy that socialism will still triumph. Another big circulation drop for *Time* came after they announced that they were no longer going to report the news but would instead "interpret" it. While they were just admitting what they had already been doing, a lot of readers decided they had enough.

Time illustrates the worst of cause-oriented journalism. After Charles Alexander of *Time* was criticized for telling an audience at the Smithsonian Institution that his magazine was enlisting in the environmental movement, there was an uproar. *Time* responded that the environment was too important to cover only through objective journalism. It had become their cause.

Lately, *Time* has pulled back a little on their crazy leftism. Last Christmas, they ran a story on Christianity and science and how the two might be reconciled. At least superficially, that was a major concession.

The other big surprise was their cover on how men and women just might be inherently different. That's such a self-evident proposition that you've got to wonder why they thought it was big news. I think selecting that issue for their cover revealed a lot about the folks at *Time*. To treat such an obvious truth as news speaks volumes about their mindset.

They are children of the 1960s. They are baby boomers settling into middle age and finally having children. So the future takes on a different meaning. They can no longer think only about themselves and their causes. The future after their deaths matters to them, because their kids are going to be alive then. So they start to think back about how their parents raised them, about the values their parents considered worthwhile, much of which they pooh-poohed. I think a lot of them are now saying, "You know, that stuff my parents believed makes sense." Maybe little girls are going to grow up to be big girls, whether you give them a G.I. Joe or a Barbie doll.

This is not to say that the media is about to embrace middle-class values or abandon liberalism. But they are slowly willing to acknowledge other points of view. Let's revisit the homeless situation for a moment. In *Time*'s April 6, 1992 issue, there was a whole page on the homeless, written, incredibly enough, as I might have written it.

Time breathlessly and finally reported that there are not 3 million homeless, contrary to the claims of homeless advocacy. There are about 600,000 homeless, the figure I have long cited from the Urban Institute. They said the expansion of shelter beds from 78,000 in 1980 to 275,000 in 1990 may have created *more* homeless people. Incredible. You wouldn't have seen that story even a year ago in the mainstream media.

I did a whole hour on that homeless story on my show. I said, "Folks, you will not see me quoted in this article but those of you who read it will recognize my words. Now, what does that mean? It means that you had better start listening to me. I'm right about the homeless. And I'll be proven right about the ozone hole and global warming. It might take four or five years, but I'm convinced The Media will slowly and reluctantly come around to my way of thinking, kicking and screaming all the way. That's why the Rush Limbaugh show is on the cutting edge of societal evolution." To the Media Elite we may be the disfavored step-child, but to others, we're setting the standard.

RELIGION AND AMERICA: THEY *DO* GO TOGETHER

AMERICA WAS FOUNDED AS A JUDEO-CHRISTIAN COUNTRY. THOSE OF you who have been to Washington, D.C., and have toured the monuments, such as the Lincoln and Jefferson memorials, know the inscriptions have been carved in stone. You cannot read one without finding the word *God* in it somewhere. But you wouldn't learn any of this by reading most of the textbooks American schoolchildren read today. The lessons most of our students learn about the religious origins of this country are so twisted they're barely recognizable. It's time that was changed.

Surveys show that Americans are the most religious people of any advanced nation. Countries such as Germany and Sweden have become so secularized that the churches survive only with government subsidies. Even in many Catholic countries, a majority of people indicate they have no great faith in God. America is different. Here, most believe a higher authority rules their lives, they attend church, and they raise their children in religious households.

But our intellectual and political elites are often either hostile or ambivalent toward religion. Religious displays have been banned from public buildings during holiday seasons unless they contain enough secular images such as Frosty the Snowman to satisfy the ACLU-lulus. People for whom belief in God is at best a charming superstition have managed to ban prayer from the public schools for the last thirty years. Is it only a coincidence that the quality of American education has declined ever since?

Not content with banning prayer, many schools have been overtly hostile to religion. A teacher was fired in Fairfax County, Virginia, for holding a voluntary Bible study for students after hours in the privacy of her home. The Supreme Court has ordered that the Ten Commandments be removed from high school bulletin boards because they are based on religious teachings. That is in spite of the fact that it is the Ten Commandments that appear on the wall of the very room where the Supreme Court meets. The Court apparently wanted to prevent harmful messages from reaching children. After all, the Ten Commandments include admonitions such as: Thou shalt not kill, Thou shalt not steal, Thou shalt not covet thy neighbor's wife. Really harmful stuff to expose to young skulls full of mush.

The confirmation hearings of Judge Clarence Thomas to the Supreme Court again brought this controversial issue to the forefront. When Thomas unapologetically told a news conference that he was grateful to the nuns who had helped raise and teach him, bedlam and hysteria ensured from the liberal left. Virginia Governor Douglas Wilder mocked and insulted Thomas's supposed relationship with the Pope.

Thomas also said in the early days of his nomination, "My mother says that when they took God out of the schools, the schools went to hell. She may be right. Religion is certainly a source of positive values and we need as many positive values in the schools as we can get."

Well, guess what happened. Thomas's comments ruffled some liberal feathers. William J. Butler, a lawyer who won a landmark 1962 Supreme Court case on school prayer, came out of the woodwork. "That's just what the fundamentalists say. You need religion in the schools to instill morality." Wouldn't it be nice if these people feared immorality and a crumbling value base as much as they fear religion?

You know, this whole notion that morality is not something which can be imposed on people is simply ridiculous. Morality certainly descends from religion and is one of the main sources of our law, although some legal scholars, humanists, and atheists do their best to scramble this premise with such doublespeak that before long those who cherish morality and its roots are defending their very right to breathe, so heinous are they accused of being. The simple fact is that morality cannot be defined by individual choice, by allowing everyone to simply do as they please as though there are no consequences to their behavior and actions. That is anarchy, and we are living it—experiencing it—in certain segments of our society today. Morality is a system of virtuous conduct based on the principles of right and wrong. If we can't teach the difference between right and wrong because some paranoid civil libertarians determine that it is an imposition of religious views, then we are adrift in a dangerous sea. There may be legitimate philosophical arguments over what is right and wrong, but they would have to be esoteric in nature. Fundamental right and wrong, such as defined in the Ten Commandments ("They are not the Ten Suggestions," as Ted Koppel likes to point out) is not arguable, nor should it be.

Now, I know a lot of people who say we can't bring religious references back into the classroom. People who want to pray to Allah or Buddha will be offended, even if the prayer is nondenominational. That's one of the reasons why I favor choice in education. Parents can send their kids to any private school they like today, but only the rich and well-to-do have that choice as a practical matter. The poor and middle class don't. It's time the government gave each parent a redeemable voucher for, say, twenty-five hundred dollars and told them they can take it to a school of their choice. Most private schools charge less than that today, and they provide a better education for about half the cost of the public schools. The competition between public and private schools would improve both institutions and no parent would then be able to complain that their kid had been forced to hear the Ten Commandments. Whatever, something needs to change. Parents are fed up and worried, so much so that many are now home-schooling their kids. Admittedly, this began in the Christian community, but it is an idea now being adopted by people from all walks of life who are unhappy with the methods and subject matter being taught their kids today.

I'll tell you what will be interesting to watch. Christopher Whittle, of Whittle Communications, intends to establish a large number of private schools over the next few years that will revolutionize education in this country. For the first time, education will be designed with market orientation. Whittle plans to have people he considers the best and brightest from a number of different fields design these schools. Whittle is doing it as a businessman, so he hopes to make a profit. This means he must satisfy his customers (parents), who will have to pay roughly fifty-five hundred dollars per year. His schools will have an eleven-month year featuring eight-and-a-half-hour days. It is simple. If he establishes a curriculum parents don't like, he will have few students and his investment will fail. If, on the other hand, parents are excited and happy about what and how their kids are being taught, you will see improvement throughout the educational system. What are the odds that there will be opportunity for students to pray? For the inclusion of teaching right and wrong and value-base reinforcement? Pretty good, I would say. We'll see.

FIRST AMENDMENT MISREADING

The assault on America's religious underpinnings is based on a distorted interpretation of the establishment and free-exercise clauses of the First Amendment. Those clauses are "Congress shall make no law respecting the establishment of religion, or prohibiting the free exercise thereof." Only a lawyer could claim not to understand the plain meaning of those words. The government is prohibited from setting up a state religion, such as Britain has, but no barriers will be erected against the practice of any religion.

Despite its plain meaning, the First Amendment has been used to forcibly remove religion from not just our classrooms but all government institutions and to dilute the religious content of much of American life. The way liberals are interpreting the First Amendment today is that it prevents anyone who is religious from being in government. They say that violates the prohibition against church and state. Regardless of the fact that the Supreme

Court has ruled to the contrary, neither the establishment clause nor the free-exercise clause was intended to preclude all interactivity between church and state. The words of those clauses have been stretched well beyond their logical extremes.

How can it legitimately be argued that for public schools to set aside a few moments in the morning for students to pray (only if they choose to) is tantamount to Congress making a law respecting the establishment of religion? Just because the schools are supported with public funds does not mean that any presence, or any hint, of religion in the classroom constitutes the state's establishment of religion. In no way does the state's allowance of a time period to enable children to commune with their Creator, whoever they deem Him to be or however they choose to communicate with Him, indicate a state preference for a certain denomination. It in no way encroaches upon anyone's religious freedoms for the students to be allowed this time. I have often wondered why no one has made the argument that to deny children the time to pray comes closer to violating their free exercise of religion than the allowance of that time violates the establishment clause. It seems to me that the free-exercise clause of the First Amendment *precludes* any prohibition on voluntary prayer in school, or anywhere else for that matter. Prayer in school, again, has nothing to do with the establishment of religion. The people who support prayer in school do not want to establish it as something everyone has to do.

When you think about it, one of the primary purposes of the establishment clause, which is the one from which the principle of separation of church and state is derived, was to prevent government from establishing a religion. Why? Because that would encroach on people's religious freedoms—i.e., the freedom to belong to any church they wanted and to worship and pray to their own God. Doesn't the prohibition against voluntary prayer in school, in the name of preserving inviolate that barrier between church and state, defeat the purpose for which that barrier was erected—i.e., to safeguard our free-exercise rights, including our right to pray? But the problem is that this concept of separating church and state has taken on a life all its own, and the secularists have succeeded in twisting its original purpose 180 degrees.

The fact that these warped, convoluted interpretations of the Bill of Rights have made their way into the opinions of the Supreme Court indicates the extent to which our society has forgotten its true roots. And it is all being done in the name of preserving those roots. Its maddening and exasperating.

We are now told that Thomas Jefferson and Benjamin Franklin didn't really believe in God (which is an outrageous falsehood), so the Founding Fathers intended that religion be kept completely apart from any public institution, especially the schools. But the truth is that the Founding Fathers sought to avoid state tyranny in the name of religion and religious oppression of any kind. They had no expectation or desire that all aspects of religion be removed from our institutions. The Declaration of Independence acknowledged the existence of a Divine Creator. Now, after thirty years of this relentless secularization, even liberals are beginning to have second thoughts. Norman Lear's People for the American Way recently issued a report that said that the study of history and civics in our schools has been so drained of religious content that children could be forgiven for thinking it played no role in the development of this nation. His group called for new textbooks that better explain the role of religion in American life. Admittedly, that's an encouraging sign.

Banning prayer in school in effect made God unconstitutional. When you look at the documents written by the men who founded this country, you find they were devoted to their God. I am certain that they did not intend for this country to be a Godless one.

I hope this chapter helps correct some of the misinformation that has been propagated about our Founding Fathers and their faith in God. I can only scratch the surface in this book, so readers who want to learn more should buy Benjamin Hart's excellent book *Faith and Freedom: The Christian Roots of American Liberty*, published by Lewis and Stanley.

JEFFERSON AND FRANKLIN

The great British essayist G. K. Chesterton once observed that "America is the only nation in the world that is founded on a creed. That creed is set forth with dogmatic and even theological lucidity in the Declaration of Independence."

Our founding document is replete with religious references. We're told that its author, Thomas Jefferson, was a Deist. That's someone who believes God exists and created all of us, but that He is now no longer involved in human affairs. Deists also do not subscribe to the view that Christ is Deity. Clearly, Deists were monotheistic. Jefferson alternated between belief in Christianity and Deism in his personal life. But he did not doubt there was a God and that He would again play a role in our lives. "I tremble for my country when I reflect that God is just: that His justice cannot sleep forever," he wrote.

The document Jefferson is best known for, the Declaration of Independence, makes it abundantly clear what convinced the Founding Fathers that they had the right to break with England. The Declaration begins by saying that "all men are created equal, that they are endowed by their Creator with certain unalienable Rights." King George compelled the colonists to revolt because he had "violated the laws of nature and of nature's God." The Declaration ends with its signatories "appealing to the Supreme Judge of the World" for guidance and expressing "a firm reliance on the protection of Divine Providence."

Jefferson had complex religious views, but he understood the importance of starting our new nation with a firm religious foundation. "Can the liberties of a nation be thought secure when we have removed their only firm basis, a conviction in the minds of the people that their liberties are the gift of God?" he wrote during the Revolution.

We are also told by some historians that Benjamin Franklin was not only a rakish fellow but a non-Christian. Yet, this is the same Franklin who in 1787 told the Constitutional Convention in Philadelphia that each of their sessions should be opened with prayers. He thought that only God's spirit would help the delegates come to an agreement. "In the beginning of the contest with Great Britain, when we were sensible of danger," he told his fellow delegates, "we had daily prayers in this room for Divine protection. Our prayers, Sir, were heard, and they were graciously answered. All of us who were engaged in the struggle must have observed frequent instances of a superintending Providence in our favor . . . and have we now forgotten this powerful friend? Or do we no longer need His assistance?"

BATTLE FOR AMERICA

The debate over whether America was founded as a religious nation is not an academic one. "To destroy a people you must first sever their roots," the great Russian writer Alexander Solzhenitsyn once wrote. Those who would undermine America and turn it into an egalitarian Utopia know they have to first chip away at the faith of Americans, at their very spiritual foundations. They will try to convince people to replace their faith in God with a belief in alphabet-soup agencies, faceless bureaucrats, and government giveaways.

But man is a spiritual being. If his faith in God is destroyed, the void will be filled with something else. Throughout history that substitute for faith has been a belief in a man-made god called the state. Untold crimes have been committed in its name, Hitler and Stalin being the most bloody recent examples.

The separation of church and state in our Constitution is not there to protect Americans from religion. It is there to protect Americans from the government. But in their desire to promote their secular humanist philosophy using the power of government, many liberals today want to alter America's heritage and remove religion from its history. Their desire is not to safeguard denominational neutrality by the state. It is to eradicate every vestige of religion from our institutions.

Liberals didn't always believe that. William O. Douglas, one of the most liberal justices ever to sit on the Supreme Court, once wrote that "we are a religious people whose institutions presuppose a supreme being." It's time we reminded ourselves and our children of that, and returned religion to its honored place in the life of this nation.

RONALD REAGAN: SETTING THINGS STRAIGHT

*I've always thought of leadership as a natural quality or character-
istic that is based on charisma and the unique ability to inspire people
to heights and accomplishments they otherwise would not attain.
This explains the phenomenon of the "reluctant" leader. Many people
aspire to leadership but fail to achieve it because it is not something
one can learn. You either are a leader or you are not.*

*I was asked to put this into a political context and would do so
thusly: Liberalism claims to have leaders: black leaders, minority
leaders, etc., but these people are not leaders at all. They advocate the
status quo of dependence and the subordination of individualism to
the group at large. There is no leadership, no inspiration or
motivation to individual greatness, but rather a continuum of
wallowing in the rut of blame and the rationalization of failure.*

*Conservatism, however, sponsors and promotes leadership by
championing and promoting individualism, from which leadership
truly descends. Reagan, vilified by so many, was a leader precisely
because of his ability, based on the strength of his personality, to make
people feel good about themselves and their country, which motivated
them to seek accomplishment and achievement beyond that which
they felt themselves capable of. Voilà! Leadership . . . which was
anathema to liberals. How 'bout that?*

—Limbaugh on Leadership

WHEN WRITING THIS BOOK I DEVOTED A LENGTHY CHAPTER TO
Ronald Reagan. After completing the book I reread the Reagan

chapter, and I found that almost every single point I made in that chapter I had covered in other chapters. As a result, I decided to abbreviate this chapter in order to avoid redundancy. Based on this fact, it should be obvious to you how important I deem Ronald Reagan to have been in shaping the future course of this nation, and indeed the world. He is a man to whom we Americans owe a debt that we will never be able to repay. In various chapters of this book I explain the contributions of Mr. Reagan, how he continues to be maligned, and how his record is continually distorted by liberals and the media.

Ronald Reagan enabled conservatives to come out of their silent-majority closet after experiencing years of derision, ridicule, and disparagement at the hands of the dominant media culture. Conservatives have always felt that they were in the minority, but Ronald Reagan inspired them with the confidence to come forward and express their views proudly and to recognize their actual majority status. You see, there was a time when many conservatives truly felt that their philosophy was doomed to minority status. After LBJ's annihilation of Goldwater in 1964, there seemed little hope for the conservative movement in terms of its ability to ultimately affect policy decisions in this country. During those bleak years it was stalwarts such as William F. Buckley, Jr., and Ronald Reagan who refused to allow conservatism to be relegated to political obscurity. For they knew that to do so would be the same as abandoning the principles upon which this country was founded. Buckley and Reagan continued to carry the torch of conservatism during its dark years, providing guidance and confidence for many who may have otherwise given up the fight. They continued to oppose the forces of socialism and collectivism, the ever-expanding governmental bureaucracy, the emasculation of our system of law and order, the assault on our nation's value base, the undermining of our spirit of patriotism, and the systematic effort to weaken our nation's economic and military prowess.

With progressive income tax rates having reached the confiscatory level of 70 percent and the estate tax code severely limiting one's freedom to transfer wealth to future generations, this country might as well have begun to call itself socialistic. Our entire capitalistic system is based on economic freedom and market economies and is undergirded by the very cornerstone of capitalism: private property. With the tax code destroying nearly all incentive to create wealth, and limiting one's ability to pass it on to his heirs, the concept of private property was in real jeopardy in this country. Karl Marx couldn't have asked for much more cooperation if he were seeking peaceful revolution. But Reagan and others persevered.

When Ronald Reagan took office he was successful in reducing marginal income tax rates and eventually lowering the highest rate to 28 percent. Plus, he was able to drive through Congress a bill that greatly expanded the estate tax credit, which significantly reduced the penalty for making gifts to heirs. Both of these were major victories for private property and capitalism and were critical to the future of this country as an economic and military world superpower.

Moreover, Reagan's vision and leadership brought conservatism into the mainstream of this nation's political thought. The advent of Reaganomics and Reagan's revitalization of our national defense enabled the conservative movement to become a driving force that was large enough (without becoming diluted in its purpose) to encompass nearly all segments of society. No longer was conservatism to be considered a fringe, extreme, or reactionary movement. I have to believe that the occurrence of this phenomenon was unimaginable to seminal conservative leaders such as Mr. Buckley and Barry Goldwater. For the first time I can remember, people were beginning to believe in the conservative ideal—they were witnessing the results of conservative governance. They were observing that conservatism in practice was not bereft of compassion and that all classes of society could benefit from fewer governmental regulations and taxes. They were proud of America again.

I couldn't submit an issues-oriented book for publication without paying tribute to Mr. Reagan and crediting him with the phenomenal difference he made in our future and that of our children.

But sadly, the disinformation about Reagan and his administration persists. The effort to destroy him continues to this day. Examples are chronicled throughout this book, from blaming him for the Los Angeles riots of 1992, for the AIDS crisis, for environmental destruction, to the unending criticism of his economic policy leveled by practically every liberal Democrat in the country. It is a ceaseless blend of cacophonous and disjointed hysteria. Why?

Quite simply, my friends, it is because Ronald Reagan is hated and despised. Strong words, I know, but I mean them. Hated because he demonstrated the folly of liberalism. He is the conspicuous symbol of its demise. Now, isn't it true that liberals, who so cavalierly accuse conservatives of being consumed with hate, are actually the ones who own its franchise? How else to explain their absolute paranoia of returning to any aspect of the 1980s? What else could sustain such a frenetic energy to discredit one man and his presidency? So beware. Liberals are arrogant and condescending and will pursue relentlessly their goal of destroying the legacy and truth of the Reagan presidency.

Reagan's presidency, coupled with the longest sustained economic boom in modern history, invalidated almost everything liberals stand for, believe in, and have been spouting for decades. Virtually every important cornerstone of liberalism was shown for what it is: wrong. The last thing liberals want is for you to understand this. Remember, their power derives from your ignorance and whatever degree of dependence they can lock you into. Of all things, Reagan understood this and sought to rebuild the self-respect of this nation. Thankfully, he succeeded.

YEAR OF THE OUTSIDERS

FOR MOST AMERICAN VOTERS, POLITICS HAS BECOME A FOUR-LETTER word. A recent bestseller, published just prior to this bestseller, was titled *Why Americans Hate Politics.* That's not surprising. The current political system has erected a curtain around the Washington Beltway that insulates everyone inside from the views of the average person. Our institutions are failing. Both major parties are failing. There is no one, neither Democrat nor Republican, who is providing real leadership. That doesn't mean the country can't survive without great leaders. I've long thought that America is a great country, not because a bunch of people in Washington have told people what to do, but because people have been free to do great things on their own. Still, you need someone to inspire, and to make people feel good about themselves to really get the country moving in the right direction. Ronald Reagan did that. There's no one like him around right now. It's therefore understandable that voters are turning to political outsiders in this election year.

There are many factors contributing to the anti-incumbent mood prevalent in America today, including an arrogant, entrenched one-party Congress, which is the paradigm of the beltway mentality. Another, in my view, is George Bush's abandonment of the Ronald Reagan legacy, without which the country would not be experiencing the economic difficulties that it is. This climate of economic despair is fertile ground for insurgent political movements, and they have proliferated at record pace in this election year.

The primary reason these movements are being launched and seriously considered is that the American electorate is at present disenchanted with Washington. Capitalizing on this widespread discontent, Pat Buchanan, Jerry Brown, and H. Ross Perot are the people who have generated the excitement in this campaign. Jack Kemp could have inspired the country this year but his loyalty to the GOP kept him out of the race. Of course, some of the outsider candidates are really phonies. Take Jerry Brown. He certainly made noise against Bill Clinton this spring, but he largely got votes because he was the only alternative to Clinton. He also attracted the support of every freak and kook organization that gravitates toward the Democratic party, and vice versa. I'm talking about animal-rights types, militant vegetarians, anti-nuke activists, peaceniks, multiculturalists, bean-curd eaters—you name it. Anyone who appeals to those constituencies the way Jerry Brown did will get a certain number of votes. In my unhumble opinion, Pat Buchanan was different. He had a clear message and was consistent in his stands, unlike Jerry Brown.

Still, the majority of people voting for him didn't support him because they thought he was the best candidate. Rather, they were disenchanted with President Bush and would have supported almost any candidate that challenged him. That's why polls showed that 30 percent of moderate and liberal Republicans backed Buchanan. This is not to say that Buchanan didn't accomplish great things. He moved the President demonstrably to the right. George Bush finally apologized for the rancid budget and forced the resignation of John Frohnmayer, the guy who viewed the National Endowment for the Arts as the arts-and-croissants version of The United Way for every sicko, perverse leftist artist in the country. Buchanan also destroyed David Duke's so-called Republican candidacy, which is something all Americans should thank him for. The Republican party should buy Buchanan *two* Cadillacs so he can get rid of his Mercedes as thanks for dispatching Duke to the ash heap of irrelevance.

Buchanan should also be credited with waking up the slumbering Bush campaign. It would have been a hell of a thing if the

Bush Boys had discovered, just before the general election, that one-third of Republicans intensely opposed the President. It would have been too late for them then. They now have time to figure out a new strategy—whether it will work remains to be seen. Buchanan also made it clear that the heart and soul of the Republican party is conservatism. I'm a Republican, and I'm terribly upset and angry about the way Ronald Reagan's record has been trashed, as described earlier. Buchanan was trying to restore Ronald Reagan's legacy, and to bring the Republican party back to the principles that won it three elections in a row during the 1980's. I will always view Pat Buchanan as one of my mentors. He is a thinking individual, nothing like the stereotypes you read about in the media. He doesn't copy anyone else's thoughts, he's out there on his own. He was willing to make real sacrifices to pursue his dreams. He gave up three high-paying jobs for an entire year. My hat's off to him. Pat Buchanan gave the liberals no quarter. He was also willing to take risks. He once told an audience in Georgia that I was his first choice to be White House communications director if he were elected! Obviously, Buchanan appreciates my quiet, in-the-background approach. *Heh–heh–heh.*

This brings us to H. Ross Perot. Quite simply a phenomenon. The campaign which may redefine American politics. In fact, it already has. Perot received 1.5 million phone calls at his 800 number in the space of 17 days last March. Not even Ronald Reagan or Jack Kennedy have excited some people as much as Perot has. The people who support Perot aren't kooks. Look at them. They are solid middle class, some upper middle class. They are enthusiastic, can't wait to vote for their guy, and are having a ball. And Perot played them like a violin.

His is one of the best psychological appeals in years. He starts out by artfully detailing the problems the country faces, which is the key ingredient in his recipe. As chronicled elsewhere in this stupendous book of major proportions, the American people are tired of hearing how all the ills in the country are *their* fault. Each day and night, the mainstream media seems to blame the middle class, ordinary people, for what's wrong with America. Nobody, it seems to most people, has the guts to point the finger of blame in the right direction. But Ross Perot does, and millions of Americans rejoice because someone in the political world is finally standing up for them and thanking them for the contributions to greatness they have made, rather than accusing them of being the reason for the nation's decline. He does this over a two-year period with well-timed speeches around the country and at the Washington Press Club, which ensures they will be televised on C-SPAN. He asks why things are so stupidly out of whack, while saying he wouldn't give you three cents for the job. He doesn't want it. He wouldn't even try it. Einstein, he says, couldn't fix what's wrong with this country.

Soon, a startling thing began to happen. By design, I am certain. People began to ask him to run for president. This is one of the many aspects of his scenario that bothers me. He asks us to believe that out of the blue, on the night of February 20, 1992, he finally caved in to the mammoth demand that he save America and become the servant of the American people. If you believe the Perot candidacy is the result of the pure spontaneity of your demand he run for president, you're wrong. Believe me, Ross Perot leaves nothing to chance. It is not his nature. This is pure deceit, yet few people seem to be bothered by it. This, in turn, bothers me. Why does it bother me? Because legions of people are motivated, enthused, and mobilized because they think they have created a candidacy, which gives Perot license to do just about anything in their name. While it is certainly true they propel the Perot juggernaut, the simple fact is they did not create it.

According to *The Kansas City Star* of June 8, 1991, there were Perot-for-President rallies in Kansas City that year. Other press accounts report similar meetings in Tampa and Orlando, Florida. It is much like telethons. Charities spend an entire year raising money, then hit the air with their telethon. The figure they show you on the screen at the outset is always zero, yet the truth is that they have raised at least 95 percent of their goal during the year, so that they need to raise only 5 percent—or less, in many cases—to "go over the top." I believe the same thing, or something very similar, occurred with the Perot for President organization. Just ask yourself this question: Is a man of such detail and planning, of such organization and dominance, going to announce his *presidential* candidacy on a cable TV show and risk the embarrassing possibility of silent telephones—that no one will care and not call his office? *Not on your life!* Come on, folks, think about it. Still, most probably say, "So what?" They seem to be not the least bit bothered. That instead of leading and instigating this, they have been duped.

The sad thing is that Perot continued to exploit these people by first quitting the race, then promising to stay involved to lead his grass-roots movement in changing not only the White House, but Congress as well. The measure of his psychological grasp over his supporters can be found in the extraordinary way they reacted to his abruptly quitting his presidential candidacy on July 16, 1992. Instead of getting angry and realizing they had been duped, they actually begged him to change his mind. This after many had sold property, quit their jobs, and spent a lot of their own money to work for his campaign. I can't think of a politician who could get away with this. Indeed, many of Perot's supporters are former Bush voters who are livid, because he broke his promise to not raise taxes. Yet, who betrayed them more? Despite the deceit, the Perotistas kept coming back, unwilling to surrender their fantasy. It is as though they all suffered from battered wife syndrome. Or perhaps a real-life invasion of the body snatchers was (is?) underway.

WHY "IT DOESN'T MATTER"

Government gridlock is the reason many people give for explaining their support for Ross Perot. Somewhere in a conversation with them you will hear them say that Perot is going to form a consensus and that is how things will get done. Well, just what do you think we've had with Bush and those precious liberal Democrats in Congress? Consensus government, friend, is an illusion, because there is no such thing. A consensus means general agreement or a collective opinion. When have we ever had that? *Never.* It is not how we do things in America. Someone or some ideology always prevails in our form of government, which leaves some people unhappy or angry.

Bush has compromised his promises and beliefs on nearly every important principle he articulated, and where has it gotten him or us? People who didn't vote for him still revile him, as does the mainstream press; as does the liberal Democratic leadership he has sought to befriend (both instances prove the folly of consensus anyway: the Democrats ought to love Bush); and now, as do many who voted for him. As for the country, just take a look: Bush has rolled over for the liberals, enacted their fix for deficit spending, clean air, and minority quotas. Look at the size of the deficit, the condition of American business on the whole, and the stability of race relations. Worse, on all fronts, than before all this consensus. I think Perot is interested in consensus because to him it means arranging things so everyone agrees with him. He said precisely this during an interview on *60 Minutes.*

One of the cornerstones of Perot's early appeal was what he called the electronic town hall. This was to be the mechanism whereby the owners of the country could tell him how they wanted him to fix a problem such as the deficit. From the outset I saw this as a sham, something that would never happen, and never work if it were tried. Indeed, Perot never specifically explained how it would actually work. This he left to the imagination of his supporters. In a *TV Guide* interview published in late June of 1992, Perot finally admitted the town hall concept wouldn't work because not enough owners of the country would have interactive electronic devices in their homes. Perot mentioned that postcards (postcards!) might have to substitute. This news sort of trickled out, causing barely a wave, yet to me it was monumental, because Perot was admitting that the primary appeal of his candidacy—direct communication with the people —was impossible. So how could the owners of the country tell him what their decisions were? Well, they couldn't, but that did not matter. I made a rather large point of this one day and promptly received bags of hate mail, most of it explaining to me how Perot was going to make the town hall work! I was in shock. Perot had just admitted it wouldn't work, yet here were a bunch of his supporters angrily telling me how it *would* work, which was common throughout the campaign: Perotistas launching into explanations of his ideas and statements that not even he had made. How did they know?

* * *

So what are we to make of all this? It is that outsiders in politics will fail just as outsiders trying to conquer any other business will fail. Contrary to what many think, politics is a profession, a business. It is not a haphazardly assembled set of principles based on goodness, kindness, or idealism born of the founding of our nation. In order to excel in the profession of politics you have to satisfy a particular and explicit set of circumstances and requirements, just as in any other business. You can't just charge to the top of some business, becoming president, without having any experience in what it takes to get there, and expect to excel. You can take singing lessons for three months, but you still aren't ready for Vegas. You can be the best pitcher in Little League, but you are still a long way from the mound in the major leagues. You can be the most successful businessman in the world, but that does not qualify you in the slightest way to be able to win elections, much less the presidency. And as Mr. Perot has learned, media popularity is not nearly the same thing as popularity with voters.

The experiences of all the candidates who labeled themselves as outsiders, primarily the experience of Ross Perot, illustrate just how tough the business of politics is, and how tough those who choose it must accordingly be. Politicians, especially candidates, are suspects. Their very desire to lead and hold office makes us suspicious of their true desires and intentions, so we look into every nook and cranny to find something that will disqualify them and show them for what we think they really are: power-seeking, insincere megalomaniacs who wish to insulate themselves from the rigors of everyday life as we must live it.

This, ultimately, is why the issue of character is so important. Liberals wig out when character becomes an issue, because many of their candidates are of dubious character. Yet, it matters greatly to voters. The Perot "candidacy" illustrates just how important character is in choosing leaders, and I find it almost laughably ironic that it was his principles (character) that the Perotistas cited most often as the reason they supported him. He made promise after promise, then broke them all. I shouted till I was without voice that his entire campaign was based on the profound deceit of manipulating people into thinking they had created his candidacy, when in fact it was he who had orchestrated the whole thing for months before anyone knew what was really happening.

Without question there is a rising clamor for change, not only in our political institutions and establishment, but in the policies and directions which emanate from them. The key to change, though, will be found *inside*—not *outside*—the system among politically experienced people who are ethical, honest, and moral—characteristics that do matter, despite how loudly they are pooh-poohed by the liberal elite.

Outsiders, and those who present themselves as such, will ultimately end up as carcasses strewn across the countryside, false prophets of a false premise.

THE LIMBAUGH LEXICON

YOU TOO CAN SPEAK RUSHIAN

I AM OFTEN ASKED BY THE UNINITIATED—NAMELY, NEW LISTENERS— to define various puzzling words, expressions, turns of phrase, and snatches of song they hear on my program. I have resisted such entreaties, telling all who ask that they must listen to my show for at least six weeks before they can comprehend its nuances. They must be patient, I tell them. However, my publisher has prevailed upon me to offer a lexicon of Rushian phrases for readers who, for some inexplicable reason, don't listen to my program or whose radios are broken. For the rest of you, loyal listeners all, this will be a good refresher course. There will be a quiz at the end.

Adult Beverages: Alcoholic beverages. Articulated in this classy way so as to avoid angering the parents of the youth of America, who also listen eagerly to my show.

Arts & Croissant Crowd: The trendy lefties who support having the National Endowment for the Arts pay for such masterpieces as a photo of Christ in a jar of urine and Robert Mapplethorpe's imaginative depictions of the human anatomy and bullwhips. Their hero is John Frohnmayer, the former head of the NEA until President Bush fired him.

Assume Room Temperature: Die; cease to inhabit the planet.

Bo Snerdley: Official Call Screener of the EIB Network.

Commie Libs: This subspecies of socialists is in danger of extinction and many members are using their chameleonlike abilities to become Environmentalist Wackos.

Dadalup, dadalup, dadalup!: The sound that precedes an EIB Update on my show. This is my attempt to approximate the stirring sound of a trumpet fanfare and alert listeners that something important is coming.

Demonstrating absurdity by being absurd: My favorite way of poking fun at liberal icons and their insane statements. By ridiculing them and exaggerating my response, I point out the utter fatuousness of the liberal philosophy.

Ditto: This developed as a timesaving greeting from listeners who would formerly waste valuable broadcast seconds praising me and the show. *The New York Times* has declared that Ditto is shorthand for, "You're wonderful, Rush, you're the best host I've ever heard. Don't ever go away."

Dittohead: An avid listener of the EIB Network. Warning to employers: If you hire dittoheads in your company, and then take away from them that which has made them dittoheads by refusing to allow them to listen to the show while at work, then you're no different from the multiculturalists out there.

Documented to be almost always right; 97.9 percent of the time: The actual figure changes from time to time as there are natural fluctuations in my accuracy. Rating is determined each month by an official Opinion Audit conducted by The Sullivan Group in Sacramento, California.

EIB: Excellence in Broadcasting. An airborne phenomenon spread by casual contact. It's addictive, yet harmless to the health. There is no cure, nor is there a vaccine or inoculation. No rehab is necessary. Millions of Americans have tested positive.

EIB Network: The Excellence in Broadcasting Network now reaches over 500 stations coast-to-coast with over 12 million listeners a week. Its only show is mine, because EIB needs no other to live up to its name. EIB's offices are in the Excellence in Broadcasting Building in midtown Manhattan.

Environmentalist Wackos: The modern environmental movement is the major remaining hiding place for socialists now that communism has collapsed. Environmentalist Wackos are fringe kookburgers and are not to be confused with serious and responsible ecology-minded people. Environmentalist Wackos believe that mankind is the greatest threat to nature, as opposed to being a part of nature. They seek to destroy private-property rights and establish a socialist regime as a means of imposing their nuttiness. They believe that whatever man does he's up to no good. Environmentalist Wackos are frequently found among the Hollywood Left, congressional staffers, and on college campuses that are hopefully nowhere near you.

The Epitome of Morality and Virtue: Me. A man whom hundreds, perhaps even thousands, of American mothers hope their daughters will someday marry. (Many of these mothers no doubt harbor the same fantasy for themselves.) I will not swear, speak sacrilegiously, demean any ethnic group, or tolerate smutty remarks on the air. Double entendres are excepted, as they are a form of genuine humor.

Feminazi: Widely misunderstood by most to simply mean "feminist." Not so, boobala. A Feminazi is a feminist to whom the most important thing in life is ensuring that as many abortions as possible occur. There are fewer than twenty-five known Feminazis in the United States.

The Frogman: Clarence "Frogman" Henry, a rock-and-roll legend and personal friend from New Orleans. His song "Ain't Got No Home" is the theme music that introduces The Homeless Updates.

The Fruited Plain: America.

General Dinkins: The hapless, ineffective mayor of New York City. A tool of every liberal group one can think of.

Governor Coomo: The current incumbent chief executive of New York State. Pronounced *Coomo* by The . . . Reverend Jesse Jackson, which is why I pronounce it *Coomo*. In this way I demonstrate my profound compassion and sensitivity for The Reverend Jackson by standing in unison with him on this pronunciation. Were I to pronounce the name *Kwomo*, as do most of you, I no doubt would be accused of making fun of The Reverend Jackson.

Gorbasm: A fake and phony feeling of bliss, euphoria, excitement, ecstasy, and nirvana when pondering all the wonderful things Mikhail Gorbachev has done for the planet.

Homeless Advocates: A group of liberal ideologues who want to exploit the homeless to further their own political agendas.

Just a Harmless Little Fuzzball: I, of course, never intend to hurt anyone or expect to affect public policy. I am just a guy on the radio who tells people what's on his mind.

Kathy Della Cava: My very resourceful secretary who handles the hundreds of faxes, letters, and phone calls that pour in each day to the EIB Network.

Kiki de la Garza: Primary Broadcast Engineer, currently on ten-month maternity leave(!) And they say they don't have equal rights?!

Kit Carson: Chief of Staff and Official Archivist of the Rush Limbaugh Show. The man who keeps me running on time (more or less) off the air. Schedules all interviews, production sessions, and most other appointments. Thinks he could do the show better than I. His real name, unless he changed it before he came to work for me.

Libosuction: Device to suck the liberalism out of callers who wish to be converted to conservatism. Sounds like a vacuum cleaner.

Limbaugh Institute for Advanced Conservative Studies: Yet another name for my award-winning, thrill-packed show, where I serve as lecturer and instructor. Questions and comments are taken from students (callers), both graduate and undergraduate. The Limbaugh Institute is the largest free educational institution in the world, providing a graduate-level course in correct public-policy thinking five days a week for three hours a day. Students who continually audit my courses and undertake the outside reading I recommend have gone on to amaze and astonish their friends with their erudition. Our senior fellows and policy analysts are hard at work seeking to obtain official course credit for those who skip their regular school classes in order to attend the Limbaugh Institute.

LoBianco: Substitute broadcast engineer who would do anything to get the gig forever. Thinks I am God.

Lover of Mankind, Protector Of Motherhood, Supporter Of Fatherhood (in Most Cases) And General All Round Good

Guy: My self-description to liberals who have bought into the propaganda that I'm a heartless conservative.

Mike Maimone: First Alternate Broadcast Engineer who is plotting ways to keep Kiki de la Garza from reclaiming the position upon her return from ten months' maternity leave.

On the Cutting Edge of Societal Evolution: I pride myself on spotting trends before others do, predicting events that few expect to come to pass, and am bringing Talk Radio into the twenty-first century. And that's just what happens before lunch.

The Only Healthful Addiction in America: My show. Millions of Americans are testing positive for EIB, and there is no known cure. Exposure of at least six weeks is necessary before addiction is complete.

Pockmarks on our Society: What bleeding-heart liberals always focus their attention on to the exclusion of all that is great and good about America.

Prestigious Attila the Hun Chair: The senior position at the Limbaugh Institute for Advanced Conservative Studies, occupied by me. Named purposely to tweak and thwart leftist critics who complain I am too far to the right.

Redefining Greatness on the Radio: What I am doing each day I am on the air.

The . . . Reverend . . . Jesse . . . Jackson: The man no one dare criticize. His name should be pronounced in a reverent near-whisper. No sense of irony intended. NOT!

Rio Linda, California: A depressing, dreary neighborhood near Sacramento (for which I have a soft spot in my heart), known for having real estate agents who despair of selling property there. Used to describe a place almost anyone would rather not be in. Most visible characteristic is that most homes have at least one car on concrete blocks in the front yard. These cars will serve as the Olympic Village when the First Annual Homeless Olympics are held in Rio Linda.

Ronald Reagan: My hero. The best President in my lifetime, and a man unjustly maligned by liberals, Environmentalist Wackos, and all the other fringe groups named above.

Rush to Excellence Tour: My national traveling stage show, starring me. I have played over ninety cities during the past three years. The Tour is currently on hiatus while other projects are started up (my new TV show) and completed (this best-selling book).

Saying More In Five Seconds Than Most Talk Show Hosts Say In A Whole Show: Another of the countless ways of describing my unequaled Talent On Loan From God (see below).

Serving Humanity: Another way of describing my incredible contribution to the human race.

Talent On Loan From God: Often misunderstood by hyper-critical and sensitive types to mean (I think) I am God. On the contrary, I believe I am what I am because of the grace of God and that my time on earth, as is everyone's, is temporary. We are all on loan from God, you see.

Uglo-American: I have been made aware that the term *ugly*, when used to describe human beings, is insensitive, derogatory, and insulting. In a sincere effort to avoid offending anyone, I have invented this new term, which I feel confident will be approved by the arbiters of what is politically correct. This term shows respect for this segment of society and does not strip them of their dignity.

Updates: Unique method invented by me as a means of keeping tabs on a critical issue which is judged by me to be one which will have a long life. They are introduced with music and sound effects. For example, the Animal Rights Updates are preceded by Andy Williams singing "Born Free," with the sounds of gunfire, explosions, and animal screams mixed in for amusement. The Barney Frank Update, popular when the Massachusetts congressman announced he had been suckered by his live-in lover who was running a male prostitution ring from the basement, was "My Boy Lollipop," by Millie Small.

With Half My Brain Tied Behind My Back To Make It Even: Denotes the degree of mental aptitude I require to engage and demolish liberals and others who disagree with me. Is based on my inherent, compassionate desire not to humiliate those who think I am wrong.

Young Skulls Full of Mush: Young American people after their brains have been pasteurized and filled with multicultural-ism, sex advocacy programs, and other twaddle by our failing public school system.

The Last Word

WE ARE WINNING

As I BRING MY FIRST LITERARY MASTERPIECE TO A CLOSE I WOULD LIKE to leave you with a request. That is to be confident, not just in yourselves but in the country and your fellow citizens. Many of you may find that curious, having just completed a book which seeks to identify a host of problems facing us today. But I believe we conservatives are winning these battles, even though it may not appear that way at first glance.

Remember that it is much easier to feel despair over what might seem like the successful attack on the institutions and traditions which make this country great than it is to see the progress we are making in defending them. I would remind you that compounding this difficulty is the dominant media culture, which does not reflect our values and concerns, which I believe to be held nevertheless by a majority of Americans. That media is constantly pounding us with doom and gloom scenarios, which often cast a negative spell over the national psyche.

Many times I get calls on my show from people who rail against one liberal outrage or another and complain that the country is going down the tubes. "The liberals are winning,

Rush," they mournfully conclude. "America is never going to be as great as it once was." I have one word for such defeatism: NONSENSE.

The truth is, as I tell people on my program, the liberal extremists are probably on their last legs. Their power source, the Democratic party, is wandering aimlessly in search of ways to revive its past rather than recognizing that it is not the people who are wrong and out of touch—it is the party and its leadership. Some would-be moderate Democrats made a run at steering the party toward the center but were cut off at every turn by the party's power brokers. Paul Tsongas's refusal to bash business was met with contempt by party bosses. Bill Clinton's earlier recognition that his party was going to have to drift right in order to become palatable to mainstream America, culminating in the Democratic Leadership Council, is all but a forgotten memory. He has had to revert to liberal, minority, and fringe pandering in order to distinguish himself from Perot, and to gain acceptance from the puppet masters calling his party's shots. The Democrats simply cannot extricate themselves from the bondage they placed themselves in by building their power base on beggar-based constituencies. But this strategy of across-the-board sycophancy has not worked because it violates the spirit and soul of humanity. The Democrats have not had an administration to steer mass quantities of money toward them for a dozen years. Remember, the feminist, environmental, so-called civil rights groups, and Naderites were all sustained during the 1970s with federal funds or contracts. They still get some, but nothing like what they need to prosper. They now exist primarily off of donations from rich, guilty liberals and whatever contributions they can finagle from the public at large. That money isn't flowing to them like it used to, as more and more people have caught on to how radical and extreme many of these groups really are.

Remember, the people who run these groups don't work for a living in the traditional sense. They survive only by inventing crises or fabricating some threat to an aggrieved minority group. That's why they appear to be more active and visible than before. If you have noticed, they are becoming more hysterical each day. They are like a screaming baby who, when it can't get what it wants, just yells louder. It can't provide for itself, so it hopes that if it makes enough fuss someone will feed it.

We are, quite bluntly, broke. We don't have the money to sustain the dreams and experiments of liberalism any longer. We have a $400 billion a year budget deficit and a $4 trillion debt. The economist Walter Williams points out that with the money we've spent on poverty programs since the 1960s we could have bought the entire assets of every Fortune 500 company and virtually every acre of U.S. farmland. Still, the left wants more. Yet, not only didn't we eliminate poverty, but today many social problems are far worse than they have ever been. You know it. I know it. And, more important, they know it.

Americans are no longer willing to pour more billions into programs that have failed to accomplish their goals. They are also growing weary of supporting a public-education system which bans God, encourages licentiousness, decries Western civilization, indicts American tradition, promotes cultural disharmony, and serves as a breeding ground to indoctrinate new little liberals. So, as the funds dry up, many leftist groups are arguing over which one of them will get a larger share of the entitlement pie. The post–Los Angeles riot battle cry, "No Justice, No Peace," is nothing more than a threat of more and more violence should the Establishment refuse to succumb to the financial demands of those who claim to represent the interests of thugs, murderers, arsonists, and looters. I contend that such threats are made out of desperation and panic. The desperation and panic result from two things: First, the realization that the largesse, in the same ridiculous amounts as has been transferred over the past thirty years, is over because the money is no longer there. Second, the sudden slap-in-the-face realization that, after thirty years of uninterrupted catering to their demands, the left's primary ideas and theories on social justice and economic fairness just do not work. They know not what to do, except yell and scream even louder and attempt to frighten and intimidate those who now seek to try other methods.

Add to all of this the massive anti-Washington sentiment (which is, in large part, a cacophonous shout of anger at those who have created and sustain this country's failed welfare state, symbolized by the phenomenal candidacy of Ross Perot, a dreaded rich guy who talks only of hard work and commitment), and you can understand even better why the agents of largesse are fraught with anxiety and horror.

The left has escalated its rhetoric because it is losing, while its various constituencies appear to be more powerful because of the prominence their concerns are given in the coverage of daily events. You must realize that they are joining forces out of desperation, not out of optimism. The most perceptive people on the left know the country is against them and that the overburdened middle class has had enough. They are retreating on all fronts. By the end of this year, the infamous *Roe v. Wade* decision that sanctioned the taking of innocent human life will likely be an historical artifact. In order to avoid this eventuality, or at least delay it, the liberals threw everything they had into the battle to defeat Clarence Thomas, including the use of lies and perjured testimony, and they STILL lost. Only 29 percent of American women are today willing to call themselves feminists. Tax revolts are springing up all over America. Over a dozen states will vote this November on limiting the terms of members of Congress.

I am convinced that the most important thing conservatives have to do to win is to just keep saying no to the left. No to their special-interest giveaways. No to their pork-barrel spending projects. No to their privileged congressional empire. If we can just deny them the fuel that runs their corrupt empire, it will wither away just like the communist empire did. Remember 1988, when George Bush defeated Michael Dukakis? If someone had told you then that the communists were on their last legs, that the Berlin Wall would soon fall, and that the Soviet Union itself would vanish from the face of the earth, would you have believed them? Of course not. The communists were able to conceal their weakness behind a barrage of propaganda and threats. That's what the left in this country is doing as well. But don't be discouraged by the left's vociferousness or its dominance of the mainstream media and Hollywood. Don't misinterpret volume for numbers. Conservatives are an ever-growing majority. So take heart, dear reader. Don't get down. Remember how I handle them. I laugh at their outrageous statements and I ridicule their latest lunacies. So should you. Laugh and move on. They are the past. We conservatives are the future.

So don't give up. Be confident. This country has not run out of opportunity. Your children can live in an America that is better, safer, more moral, and more prosperous. Those who would tear down the great traditions of this country are, in fact, losing. Don't misunderstand. They haven't lost—they won't ever be totally defeated—but they can be greatly deemphasized. This is a never-ending battle and if you want to follow the chronicling of their demise and learn about the people who are helping make America great again, I can think of no better way than for you to tune in to my radio and TV shows. I must warn you, however. Both are highly addictive.

ALSO BY ROBIN SLOAN

Mr. Penumbra's 24-Hour Bookstore

Ajax Penumbra 1969

SOURDOUGH

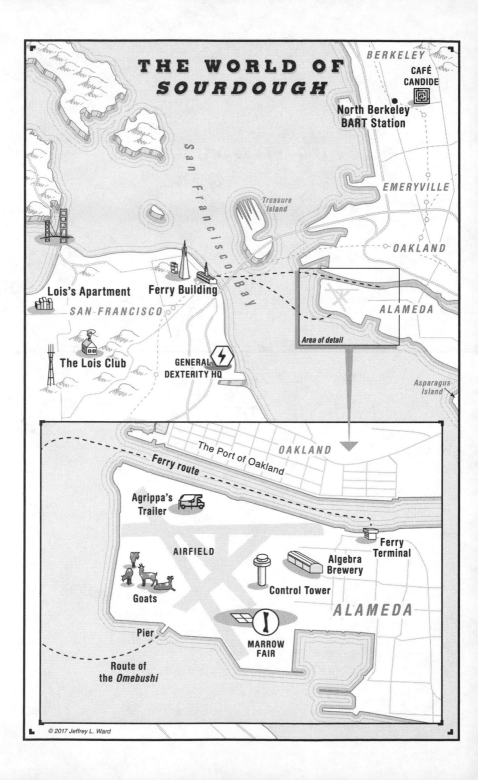

SOURDOUGH

A NOVEL

ROBIN SLOAN

MCD

FARRAR, STRAUS AND GIROUX

NEW YORK

MCD
Farrar, Straus and Giroux
18 West 18th Street, New York 10011

Copyright © 2017 by Robin Sloan
Map copyright © 2017 by Jeffrey L. Ward
All rights reserved
Printed in the United States of America
First edition, 2017

Library of Congress Cataloging-in-Publication Data
Names: Sloan, Robin, 1979– author.
Title: Sourdough / Robin Sloan.
Description: First edition. | New York : MCD / Farrar, Straus
    and Giroux, 2017.
Identifiers: LCCN 2016059400 | ISBN 9780374203108 (hardcover) |
    ISBN 9780374716431 (e-book)
Classification: LCC PS3619.L6278 S67 2017 | DDC 813/.6—dc23
LC record available at https://lccn.loc.gov/2016059400

Open Market edition ISBN: 978-0-374-90334-3

Designed by Abby Kagan

Our books may be purchased in bulk for promotional, educational, or
business use. Please contact your local bookseller or the Macmillan
Corporate and Premium Sales Department at 1-800-221-7945, extension
5442, or by e-mail at MacmillanSpecialMarkets@macmillan.com.

www.fsgbooks.com
www.twitter.com/fsgbooks • www.facebook.com/fsgbooks

1   3   5   7   9   10   8   6   4   2

For Kathryn

ACKNOWLEDGMENTS

Thanks to Dan Bouk, Patrick Ewing, Andrew Fitzgerald, Wilson Miner, Kiyash Monsef, Jim Ray, Sarah Rich, Brad Thomason, and Kathryn Tomajan: first readers.

Thanks also to Norma Barksdale, Maya Binyam, Rebecca Caine, Rodrigo Corral, Rebecca Gardner, Brian Gittis, Debra Helfand, Naomi Huffman, Abby Kagan, Roberta Klugman, Spenser Lee, Will Roberts, Jeff Seroy, Lisa Silverman, and Rob Sternitzky: collaborators.

Thanks, most of all, to Sarah Burnes and Sean McDonald: instigators.

SOURDOUGH

NUMBER ONE EATER

IT WOULD HAVE BEEN nutritive gel for dinner, same as always, if I had not discovered stuck to my apartment's front door a paper menu advertising the newly expanded delivery service of a neighborhood restaurant.

I was just home from work and my face felt brittle from stress—this wasn't unusual—and I would not normally have been interested in anything unfamiliar. My nightly ration of Slurry waited within.

But the menu intrigued me. The words were written in a dark, confident script—actually, two scripts: each dish was described once using the alphabet I recognized and again using one I didn't, vaguely Cyrillic-seeming with a profusion of dots and curling connectors. In either case, the menu was compact: available was the *Spicy Soup* or a *Spicy Sandwich* or a *Combo (double spicy)*, all of which, the menu explained, were vegetarian.

At the top, the restaurant's name was written in humongous, exuberant letters: *CLEMENT STREET SOUP AND SOURDOUGH.* At the bottom, there was a phone number and the promise of quick delivery. Clement Street was just a few blocks away. The menu charmed me, and as a result, my night, and my life, bent off on a different track.

I dialed the number and my call was answered immediately. It was a man's voice, slightly breathless. "Clement Street Soup and Sourdough! Okay to hold?"

I said yes, and music played—a song in some other language. Clement Street was a polyglot artery that pulsed with Cantonese, Burmese, Russian, Thai, and even scraps of Gaelic. This was none of those.

The voice returned. "Okay! Hello! What can I make for you?"

I ordered the double spicy.

I CAME TO SAN FRANCISCO from Michigan, where I was raised and educated and where my body's functioning was placid and predictable, mostly.

My father was a database programmer for General Motors who liked his work and had endeavored to surround me with computers from toddlerhood onward, and whose plan succeeded because I never thought of anything except following his path, especially at a time when programming was taking on a sheen of dynamism and computer science departments were wooing young women aggressively. It's nice to be wooed.

It helped that I was good at it. I liked the rhythm of challenge and solution; it felt very satisfying to solve programming problems. For two summers during college, I interned at Crowley Control Systems, a company in Southfield that provided motor control software for one of Chevrolet's electric cars, and when I graduated, there was a job waiting for me.

4

The work was minutely specified and cautiously tested, and it had the feeling of laying bricks: put them down carefully, because you won't get another chance. The computer on my desk was old, used by at least two programmers before me, but the codebase was modern and interesting. I kept a picture of my parents next to my monitor, along with a tiny cactus I'd named Kubrick. I bought a house two towns over, in Ferndale.

Then I was recruited. A woman contacted me through my stubby LinkedIn profile—her own identifying her as a talent associate at a company called General Dexterity in San Francisco—with a request for an exploratory phone call, which I accepted. I could hear her bright smile through the speaker. General Dexterity, she said, designed industry-leading robot arms for laboratories and factories. The company needed programmers with a background in motor control, and in San Francisco, she said, such programmers were rare. She explained that a software sieve had flagged my résumé as promising and that she agreed with the computer's assessment.

Here's a thing I believe about people my age: we are the children of Hogwarts, and more than anything, we just want to be sorted.

Sitting there in my car in the little parking lot behind Crowley Control Systems on West 10 Mile Road in Southfield, my world cracked open a tiny bit. It was only a hairline fracture, but that was enough to see through.

On the other end of the line, the talent associate conjured difficult problems suited to only the fiercest intellects. She conjured generous benefits and free food and, oh, was I vegetarian? Not anymore, no. But maybe I could try again,

5

in California. She conjured sunshine. The sky above the Crowley parking lot was gray and drippy like the undercarriage of a car.

And—no conjuring here—the talent associate made an offer. It was a salary that represented more money than both of my parents currently earned, combined. I was a year out of college. I was being wooed again.

Ten months into a Michigan-sized mortgage, I sold my house in Ferndale at a very small loss. I hadn't hung a single thing on the walls. When I said goodbye to my parents, I cried. College had been less than an hour away, so this was the real departure. I set out across the country with all my belongings in the back of my car and my desk cactus strapped into the passenger seat.

I drove west through the narrow pass in the Rockies, crossed the dusty nothing of Nevada, and crashed into the verdant, vertical shock of California. I was agog. Southeastern Michigan is flat, almost concave; here was a world with a z-axis.

In San Francisco, a temporary apartment waited for me, and so did the talent associate, who met me on the sidewalk in front of General Dexterity's brick-faced headquarters. She was tiny, barely five feet tall, but when she took my hand, her grip was viselike. "Lois Clary! Welcome! You're going to love it here!"

The first week was amazing. Grouped with a dozen other newly Dextrous (as we were encouraged to call ourselves), I filled out health insurance forms and accepted a passel of phantasmal stock options and sat through recitations of the company's short history. I saw the founder's original prototype robot arm, a beefy three-jointed limb almost as tall as me, set up in a little shrine in the center of the cafeteria. You could call out "Arm, change task. Say hello!" and it would wave a wide, eager greeting.

I learned the anatomy of the software I'd be working on, called ArmOS. I met my manager, Peter, who shook my hand with a grip even firmer than the talent associate's. An in-house apartment broker found me a place on Cabrillo Street in San Francisco's Richmond District for which I would pay rent fully four times larger than my mortgage in Michigan. The broker dropped the keys into my hand and said, "It's not a lot of space, but you won't be spending much time there!"

General Dexterity's founder, an astonishingly young man named Andrei, walked our group across Townsend Street to the Task Acquisition Center, a low-slung building that had once been a parking garage. The cement floor was still mottled with oil spots. Now, instead of cars in long lines, there were robot arms parked thirty to a row. Their plastic cladding was colored Dextrous blue, the contours friendly and capable with just the faintest suggestion of biceps—gentle swells marked with General Dexterity's logo, an affable lightning bolt.

The arms were all going at once, sweeping and grasping and nudging and lifting. If it was supposed to impress us: it worked.

All of these were repetitive gestures, Andrei explained, currently executed by human muscles and human minds. Repetition was the enemy of creativity, he said. Repetition belonged to robots.

We were on a quest to end work.

And it would involve: a shit ton of work.

My orientation week ended on Friday night with celebratory beers and a ping-pong tournament against one of the

7

robot arms, which of course emerged victorious. Then my job began. Not the following Monday. The next morning. Saturday.

I had the feeling of being sucked—*floop*—into a pneumatic tube.

The programmers at General Dexterity were utterly unlike my colleagues at Crowley, who had been middle-aged and chilled-out, and who enjoyed nothing as much as a patient explanation. The Dextrous were in no way patient. Many of them were college dropouts; they had been in a hurry to get here, and they were in a hurry now to be done, and rich. They were almost entirely young men, bony and cold-eyed, wraiths in Japanese denim and limited-edition sneakers. They started late in the morning, then worked past midnight. They slept at the office.

I hated the idea of it, but some nights I, too, succumbed to the cushy couches upholstered in Dextrous blue. Some nights, I'd lie there, staring up at the ceiling—the exposed ductwork, the rainbow braids of fiber channel ferrying data around the office—and feel a knot in my stomach that wouldn't loosen. I would think I had to poop and I would go squat on a toilet, doing nothing. The motion sensor would time out and the lights would click off, leaving me in darkness. Sometimes I would sit like that for a while. Then a line of code would occur to me, and I would limp back to my desk to tap it out.

At Crowley Control Systems in Southfield, the message we received from Clark Crowley, delivered in an amble around the office every month or so, was: Keep up the fine work, folks! At General Dexterity in San Francisco, the message we received from Andrei, delivered in a quantitative business update every Tuesday and Thursday, was: We are on a mission to remake the conditions of human labor, so push harder, all of you.

I began to wonder if, in fact, I knew how to push hard. In Michigan, my colleagues all had families and extremely serious hobbies. Here, the wraiths were stripped bare: human-shaped generators of CAD and code. I tried to emulate them, but something hitched inside me. I couldn't get my turbine spinning.

In the months that followed, I had the sense of some vital resource dwindling, and I tried to ignore it. My colleagues had been toiling at this pace for three years without a pause, and I was already flagging after a single San Francisco summer? I was supposed to be one of the bright new additions, the fresh-faced ones.

My face was not fresh.

My hair had gone flat and thin.

My stomach hurt.

In my apartment on Cabrillo Street, I existed mostly in a state of catatonic recovery, brain flaccid, cells gasping. My parents were far away, locked in the frame of a video chat window. I didn't have any friends in San Francisco aside from a handful of Dextrous, but they were just as traumatized as I was. My apartment was small and dark, and I paid too much for it, and the internet was slow.

TWELVE MINUTES after I had called it in, my order from Clement Street Soup and Sourdough arrived, carried to my door by a young man with a sweet face half hidden inside a ketchup-colored motorcycle helmet. A soft *oonce-oonce* of music emanated from within the helmet, and he bobbed to the beat.

He boomed his greeting in a heavy, hard-to-place accent: "Good evening, my friend!"

Greatest among us are those who can deploy "my friend" to total strangers in a way that is not hollow, but somehow real and deeply felt; those who can make you, within seconds of first contact, believe it.

I dug in my pocket for cash, and then, as I paid him, I thought to ask, "What kind of food is this?"

His face lit up like a neon sign. "It is the food of the Mazg! I hope you like it. If not, call again. My brother will make it better next time." He jogged toward his motorcycle but, halfway there, turned back to say, "You will like it, though." Above the rev of the engine he waved and repeated: "You will like it!"

Inside my apartment, on my kitchen countertop—utterly bare, free from any sign of food preparation or, really, human habitation—I unwrapped the sandwich and opened the soup and consumed the first combo (double spicy) of my life.

If Vietnamese pho's healing powers, physical and psychic, make traditional chicken noodle soup seem like dishwater— and they do—then this spicy soup, in turn, dishwatered pho. It was an elixir. The sandwich was spicier still, thin-sliced vegetables slathered with a fluorescent red sauce, the burn buffered by thick slabs of bread artfully toasted.

First my stomach unclenched, and then my brain. I let loose a long sigh that transformed into a rippling burp, which made me laugh out loud, alone, in my kitchen.

I lifted the lone magnet on my refrigerator, allowed a sheet of shiny pizza coupons to fall to the floor, and stuck the new menu reverently in its place.

I CALLED CLEMENT STREET SOUP AND SOURDOUGH again the next night, and the next. Then I skipped a night, feeling self-conscious, but I ordered again the night after that. For all its spiciness, the food sat perfectly in my traumatized stomach.

In the month that followed, I learned about it bit by bit:

- The restaurant was operated by two brothers.
- Beoreg, with the sweet voice and the perfect English, answered the phone and cooked the food.
- Chaiman, with the sweet face and the earbuds never not leaking dance music, rode the motorcycle and delivered the food.
- When pressed for more information on "the food of the Mazg," Chaiman would only laugh and say, "It's famous!"
- Beoreg and Chaiman had been slinging spicy soups and/or sandwiches in San Francisco for just over a year.
- They possessed no storefront: they cooked where they lived, in an apartment whose precise location they were reluctant to disclose.
- Chaiman said, "It is okay. Just not legal. Definitely okay, though."
- With the double spicy, one bonus slab of sourdough bread was included, always, for dunking in your soup.
- That bread was the secret of the whole operation. Beoreg baked it himself every day.
- That bread was life.

Most nights, I called ahead and waited on hold (though I was recognized, and the greeting from brother Beoreg was not "Okay to hold?" but "Lois! Hi! I have to put you on hold. Just a second, I promise") with the music in another language I'd grown to appreciate—it was sad, in a nice way—and then, rescued from purgatory, I placed my order (the same order every time), and when brother Chaiman brought it on his motorcycle, I greeted him warmly and tipped him generously, then carried my double spicy inside to eat it standing, my eyes watering from the heat and the happiness.

One Friday, after a particularly shattering day at the office, in which my code reviews had all come back red with snotty comments, and my manager, Peter, had gently inquired about the pace of my refactoring ("perhaps not sufficiently turbo-charged"), I arrived home in a swirl of angst, with petulance and self-recrimination locked in ritual combat to determine which would ruin my night. On the phone with Beoreg, I ordered my food with a rattling sigh, and when his brother arrived at my door, he carried something different: a more compact tub containing a fiery red broth and not one but two slabs of bread for dipping. "Secret spicy," he whispered. The soup was so hot it burned the frustration out of me, and I went to bed feeling like a fresh plate, scalded and scraped clean.

Is it an exaggeration to say Clement Street Soup and Sourdough saved me? At night, instead of fitfully reviewing the day's errors while my stomach swam and churned, I . . . fell asleep. My course steadied. I had taken on ballast in the form of spicy broth and fragrant bread and, maybe, two new friends, or sort-of-friends, or something.

Then they went away.

It was on a Wednesday in September that I dialed the number and was greeted by Beoreg, who said "Okay to hold?" as if he didn't recognize me, then abandoned me to the sad-but-nice music for a very long time, so long in fact I suspected he'd forgotten me. When he came back on the line, he accepted my order dutifully and told me his brother would bring it soon. "Goodbye," he murmured before hanging up. He'd never actually said that before.

When Chaiman knocked on my door, his sweet face was morose. He wasn't listening to any music. The night seemed suddenly oppressively quiet

"Hello, my friend," he said limply. The bag containing my double spicy dangled limply from his fingers.

I took the bag and cradled it, felt the warmth of the soup across my chest. "What's wrong?"

"We are leaving," he said. "Visas, you know?"

This was unacceptable.

"We cannot stay. I would try, but Beoreg says . . . he does not want to be hidden forever. He wants to have a real restaurant. With tables." Chaiman rolled his eyes, as if wishing to serve customers in a physical establishment constituted Versailles-level extravagance.

"We will miss you," he said. "Me and Beoreg both."

The bag in my arms crinkled, and so did the skin around my eyes. I wanted to wail, *Don't leave me! What will I eat? Who will I call?* But all I could muster was "I'm so sorry to hear about this."

He nodded. I did, too. It was September, and the air was very cold. He said, "I should tell you . . . Beoreg and I have a joke. When he gives me the bag"—he poked at the food in my arms—"and says, for Lois on Cabrillo Street, we always say together: the number one eater!"

I didn't know what that meant, but I knew I had never been one before.

"It's supposed to be nice. Because we like you. You know?"

I did.

Astride his motorcycle, Chaiman raised a hand and shook his index finger emphatically. Above the rev of the engine, he cried again: "Number one eater!"

THE SLURRY TABLE

WORK LOOKED LIKE THIS: me, sitting for twelve hours at my desk in the basement of a converted macaroni factory near the park where the Giants play. My company-issued laptop was hulking and loud, the roaring fan necessary to cool the superfast GPU within. At my desk, I hooked it into a pair of monitors, a keyboard, a tablet with stylus. No mouse. I'd learned the tablet trick from one of the patient programmers at Crowley, who recommended it as a ward against repetitive stress injury. Here at General Dexterity, the wraiths regarded it strangely. They could not yet imagine their bodies betraying them.

ArmOS was comprised of two lobes.

First there was Control, the code that told the arms how to move. It read their super-precise sensors, flexed their motor-muscles. The code was very compact and highly optimized, because any improvement to Control—a faster sensor reading, a firmer grip—applied to everything the arms did.

Then there was Task, the code that told the arms *why* to move. Task was a thrilling jumble of heuristics and hacks.

If Control was all about one thing—moving in space—then Task was about a thousand things. The module called Stacking gave the arms a theory of gravity, balance, and layers, and right next door there was the module called Glassware, a hard-coded cheat sheet containing the dimensions, to the micrometer, of the world's ten thousand most common scientific flasks and vials.

(In addition to Task and Control there was also Interface, the code that allowed users to control their arms and apply continuous ArmOS upgrades, all with a simple web app, but the other teams pitied Interface, because its work was so easy.)

My manager, Peter, had recently been promoted to oversee all of Control. I worked on the submodule responsible for Proprioception, which is, I think, a beautiful word—*pro-pri-o-cep-tion!*—and also the process by which organisms judge the position of their own body parts in space. It's a crucial sense; definitely more important than a few of the Big Five. When you walk, you look forward, not down at your feet, because you are confident they are where you expect them to be, obeying your commands. That's a pretty cool feature.

It was an unanticipated consequence of working on robot proprioception that I would often sit at my desk snaking my arms around in the air, trying to pay very close attention to what was happening. I'd close my eyes, extend a hand, lift it slowly while rotating it at the same time. What was I feeling? The weight of my own limb, yes; but also . . . a tendril of strange information. Not touch, exactly. Something else. Proprioception!

I did this quite a bit, for reasons both technical and therapeutic, and once, I opened my eyes to find Peter standing there, silently watching me propriocept. I yelped.

My persistent stomachache had been diagnosed after a consultation at General Dexterity's in-house clinic (next to the dentist and the masseuse) as stress-related. The nurse plucked a brochure from a thick stack; its title, printed in Dextrous blue, was *Taking Care of Yourself While You're Changing the World.*

It was Peter who recommended switching to the liquid meal replacement that he and many of the other programmers preferred, and that seemed easier to digest under the circumstances, which were extreme and unrelenting.

"Slurry," he said. "It's outstanding."

Slurry was a nutritive gel manufactured by an eponymous company even newer than General Dexterity. Dispensed in waxy green Tetra Paks, it had the consistency of a thick milkshake. It was nutritionally complete and rich with probiotics. It was fully dystopian.

I signed up for a trial month using a coupon code obtained from Peter and had my subscription delivered directly to the office. I was not alone. On the day I picked it up in the mail room, there was an enormous ziggurat of green Tetra Paks waiting on a shipping pallet. The gel tasted like burnt almonds and it did sit better in my stomach than the regular food in the cafeteria; it also rescued me from the endless teeter-totter between salad bar and paella station.

There was another benefit, which was social. At mealtimes, I sat in the Slurry corner of the cafeteria, where a not-insignificant fraction of the Dextrous gathered to furtively slurp our gray gel. The group around my table became my first shaky scaffolding of office friendship. Peter was our chieftain, and he was in fact sponsored by Slurry, his deluxe subscription provided free as long as he continued to place in the top five in his age group at approved athletic events (10K races, triathlons, caber tosses) and do so wearing bright green Slurry-branded spandex. His subscription was a bleeding-edge formulation with occasionally noxious side effects; he consumed it three times a day, seven days a week.

The rest of us ate Slurry only two or three days a week. The other days, we slunk into the lunch line to select our preferred fried chicken parts under Chef Kate's woeful gaze.

Besides Peter, there was Garrett, a pale and intense programmer on the internationalization team; Benjamin, a security specialist who worked to ensure that the robot arms couldn't be hacked; Anton, a sales associate burdened with a deeply unfortunate Bluetooth earpiece; and Arjun, a sprightly interface designer, also from Michigan, who became the first of the Dextrous I dared to call my friend. In addition to our interactions at the Slurry table, Arjun and I sometimes migrated to a bar farther down Townsend Street after leaving the office for ten p.m. beers and cheese fries. Peter did not approve.

During a lull in the conversation around the table—they were many; we were awkward—I told my comrades in slurpage the sad news about Clement Street Soup and Sourdough.

"I don't eat bread," Peter said preemptively.

"Didn't it hurt your stomach?" asked Garrett.

It had not. "The soup was really spicy, but it was balanced somehow. And I really liked the guys who made it." My cheeks felt tight, and I knew I was emitting a pulse of emotion that was too much for this crowd, so I said, "Back to Slurry for dinner!" and took a gurgling slurp from the Tetra Pak.

I COULDN'T FACE Proprioception or ArmOS or any of it, so I walked across Townsend Street to the Task Acquisition Center.

All the arms faced different scenarios erected on workbenches wheeled and locked into place: one was an array of test tubes, as in a lab; another, a disassembled phone, as in a factory; another, an open cardboard box, as in a warehouse; and on and on. Arms had vacuums, arms had drills, arms had nothing but their bare six-fingered hands. The training floor clicked and whirred and whined and thwacked. Above the din, the occasional human curse.

At each bench there was an instructor, moving an arm through a sequence of motions, demonstrating how a procedure unfolded: the lift and shake of a test tube; the pick and place of a phone assembly; the pack and seal of a box, which was a job for two arms together, punctuated by the *skritchhh* of tape.

The trainers were contractors, very well compensated— but only temporarily. Each lab technician or factory worker or logistics specialist would teach one robot arm how to perform one task impeccably, under many different conditions, variously adverse. When the task had been mastered, it would be integrated into ArmOS, and in that moment, every General Dexterity arm on the planet would become that much more capable.

There were trainers outside this building, too. In addition to all the built-in capabilities of ArmOS, there was a marketplace for skill extensions—things more niche than we could ever imagine. How to swirl a petri dish containing a particular strain of bacteria. How to insert a fuel rod safely into a nuclear reactor. How to sew the laces into a football. Whole companies had formed around some of these tasks. The fuel rod people had just three customers, and they were rich.

I paused for a moment to watch the arms at work, and in their subtlest motions I could see my contribution. When they swiveled in two dimensions at once, the motion was smoother than it had been a few months ago. I'd spent a lot of time poring over the PKD 2891 Stepper Motor data sheet to figure that out.

One arm, working under the supervision of a burly, bearded trainer, faced a mock kitchen countertop, bare except for a mixing bowl and a carton of eggs. *Oh no.* I pitied it.

The arm plucked an egg, brought it to the bowl, tapped it against the rim: once, gently (too gently); again, harder (still not enough); and a third time, too hard (much too hard), shell exploding against the bowl, yolk falling in orange ribbons through its fingers down both sides of the bowl, pooling on the countertop.

I was glad not to be working on Force Feedback. Even after years of work, ArmOS struggled with its gentlest touch. We would solve everything else before we solved the egg problem.

THAT DAY, I left General Dexterity earlier than I ever had before, with the sun still shining on the sidewalk outside. I activated the standard suite of office chaff: left a data sheet on my desk, opened to its third page, seemingly mid-consultation, and draped my jacket artfully across the back of my chair, indicating that I hadn't left the office—never that—but was only attending a meeting or crying in a bathroom. Normal stuff.

In fact, I hopped aboard the Muni train bound for downtown. Riding across the city, I had a knotty feeling in my chest that I briefly worried might be cardiac, but by the time the 5 bus arrived in the Richmond District, I understood it was simply sorrow.

THE CLEMENT STREET STARTER

I HAD MOURNED MY LOSS and slurped my Slurry and was buffering a dark serial drama through my slow internet connection when I heard a knock on the door, light and confident. I knew that knock.

It was Chaiman, for the first time unencumbered by his motorcycle helmet. His hair was sandy brown.

"Number one eater!" he cried.

Another figure was standing behind him, farther down the steps. This man had the same sweet face and the same sandy hair, but his skin was darker and he was thicker around the middle.

Chaiman turned to him. "Beoreg, you are too shy. Come on."

The voice on the phone! Beoreg. Chef and baker, master of the double spicy, author of my comfort. I felt like I should bow.

"We are leaving now," Chaiman said. There was a brown taxi idling in the street behind them. "But Beo had the idea to give you a gift."

"That's sweet of you," I said.

Beoreg smiled, but his gaze was fixed somewhere around

my shins. He offered an object wrapped in a scratchy kitchen towel. It was a ceramic crock, about as big as a family-size jar of peanut butter, dark green with a matching lid, the glaze shimmering iridescent.

"What is it?" It looked like the kind of vessel that might contain an ancestor's ashes, which I definitely did not want.

"It's our culture," Beoreg said softly.

Nope, I definitely did not—

"I mean 'starter,'" Beoreg corrected himself. "For making sourdough bread, you know? I brought it so you could bake your own."

I had no idea what to do with a starter.

Chaiman sensed my unease. "Beo will show you," he said. He craned his neck to peer into my apartment. "If you have a kitchen?"

I had a kitchen. I led them inside.

"It's very clean," Beoreg said. His English was flawless, with a faint clip like something from a BBC show—a new one, not a historical drama.

"I never cook," I confessed.

"Because you are the number one eater!" Chaiman hooted. He pointed gleefully at their menu, still stuck to the refrigerator.

"Do you have flour?" Beoreg asked softly.

I almost laughed. "No flour," I said. "Really. I never cook."

He nodded sharply. "No problem. I'll give you everything you need." He jogged to the door.

Chaiman had opened the refrigerator without asking and was rooting around inside. He pulled out a waxy Tetra Pak of Slurry and looked at it like it was a dead mouse.

23

Beoreg returned a moment later dragging an enormous wooden trunk, scarred and stickered, something from another era of travel. He unhooked its clasps and threw back the lid; inside, arrayed in a jumble, were all the accoutrements of a kitchen.

There were small long-handled cups and broad, flat pans. I saw a thick clutch of wooden spoons, their edges stained and charred, and a collection of mixing bowls nested one inside the other, padded with newspaper. There were murky glass vessels holding baby Xenomorphs (possibly they were pickles) and bright colorful boxes with labels in Arabic and Hebrew and other scripts I didn't recognize. There were tiny unmarked jars holding red and yellow powders; precursor ingredients, no doubt, to the "secret spicy." There was a cutting board upright along the back of the trunk, its surface mottled with spills and streaks and deep-notched evidence of cleaver work.

While he rummaged, Beoreg asked, "So, do you know how bread is made?"

"Sure," I said. "Basically." I knew there was flour involved. "Not really." I was an eater, not a baker.

"There's a living thing, a culture. I guess it's more American to say 'starter.' You mix the starter with the flour, along with water and salt, and it makes gas, which makes the dough rise. It gives it a certain flavor, too." Beoreg stood, holding a selection of tools. "You've had pets?"

I shook my head ruefully. The only living thing I had ever managed to support was myself, and then only barely, except for—

"Maybe a plant?"

"Yes!" I said. "I have a desk cactus."

"Okay! This culture—starter, sorry—it's like that. It's alive." He lifted the crock's lid. "See?"

The gray slime inside looked distinctly not alive. It looked like an enemy of aliveness. Like something alive things crossed the street to avoid.

"Smell," he commanded, and offered the crock, tilting it toward me. "Can you detect it?"

I took a guarded sniff, allowing no more than two or three molecules from the decrepit vessel into my nose. I equivocated. "What is it supposed to smell like?"

"Bananas, a bit. It's a very nice smell."

I sniffed again, still detected nothing, but nodded my head agreeably. "You're right. That is nice." It was the same strategy I employed at wine tastings.

Beoreg beamed. "But you have to feed it, okay? Keep it going. I'll show you how."

He plopped his selection of tools onto the countertop. First was a stout, thick-papered sack of flour, the top neatly folded and chip-clipped. "Whole flour," he said. "It has to be whole." Next came a small mixing bowl and a long-handled cup. "Measure twenty grams—just this much." He lowered the cup into the sack, leveled it with his finger. "See?" He dumped the flour into the mixing bowl, then filled the same long-handled cup with water from the tap. "The same amount." He added the water to the bowl, snatched up the last of his tools, a short wooden spoon, and started to stir.

Chaiman had been fishing around in the trunk, and he stood holding a CD jewel case. "You must play the music of the Mazg, too!" he declared.

I dug out my hulking General Dexterity laptop and felt along its edge for the CD tray I had never once used. Inside

Chaiman's jewel case there was a plain disc with its title handwritten in the mystery script of the menu. I dropped it into the tray. The laptop cleared its throat, whining and clicking, and sound began to flow from its speakers. It was the brothers' hold music, sad and inimitable, crooned in that unfamiliar language. The language of the Mazg. As it played, Beoreg and Chaiman seemed to slow down and synchronize. Chaiman's posture relaxed and Beoreg's eyes softened as he stirred.

"This is the starter's food—see?" Beoreg said, showing me how the water and flour had combined into a pale paste. "It's important to feed it every day. If you skip a day, it will be okay, but not any longer than that."

This was seeming like more and more of a commitment.

Beoreg looked me in the eye for the first time, his gaze suddenly searching. "You'll keep it alive?"

I should have backed out. I should have thanked the brothers one last time for all the combos (double spicy) and escorted them back to their taxi waiting in the street. Instead, I said: "Of course I will."

Beoreg beamed. "Good! And you can bake with it. That's great." His eyes flickered down. He handed me the mixing bowl with its pasty contents. "Here, you can feed the starter now. Your first time."

I scooped up the floury paste with the spoon, held it for a moment over the shimmering maw of the crock, then plopped it in.

"Do I stir it together?"

"Yes, until it's all mixed."

The pasty food marbled into the dark starter, and then the combined mixture faded to an even gray. I kept stirring, and stirring, until Beoreg said gently, "That's enough." He took the spoon, washed it quickly under the tap, then laid it neatly beside the mixing bowl and the long-handled cup. "All of these, you can keep."

He set the crock's lid into place with the gentleness of a parent tucking a child into bed.

I wondered what else was inside that trunk. "What about the spicy soup? Can I make that, too?"

Beoreg looked sheepish. "It's more complicated. I can write it down, maybe. Here." He scrounged for a pen, crouched in front of the refrigerator, and wrote an email address along the bottom edge of their menu. It was the same dark, sure script; that was Beoreg's handwriting. "Send me a message."

The brothers shuffled out of my apartment and into the taxi, still waving as its door clomped shut. The taxi's tires squeaked as it leapt forward into the night, carrying them to the airport or the bus station or, who knows, maybe to a boat waiting at some lonely pier.

Back in the apartment, the CD was still playing, sweet and sad.

SPARTAN STIX

L ET ME JUST ESTABLISH where I was at with the whole cooking situation.

When I was a child, my family had no distinguishable cuisine. I remember Happy Meal hamburgers and Hungry-Man fried chicken. I remember the Denny's menu; we knew that backward and forward. I remember tubs of popcorn at the movies. Tubs of popcorn for dinner.

We possessed no stock of recipes, no traditions, no ancestral affinities. There was a lot of migration and drama in our history; our line had been broken not once but many times, like one of those gruesome accident reports, the bone shattered in six places. When they put my family back together, they left out the food.

There was one exception. My grandma Lois, for whom I was named, did not deign to cook—she was my mother's mother in that regard—but she did, on special occasions, bake bread. Specifically, she baked Chicago Prison Loaf, a comically hard and dense but apparently nutritious substance that she had learned to produce working part-time at an industrial bakery that served the Illinois Department of Corrections. In my family, Chicago Prison Loaf was a joke—a grim surprise often wrapped up for Christmas in a box chosen for its resemblance to a nice sweater or a video game console. Grandma Lois did seem to genuinely enjoy eating it, toasted and slathered. The rest of us, we buttered the bread we bought at the grocery store.

My high school cafeteria offered a rotating daily menu item, but I can assure you that I never chose it. Instead: fries, fries, two orders of fries! Fries so perfectly crisp they put fast-food fries to shame, fries crusted with salt and eaten one by one, fries not merely consumed but circulated as social currency: peace offerings, seductions. Four years in that cafeteria and I ate nothing but fries. The teenage body is a miracle. How did it scrounge from those sticks of burnt starch enough vitamins and minerals to sustain me, and not just sustain me but make me grow, and grow absurdly, grow six inches, grow boobs and hips? It was a disgusting diet. I realize that now. I bow down before that body.

In college, I did not immediately realize that it was behind me. The summer before freshman year, the One Campus, One Book selection had converted me to vegetarianism, which meant the things I ate never seemed to fill me up. Armed with a dormitory meal plan, I consumed the equivalent of nine meals a day, all of them shaded brown, textured crispy. You would expect a vegetarian, perhaps, to eat vegetables; you would be disappointed. There was never on my tray a single tuft of green.

I sat in various dorm rooms with my computer science cabal, plowing through problem sets, eating whole pizzas and so-called Spartan Sticks—named for the school's mascot, and upon reflection, it may have been spelled Stix—which were just pizzas that omitted tomato sauce and compensated for its absence with more cheese and even more cheese and a flaky garlic powder that carried a hot chemical burn.

Four years of this. By the end, I was a puffy caricature of myself. As my senior year started, I did finally realize that something had gone wrong; that the teenage machine had broken down, and that my body—desperate, pushed beyond any reasonable nutritional tolerances—was simply building new parts out of salt. I tried to improve my diet, but only in the most marginal and clueless ways. I stopped ordering whole pizzas and bought family-size tubs of hummus. I consumed baby carrots by the pound.

Later, back in Southfield, I cleaned up my act somewhat. Before I was the number one eater at Clement Street Soup and Sourdough, I was a very familiar face at the Whole Foods salad bar on West 10 Mile. My creations tended to go heavy on croutons. One day, a single chicken tender found its way into the nest of lettuce. It was delicious. So closed a brief and disastrous era.

In San Francisco, I switched to Slurry, and my refrigerator looked like something out of a sci-fi movie, tight rows of shimmery Tetra Paks replenished every two weeks.

This is all to say: I'd never baked bread in my life.

THE LOIS CLUB

I CLIMBED THE HILL behind the hospital to attend a meeting of the Lois Club.

Do other names boast affiliated clubs? Certainly there is no Rachel Club. Maybe Persephones have a club. We Loises do. It's real! There are chapters scattered around the country.

My grandmother Lois LaMotte was a member of the first-ever Lois Club, in Milwaukee. Later, after she moved to Detroit to be closer to her daughter and eponymous baby granddaughter, she met another Lois waiting in line at Meijer and together they formed the Metro Detroit chapter. They advertised it in the newspaper! I attended an early meeting as an infant; there is a photo I still possess, scanned and saved, that shows a group of six white-haired women all named Lois gathered around a swaddled baby burrito who is also named Lois, their faces frozen in coos of delight. Little burrito Lois is crying.

My only conscious memory of that Lois Club comes from when I must have been nine or ten years old. I can remember the dry floral scent of someone else's grandma's house, and what then seemed to me—a shy kid—an overwhelming cacophony of laughter; unrelenting cackles. I retreated into an adjoining room, where I played my Nintendo DS. One of the Loises—I have no idea which one—stumbled upon me there, and for at least ten minutes she watched the shimmering screen silently over my shoulder.

Grandma Lois died when I was twelve, and throughout my teens my mother would gently inquire, once every couple of years, if I ever thought about attending a meeting of the Lois Club. I did not. Without Grandma Lois? Unthinkable. In any case, I'm not sure the Detroit chapter lasted long without her.

So, my first thought upon arriving in California was not: *I ought to look up the local Lois Club.* Nor was it my second thought, or my three hundred and fifty-third. It was my mother who sent me the link. "I thought of Gram's club the other day," she wrote, "and look what I found!" It was a page on the Lois Club website advertising the existence of a San Francisco Bay Area chapter.

I might not have been so eager to meet the Loises if I hadn't been spending all day with the cold-eyed wraiths at General Dexterity. By comparison, hanging out with a bunch of middle-aged ladies with the same name as me sounded pretty alluring.

The meeting was held in a dark-shingled house in a twisty neighborhood reached by a hidden staircase that wandered up from Parnassus Avenue. I hiked from the Farnsworth Steps to Edgewood Avenue to a cul-de-sac that backed up against the eucalyptus forest that crowned the hill.

A handwritten sign on the door read: *Welcome, Lois!*

It made me smile. I could tell that whoever wrote it was very pleased with herself. Not without reason.

The house was large and deeply lived-in, all the shelves

and surfaces stacked with books and boxes, framed pictures, old greeting cards set up like tent cities. If there was a spectrum of spaces defined at one end by my barren apartment, this marked the other extreme. Every single surface told a story. A long one. With digressions.

The Loises were in the dining room open to the kitchen, five of them clustered around a long table beside a wide window that showed a panorama of the western city—Golden Gate Park, my neighborhood beyond it, the fuzzy gray bar of the ocean beyond everything. Their hair, bleached by age, glowed in the afternoon light.

If you ever wonder about the difference between Metro Detroit and the San Francisco Bay Area: compare their Lois Clubs.

The hostess, whom I thought of as Hilltop Lois, had owned her house since 1972—an impossible span. She had once run a cheese shop at the base of the hill, and her taste had not grown less discriminating; she served us the stinkiest cheese I have ever been offered at a casual gathering. Nibbling with varying degrees of enthusiasm were also:

- Compaq Lois, who had been a marketing executive at that company in its boom years. Her wrists dripped with bracelets and chunky bangles, all gold; they piled up onto her forearms. She looked like a Valkyrie queen.
- Professor Lois, who taught anthropology at the University of San Francisco. Through the window, she pointed to the spires of St. Ignatius: "I've been climbing that hill for a decade." She was lean like a goat.
- Impeccable Lois, who possessed the kind of sartorial style that stops you on the street. She was wearing

jodhpurs—with confidence—and above them an inky denim jacket that any of the cold-eyed wraiths would have killed her to acquire. Literally murdered her. "Don't wear that down by the ballpark," I warned.

• Old Lois, who deserved a better nickname, but truly: she was old. Somewhere past ninety. Physically she seemed barely there, curled into herself, but her eyes were bright, and when I walked into the dining room and introduced myself, she crowed: "I didn't know they were still making Loises!"

They were interesting and lively, their relationships worn-in and comfortable. They had been gathering for two decades. I sat and listened and smiled and genuinely enjoyed myself, though afterward, as I padded down the Farnsworth Steps, I worried that I'd been too quiet—too boring. The other Loises had sharp opinions. They took up space.

They reminded me of Grandma Lois, and I thought about her Chicago Prison Loaf. The absurd density of it. It was the single culinary tradition my family possessed, and it was horrible.

But she had baked it all the time.

As I walked through Golden Gate Park, it struck me: the mystery of that woman's life. I hadn't ever known her, not really. I sucked in a deep breath. She had relocated from Wisconsin to Michigan, but before that she'd lived in Chicago and performed with an experimental-theater company, bunking with three other women in a tiny apartment, and not only baking that awful bread but bringing it home to share, because it was free and more or less nutritious. In later years, when she baked Chicago Prison Loaf, it must have conjured that other place, that other time. Four women in bunk beds. Midnight shows. Crimson wigs.

I sat at a computer twelve hours a day and slurped nutritive gel for lunch and dinner.

After my success in college, my neat acquisition of a job, and my precocious home purchase, I had considered myself a child of whom parents and grandparents could be proud. But it struck me then: the starkness of my apartment. Of my life. Grandma Lois, if she could have come to visit—and for the first time ever, I felt a pang, a deep wish that she could visit me here, just her alone, alive—if she could have, and if she had seen me here in San Francisco, she wouldn't have been proud of me. She would have been sad, and maybe a little bit worried.

I needed a more interesting life.

I could start by learning something.

I could start with the starter.

JESUS CHRIST IN AN ENGLISH MUFFIN

I WALKED TO THE BRIGHT BOOKSTORE on Clement Street and obtained a used copy of *The Soul of Sourdough*, written by a baker named Everett Broom, whose forearms graced the cover, taut and darkly gleaming, cradling a loaf of bread that was likewise burnished.

The book's introduction ran for twenty-two pages. It was a baker's bildungsroman, chronicling Broom's youth in Sacramento, his visits to his grandfather's bakery, his flameout as a professional skateboarder, his addiction to a home-cooked drug known as spaz rocks, and finally his retreat to a bread-baking shack on the beach and his reformation there. There were photos, all monochrome: a young man with a thick black beard below a face so clean and cherubic it made the beard appear glued on. In a photo spread across two pages, he leaned against a homemade brick oven, for which the adjective *rustic* was a favor; it looked like a pile of rubble. Scattered in the foreground were various signifiers of bohemian tranquility: a guitar, a surfboard, a book with VOLTAIRE on the spine.

He was out there learning, in his words, "to bake without

dry yeast, without desiccation, without death." Well, sure. Nobody wants death bread. Instead, he sought the alchemy of sourdough: "Wet, living, fragile, sensual. The funk of life. I smelled it on the beach, and in the forest glades where I gathered mushrooms, and in the embrace of Lucia, who was at that time my lover. And I smelled it in my starter, too."

After twenty-two pages of funk versus death, the painstaking construction from found materials of his oven, the hollow of Lucia's clavicle, et cetera, Broom figured it out. A photo showed a very young man with a very large beard grinning manically into the camera, hoisting a loaf of bread in the air like a trophy. The loaf was as big around as his chest, and, to be fair, it looked totally awesome.

He came to San Francisco, where he opened Boulangerie Broom—now a chain with three locations—and wrote this book. He shaved his beard and traded the shack for a house in Noe Valley. He married a product manager named Olivia and had two kids.

End of introduction. Next, Broom got down to business.

Sourdough bread begins with sourdough starter, which is not merely living but seething. It is a community of organisms comprised of, at minimum, yeast, which is a fungus, and lactobacillus, a bacteria. They eat flour—its sugars—and poop out acid—thus, sour—in addition to carbon dioxide, which, trapped by stretchy, glutenous dough, gives the bread an airy structure, the so-called crumb, at its prettiest a dazzling network of gaps and chambers.

Broom's first chapter described the capture and cultivation of a wild sourdough starter, a process that could take a week or more. I already possessed the Clement Street starter, so I skipped ahead.

Broom lamented the fact that we, his readers, could not bake with the benefit of a beachside shack or a rough-hewn brick oven or an Argentine lover. But he said we could still make a pretty good attempt at it, and he listed the equipment we would need:

- A digital scale, to weigh the ingredients
- A bench knife, to scrape and divide the dough
- A bread blade, to score the loaf (with a baker's mark that, ideally, matched our wrist tattoo)
- A baking stone, to absorb and emit heat in a loose simulation of Broom's brick oven (though he counseled that there was, in fact, no substitute and that, basically, he pitied us)

I opened my laptop, called up the website of an expedient internet retailer, and pecked in the name of the scale—the precise brand and model that Broom recommended. The site immediately responded: CUSTOMERS WHO BOUGHT THIS ITEM ALSO BOUGHT . . . followed by the bench knife. And the bread blade. The baking stone. King Arthur flour and Diamond Crystal salt, just as Everett Broom recommended. And finally, Broom's book itself.

The internet: always proving that you're not quite as special as you suspected.

Two days later, a UPS driver delivered the tools and ingredients to my apartment. She also delivered one apron that I had purchased from a different internet retailer, a craftier one. The apron was squarish, made from heavy denim. It looked like something a blacksmith might wear. It was the first apron I'd ever owned. I loved it.

I set out my tools. I donned my apron. Everything was in order, and I was ready to produce a beautiful, burnished loaf just like Broom's on the cover of his book.

There were detailed instructions. I love detailed instructions. My whole career was detailed instructions. Precisely specified actions, executed in order. A serene confidence settled over me.

I mixed the ingredients together, and immediately the project collapsed into chaos and disaster.

Where the bread book showed a lump of dough folded elegantly into itself, I looked upon a twisted mutant mass.

Where the bread book showed Everett Broom's clean fingers deftly maneuvering said lump, my hands soon wore thick gauntlets of glop. I waved them over the sink, tried to shake some of it loose

Where the bread book showed a rustic work surface smartly maintained, I looked upon a cramped and dingy countertop filmed with slime.

There was dough on the cupboards. Dough on the faucet. Dough on the floor. It looked like the scene of a glutenous murder committed by a careless killer.

With each step, reality diverged further from the shining ideal pictured in the bread book, and by the end of it, I wasn't even following Broom's directions anymore, just doing whatever I could to keep the dough in one piece. It was too wet, so I added flour, then it was too dry, so I added water, and it became gloppy again, so more flour was required, and the dough grew and grew, bloblike.

There was a malevolence to it. It was not on my side.

Broom's directions indicated that it was now time to retreat while the starter did its work to make the loaf ferment and rise, and I did this gratefully. I washed my hands, tore off the apron, set the oven to preheat, opened an Anchor Steam, and flopped down in my living room. I found my laptop and set Chaiman's CD to playing. I knew every song. I'd heard them all, waiting on hold night after night.

When the timer beeped, I discovered that the dough had indeed expanded in size, and it had also firmed up somewhat. Its skin was soft but not gloppy. Glossy. I quickly folded it over onto itself, opened the oven—which was really very hot inside; was this safe? Were you truly supposed to set the temperature this high?—and dropped it onto the baking stone. Then I pushed the oven's rack back into place and slammed the door, just as a warden might slam the door on a prisoner, supremely evil and objectively irredeemable, banishing him to solitary confinement forever.

I set the oven's timer, opened another Anchor Steam, and played Chaiman's CD again. It had seven tracks, each almost ten minutes long. The music of the Mazg was entirely a cappella—a tight cluster of voices. Their language sounded Slavic, but every so often there was a hard stop, like the hitch of a sob, or an ear-bending slide between notes that spun the sound into some other, more distant dimension.

I wondered if the brothers had arrived at their destination. I thought about emailing Beoreg, but I didn't know what I would say. Our relationship had been constrained entirely by the menu. If not "Double spicy, please," then what?

FORTY MINUTES, four songs, and three beers later, the timer beeped. I opened the oven door and pulled out the rack to assess the damage.

Against all odds, the malevolent loaf emerged from the oven round and buoyant, its crust split by deep fissures. It was perhaps not as perfectly photogenic as the one on the cover of the bread book, but it was . . . not too bad.

In my exasperation, I had skipped one of Broom's steps, the one where he exhorted you to carve a baker's mark, some symbol of your own choosing. (His mark was a heart with an X through it, which was also the logo of Boulangerie Broom, seen on T-shirts and tote bags throughout San Francisco.) I had not signed my sloppy work, but there was nevertheless a clearly defined shape in the cracks and whorls of the crust.

You couldn't not see it.

The loaf had a face.

It was an illusion, of course. Jesus Christ in an English muffin. It's called pareidolia. Humans see faces in everything. Even so, the illusion was . . . compelling. This face was long and twisted, wide-eyed and openmouthed, Edvard Munch–like. Where the crust cracked, it formed furrows in the face's brow, lines around its howling mouth.

I reached down with oven mitts and lifted the loaf from the baking stone, almost expecting the face to relax in relief. Its expression remained fixed, because it was, of course, not a face but a crispy crust. I plopped it down on the countertop, fished out my phone, and snapped a picture. I was about to send it to Arjun, but something made me pause. There was real pain in the phantom face. It wasn't funny. It was disturbing. I deleted the photo.

In the bread book, Broom counseled that it was essential now to wait, to let the bread cool, to allow the glutens to complete their final binding, but I was hungry and I didn't want to stare at the face any longer. With my bread knife (which CUSTOMERS WHO BOUGHT THIS ITEM ALSO BOUGHT), I sawed through the loaf at its widest point and, like a vision in the clouds twisting apart in the wind, the illusion broke. I looked at the bread's cross section, the crumb, and I giggled a little. It didn't look like the pictures in the book; this sourdough was not so perfectly inflated, its bubbles not so lacy. But, seriously . . . not too bad!

I made another cut, peeled away a rough slice, and blew across its surface, tossing it from one hand to the other. It was too hot to eat, but I began to eat it anyway, and it tasted just like the bread that came with the double spicy.

This was Beoreg's sourdough. There was no disputing it. But as I took one mincing bite after another—I'd been waiting hours—the fact asserted itself: I'd made it myself, from nothing but flour and water and salt and a dollop of the Clement Street starter. The net cost of ingredients couldn't have been more than a dollar, and now I had this enormous loaf of bread, my favorite bread, my serenity bread. I was disappointed not to have any spicy soup for sopping. I didn't even have any butter. I ate it plain.

That loaf of bread was the first thing I'd ever prepared myself that did not come out of a box with instructions printed on the side. My apartment was suffused with its smell, the smell I knew and loved. I wanted to fish out my phone and dial the old number and cry out to Beoreg before he could put me on hold: *I did it!*

Instead, I wrote an email. Just a short message—*Look what your number one eater made!*—dispatched to the address he'd written on the menu, to which I attached a photo of myself, proudly holding up a sliver of a slice of sourdough, my cheeks full of the rest. Was it cute? It was cute. I sent it.

The twisted face in the crust was forgotten as I carved and ate, carved and ate, until the whole loaf was gone.

SHARING THE MIRACLE

THE NEXT MORNING it felt like it had been a dream, but there was the mess I'd left on the countertop, and there was the aroma, still lingering: evidence of the work I'd done, the thing I'd produced. I emailed Peter at General Dexterity to invoke one of my theoretical vacation days—I could almost hear his gasp across the city—then switched my phone to airplane mode and baked two more loaves.

This time, the dough was not so gloppy, the process not such a disaster. I waited serenely, watching three episodes of the dark serial drama while the dough fermented and rose, and another episode while the twin loaves baked.

But when I opened the oven door and pulled out the rack, I had to suck in a sharp breath. My first thought was: *You have had a tiny stroke. Possibly stress-related.* I'd read about neurological conditions that made it so you couldn't recognize people's faces; was I suffering from the opposite? Some sort of hyper-recognition? I looked around the kitchen, fixed my gaze on random objects: Cupboard. Faucet. Refrigerator. Did I see faces? I did not see faces. The power outlet looked like a little dude, but power outlets always look like little dudes.

I looked down again at the loaves on the baking stone, which, just as before, carried in their crusts the overwhelming illusion of dark eyes, upturned noses, fissured mouths.

Upon closer inspection, these faces were different from the last loaf's. They weren't disturbing. Their eyes squinted merrily and their mouths curled into ragged, jack-o'-lantern grins.

The bread knife was the solution to all my problems. I sawed and sawed until the faces were no more.

IT'S ALWAYS NEW AND ASTONISHING when it's yours. Infatuation; sex; card tricks. How many humans have baked how many loaves of bread, across how many centuries? I'm sure Beoreg baked calmly, matter-of-factly, without paroxysms of cosmic delight. But that didn't matter. For me, the novice, the miracle was intact, and I felt compelled by some force—new to me, thrillingly implacable—to share. I tied the sliced loaves into neat bundles with twine and bounded outside, still wearing the sweatpants I'd slept in.

My apartment was the lower of two units carved out of a dingy house on Cabrillo Street. My neighbor Cornelia lived upstairs. Our front doors were side by side on the face of the house, and I knocked on Cornelia's now. We didn't see each other that often, so when she appeared, her expression was cautiously curious.

I presented the twine-wrapped loaf and explained: "I . . . baked this for you?" Had I really? Was it possible? Did the universe permit feats of such profound creative alchemy? Apparently, it did.

Cornelia was, if not quite as impressed with me as I was, still at least medium-impressed. "What a nice surprise," she said, accepting the gift, and lifted it to her nose, murmuring "Mmm" appreciatively, which is exactly the right thing to do when someone presents you with the second loaf of sourdough they've ever baked in all of history.

"I didn't know you were a baker," Cornelia said.

I told her I had not been until yesterday. She raised an eyebrow, seemed to reappraise the loaf in her hands; her impressed-ness modulated upward a degree.

There was still another loaf to share. I went to the house next door, its resident unknown, never before seen or even considered. No one was home—or they were, but they were spooked by the appearance of a wild-eyed woman in sweatpants alive to the miracles of the universe, cradling a mysterious bundle, with traces of dough drying on the front of her tech company T-shirt.

The next building, then. There were three doors, and I rang the bell attached to the first. A man came to the door, flabby and whiskered, a bit drowsy looking. Behind him, deeper in his apartment, I saw a television paused on a frame of a movie; from the color palette and aspect ratio, I guessed early 2000s superhero.

"Hello," I said. "I live down the street. I was baking. I made too much." I held out the loaf.

He looked skeptical. "Nah, thanks. That's okay."

I wanted him so badly to take it. "I used the starter from Clement Street Soup and Sourdough. Did you ever order from them? Two brothers? Double spicy?"

The movie-watcher shook his head slowly, and the muscles under his eyes were wary. "Sorry. I've got to go." He closed the door, and I heard one, two, three latches click into place.

If I wanted to share this miracle—and I did—it would have to be with people who knew me.

AT THE SLURRY TABLE, when I unveiled my gift, Peter scooched his chair back apprehensively. "I don't eat bread," he reminded us. He said it like a ward against evil.

The other Slurry slurpers had no such compunctions. The slices I had sawed were thick and fluffy, and we slathered them with plum jam swiped from Chef Kate's fancy toast station.

Garrett relished the sourdough most of all. The sounds he made were borderline NSFW.

"You *made* this?" he said, mouth agape. "Like, from a kit? Does it come frozen?"

Garrett lived in one of the new micro-cube apartment buildings on Sansome Street, and his living space didn't have any kind of kitchen. Instead, it offered a wall-mounted touch screen connected to various delivery services expedited to sub-five-minute timescales through a contract with the building's owner. Garrett operated at a level of abstraction from food that made me look like Ina Garten.

I explained the process by which living sourdough starter gave the bread its texture and flavor. Garrett's eyes were wide with disbelief. "It was . . . alive," he said softly. Wonderingly. He, like me, had never before considered where bread came from, or why it looked the way it did. This was us, our time and place: we could wrestle sophisticated robots into submission, but were confounded by the most basic processes of life.

Chef Kate was making the rounds, chatting amiably with her lunchers. Generally, when she did this she avoided our table, reticent to confront the disgustingness of our food preferences. Today, Arjun called out to her—"Chef Kate!"—and she changed her course to approach us, her gaze darkening.

"Lois bakes bread now," Arjun announced.

"I didn't think you kids ate solid food," Kate said.

"That's only Peter."

"Correct," Peter said.

"Well," Kate said. "Can I try some?"

All gazes swiveled to Garrett, who had just consumed the last slice. He looked guilty but in no way repentant.

Chef Kate hooted. "I never thought I would see the day. One of the Slurry kids baking bread. The rest eating it. *Dude.*" Her "dude" was a thumping approval. "Lois? Bring me some. I want to taste your wares."

THAT NIGHT, when I returned home: a new disaster.

The Clement Street starter had dried out. It was now less a slime and more a crust on the walls of the crock. Its surface was dark and rippled. It smelled like nail polish remover. It looked dead.

In a panic, I threw together a batch of the flour-water starter food. It felt like I ought to drip it in slowly, just a bit at a time, as if I were bottle-feeding an ailing kitten. (I have never bottle-fed an ailing kitten.) (I did once coax Kubrick back to life with a spray bottle.) (You have to work pretty hard to push a cactus to the brink of death.) I dripped, dripped,

dripped the floury paste into the crock, and as I did, I spoke to the starter.

"Come on," I murmured. "It was just one day. You're supposed to be able to handle that. The bread book said I could leave you alone for a week."

You must play the music of the Mazg, Chaiman had said. I set his CD to playing on my laptop and tapped a key to increase its volume—*plink-plink-plink*. As I fed and coddled the starter, it began to perk up. Its color lightened. One tentative bubble formed on its surface.

Relief. But also exasperation: Beoreg and Chaiman had gifted me with a starter that was strange and potent, and also extremely high-maintenance.

I left the starter to recuperate and fished from the cupboard a bottle of pinot noir (purchased for the hedgehog on its label), then retreated into my living room to sit with my eyes closed, sipping. The wine tasted vaguely like dirt. Not in a bad way. When Chaiman's CD ended, I poured the last of the wine into my glass, then played it again.

The CD's seven songs were slow and meandering and seemed to fade one into the other. Some were sung by groups of women, others by groups of men, and one was a mixed chorus. The style was all the same: sad, so very sad, but matter-of-factly so. These songs did not blubber. They calmly asserted that life was tragic, but at least there was wine in it.

I realized suddenly that my apartment reeked of bananas. I followed the scent to the kitchen, where the Clement Street starter had more than doubled in volume and was surging out of the crock, puffy tendrils oozing down the green ceramic. I heard a crispy, crackling *pock-pock-pock*; the starter was not merely bubbling but frothing.

It is only barely anthropomorphization to say it looked happy.

I could understand that.

I retired to my bedroom, where I kicked off my pants and flopped down onto my futon. I was drunk and tired and happy. More than happy: delighted. Proud of myself—not just for making the bread, but for sharing it, and for making a few friends, even if they were all programmers and Loises. Maybe programmers and Loises are all you need.

I WAS MIDWAY TO SLEEP when I heard a sound in my apartment—a whispering creak, like the bending of a board. It sounded again, louder. A dose of danger-chemicals flooded into my blood and I snapped wide-awake, eyes sharp, nose flaring.

I think some people call out "Hello?" when they hear strange sounds in the night; this has always seemed foolish to me. If the strange sound does indeed emanate from something fearful, then it already has the drop on you. Better to stay quiet; better to even the odds. I hopped up onto the balls of my feet, crept to the doorframe, slowed my breathing, and stretched my senses to listen.

The sound continued. It was less a creaking and more a high back-of-the-throat sound. *Mmm-mmm-mmm.* My pulse was throbbing in my neck.

I peeked out into the main room. My eyes flicked from the front door to the back window. Everything was shut tight. This is one virtue of a small domain: you can survey it all at once.

The sound was resolving into something residential, but

I still didn't know what. The wind whistling through a crack somewhere? I relaxed and padded out to investigate.

I followed my ears into the kitchen, where the sound was louder. Up to the countertop; louder still. I zeroed in on the source: the Clement Street starter in its crock.

As I watched, the surface of the starter trembled. It had become smooth and glossy in the moonlight.

It went, *Mmm-mmm-mmm.*

Even up close, the sound was faint. I leaned my face in, trying to discern its source. Was the crock itself flexing as it cooled in the night? Was the sound coming from a pipe behind the wall? I lifted my hand to move the crock so I could find out if the sound moved with it, and just as my fingers touched the ceramic, the *Mmm-mmm-mmm* rose and became a coherent note, then two, then more, soft but clear.

The starter was singing.

Its surface was vibrating like a pot just before boiling. This cold-simmering substance was somehow sustaining a quavering harmony.

It was singing in the key of Chaiman's CD, the key of the choirs of the Mazg.

It crooned into the darkness, then faded.

There was a silence in which I processed the fact that this crock of gray slime had been singing; in which it followed its performance with a tidy farting noise; in which it settled into quiescence; in which I moved first my fingers and then myself away from the crock, across the room, to stand against the far wall.

I wish I could say the moment was hazy or dreamlike, but I was sharp with the battle-readiness familiar to all humans of all eras awoken by strange noises in the night.

I approached the crock again, peered inside, and whispered, "Hello?"

The starter's surface had lost its shiny tautness. It sang no more.

I considered the possibilities. An accident of gas could, I reasoned, produce a sound—boiling pots bubbled merrily—but it would be plosive. It would go *pop, poof,* or *plop*. Possibly *boof* or *bloop*. Maybe—*maybe—ffft* or *frap*; a farting sound could be explained. I let my tongue and vocal cords go slack, forced air out of my lungs, and simulated these airy sounds. *Boof. Plop.*

But the starter had not gone *boof* or *plop*. It had murmured *Mmm-mmm-mmm* in a clear, coherent voice. You needed lips to make *Mmm*, you needed a brain to find a note. That was complicated equipment.

I looked down at the Clement Street starter. It was not complicated.

I set the crock's lid in place and padded back to bed. Sleep came slowly.

IT'S A MESS when strange events smack into the windscreen of a resolutely rational mind. It would have been tidy to believe that it was a ghost speaking to me through the malleable medium of goopy dough. There's a whole story there: I could have organized a séance, hired a specialized kitchen exorcist, et cetera. But, of course, I do not believe in kitchen ghosts, or sourdough angels, or 500-degree devils, and so the event I had witnessed had to be explained by actually existing physical and/or mental phenomena. I simply could not come up with any.

The next day was Saturday, and I spent most of it trying to devise a way in which the starter's song might have been a bit of dream shifted into waking—the mental equivalent of an off-by-one error. But the sound was sharp in my memory.

I ejected Chaiman's CD and turned it over in my hands. Its title was handwritten. There was no label, no publisher, no bar code. There were no clues.

I opened my laptop and searched in vain for information on world writing systems. I found a comparative table of scripts, but at the top of the page it warned that there were thousands of written languages on Earth, some of them with just a handful of writers, and it would be impossible to list them all. Nothing in the table matched the script on the CD, the script on Beoreg's menu.

I'd received no reply to my email.

The starter did not sing that day. It did not evince any special glossiness. It did not respond to questioning. I didn't try to bake. Instead, I watched it closely, stirred it with a spoon, stuck my nose into the crock. It was mute, though fragrant.

Bananas.

CHEF KATE

O N MONDAY, I rose early and baked two loaves that emerged from the oven with faces happy-cheeked, cherubic. I wrapped them in paper towels and stuffed them into my backpack.

I also carried the crock with its fragile passenger along to the office and set it on my desk next to Kubrick the cactus. I threaded a pair of earbuds between my laptop and the crock, dangled them inside, and played Chaiman's CD at minimum volume.

The cafeteria was nearly empty, with only a few early risers (or never-slepters), who sat quietly with code and yogurt. In the kitchen, Chef Kate and her small staff were subdividing a pile of potatoes, collecting tater-tot-sized pieces in plastic tubs. Reggae played on a whoomphy Bluetooth speaker.

Chef Kate had come to oversee the feeding of the Dextrous by way of a cool restaurant on Valencia Street, wooed away from fine dining by lavish stock options and normal work hours. For Andrei, she was a trophy. His chowhound ways were well-known, as was his dream of seeing his robot arms working smoothly alongside sous chefs in all the open kitchens of the city.

I lifted my swaddled loaves in greeting. Chef Kate cleared a space among the potatoes.

She brought a loaf to her nose, then thunked its backside with her finger and listened to the report. "Very nice." She produced a serrated blade and commanded me to cut while she stepped away in search of something else.

Once every quarter, Andrei insisted that Chef Kate employ the robot arms in her kitchen, and once every quarter, the robot arms failed her horribly. The latest tryout sat in the corner, powered down with a broom leaned up against it, waiting to be wheeled back across the street to the Task Acquisition Center. We would solve everything else before we solved the egg problem.

I followed Kate's instructions and sawed off two rough slices. She returned with butter and salt and generously dressed both of them. "There." The bread was now blanketed with bright yellow butter. It glittered with a crust of flaky salt. It seemed excessive.

Kate hoisted her slice in a salute and said, "You'd be better off eating *this* every day than that Slurry shit." She took a bite. "Dude." Chewed. Took another bite. Said again: "Dude." Swallowed. "You could sell this."

I told her Arjun said the same thing.

"Arjun doesn't know anything. I do. This is a solid product. Dude. Sell me some."

She fixed me with a challenging gaze. This was not the empty jollity of a friend's "You could sell this"; this was the hard-eyed appraisal of someone who spent a lot of time thinking about what was and wasn't commercially viable.

This was, in other words, a real offer.

I told her okay. I would sell her some.

"What's your capacity?"

"Not much? I can bake two loaves in my oven. So I can do four, I guess, in a couple of hours."

"I need at least eight. You kids eat a lot."

I told her I would find a way to do eight. I had no idea how, but that's what I told her.

"Bring them next week," Chef Kate said. "Trial run, Monday through Friday. Cool?"

Cool, I agreed, and I could not account fully for the thrill of the prospect. Maybe it was the miracle of baking, still alive for me; maybe it was the fact that I'd never produced anything that earned such a visceral reaction before. Visceral was nice. Visceral was fun.

"I pay Everett Broom five dollars a unit, which is absurd, but I'll pay you the same, on the strength of this loaf. Thirty days net. Bring me an invoice."

Units! Net! Invoices! I was drunk with it.

"See you next Monday," Chef Kate said. "Early!"

Back at my desk, I sat smiling—grinning goofily, in fact— and wondered if it was the first time I had ever done so sitting at that desk. The Clement Street starter was happy, too— burbling merrily—and my workspace was permeated by the faint smell of bananas and the croon, even fainter, of the choirs of the Mazg, whoever they were.

<FROM: BEO>

HELLO, NUMBER ONE EATER! Your sourdough looks splendid. I'm very happy to see it. Does it smell like bananas—just a tiny bit?

Chaiman and I are back in Edinburgh, crowded into Shehrieh's small apartment here. (That's my mother. Mazg don't say "Mom" and "Dad." I don't really know why not.) I'm cooking for everyone. After a year of practice in San Francisco, I think it's happened: I'm finally a better cook than my mother. She won't admit it, of course, but I can tell she's nervous. I have a batch of spicy soup going now, with an ingredient that is, wickedly, new to her: FRESNO CHILI! I discovered it on Clement Street. Yes, I think this is going to be the night she concedes. Please picture me rubbing my hands together like a villain.

Send more messages!

THE JAY STEVE VALUE OVEN

THE CHALLENGE from Chef Kate smoldered in my brain. It was a familiar burn. I broke down the tolerances, the timings. To produce bread in the quantity she required, I would either have to start at three in the morning and bake loaves two at a time for four hours . . . or I would have to acquire a bigger oven.

Midway through *The Soul of Sourdough*, in a sidebar, Everett Broom alluded to the deep satisfaction of building a brick oven of one's own. "A full exploration of the design considerations is beyond the scope of this book," he wrote, "but you'll find a helpful community online at Global Gluten."

Global Gluten turned out to be a collection of forums populated by a kind of person I hadn't known existed: the carbohydrate nerd. They talked about hydration ratios, pH levels, dough temperatures. They traded recipes and swapped starters.

And, as Broom had promised, they gathered in a subforum devoted to the design and construction of elaborate wood-fired brick ovens. Here, the carb nerds shared blueprints.

The ovens they built were beautiful, architectural, like miniature Byzantine churches. For each design, there was a corresponding "heat curve" that swelled to 800 degrees or more, then eased down slowly for hours. The carb nerds got very, very excited about the shapes of these curves.

There were a few message threads pinned to the top of the forum—perennial references. One of them had been created six years ago and boasted seventy-nine pages of commentary. Its title was: THE JAY STEVE $200 VALUE OVEN (VERSION SIX).

I investigated. There were pictures, captured in a backyard that presumably belonged to Jay Steve. The grass was brown and patchy. There was a chain-link fence and a plastic dog dish.

And there was an oven, neither Byzantine nor beautiful. Instead, it was fully *Mad Max*: a squarish jumble of brick and metal. If I'd stumbled across the picture in a different context I would have assumed I was looking at the remains of a very small shanty following a great conflagration. The lines were askew; the metal was rusted; the bricks around the door were stained black with char.

Following Jay Steve's initial post (his profile picture was the affable snout of a golden retriever) were the seventy-nine pages of comments in which the carb nerds proposed tweaks of all kinds—different dimensions, different materials—but at some point all conceded: this was a badass little oven.

I could acquire all the materials at the expedient big-box home-supply store. Unfortunately, my car was minuscule and its tiny engine moaned even when it was carrying just me and zero home supplies over San Francisco's hills. I knocked on my upstairs neighbor's door, and when Cornelia appeared, I asked her if I could borrow her car.

"Nobody drives it but me," she said. "You need to go somewhere? I'll drive you. What day is it? Yeah. I should get out."

Cornelia's car was her defining feature. I saw it approximately a hundred times more often than I saw her: a battered green Honda CR-V that was always parked directly in front of the house, except for when Cornelia was working, when she replaced it with four traffic cones. As I watched, she removed them from the trunk and plunked them down.

The car's windshield was bordered with the badges and shields of every extant on-demand delivery service, along with several that were now defunct. While she navigated us to the expedient big-box home-supply store just south of the city, she swiped through a long carousel of apps with one hand and, I sensed, ninety percent of her attention. "Nah," she murmured. "Nah. Nah. Nah."

Cornelia was a highly strategic pawn in the on-demand delivery marketplace. Most hours of most days, she lounged at home in her sweatpants. But she was at all times monitoring the apps, and at the moments when demand burned blue-hot—Friday nights, often, but also random Tuesdays when the fog was at its thickest, suggesting to people that they ought to stay home and ponder their lives over delivered Burmese food—Cornelia would spring into action and earn a thousand dollars in a tire-screeching rally worthy of *Bullitt*. When it rained, she paid her rent in a day.

At the expedient big-box home-supply store, I wound my way through the towering aisles, following the shopping list provided by Jay Steve. I amassed thirty-six cinder blocks; two hundred and twenty-six plain red bricks (not firebricks, which Jay Steve claimed were for "luxury ovens only"); one bag each of clay and sand; one two-by-four cut to measure; and a supply of kindling, which the store sold in neat boxes.

When I returned to the car with three polo-shirted helpers pushing three different carts laden with materials, the trunk of Cornelia's CR-V was already open and she was perched on the bumper, swiping through her phone, wearing a satisfied, catlike look. While I had shopped, she had completed two delivery missions, earning fifty dollars.

She ferried me and my materials back to Cabrillo Street, the CR-V riding noticeably lower to the ground, and there we hauled my acquisitions one by one around the side of the building into a heap in the backyard.

"What are you doing out here?" Cornelia huffed at last.

I told her, with as much confidence as I could muster, that I was constructing a wood-fired brick oven in our backyard.

"How . . . crafty."

She retreated to the front of our building. I considered its bulk. It was charmless, a blank expanse of stubbly pseudo-stucco broken by just two windows: mine at eye level, Cornelia's above. The appropriate next step in this project would have been to contact the property management company, explain what I wanted to do, perhaps offer to increase my security deposit by some as-yet-unknown amount, and hope for official assent.

It was early evening.

The sky was a low ceiling of fog.

I shooed away the Cabrillo Street cats.

I beat back the weeds.

I built the oven.

It was shockingly easy because the instructions had been refined by Global Gluten's collective cleverness into something approaching IKEA-grade ease, and also because it was just a box. A box for fire.

I stacked the cinder blocks to mid-thigh, forming the oven's base. Then I assembled its floor and walls and ceiling, three bricks thick all around, leaving a gap a few bricks wide for the door. Finally, I mixed the clay and sand with water to make a mortar that I slathered into the cracks between bricks. I did this with my bare hands, as Jay Steve recommended. Whatever mortar remained I painted onto the oven's top and sides.

The bricks were the crux of it, Jay Steve explained. Prior to this just-in-time education, I had assumed that in a wood-fired brick oven, the flames of the fire baked the bread. I mean, of course, right? Wrong. Baking in this oven would be a two-step process, and the first was for the fire to charge those thick walls with heat. The thicker the walls, the more heat they could absorb and then return. In an oven like this, it was the bricks, not the fire, that baked the bread.

My oven looked like a gloppy cube, without even the crudest approximation of the graceful heat-reflecting domes that topped the fancier designs. But Jay Steve was insistent: *Ugly ovens bake great bread.*

The crowning touch was the door, a plug of thick wood built from the two-by-four cut to measure.

The sun had set. Fog was rolling into the yard, cold and dense. The oven was done. I stepped back to appraise it. It looked like a pile of junk. It was a success.

I wanted badly to try it out, but here, Jay Steve cautioned, impatience spelled doom. Before I could bake with it, I had to cure the oven by building a very small fire, then growing it larger, and larger still, all over the course of several hours, until I had reached peak flameage (about 800 degrees), and, in the process, coaxed the latent moisture out of the bricks. If I rushed the process and baked at full strength right away, the oven would crack. It would become even uglier, and, worse, it would never bake in fully badass fashion.

I pushed a few logs inside, arranged them in a loose triangle, tucked some kindling into place, and lit my first fire. It smoked and fumed. A lick of flame appeared, inspected its nest, proclaimed it satisfactory, and began to crackle.

There were four ancient lawn chairs lying in a tangle behind the recycling bin, evidence of long-departed residents, with vines growing through their seats. I ripped away the vines, carried one of the chairs to the oven, plopped it down, and sat.

I waited.

It was cold, maybe forty degrees. I dashed inside to retrieve a blanket, my jacket, and an additional sweater, and when I returned to the lawn chair, I piled them all on top of myself. I slithered one hand through the heap to grasp and manipulate my poker (a long straight stick gleaned from the back of the yard) while keeping the skin–air interface to a minimum.

I had another thought, and with reluctance I dismantled my insulating heap to go back inside and retrieve the Clement Street starter in its crock. Wary of the cold, I wedged it into the lawn chair next to me, then built the heap on top of it. I figured the starter ought to be present for the beginning of this important next phase in our work together.

On the back of the building, the upper window flickered with the movement of blinds. They snapped up and the window slid open with a sharp squeak. A Cornelia-shaped silhouette appeared. I heard a curious "Hmm" and the silhouette retreated. A few minutes later, Cornelia emerged around the side of the building. She extricated another lawn chair, dragged it over, and plopped herself down.

"Be a shame if the management company heard about this," she said.

It would be a shame, indeed.

"You could keep your neighbor quiet pretty easy, though. Bribe her. I bet she just wants more of that bread."

Did she now.

"Mm-hmm." She leaned toward the oven, opened her palms to the heat. "Why bake it out here? Does it make a difference?"

I began to list the virtues of the Jay Steve Value Oven as I had learned them on the message board, not least of which was its capacity: for $200 of raw materials and a few hours of labor—not including these hours of fire-watching, which were decidedly unlaborious—I had doubled my baking capacity. I could fit four loaves inside this oven. Four! And they would come out better. This was a wood-fired brick oven, the kind used by Everett Broom, and also by the artisan bakers of ancient days . . .

I stopped talking, and we were quiet, watching the fire burn.

After a while, Cornelia hoisted herself up with a little grunt, said good night, and padded into the building. I saw her silhouette in the window. She waved, then disappeared, and the light went out, but the window was still open to the cold night air and the smell of the fire.

I fell asleep; for how long, I wasn't sure. When I woke up, the oven was still going strong. The bricks weren't steaming and crackling anymore. The curing process was well under way.

The crock wedged next to me was vibrating with the starter's tremors of growth, even though I hadn't fed it. Was it responding to the warmth? I peeled back a sweater and the blanket and heard its quiet musing leaking out into the night.

The air was heavy and cold, and when I looked up, I saw a surprise. The oven's heat, rising in a steady plume, had bored through the fog and cleared a channel to the sky.

I saw stars.

YOU ASKED what makes the Mazg the Mazg. I've been thinking about it, and I've come up with three things.

First is our food. Most Mazg would say the culture—the starter—is the crucial thing, and of course the sourdough. Honestly . . . it's not my favorite. I like the spicy better. But I think you already knew that.

Second is our singing! Easy one.

Third is our reticence. There are Mazg neighborhoods in cities all over Europe, but you would never know it, because we never have signs or storefronts. You will never, ever see our beautiful script on the street.

It's a shame.

THE PROBLEM WAS ONGOING

I ROSE BEFORE DAWN, carried the loaves into the backyard, started a fire in the Jay Steve, let it roar. When I reached in to push the coals to the back, the intensity of the heat made it suddenly clear the oven in my kitchen was no oven at all. The tiny hairs on my arms all vaporized. Four loaves went in and I jammed the wooden plug into place. Then I did a little jig.

Forty minutes later, my hands shielded by thick mitts, I yanked the plug.

The loaves were bigger than before, colored a deeper gold. Clearly visible in the cracks and crevices of the crust were the wide smiles they wore.

Everybody was happy.

The simple math of it was astonishing, and I felt the giddy leverage of technology—more palpably, I should add, than at any moment during my General Dexterity orientation. This was simple and direct: Before the machine, I could make two loaves. After the machine, I could make four. For the first time in my life, I realized why a person might be interested in capital. This was capital!

I slammed through one batch of four loaves, then another. It took every ounce of restraint not to cut into the sourdough myself.

It wasn't even six a.m. and I had a set of loaves, rough octuplets, all smiling. I had stopped worrying about the faces. I wrapped the loaves in paper towels, resolved to buy more appropriate swaddling—what was the appropriate swaddling?—and hustled out the door.

It was still dark outside. To the east, downtown San Francisco was obscured by hills, but the lights glowed splotchy purple on the underbelly of the marine layer.

The General Dexterity office was quiet but not deserted. Chef Kate was in her kitchen, bent over a notebook, building a tall, skinny to-do list. Her two sous chefs stood at their stations, rapping their knives through thick heads of cabbage and long green onions. This morning, it was slow-rolling hip-hop on the Bluetooth speaker.

"Here's your first shipment," I said, presenting the loaves.

Chef Kate inspected them one by one. "These look pretty good," she said. "Consistent. But this—the crust." She indicated the whorls of the faces. "How the hell do you do that?"

I told her it had been an accident the first time, and I'd repeated the steps every time since, which was technically the truth, if not entirely forthright.

"It's weird, dude. But I think I like it. You got an invoice for me, or what?"

Later that day, I carried it to her, warm from the office printer. Forty dollars. I made more than that in fifteen minutes of programming, but this money felt special.

It was a decidedly different kind of work.

At General Dexterity, I was contributing to an effort to

68

make repetitive labor obsolete. After a trainer in the Task Acquisition Center taught an arm how to do something, all the arms did it perfectly, forever.

In other words, you solved a problem once, and then you moved on to more interesting things.

Baking, by contrast, was solving the same problem over and over again, because every time, the solution was consumed. I mean, really: chewed and digested.

Thus, the problem was ongoing.

Thus, the problem was perhaps the point.

On Tuesday morning, I baked eight more loaves.

Every day after work, rather than migrate to the bar down the street with Arjun, I went straight home. I timed the bus perfectly, ran from the stop on Fulton Street to my front door, barreled into my apartment—because I had so much to do. I had to mix fresh dough, let it sit, work it again, shape it into loaves. All before bedtime, and bedtime was early, with a bar of sunlight still crossing the foot of my futon. It felt strange but good.

Wednesday: eight more loaves.

My hours at my desk became a blur. The moment I left the office, my brain shifted gears; the interlocking complexities of ArmOS were gone, evaporated, and all that existed was the labor ahead.

Thursday: eight more loaves.

Chef Kate made grilled cheese sandwiches using my sourdough and I saw them consumed in the cafeteria. I saw roboticists' faces rapt with pleasure. I saw Andrei, the CEO, carrying one on his tray.

I took loose slices of sourdough, buttered luxuriously in the Chef Kate style, over to the Slurry table. Peter sharply declined, of course, but Arjun and Garrett both snatched them up greedily. "This is so good," Garrett said. "Can I order it online?"

Friday: eight more loaves.

Some mornings, the repetition felt Zen-like; others, Sisyphean. But in either case, it felt good to use my arms, not my fingertips. My nose, not my eyes.

On Friday afternoon, Chef Kate told me the sourdough had been "pretty freakin' good, dude"—I squealed—and asked me to keep it coming.

<FROM: BEO>

As I MENTIONED BEFORE, nearly every large city in Europe has a community of Mazg, but they can be hard to detect. The Mazg like to live in alleys and courtyards, or up above the street. One of my uncles calls us "the second-story people," which has a nice sound to it, I guess.

Here's the thing.

I think many of my relatives like being obscure because it means they can't be ambitious either. It lets them off the hook.

I think more people should know about the Mazg—particularly our cuisine. I think we should have restaurants with signs and front doors.

I think a lot of things.

A CATALOG OF PHENOMENA

THE RHYTHM WENT LIKE THIS: In the evening, when I got home from General Dexterity, I would play Chaiman's CD and feed the Clement Street starter. I would wait for it to bubble and grow and suffuse the apartment with its banana scent. Then I would section off half of the mass, mix it into my dough, and form the loaves, which I would set beside the open kitchen window to rise slowly overnight in the naturally occurring refrigerator that was the Richmond District.

I went to sleep, but that wasn't the end of the day for the starter. Many nights—not all, but many—it woke me with its grumblings and exhalations.

A catalog of phenomena:

- Tiny winking bubbles produced not randomly but in a perfect grid across the starter's surface, like turbines on a power plant floor
- A dusting of pinprick lights, luminous powdered sugar
- Stronger lights emanating from deeper within the starter's bulk, blurred like the sodium glow of a city

viewed from a window seat on an airplane landing in low clouds
- A fine mazelike patterning on the starter's surface, retracting into smoothness upon my approach
- Songs, various: all in the key of Chaiman's CD
- Scents, various: with banana as the backbone, always, but adding other fruity currents as well as, on one memorable night, the smell of smoke so potent I thought for a moment the Jay Steve had lit the backyard on fire

Always that glossiness; always the moment when it wasn't slime but something firmer, more self-possessed.

Always I saw these things in darkness, usually past midnight, in various states of wakefulness. Some of the encounters felt dreamlike, and in fact I suspected at least one really was a dream; others were as sharp and vivid as that first song.

When I saw the pinprick lights, I tried to snap a photo with my phone, but in the morning my camera roll was just a line of swampy rectangles, the outline of the crock barely darker than the countertop, the lights I had seen with my eyes not sufficiently bright to register pixels on the camera's sensor.

Another night, with the city-like extrusions, I tried again, this time using my phone's flash, and it bounced back brightly from the shiny ceramic crock, blinding me. A moment passed, my eyes swam pink, and then the starter, summoning some hidden energy, flashed back. It was the faintest flicker of green, but it registered like a signal flare across a vast abyss. A message from Alpha Centauri. The resulting photo was awful and alien, like the time I tried to take a picture of the inside of my mouth to check on a blister that was forming. (Sorry, but I did.)

When the starter sang, I tried to record it, but these recordings, like the pictures, were all inscrutable in the morning. Either my phone's mic didn't pick up anything, or my own ragged breathing drowned it out, or there was a note faintly audible, but so what? Who was I going to play it for? On what website was I going to post it? Global Gluten? New thread: *Does anyone else's starter sing? Here's a clip.*

I stopped getting up. The rattle of the crock's lid would rouse me, and I would listen for a minute, then roll over and go back to sleep.

AT THE CLOSE OF THE THIRD WEEK, Chef Kate summoned me to her kitchen.

"So, I love this bread, but these kids can't tell the difference, and it's bumming me out." She waved her hand dismissively at the cafeteria.

I felt a twinge of shame. Was this Chef Kate's life? Preparing great food for a terminally unappreciative clientele? No one ever ate the creative salads. Meanwhile, the tater tots were depleted in minutes.

"It's really special," Kate said. "You know that, right?"

I had suspected it, but hearing her say it plucked a string inside me.

"I think you should try to get a spot at a farmers market. The faces in the crust, they're weird. People like that shit. Do you know how the markets work? No, of course you don't. There's an audition every month. Fancy judges. Mostly insufferable, but Lily Belasco is okay. If they like what you bring, they assign you to a market. Lake Merritt, if you're

74

lucky. Colma, if you're not. I'm pretty sure you'll get a spot if you try."

I told her I would think about it, and she was quiet a moment.

"I'm sure you like your work here," Kate said. "I have no idea what you do. No, please don't try to explain it. But I feel like I have to tell you, for what it's worth . . . feeding people is really freakin' great. There's nothing better."

Even feeding people as ungrateful as the Dextrous?

She began to reply, but something caught her eye, and instead she shouted to one of her sous chefs: *"Mario! We need a bacon refresh!"* She turned back to me. "Trust me, if I could pay for my kid's school with farmers market dollars, I'd be there right alongside you."

THE LOIS CLUB (CONTINUED)

I MESSAGED HILLTOP LOIS and told her I would bring bread to the next meeting of the Lois Club.

I'm so glad you're coming back!! she replied. *We were afraid we might have scared you off. Flashy Lois can be a bit much . . .*

It was nice to know we each had our own system for Lois disambiguation. Who was I to them? Young Lois, I supposed. Better than Boring Lois, or Lois Whose Stomach Hurt.

In fact, my stomach had been feeling pretty good lately.

So it came to pass that the Loises of the San Francisco Bay Area built open-faced sandwiches, piling prosciutto and fig over soft slathers of goat cheese all atop slices of my bread. They ate all of it, every crumb, and they oohed their appreciation.

"I've been baking bread for twenty years," Professor Lois said, "and it never turned out this good."

"My starter is unique," I said.

She snorted. "I get mine in the mail from King Arthur—the flour company. Every three months it dies and I order a new one."

The Loises shared their updates. Compaq Lois was organizing a fund-raiser for a turkey vulture research center; Professor Lois had just returned from an academic conference in Montreal; Impeccable Lois would soon acquire a vintage Moog synthesizer for a very good price; and Old Lois was still alive.

I told the Loises about my baking adventures—they interrupted to say, "It's really great," and "Truly, Lois, dear, you have a gift"—and also about Chef Kate's challenge.

"I love the farmers markets," Professor Lois cooed. "You should do it." The other Loises nodded in agreement.

Compaq Lois spoke. Her voice was not kind or coddling, but stern. "Do you like your job?"

My hesitation answered for me.

"I know I have strong opinions about everything—I can't help it, I do—but this one's the strongest. I waited too long to get out of that office. Much too long. I weep for those years."

The seriousness of her statement quieted the room.

"If this is fun for you—and I think it is fun for you? Damn, you're good at it. You should try out for those markets. See what happens."

The other Loises murmured their assent. Everyone wore inward looks, perhaps contemplating the things they wished they'd done sooner.

"Thanks," I said. "I appreciate the advice."

The wine was gone, so Hilltop Lois, wearing a mischievous look, uncorked a bottle of port. I got the sense this did not happen at every meeting of the Lois Club, but the ones at which it did: those were the good ones.

"I envy you, Lois the Younger," sighed Compaq Lois.

"No, no, she's Computer Lois," said Hilltop Lois.

"We all have names? Who am I?" Old Lois interjected.

There was a pause. "You're Most Respected Elder Lois," said Impeccable Lois, who was today wearing a tweed suit tailored close to her body with pleats of intimidating sharpness.

Old Lois sniffed. "I don't like it. Anyway, I think she has to be Lois the Baker now."

"The bread was awfully good," Compaq Lois agreed. She flipped the last remaining sliver of fig into her mouth and looked at me pointedly. "See what happens," she said.

The setting sun lit the house in orange and pink and it made all the Loises look great. Emerging from the bathroom, I caught a glimpse of myself in a hallway mirror. My hair was longer than it had been in years, and it glowed in the sunset, the ends alight like burning filament. Lois the Baker looked great, too.

Cars appeared. One was from the expedient internet car service and Compaq Lois waved as she stepped in, her bracelets glittering. The other cars were piloted by various Lois associates. Professor Lois's husband read *The Atlantic* while he waited. Old Lois's daughter helped her into the passenger seat of a Toyota, laughing at some quiet joke. Impeccable Lois's girlfriend drove an old Ford pickup truck.

On top of the city with my Loises all around me, I felt a tremor of something. Was it possible?

I had become interesting.

I KEEP WRITING "the Mazg" like it's such a definite thing. In fact, Leopold (my father) is Dutch. Shehrieh's mother was Italian. Truthfully, Chaiman and I could, if we wanted, decide not to be Mazg. I have a cousin who did that. She makes dresses in Barcelona now. But Chaiman and I have . . . attachments. For me, it's the food, and for Chaiman, it's the music, and for both of us, it's Shehrieh, who is Mazg through and through, whatever that even means. We are both always trying to impress her *and* not disappoint her, which can be a tricky combination.

THE GREATEST OF ALL THE MARKETS

I'D NEVER SEEN SO MANY PICKLES in my life.

We were lined up, a hundred of us, all with our samples like offerings for a queen or a newborn prophet. Boxes and baskcts and bottles and jars—so many jars: some jars plain, others with clever labels already designed and printed in anticipation of a bright future at one of the Bay Area's many markets.

Not all of those labels would be needed.

The woman in front of me was clutching a jar of Japanese pickled plums between her breasts, staring into space, moving her lips, subvocalizing. Rehearsing.

Behind me was another woman who seemed somewhat more serene. She'd brought a tall bottle of olive oil labeled with a strip of masking tape that read PICHOLINE. In a cardboard carrier, she had eight tiny blue tasting glasses shaped like tulips.

"It's amazing, isn't it?" she said, her eyes roaming the space.

The Ferry Building was more than amazing; it was mythic.

This grand structure on the city's edge, perched on pylons,

built a hundred years ago and in the middle of that century, not merely abandoned but actually walled off by a dark freeway that curled around the Embarcadero like a rampart. Then, an earthquake came and it was like something out of a fairy tale: the wall tumbles, the spell fades, and the townspeople realize what a gift they've possessed all along.

The Ferry Building was rebuilt, reopened. It was better than ever, and best of all on Saturdays, when it unfurled itself into a farmers market that filled up the plazas, reached out onto the piers. Trucks converged from a hundred miles in every direction carrying fruits, nuts, vegetables, flowers, fresh meat; the whole bounty of California. The sun glittered on the bay and the big bridge to Oakland bracketed the scene like a picture frame.

This was the greatest of all the markets, and basically no one in this line had a chance of getting a spot here. I'd learned this online, searching for information about the tryout. You started on the periphery and made your way to the bright bustling core.

It was Wednesday, so there was no market, but even during the week, the Ferry Building was a prodigious hub of gastronomical commerce. We petitioners were lined up on a catwalk above the building's main concourse, where shops sold cheese and chocolate, beef and beans, knives and cookbooks and garden gloves. Midday sunshine streamed in through skylights that ran the length of the building. Tourists and locals alike gathered around Greenlight Coffee, watching the baristas take their time.

In San Francisco, there is a particular trajectory available to food-related enterprises. Your little venture—maybe it's

81

called Greenlight Coffee!—begins with a ramshackle cart at the outermost corner of a far-flung farmers market. Colma: market of the dead. In a year or two, having established your dedication, you are invited to the Ferry Building. This is your audition. The right person sees you—and the right person is assuredly here, canvassing the stalls—and you are springboarded, granted a small storefront in a rapidly gentrifying neighborhood. If the storefront is successful—if it assists with the greater aims of gentrification, is written up in national food and/or lifestyle publications, including, ideally, *The New York Times* (the local paper can't help you here)—then you will be permitted to open a larger, more boldly designed flagship along one of the city's Certified Cool Thoroughfares. In a few years, you will have expanded into a few additional locations, including a permanent spot in the Ferry Building—a gleaming café bathed in that midday light. You will have become a celebrated local mini-chain. Finally, you will sell your company to Starbucks for nineteen million dollars. And remember: You began with the cart at the outermost corner. You began here, in this line.

That's why I was petitioner number forty-three, with more people behind me than in front. This tryout occurred once a month. We would have had better odds applying to Stanford as adult learners.

When I reached the front of the line, a bright-eyed Ferry Building functionary explained what I was about to experience. The deal, she said, was this: Three minutes with the panel. Offer a taste; just a taste. Explain what makes you different. Be eloquent but concise but confident but deferential. Much of this is beyond your control; if you make pickles but the markets are overflowing with them, it won't matter how great your pickles are.

The woman with the Japanese pickled plums was inside now.

The loaf I had baked that morning had cooled completely, and suddenly I wished I'd carried it in some kind of insulating sleeve. But then, I supposed, it might have turned soggy. How *do* you store and transport bread? I didn't know anything. That was the absurdity of this: I was standing in line with people who were masters of their craft. People who pickled plums, pressed olives, raised chickens, kept bees. I was just lucky: gifted with good raw materials and, perhaps, charitably, a sense for how to use them.

The Clement Street starter was waiting back at my desk.

"Smells good," the functionary said, catching a whiff of the bread. I wished suddenly that I'd brought the starter itself. I wished I'd trained it to sing on command. I could have put it in front of the panel and said, *Have you ever seen anything like this?*

The functionary explained that the panel would taste my sourdough and hear my plea, then announce its market placements later in the afternoon. Placement was conditional on my willingness to sign certain agreements and also on certain logistical double checks that she, the functionary, would make. If I wasn't placed anywhere—well, most of the people in this line had been turned down many times already. You can always try again, the functionary said. You were allowed to return once a season. People applied and reapplied, groveled and waited, for years. The Greenlight Coffee people had done that. Nineteen million dollars.

83

The door opened. The pickler of plums emerged, her face a tangle of vexations. I tried to catch her eye, to give her an encouraging look, but she was all wrapped up in herself, carrying her jar toward the stairs that would lead her down to the main concourse, where perhaps she would acquire a cone of cardamom ice cream to assuage her anxiety.

The bright-eyed functionary held open the door to the panel's chamber and wished me good luck.

TONIGHT, CHAIMAN AND I counted through all the places we've ever lived: Brussels, Budapest, Turin, Avignon, Edinburgh, San Francisco. That's six—about average for a couple of Mazg. I don't know if I should count Edinburgh twice, now that we're back here. Chaiman's favorite city is San Francisco. ("FOR SURE," he is shouting.) I don't think I've found mine yet.

THE PANTHEON

T HE ROOM WAS WIDE and well windowed with a blinding view of the bay, Yerba Buena Island directly ahead. Seven judges sat in a line at a long table, four women and three men, swaddled and comfortable, wrapped in scarves and caftans. Plain fabrics, generous cuts. They had different-colored skin and different-colored hair, but they shared a satisfied plumpness. It looked like a committee of harvest gods drawn from all the pantheons.

All except one, seated at the end of the table, who seemed less Demeter or Dionysus, more Hades. Her hair was shiny and slicked back; she wore a slouchy black leather jacket over a shimmering black T-shirt. Maybe she was the token goddess of death, and also of street fashion.

Welcome, the gods murmured together. What do you have for us today?

They were smiling, apple-cheeked, with friendly wrinkles around their eyes. They were wide-framed and golden-whiskered. They didn't seem like cruel, uncompromising judges at all. Even the queen of the underworld was smiling.

Let's have a taste, they said.

There was a bread knife waiting in a tray alongside other knives as well as spoons and cups. The instruments of ritual. Using the Ferry Building knife, I sawed seven generous slices.

Tell us about this bread you've made, they said. We do have many bakers already. But, Jacqueline, you never know. The Inner Sunset could use a good sourdough. That's a fair point, Marco. Let her speak. Tell us about it.

"It's unique," I said. "That's why I brought it. Sourdough depends on its starter, right? This starter is special, and I thought you would appreciate it." A bit of flattery. They received it well. There was fluttering and cooing and those with whiskers stroked them.

I watched them eat. They did so carefully, all at their own pace. They sniffed the bread, flipped it over, tore it into smaller pieces. One gray-haired goddess held it up to the light, peering through the crumb of the bread as if it were a stained-glass window.

This is good, they said. Very good indeed. But we do have bread already. We have many fine sourdoughs. Is this superior? Is there a market where it fits?

A bearded god of wine and festivals asked pointedly: To what baking tradition would you say this belongs?

That stumped me. I would have been very comfortable lying, but I didn't know any baking traditions at all. I was about to say I learned from Everett Broom, but I stopped myself; every baker who walked into this chamber must have learned from Everett Broom.

"Actually, I work at a tech company," I confessed. "General Dexterity, do you . . . ? Okay, no. I served this in the cafeteria there, and Chef Kate . . . I mean, Kate . . ." I realized I didn't know her last name.

"Kate Rossi," said the goddess of the dead. "Did she send you here? That's interesting."

From beneath a luxurious beard came a gentle query: "A tech company, you said? Are you . . . technical?"

I told them I was a programmer.

"And which do you prefer? Baking . . . or programming?"

"Do I have to choose?"

You might, they said. The day may come. Lake Merritt, it's very busy, it demands everything of a vendor . . . Do you think she's right for Lake Merritt? Oh no, no no no, I was just making a point.

The central goddess, a woman wrapped in a light blue shawl, had been silent. Now she quieted the rest with the tiniest motion of her hand. She had barely nibbled the bread. There was no charity in her eyes when she looked at me and said, "That will be all."

"Okay," I said. "Thanks."

Thank you for bringing this to us, they said. Thank you for bringing yourself.

LATER, I WAS WAITING for the announcements, walking in circles around the perimeter of the Ferry Building, two licks into a cone of soothing pistachio ice cream, when a voice called out to me. "You, with the bread."

Me, with the bread?

It was the queen of the underworld. She stood in the shadow of the pillars that supported the Ferry Building's great roof, smoking a cigarette, looking exquisitely renegade. She was positioned precisely one inch beyond the sign that demarcated the building's no-smoking zone.

"General Dexterity makes robots, right?"

I turned to tell her yes, the company designed industry-leading robot arms for laboratories and—

"You program robot arms, and you bake bread."

"That's right," I said.

"Interesting."

"Is it?"

"Oh, definitely. People here tend to go the other way. They're suspicious of technology."

A jag of excitement skittered through my chest. Was this a hint? "Do you think I'll get a spot?"

She lifted her head in what I thought was going to be the beginning of an affirmative nod, but instead her chin just hung there as she regarded me quietly.

"We'll see."

THE PICKLE PRODUCERS and miscellaneous others all gathered on the main concourse as the Ferry Building's giant clock bonged the hour. Three echoing bongs. The bright-eyed functionary was standing on the catwalk above, and she read off names like a herald calling out the queen's decrees.

I surveyed the crowd. Some faces were plainly tortured with anxiety, on the verge of tears and/or unconsciousness; others appeared placidly pessimistic.

"Gilroy," the functionary called out. The farthest market. She began reading names and products. "Sonja Tarkovsky, tea." There was a little whoop from the very back of the crowd; hundreds of eyes whipped around to find Sonja, some glittering with envy, others with naked malice.

The list went on, Alex and Graham and Jenna, cheese

and coffee and bread—I winced at the bread—and as the crowd shrank, the stakes grew higher. The list was moving north and west, from Gilroy to Los Altos to Colma (a sausage maker slotted there emitted a quiet groan), from Orinda to Moraga to Lake Merritt, closer and closer to the ground on which we stood.

Each vendor accepted made his or her way to a table positioned beside the heirloom bean emporium to receive an orientation packet. The rest of us waited as the markets grew more prestigious and the list grew shorter.

At this point, I maintained no illusions. I would not be chosen.

The functionary came to the end: "For the Ferry Building Farmers Market"—the crowd was silent, levitating an inch off the ground—"we have no selections at this time."

Everyone on the concourse exhaled together, withering disappointment mixed with clean, clear relief. The crowd disintegrated—the force holding it taut was spent—but the functionary wasn't finished. "There's one more," she called out. Most people ignored her; a few turned curious faces toward the catwalk. What could possibly follow the Ferry Building? "For the Marrow Fair," she said, "we have one selection." No one cared. Never heard of it. "Lois Clary, sourdough bread."

It barely registered with any of the others, who were all caught up in celebration or mourning. What was the Marrow Fair? I stared at the functionary. I wasn't sure how to feel; excitement and confusion were duking it out, with horror quietly circling the ring. The functionary caught my gaze and pointed to the table by the beans, where the queen of the underworld waited.

I was so confused I didn't know what questions to ask. Was it real? Was it worth my time? Where was it?

"Hello, baker," the queen of the underworld said. "You weren't selected for one of the main markets, which means I'm free to make an offer. I'm Lily Belasco. I manage the Marrow Fair."

"What . . . is . . . the Marrow Fair?"

She fished something out of her leather jacket. It looked like what was left after you finish a chicken drumstick, but when I accepted it, I realized it wasn't real bone. Instead, it was made from beige plastic, some kind of high-grade polymer, warm and smooth, almost buttery. There was a ring attached to one end, as if to dangle it from a key chain.

"That's a key to my market," Lily Belasco said. "This offer is contingent. But I want you to see the place before you decide."

"Contingent? On what?"

"I'll send you directions. Just come visit. Then decide."

A LOT OF MAZG WORK in kitchens because (not to sound too haughty, but) we're really very good at it. All the restaurants with Michelin stars, where you can eat salted moss and turnip foam—I guarantee you'll find Mazg working there! I did that in Edinburgh before, at a really excellent restaurant. The owner just found out I was back, and he asked me if I wanted to return. I turned him down. (Nicely.) I've decided I want to open my own restaurant, like in San Francisco, but this time I'm not going to be so cautious about it. I'm not going to be so Mazg!

Lois, I'm telling you before anyone else:

I'm going to have tables.

ALAMEDA

IT WAS SEVEN P.M. when I slunk out of the office with the Clement Street starter in its ceramic crock. Instead of heading home, I walked around the curve of the Embarcadero to the Ferry Building. This time, my destination wasn't the gourmet arcade inside, but the piers beyond. I boarded the boat bound for the skinny island shouldered up against Oakland on the far side of the bay: Alameda.

The trip was shorter than I expected. Soon, we were passing the Port of Oakland and its loading cranes. They looked like the bleached skeletons of prehistoric quadrupeds, Godzilla-scale, with monstrous pulleys in their guts lifting bright containers out of long freighters that dwarfed the ferry.

We bumped up against the dock at Alameda. I disembarked onto a wide parking lot, now mostly empty, and hiked up the road toward the coordinates I'd been given.

I'd never set foot on Alameda before. It had once been home to a sprawling naval base, but that had been decommissioned decades ago, and what remained in its place was a weedy moonscape dotted with military-scale buildings inhabited by small businesses, like hermit crabs in over-large shells. I passed a distillery, a furniture emporium, and a drone manufacturer, each in its own aircraft hangar.

I stopped to check my directions. YES, KEEP WALKING, Lily Belasco had written.

Behind the hangars, there was a huge expanse of aban-doned asphalt, cracked and overtaken by vegetation. There were tall grasses and low, tight shrubs with gray-green leaves and bright white blossoms.

I walked across the broken surface, feeling illicit; but there were no fences, no signs telling me to KEEP OUT. It seemed derelict. I passed a hangar-turned-brewery; this was Algebra, whose beers I'd tasted at fancy bars in San Francisco. Their flagship brew was the x^2 Saison.

Out on the airfield, a herd of goats was grazing. They bleated and cried and retreated as I approached, little bells jin-gling around their necks. It was an unexpected sight: the goats scattered across the vast empty asphalt, gnawing on the patchy grass, and behind them the mirrored quadruped forms of the cranes, snuffling their noses in the holds of the great freighters.

Maybe the cranes would also be improved by bells around their necks.

Among the goats, there were two taller figures. One was an alpaca. It stood in the center of the flock, its gaze tracking me coolly. The other figure was a young man with a rumpled skater look.

I waved, as if signaling a ship, and called out to him. "Hello?"

The man waved lazily, but remained as silent and

baleful as his alpaca accomplice. They both cast very long shadows.

"I'm looking for a market," I shouted. Standing there on the asphalt, it seemed like an absurd statement.

He nodded slowly at this. We were still standing very far apart. The man's aspect and the alpaca's were approximately equivalent: wary, not unfriendly, but fundamentally alien. After a long pause, the man pointed toward the old control tower.

I waved again and walked in that direction.

When I reached the tower, its front door was propped open. I poked my head inside; it appeared long abandoned, scraped clean of furniture and ornament. Spiraling metal steps wound their way upward. Climbing them, I found myself on the tower's bulbous deck with a panoramic view of the airfield and the island and the bay. The window's edge was decorated, through all 360 degrees, with beer bottles, all with Algebra labels. The last of the day's sunlight filtered through them, casting blobs of green light around the room.

The spiraling metal steps returned me to the tower's front door and also continued down into the ground. There was a landing below. I descended and found another door, this one locked tight, blank and gray except for a palm-sized outline stenciled in creamy white paint.

The stencil's shape looked like what was left after you finished a chicken drumstick.

The door offered no knob, no handle, no doorbell, no speakeasy slit. I tried to knock, but the metal hurt my knuckles. I thumped it with my palm. Nothing.

I drew out the buttery plastic bone token I'd received at

the Ferry Building and pressed it against the stencil. From unseen speakers, a synthesized voice bellowed like a buzz saw:

STILL—
TOO—
SKINNY.

And the door opened.

<FROM: BEO>

WHILE I WAS IN SAN FRANCISCO with Chaiman, I sometimes had the thought that perhaps the two of us were like the bacteria and the fungus in the starter—a tiny self-sufficient community.

(In that analogy, I am the bacteria and Chaiman is the fungus. Never tell him I said that.)

Chaiman hardly ever comes out of his room anymore. He's working on his album nonstop. He's been talking about it for two years, but something happened after we left San Francisco. He got serious. He follows all the excruciatingly cool music—I don't even understand where he finds it—and he says, "Mazg singing will blow their minds." He's taking the old recordings, cutting them up, transforming them. And, of course, adding a beat. He loves making the beats.

The bacteria stands alone.

PINK LIGHT

I WALKED INTO A SPACE that was long and narrow with the powered-down gloom of a high school at night, a raw concrete concourse with portals all along its edges. Bars of pink light streamed in from those portals and made me think of the prom spilling out of the gym, except here there were many proms, and many gyms, and all were silent. The smooth floor was marked with stripes of paint that had flaked into segments—directions that no one had followed in a long time.

It felt, also, like an empty spaceship, and, as a rule, you do not enter an empty spaceship without first knowing the fate of the crew.

But the floor offered fresher directions, too. Extending away from the door, long strips of yellow tape marked an angling path, and along that path workstations were set up, built from unstained lumber bolted across metal frames supporting kitchen gear and lab equipment. Some workstations had ranges with burners chunky like the grilles of semitrucks. Ventilation hoods whirred softly.

Where—was—the crew?

The workstations had a rough-and-ready look, but this was no shantytown. The floor gleamed; I saw shoe prints over the swirled track of a mop. Power cords snaked across the yellow-tape road, routed securely beneath plastic channels. The arrangement was improvised but not anarchic. There was a power grid. There was a plan.

I stepped off the yellow-tape road to investigate one of the portals and its prom light. Beyond, there was a squarish space about as big as my apartment, the far wall marked *A3* in paint with the same level of flakeage as the stripes on the floor, and both sides of the room were packed with bushy vegetables in trays on tall racks fitted with lights blaring fuchsia. Was that lettuce? Kale? The greens looked black in the weird light. The next portal opened into room A4, which definitely held broccoli. Cauliflower? No, broccoli.

When I turned back to the concourse, it took a moment for my eyes to adjust. I heard the hum of air circulation, the chirp of unseen electronics, and above the hum, below the chirp, I detected murmurs. Voices. The crack of laughter.

I returned to the yellow-tape road, passing more workstations and more pink-light portals on both sides and, in one place, a line of glass-faced industrial refrigerators grumbling and clicking. The road ran straight through them, like a grocery store freezer aisle. The refrigerators were full of tubs and boxes, all with handwritten labels. I shivered.

Ahead, the road bent sharply around a line of enormous planter boxes supporting bushy, dark-leafed trees, their branches heavy with lemons. Above them, the ceiling broke open and admitted a cylinder of hazy sunlight through a smudgy grid of glass.

On the other side of the pop-up lemon grove, I found the

crew—dozens strong, all sitting together at a superlong picnic table, talking and eating. Tattoos flashed on wrists and forearms as they passed dishes and poked forks. Men and women, mostly young, but a few with gray hair or bald heads.

Near the middle of the table, a figure rose. It was the queen of the underworld in her slouchy black leather jacket: Lily Belasco.

"Baker!" she called.

A few heads swiveled, and those few regarded me amiably. Belasco beckoned, and I went to her, holding my bone-key token in front of me as I approached, as if it were an amulet of protection. "You invited me here," I said. A reminder, and maybe also an accusation.

Belasco wiggled her hands and the people sitting across from her scooched apart dutifully. I wedged myself between them—a man and a woman. The man, who was broad-bellied and round-cheeked, began building a plate. The woman, who was as tiny as an elf, reached for an unlabeled growler and filled a jam jar with dark beer.

"This is Lois," Belasco said to everyone within earshot, "a very talented baker." This was followed by silence. I got the sense maybe everyone within earshot was a very talented baker. Belasco continued: "She also programs robots." That earned a raised eyebrow from the elf girl and a few murmurs of interest farther down. "Lois, this is Horace"—the round-cheeked man—"who managed the bookstore at the Ferry Building before joining us as our . . . What are you, Horace, the archivist?"

"Librarian," Horace said neatly.

"And this is Orli"—the elf—"who sells cheese."

I looked down at the plate Horace had built for me: brown rice with green onions and sesame seeds, dark glistening greens, a curl of what appeared . . . to be . . . octopus. I'd never eaten octopus. I looked up at Lily Belasco. "What is this place?"

She waved the question away. "First, eat. Gracie was just showing us her new acquisition." She turned to the woman next to her, wide-framed with dark freckles, who cupped a jar on the table in front of her.

"Chernobyl honey," Gracie said.

"Surely not," Belasco scoffed.

Gracie nodded firmly. "It's gone back to nature," she explained, "and the bees, they filter out the radioactivity. Most. Enough." She unscrewed the jar, offered a taste. Belasco dipped her spoon and lifted it, trailing a strand that seemed to glow faintly. Put it between her lips, let it sit. Her eyes glittered. "Try it," she said to all of us seated around her. "Try it, try it."

The elf—Orli—dipped her spoon. Horace dipped his, too, and from him the Chernobyl honey earned a rumble of appreciation that was conducted by the bench into the soft flesh of my thighs.

Gracie tipped the jar toward me. "Try some, baker." The gesture was solicitous, but her eyes glinted challenge.

In every legend of the underworld, there is the same warning: Don't eat the food. Not before you know what's happening and/or what bargain you're accepting.

Along the length of the table, wide dishes bobbed up and down, orbiting on currents of camaraderie. I saw faces smiling and serious, all lit by the hazy light from above, but haloed with pink from the portals on both sides. Across the table, Lily Belasco watched me with dark eyes. I had come this far.

I dipped my spoon.

<FROM: BEO>

IN SAN FRANCISCO, there was an older woman, a Russian, the sister of Shehrieh's landlord in Brussels from long ago, back before either Chaiman or I was born. (I'm laughing here, because this is how every Mazg story starts: "My old landlord." The Mazg are inveterate renters.) Anyway, this Russian owns many buildings on Clement Street. She offered us an apartment, but the kitchen had no oven, just a hot plate, and when we asked for a different one, she said, You're going to get me in trouble! But she couldn't refuse, because many years ago, Shehrieh did something very kind for her sister.

This is such a Mazg story, it's sort of embarrassing.

Anyway, Chaiman and I got an apartment with an oven. It wasn't very big, but I felt comfortable there, and that's where the phone rang when you called me all those times.

THE FAUSTOFEN

THE MARROW FAIR is a new kind of market," Lily Belasco explained. Picnic dinner was over and everyone who had tasted the Chernobyl honey was still alive. I was following her away from the lemon grove, back up the yellow-tape road, the way I'd come. "It's an experiment, a place for new ideas. New tools. New food."

"What is this *place*, though?" I asked.

"Oh. Back when the base was operational, this was a munitions depot. Don't you love it? Long and skinny, like a mirror-image Ferry Building."

Like an *underworld* Ferry Building. Yes, I could see why this space appealed to Lily Belasco. As above, so below!

"They kept missiles down here," she continued. "Lifted them up through there"—she pointed back toward the skylight—"into planes, I guess? Don't worry. The floor isn't radioactive anymore."

There was a lot of weird light for a place that wasn't radioactive . . .

"Those are grow rooms. All pink LEDs! Apparently, plants

absorb that portion of the spectrum more efficiently. Ask Kenyatta, he'll tell you more."

Belasco pointed out workstations as we passed them: "That's the coffee bar. Naz Kalil runs it—he was Greenlight Coffee's first barista. Over there they make a new kind of smoothie. Look closely before you try one. Around that corner—cricket cookies. I can smell them. Mmm."

We arrived at a place close to the door where I'd entered, far from the light of the lemon grove. There was a workstation here, shadowed and bare. "Here we are. This is where I want you and your robot."

There had been a misunderstanding. "I don't have a robot, I just work on them."

Belasco groped the depot's wall to find a switch that brought cold fluorescent tubes sparking to life above the workstation. It was outfitted with the same basic accoutrements as the rest—a countertop, some wire shelves, an industrial sink—and it boasted, in addition, a ping-pong table with no net, one folding chair (currently folded), and, finally, an elephantine bread oven, gray and stoic, the size of a small car.

Belasco gave me a frank look. "A market in the Bay Area needs, at minimum, three things. It needs fancy coffee, weird honey, and sourdough bread. Naz has been here from the start and he roasts his beans with lasers. Gracie gets me my honey. You might be my baker. But like I said, this is a place for new tools." She smiled. "I want robot bread."

"I don't. Have. A robot."

She looked at me innocently. "Get one."

"Why can't I just bake bread normally?"

"Go to Colma if you want to do that. I need you to do something different here. The new ideas, they're not always . . . Have you seen cricket flour? It looks like flour. Once you explain it, people get interested, but as we approach our opening, I am mindful of the need for a bit more pizzazz. You, baker, could provide this pizzazz."

I had never before been invited to provide the pizzazz.

"Get a robot and this spot is yours. You'll have the exclusive sourdough franchise. The market runs previews Wednesday mornings. Look, you're right by the door! You'll sell out. Get a robot."

MY DISGRUNTLEMENT DISSOLVED on contact with the problem, the way it had hundreds of times at Crowley and General Dexterity. Maybe that was my great weakness: if a task was even mildly challenging, any sense of injustice drained away and I simply worked quietly until I was done.

I guess I learned that in school.

The elephantine bread oven's manufacturer was etched on the thin lip of metal above the baking bays; it was a FAUSTOFEN, from MUNICH. I looked it up on Global Gluten— the depot had very fast wireless internet, network name: CRUCIFEROUS—and discovered that the oven was considered a boring but reliable workhorse of industrial bakeries.

A Faustofen definitely did not provide pizzazz.

It took me a bit of poking around to find an open pantry stocked with staples, including flour and salt, the latter Diamond Crystal, which made me feel for a moment like I was somewhat in the loop. I mixed the flour with water and fed the Clement Street starter, watched it bubble and fizz. It was late, nearly midnight, but I was wide-awake, buoyed by curiosity. We would see about pizzazz. I mixed some dough and set it to rest.

I stood and faced the Faustofen. The controls were all in German, but how difficult could they be? Very difficult, it turned out. It took me ten minutes to deduce the combination that commanded ignition. When I did, the deep *whoomph* of the burners inside sent me leaping backward.

As I turned the dough, I paid special attention to what my joints were doing. I imagined myself a General Dexterity robot arm. I made low, rumbling robot-arm noises.

A smell wafted over from farther up the concourse, fishy and marine. I heard the clink of glass. I watched a sheet of steam rise in the distance. I saw a woman in a short lab coat, stunningly beautiful, dark-skinned with darker slashes under her eyes, wandering slowly up the yellow-tape road carrying a bright blue mug, her lips moving slightly, twitching at moments into a smile. Then, suddenly, she spun in place and sprinted back to wherever she'd been working.

I knew that feeling.

While I waited for the dough to rise, I wandered back to the lemon grove and the coffee bar. The barista, Naz, alternated his attention between a rig upon which a laser tracked slowly across a scattered bed of coffee beans—their roasty smell rising—and a laptop that showed a long playlist.

"Any requests?" he asked.

It was only then that I became aware of the depot's soundtrack: currently an ambient swell so deep it could have been the far-off foghorns that guarded the Golden Gate.

Was it the far-off foghorns?

"She calls herself Microclimate," Naz explained. "She

samples the foghorns up close, then she plays with the sound, turns it into drums, voices, everything."

So Naz chose the Marrow Fair's music.

"The acoustics in here," he began, and then words failed him, and he just shook his head in awe.

I sat with my cappuccino in the folding chair alongside the ping-pong table. The acoustics of the concourse carried not only Naz's playlist but also scraps of sound from other workstations. I heard low beeps, sharp scrapes, muttered conferences, and the occasional laugh. The depot was wreathed in gentle effort. It percolated.

My dough had risen, so I formed a loaf. Technically, I should have let it sit, but I was impatient. I slung it into the Faustofen's top baking bay and commanded the stoic monolith to bake.

The Faustofen had, in addition to its temperature dial, a humidity control, and I'd never controlled an oven's humidity before. I made my best guess and resolved to check Global Gluten later. Then, through cloudy glass, I watched the solitary loaf bake. It felt transgressive; a process previously private, protected by walls three bricks thick, now starkly visible.

Naz must have switched albums, because the foghorn faded to nothing and was replaced by electronic drums—slow taps blurred by the width and breadth of the concourse into massive echoing thuds. I imagined the loading cranes at the Port of Oakland lifting their legs to plod across the airfield above.

Inside the Faustofen, the loaf inflated.

The crust darkened. Cracks formed.

A face emerged, wearing just the faintest smile.

I looked around. I liked this spot, right next to the door. I liked the folding chair. I liked the ping-pong table. I liked the pink light and the cool soundtrack and the wandering geniuses.

It couldn't be that difficult to acquire a robot arm.

SO, YOU ASKED ABOUT THE STARTER.

The Mazg have many stories explaining how it came to us, and they all contradict each other. Every family maintains their own starter, always in a ceramic crock like the one I gave you. Sometimes the crocks are very old. That one was pretty new. I bought it in Daly City.

Here in Edinburgh, in the little Mazg neighborhood, when I go walking in the morning, through all the second-story windows I can hear the starters singing.

REFURB

I TOLD PETER I wanted to borrow a robot arm so I could teach it to bake bread.

"I don't eat bread," he reminded me.

That was well established.

"I didn't think the arms could do kitchen stuff," Peter said.

"They can't. Not yet. I can figure it out."

He pressed his lips together and I saw the muscles of his jaw working. This was Peter's being-a-manager face. It meant he was figuring out how to help you. "There's never enough arms, and Task allocates them. But if you really think you can do it . . . Huh. That would be a big deal, right? It would be. We could pitch it to Andrei."

For all his reality-bending intensity, our CEO was accessible and approachable. He ate his lunch in the cafeteria with the rest of us, sitting with a different group every day. You could tell where he was without looking because Andrei's table always laughed a little too loud.

Peter and I went to lunch early. We migrated between the stations of the cafeteria slowly, smoothie to salad to waffle maker, circling vulture-like, waiting for Andrei to appear.

Peter looked very suspicious circling with just a single green Tetra Pak.

When Andrei appeared, Peter hooted an alert, and I tracked the CEO out the tail of my eye. It took him a long time to fill his tray—every step interrupted by a greeting, an admonition, a whispered report. I had never watched him this closely. Passing through the cafeteria, he left a wake of keyed-up expressions—smiles and grimaces. He was a walking amphetamine. Peter and I loitered together at the paella station. My pulse accelerated.

Finally, Andrei selected a seat at a half-empty table.

"Go, go, go!" Peter commanded. We sprinted across the cafeteria, Peter angling neatly between the Dextrous, me smashing into them, to bring our butts—his sliding, mine crashing—into the table's last available chairs. Two cold-eyed wraiths had been vectoring for the same spots. I glared at them and sounded a warning hiss.

"Peter!" Andrei boomed. "And Lois!" He looked around the table. "Do you all know Peter and Lois? Peter runs Control, and Lois works on Proprioception. Very cool stuff."

Andrei knew everyone's name and role. Everyone's. It was said he used flash cards.

Peter and I had planned to begin with three to five minutes of small talk before easing into our overture, but looking at the group of Dextrous we had joined, I understood suddenly that everyone at the table had exactly the same plan. We were not the only birds of prey in this cafeteria.

"*The eggs!*" I blurted.

Andrei raised an eyebrow.

"I want to solve the egg problem," I said. "I mean. Cooking. Specifically, baking."

Andrei lifted a curl of fennel from the top of his salad and popped it into his mouth, where he chewed it thoughtfully.

Peter daintily removed the seal from his Tetra Pak.

The other Dextrous glowered.

"We've been working on that for a long time," Andrei said.

"Right. But I know the Control codebase, and I know the task."

"An integrated approach," Peter interjected.

I nodded. We had practiced. "Task and Control together."

Peter couldn't help himself. "But if it works, Control gets the credit."

We had the rest of the argument ready to go—an appeal to the skunkworks spirit, a preapproved interjection from Peter praising my most recent bug fix—but none of it was needed. Andrei nodded, picked up his phone, and tapped a short message.

"Okay. You can have a refurbished arm. Lois, this is your job now. Peter, you'll oversee?"

Peter slurped affirmatively.

"Great. Make it work."

I told him thank you, and that I was going to sit somewhere else to actually eat my lunch. Andrei laughed (followed by everyone else at the table, too loudly) and waved me away.

Later, I crossed Townsend to meet my new robot at the Task Acquisition Center. I walked through the rows of arms, watched them lift boxes and knock over glass bottles. I walked all the way to the back of the building, to a work area set up against the far wall, where several arms stood slack, all of them marked with wide red stickers that said REFURB.

A woman was sitting at a small desk there in the shadows: Deborah Palmer-Grill, queen of the training floor.

DPG narrowed her eyes. "So I hear you're going to solve the egg problem."

I nodded slowly.

"We've broken a lot of eggs in here."

"I'm going to try something different."

"More eggs than you can imagine. Garbage bins full of shells. Full of them!"

"I'm going to bring you a loaf of bread," I said with more confidence than I actually possessed. "It's going to be perfect, and it's going to be baked by this . . . fellow . . . right here." I patted the closest arm.

"Not that one," DPG said. "That one's new. The one on the end—that's a Vitruvian 3 from a year ago. Fill out this form. They used that one at the CDC, so if I were you, I'd wipe it down extra good."

THE ARM ARRIVED on the airfield borne on a pallet, mummified in plastic wrap, delivered by a courier waiting confusedly on the asphalt whose relief showed clearly when we appeared from inside the control tower. Lily Belasco and I extracted the Vitruvian, released the brakes on its wheeled base, and brought it slowly down the vehicle ramp into the depot, Belasco cackling the whole way.

IS IT STRANGE that a sourdough starter sings?

It didn't seem strange when I was a child. I'm now twenty-three years old (how old are you?), and yes, I understand that most starters don't behave this way. But I still don't think the singing is the most remarkable thing about it. (I'm not being evasive—this is the truth.) Every time I feed my family's starter, I feel a sense of awe, because from your starter to mine to my mother's and her father's, it's all the *same stuff,* and it goes back a very long way. Immortality is stranger than singing, if you ask me.

Anyway, Leopold says it's just a weird thing with the CO_2 bubbles.

In other news, I have officially received permission from Chaiman to share one of his new tracks. It's attached.

CATHEDRALS

THE MARROW FAIR'S ORIENTATION wasn't as involved as I'd expected, given that I was being granted space in a repurposed munitions depot slightly below sea level. Lily Belasco showed me the bathrooms, told me there were emergency exits in most but not all directions, then pressed a flashlight into my palm. She explained that the depot connected to other bygone facilities that were not fully mapped.

"But really," she said, "nothing's radioactive anymore."

I resolved to orient myself. The concourse was the spine of the Marrow Fair, and the lemon grove, with the skylight above, its central chakra. Beyond that, portals opened not into pink light but darkness, and long corridors. Exploring them, I discovered:

- A mushroom grotto where dense clusters of broad-brimmed fungi protruded from transparent plastic sacks bulging with dark dirt.
- The cricket farm! I did not see the bugs, but I heard them, chittering enormously in the darkness. I turned and retreated.

- A single lemon, forlorn and desiccated.
- A ladder that rose to a hatch. When I poked my head through, I found myself nearly nose to nose with one of the goats grazing on the airfield. It regarded me with flat skepticism. (Goats only ever give side-eye.)
- An enormous vehicle ramp, wide enough for whatever kind of truck carries (nuclear?) missiles. I hiked its gentle rise to find myself at the back of the Algebra hangar with its gleaming vats. Brewers rolled kegs on dollies and bantered about the recent performance of the Golden State Warriors. I wandered out through the brewery onto the airfield and saw the goats again in the distance.

I went back down and followed the concourse to its terminus, a blank concrete wall with another gray door marked with a stencil and unlocked by the bone key: *STILL—TOO—SKINNY.* This door opened onto the glittering water and the night sky and a tiny concrete pier at which a wide-bellied boat waited with a few passengers, familiar from inside, already seated in her stern. I returned to San Francisco on that slow, easygoing craft, and learned from its pilot that he operated a daily ferry service for the Marrow Fair. He gave me a slip of paper on which his schedule was printed alongside his name, Carl, as well as the name of his boat, the *Omebushi.*

His schedule started at six a.m. "Is that the earliest?" I asked.

"You need me to go earlier?"

I told him I might.

He nodded gravely. "Just means more hours for me and the *'Bushi.* I'll tell Belasco."

LATER, I FOUND MY ROUND-CHEEKED NEIGHBOR from the picnic table. His full name was Horace Portacio and he was the Marrow Fair's librarian. He also compiled the weekly e-newsletter.

In a prime spot just across the yellow-tape road from the lemon trees, he tended his own dark grove of bookshelves, and beside them a field of legal boxes, which held thousands of menus from restaurants famous and obscure. Whenever I passed Horace's collection, there was someone flipping through the menus with the furious intensity of a DJ digging in the crates.

When I introduced myself again and explained I'd officially joined the market, Horace raised a finger—*Just a moment!*—then disappeared into his shelves. He emerged again with a teetering armload of books. It seemed impossible that he had gathered them so quickly. Did he have thematic stacks presorted, awaiting the right recipient? He sat to enumerate the volumes.

"Here we have a reproduction of a pamphlet printed by the bakers guild in London, around, let's see, 1600, very nice. And *A History of Food*, it's quite contemporary"—he said that with palpable regret—"but there's a good bit on baking. And here, oh yes, these"—he plopped a folder onto the table—"are Edward Brown's notes toward *The Tassajara Bread Book*. Lovely handwriting, don't you think? Keep those pages together. And of course you must read Ibn Butlan. Here is his classic *Tacuinum Sanitatis*, an edition printed around 1500. There's a section where he strongly recommends whole wheat, and I, for one, am inclined to obey. And of course . . ." He flipped through *Tacuinum Sanitatis*, searching for a page, and when he found it, he spun the book around to show me. "That," Horace said, "is the first identifiable published illustration of a carrot." He was beaming.

The book looked very old. I didn't want to take it.

"Oh, you must, you must!" he said. "It is an absolutely foundational document."

I squinted at the text below the illustration. "I can't read Latin."

Horace sobered. "All right. I'll keep this one. But take the rest."

THE NEXT DAY, I rode the *Omebushi* from San Francisco to Alameda, used my bone-key token to enter through the bay door, loaded the master development branch of ArmOS into my refurbished Vitruvian 3, and spent the next six hours teaching it to stir.

With my fingers on its elbows, I led it through the motion. This was Task Segmentation. Whenever I paused and said, "Like that," the Vitruvian emitted a whispering beep of acknowledgment, recording not only the motion but also its understanding of the context—what it saw through its cameras (visible and thermal) and felt through its pressure sensors. After finishing the sequence, I stepped back and spoke again. "Now you try."

And so it came to pass that a late-model Vitruvian, loaded with the master development branch of ArmOS, reenacted all the horrors of my first attempts at baking.

Except this arm was five feet long, with strength commensurate, and every error was multiplied. It sent the bowl clanging across the concrete, leaving a powdery trail of unmixed flour.

I did, in time, teach it to stir, and so we progressed, briefly, to kneading and shaping, but then it was launching disks of dough through the air like gooey artillery. The arm was strong; they went a long way. One of the disks missed the coffee bar by inches. One of them, I never found.

For now, we would stick to stirring.

THE FLUX OF PREVIEW CUSTOMERS in the Marrow Fair when the doors opened the following Wednesday morning was immense. Had these people all been waiting out on the airfield, jostling with the goats? Between eight and nine a.m., the depot transformed from a spaceship into . . . a farmers market on a spaceship. The customers looked, for the most part, very rich. I saw the toothsome plaids of tech wealth, and I saw the supple leather handbags of something older.

The customers came gliding through the control tower door, none in any rush, some walking alone, others in pairs or small groups whispering among themselves. I hadn't yet taught the Vitruvian to do anything of value, so my workstation stood quiet and dark while they passed.

Horace approached me. "Shall we wander?" he asked. "It's always interesting to see what everyone is offering."

There was Gracie with her Chernobyl honey; the cave-dwelling mushroom monger; a man and a woman decanting smoothies that appeared to have . . . *things* swimming inside them. Orli, the elf, presided over a table piled with cheeses, some ghostly pale, some brown like leather, and some veined not only with blue but also bright green and hot pink. The larger wheels she had carved into pieces at irregular angles, so the resulting hunks looked like soft, fat jewels.

There was a workstation selling algorithmically optimized bagels, their outsides perfectly smooth like computer renderings. A printed banner said NEWBAGEL; it was surprisingly well designed.

There was a man selling barramundi that lived their whole lives in watery tubes extending deep into the depot's corridors. Next to him, another man cleaned those fish and fried them into tacos on the spot, filling tortillas made from cricket flour and topping them with slaw made from cabbage grown in the pink-light rooms. Horace and I requested two tacos each and agreed that the collaboration was impeccable.

We came to the cricket bakery and Horace greeted its proprietor. "Anita! This is Lois, a baker of great skill. She employs a robot." To me, Horace said, "You must try one of Anita's cookies." It was light brown, threaded with darker grains. "There are cave paintings in Spain, thirty thousand years old, that depict the collection and consumption of insects." He popped a cookie into his mouth.

When we moved on, I asked him, "So who are these customers? If one of them says, 'Sure, Anita, I'll take a dozen boxes of bug cookies . . .'?"

Horace leaned closer, clearly delighted to be conspiring. "I believe we have here representatives of many of the greatest restaurants in the world—from San Francisco, New York, London, and Tokyo. Who better to assess the market's progress? They bring their findings to their diners. Perhaps they report back to Mr. Marrow, as well."

We approached the lemon grove. Just ahead, a young woman held court before several of the customers. She was the one I'd seen the first night, walking the quiet concourse carrying a mug of coffee and an inward look.

"—a nutritionally complete food product," she was saying. The stitching on her lab coat named her DR. JAINA MITRA.

The woman was passing around a platter stacked with blocks of apparently edible matter. Each was wrapped in silvery-green paper, but the matter itself was as white as a grub. The blocks resembled ghostly Rice Krispies Treats.

The customers moved along, one whispering to another. Jaina Mitra's gaze followed them. She chewed her lip a little.

"Hello, Dr. Mitra," Horace said. "This is Lois. She has a robot."

Jaina Mitra said hello, her eyes still following the customers, and absently offered the platter to us.

I lifted a slab and gave it an exploratory sniff. It smelled like dirt. Not in a bad way. "You said it's nutritionally complete. Is this anything like Slurry?"

Jaina Mitra's gaze snapped around. "No," she said, her face taut. "This is Lembas. It's much better. Have you tried Slurry?"

When I told her that I had, in fact, subsisted on it, she looked surprised. "Lembas is a very different concept. I'll explain, but please, taste it first."

I took a bite, expecting the slippery, chemical tang that I knew from Slurry. Instead, the taste was warm and definite. The closest comparison was an immense tater tot, but it went beyond tot; in this substance, the balance of sponge to crisp was perfected.

I ate the whole piece.

Jaina Mitra smiled. "You like it?"

It tasted great, and the initial texture was top-notch, but

once inside my mouth it seemed to surrender to my saliva too easily. I could feel it adhering to my molars.

"Itsh good," I said, "but"—swallowing—"itsh a bit shticky."

"Mmf," Horace mumbled in agreement. He was struggling to unstick his jaws.

"That's the new enzymes," Jaina Mitra said darkly. "I should make a note." She scrambled back to her workstation, typed something into her laptop, then turned back.

"Whatsh it shupposed—" I started. "Wait." I squeegeed my teeth with my tongue. "What's it supposed to taste like?"

Jaina Mitra's gaze sharpened. "Nothing. It's not intended to be a simulation. I think food should taste like what it is, don't you? And what this *is*, is a super-nutritious cellulosic suspension manufactured in situ by a community of microbes."

Jaina Mitra was, I decided, very impressive.

"It's got all the vitamins, minerals, and macronutrients you need," she said, "all in the right ratios. Plenty of protein. Tons of fiber. *Tons*."

Horace had regained his powers of speech. "Dr. Mitra, you are the heir to Pasteur!" he exclaimed. "Mistress of microbes. I believe Bruno Latour would be tickled by this. I have a book of his you should read . . ."

Jaina Mitra turned to the machine that stood behind her, occupying most of the workstation: an enormous steel cylinder with a bright, swirly logo on its breast, from which burst a tangle of pipes and cables. One large pipe connected the cylinder to a wide beige box with the plain *Who, me?* look that all biotech gear seemed to share.

"This is my bioreactor," she said, accents of pride evident on both *my* and *bioreactor*. She looked at me, ready to make a point. "As you might know, Slurry is assembled from various organic precursors. Basically thrown together in a blender." Her voice made it clear she did not respect mere blending. "My Lembas cakes are manufactured whole by living microorganisms."

I pointed to the shiny cylinder. "Right there in that tank?"

"Bioreactor. Yes. I grow the cultures here, and they assemble the cakes here."

She opened one of her huge cabinets, which was populated by racks that looked like shallow muffin trays. In each one, a Lembas cake was blooming: the light, airy structure rising like scaffolding. Around their edges, they glistened wetly.

"The form recalls a Breton cake," Horace mused. "It almost has the finesse of a kouign-amann."

"I think of them as microbial cathedrals," Jaina Mitra said.

I wondered if that comparison made her the architect or the deity.

"Why not just leave it liquid like Slurry?" I asked.

Jaina Mitra ticked off the reasons: "Mouthfeel. Dental health. Market research indicates people associate liquid superfood with pessimistic science fiction." That was a good point. "And, I should clarify, I don't want people to eat Lembas all day, every day," she said. "It's your quick lunch. It's what you eat in the car. It solves food security, because once I get the microbial community stabilized, we'll be able to produce it literally *anywhere*. Trust me, I have no desire to replace all of this." She lifted her hands to encompass the Marrow Fair. "It's fast food I want to replace, and all the other terrible stuff people eat when they get impatient."

"Starbucks breakfast sandwiches," I said ruefully.

"*Curse* those breakfast sandwiches," Horace muttered.

Jaina Mitra offered the platter again. "Another one?"

I ran my tongue around my teeth, found bits of cathedral still stuck there. "I'm fine for now."

"Come back for the next batch," she said. "I'm going to get those enzymes dialed in. It's almost ready. Almost, almost, *almost* ready."

RIGHT NOW, I'M MAKING SPICY SOUP, the kind you like. Chaiman brought his laptop into the kitchen (Shehrieh told him he was being a weird hermit) and he's hunched over the table, composing. I can hear the *oonce-oonce* in his headphones. As for my mother, she's rolling noodles on the countertop, humming while she does it.

It always begins with the humming. Chaiman and I joke about this. It sneaks up on her. In another minute, she'll be singing with her full voice. She can't help herself. Right now, she's humming her favorite song, which is about leaving places behind, and how it's sad but also happy.

It's very Mazg.

Lois, the picture you sent—the robot with the mixing bowl—it inspired me. I think I've gotten complacent with my cooking. I need to experiment more! This morning I separated a bit of my starter and mixed some Fresno chili into its food.

It died instantly.

But I'm not giving up! If you want to experiment, too, we

could compare notes. For one thing, I recommend feeding your starter better flour. It's hard to get good flour in the U.S., but it makes a big difference.

My stockpile of Fresno chilies is dwindling, by the way.

THIS NEW DARKNESS

THE NEXT WEDNESDAY, I was ready. When the preview customers streamed in, their eyes snapped onto the Vitruvian, and they murmured appreciative sounds to one another. Not many stopped; there were stranger delights than sourdough bread waiting within. But this is what they wanted to see. This is where they wanted to be.

I understood Belasco's objective now. I was a mascot. I was the pizzazz.

I saw faces I vaguely recognized from the world of General Dexterity. A young tech CEO; several well-known investors; a programmer with a wine blog.

Two men stopped to assess the Vitruvian. It was, in fact, a pair of the cold-eyed wraiths I worked with at General Dexterity. I knew them by their sneakers.

"Oh, *sweet*," hooted one. "Didn't expect to see a V3 here."

"Look at that beast," said the other.

"It's so clunky, dude! The old motors were super slow."

"Actually," I said—oh, it felt good—"the Vitruvian 3's motors are exactly the same as the V4's. They're all PKD 2891s. It's just that the V4's chassis is lighter."

The wraiths noticed me for the first time. "Wait," said the first. "I know you, right? You're . . . one of our marketing people?"

My face burned hot, but through force of will, I cooled my gaze to absolute zero kelvin. "Actually." Yes. It felt very good. "I work on Control."

The wraiths pulled knives from their waistbands and committed ritual suicide.

Actually, they backed slowly away, and I never saw them again.

A pear-shaped, plaid-shirted customer stopped to admire first the Vitruvian and then the loaves with their merry faces. "What's, uh, going on with these, exactly?" he asked.

I explained to the pear-shaped man in plaid that I was offering sourdough bread made from a starter strange and potent that had come into my possession unexpectedly. I explained that I found the bread delicious and also mood-stabilizing. I explained that the faces were a trade secret.

Oh, and a robot mixed the dough.

He lifted a loaf, tapped it on its back with his finger, listened to the sound, and for a moment, his expression matched the loaf's. He dug for his wallet. I was officially in business.

By nine a.m., the loaves were gone. I had to turn away a customer, and in her eyes I saw a glint of covetousness. She would be back next Wednesday, I understood suddenly. She would be here earlier.

I darkened my workstation and walked, buzzed on commerce. Did I need another Faustofen? How much bread could one morning market absorb? Could this grow into a real business, a real bakery? Would I have my nineteen million dollars?

Up and down the concourse, the Marrow Fair had been sucked dry. Orli's table was bare, her gemlike cheeses all claimed for various hoards. The pink-light farmers had retreated into their grow rooms to tend their crops. The fishmonger's cooler was empty, and only crumbs remained at the bug bakery. Even Naz's stock was depleted. He'd run out of milk and could offer only unadulterated espresso.

The only person with anything left was Jaina Mitra. She stood beside the yellow-tape road with her platter of Lembas cakes, smiling at the last straggling customers as they skirted her lab on their way toward the exit. Her cathedrals were fascinating . . . but not yet appealing.

After that, my days were cleaved in two.

I rose earlier than ever before and experienced a portion of the morning that was new to me. I heard the chirping of unfamiliar bird species—negotiations that had, until now, been concluded long before I woke. The bus didn't run that early, so I bought a used bicycle, paying $50 cash to a woman outside Velo Rouge Cafe, and pedaled my new route: cutting south from Cabrillo Street to ride through Golden Gate Park on my way to the Wiggle, which would take me to Market Street and, at its terminus, the Ferry Building, locked tight.

In this new darkness, I pushed my bicycle to the pier where the *Omebushi* waited. Carl offered me coffee from a family-size thermos. It was just the two of us crossing the bay, and when the fat little boat puttered below the bulk of the Bay Bridge, I felt like we were astronauts in transit across the back side of the moon.

In this new darkness, the Marrow Fair welcomed me. The computerized *STILL—TOO—SKINNY* became rote and comforting. Naz's morning playlist echoed through the concourse, lazy and hopeful. Even in those hours, the depot was never empty. There was always someone—multiple someones—who had spent the night working. Aromas wafted. Timers beeped. Crickets chirped.

In this new darkness, my team greeted me. The Faustofen woke with the *whoomph* of burners. The Vitruvian snapped to life with a friendly chime and leapt instantly to work, arranging its tools in a neat line. The forming of the loaves still eluded it, but I'd taught it to reach the sink and wash the mixing bowls. That was something.

In this new darkness, the Clement Street starter greeted me like a puppy, yapping and leaping, excited to be alive.

In this new darkness, a catalog of phenomena:

- Ripples across its surface like laughter
- Bursts of luminescence, like the signal flare from before, but brighter, shifting from green to pink
- A tiny pseudopod rising slowly like a periscope, wobbling back and forth, then retracting into the crock
- Songs, various: wider-ranging, not just imitations of Chaiman's CD, but new sounds it was picking up in the depot, including a soft but unmistakable foghorn
- Scents, various: still banana, always, along with smoky smells, like far-off fires, and occasionally the scent of gasoline

In this new darkness, I baked as fast as I could: taking dough from the Vitruvian, forming loaves, slamming them into the Faustofen.

Then, while the Vitruvian stirred another batch of dough and the Clement Street starter performed its last labors in the oven, I cracked my laptop and did the work of the Dextrous, responding to emails, reviewing code. I was preternaturally productive in those hours. At first I theorized it was something about the rhythm of baking, the quick bursts of attention alternating with mandatory pauses, but then I decided it was probably something simpler: I was happy.

Most days, I gathered my loaves and rode the *Omebushi* back to San Francisco, still in darkness, to deliver them to Chef Kate.

On Wednesdays, I kept baking while the market opened for its preview hour. I called out, "Arm, change task. Say hello!" and the customers waved back. Loaves came out of the Faustofen and disappeared in moments. Pizzazz! As soon as I sold out, I patted the Vitruvian on the shoulder, powered it down, covered the starter in its crock, made for the *Omebushi*, and watched the sun rise over the Oakland hills from the middle of the bay.

My work complete, I went to work.

At lunchtime, I sat with the Slurry contingent in the General Dexterity cafeteria, but it had been weeks since I consumed any of the nutritive gel myself. I ate my own product: sourdough bread slathered with butter or soft avocado, consumed with gusto while Peter looked on ruefully.

AT BEO'S URGING, I upgraded my flour. The cheap stuff had served me well, but this new phase called for a finer grain. There was a mill just fifty miles away, in a farm town west of Davis, that sold flour ground from wheat grown nearby. It cost more than twice as much as King Arthur flour, so I started small, with just a little bag, a test run.

The Clement Street starter loved it. It groaned and luxuriated. It belched ecstatically.

There was more to upgrade. I went to a shop in downtown Oakland that sold salt of every kind and color, black and pink and blue. Each variety sat shimmering in a glass canister, priced by the ounce, with a handwritten card recounting its biography: here, salt from the beaches of Gujarat; there, salt from the pans of Brittany; behold, salt from the suburbs of Portland.

I backed slowly out the door. I would stick with Diamond Crystal.

At the Marrow Fair, I sought out Gracie, the woman with the Chernobyl honey, and the starter's next feeding included a thin drizzle of the stuff. The morning after that, it glowed brighter than ever before, and when the loaves emerged, their expressions looked slightly wonky. I took a picture and shared my findings with Beoreg.

I WAS GETTING HEALTHY.

My arms were stronger, from working the dough. My legs were thicker, from riding my bicycle. My butt showed a heretofore unimagined definition. Even with all the bread I was eating—and it was not a small amount—I lost ten pounds. I felt lean and purposeful. Scoping myself out in my stand-up mirror, I turned and gently twerked.

In the evening—it was possibly more accurate to call it late afternoon—when I fell into my bed, I was truly tired; not merely the brain-spent *Well, I guess I'll give up now* tiredness of a day at the robot factory, but something deeper, actually muscular.

Weeks passed in a haze of happy exhaustion.

In this new darkness, once every two weeks, I found waiting on the ping-pong table an envelope, and inside a check issued by the Patelco Credit Union under the authority of an ALAMEDA TEST MARKET, LLC, bearing the angular signature of *Lily Belasco*. My earnings, minus the market's percentage. The amount was not staggering—barely a tenth of my General Dexterity paycheck for the same amount of time—but this money felt more truly mine, somehow.

In this new darkness, I stood behind the ping-pong table, considered the Clement Street starter in its crock and my partner the brawny Vitruvian. The hardy Faustofen, too. I looked out across the depot, awash in pink light, the tang of tube-fish rising, and realized it was the hidden root of something interesting and maybe important, and I, improbably, was part of it.

WE'RE MOVING AGAIN!
Shehrieh decided suddenly, and when you're Mazg, you don't question this feeling. Our destination is Berlin. It's actually going to be perfect. Even though Berlin is a bigger city than Edinburgh, the Mazg community there is smaller. I'm thinking strategically, you see.

I just finished packing our kitchen things into boxes. I wish we could take the oven. It's a good one—a very old and beautiful English model. I told our landlord she could sell it on the internet. Someone in California would buy it in a second, then pay just as much again to ship it across the world.

I still haven't told anyone else about my restaurant. This is good practice, to say it, or write it. I'm nervous. Shehrieh will be worried because we're supposed to be "the second-story people." Leopold will be worried just because he worries. But I want those tables! I want a sign, written in German *and* in Mazg. I want a front door with a little bell that rings when people step inside.

I'm starting my own restaurant.

I'm starting my own restaurant!

THE EATER'S ARCHIVE

I T WAS WEDNESDAY MORNING at the Marrow Fair, the customers all gone, the doors closed again. Horace sidled up to my workstation while I was cleaning, and I could tell by his quiet calm—no incipient factoid, no swirling ecstasy of trivia—that something was afoot.

He lifted a loaf of the sourdough, held it at arm's length, regarded it with a new sharpness.

"You cut these faces into the crust, do you? You learned the technique from someone? From a book?"

I wiped my hands on my apron. "No," I said carefully. "I didn't learn it from a book."

"I suspected as much." He lowered his voice. "I found something."

"What kind of something?"

"What do you think?" He waggled the loaf, then tucked it under his arm like a football. "Come along." I began to protest, but he was already on his way. "Come along! You'll want to see this."

HE LED ME THROUGH THE LEMON GROVE and into his library, but he did not pause in the shelves. Instead, he plunged through them, and beyond, into a portal I had never before noticed—or, if I had, I assumed it led into one of the depot's innumerable dark corridors.

It did, but this corridor was lined with shelves. Horace's library continued.

"Yes, of course it does," he said. "At the time I moved here, I had two thousand linear feet of materials, and to store such a collection in archival-grade conditions . . . it was not cheap. Mr. Marrow was able to entice me primarily with the prospect of unlimited storage." He said those last words with palpable relish.

I followed him as he plunged down the corridor, which was not wide to begin with and made narrower by the shelves and legal boxes on both sides. Cold white lights above were set up on motion detectors, and they snapped to life as we approached.

As we walked, Horace's fingers danced from the lips of shelves to the lids of legal boxes. I saw annotations on the fronts of the boxes. The years ticked back like a time machine: *1992, 1991, 1990*. Horace's handwriting gave the nines long elegant tails.

Behind us, the motion-activated lights snapped off.

We passed through a tunnel of memory in a bubble of light.

"It began with a windfall," Horace said. "I used to haunt estate sales. It was my hobby. I was less focused then . . . I was interested in fin de siècle pottery, rejected applicants to the Oulipo, siege weaponry of the Gironde. But this collection that I found, it was something entirely new to me. He was a great eater, you see! John Eliot Sinclair of San Francisco. Born in 1913 and died in 1998, during that wet, wet winter, alone in his enormous house on Sacramento Street, and in the time between, he made it his mission to eat at every restaurant that opened in his city. And"—Horace turned to me, alive with astonishment—"he kept the menus. He kept all the menus!"

I didn't think you were, strictly speaking, supposed to keep the menus.

"John Eliot Sinclair must have been very charming. Or clandestine. Or both. Probably both."

"How many menus are we talking about here?"

"He was not the only one with this passion. After I acquired the Sinclair collection—for the price of hauling it away, not a penny more—I began to wonder if I hadn't stumbled onto something. The archives of the great eaters. That is what I am assembling. Here!"

He stopped short and selected a volume, fat and puffy like a photo album. He held it against the shelf and flopped it open; inside, protected by plastic overlays, were wine labels, fastidiously peeled from their bottles and flattened, each with an accompanying note written in a spidery hand. More albums waited. The wine drinker's liquid autobiography occupied four entire shelves.

When I thought of archives—documents stored and studied—I thought of poets, writers, politicians, scientists. But why shouldn't the archives of the eaters also have avid keepers?

Horace kept walking, the lights snapping on ahead of him, and I followed. The years ticked back, and around 1979, there was evidence of a transplant in process, documents being moved out of old boxes, foxed and rippled with age, into new ones, freshly assembled.

A cup from Naz's coffee bar sat on the corridor's floor beside one of the boxes.

Horace turned. "I was revisiting the Louise Bouk collection, which is of particular interest because she overlapped with John Eliot Sinclair in San Francisco. Sinclair loved the steak houses. Bouk was different; she was enthusiastic about California cuisine."

"Raw turnips drizzled in olive oil? That sort of thing?"

"I'm not sure the cuisine's adherents would call that its most soaring exponent, but yes, you have the idea. In Bouk's collection, I found . . . No, not this one . . . Where is it . . . ?"

He was pulling out menus as big as newspapers, hand-lettered and reproduced using some antique process on heavy brown paper, with fine-lined illustrations that made them look like pages from a Victorian children's book. The menus were all dated 1979.

I saw one menu titled JAPANESE DEATH POEM. Another called THE PLUM'S LAMENT. I saw a tiny, perfect sketch of a clutch of carrots with shaggy tops. Another of a very handsome goose.

Horace found his quarry. "Here," he said, offering it. "December 1979."

The menu was titled A FEAST FOR THE UNREQUITED, and it began with a dish called Sourdough à la Masque served with smoked salt and bone marrow. It was accompanied by a very respectable rendering of a loaf of bread, darkly crosshatched. The loaf was oblong and rustic and unmistakable: because a face leered out of the crust.

The name of the restaurant was written in tiny script at the bottom of the menu, almost reluctantly. I read it aloud: "Café Candide." I looked at Horace. "Have you heard of it?"

He blinked. "Yes, Lois. I have heard of it." He looked at me strangely. "Never? Truly? Perhaps . . . the Café Candide cookbooks . . . simple black covers, very elegant . . . ? She sold two million of them?"

Had I seen them at the bookstore on Clement Street? It was possible, but . . .

"Lois. Café Candide is a very important place. It is the wellspring." He shook his head. "Surely you've heard of Charlotte Clingstone."

"Is she on TV? I don't really watch—"

"I'll tell you this." Horace snorted. "You have dined, apparently without realizing it, in restaurants established by alumni of her kitchen. I know this for a fact because *all the restaurants* are established by alumni of her kitchen. It is the greatest and farthest-reaching culinary mafia since the twelve pupils of Apicius, who went out like disciples . . . Wait! You have read Everett Broom!"

The tattooed baker whose book taught me the basics of sourdough. Yes, of course.

Horace raised a finger, triumphant. "He, too, hails from the Candide clan!" Then his look grew admonishing. "Lois, it is a lazy thing not to know whose world you live in. This is Charlotte Clingstone's."

He held up the menu with its leering sourdough.

"And you see, that makes this *interesting.* Café Candide, of all places! How did a loaf with this . . . *look* arrive at Charlotte Clingstone's table? How did it come into your possession, more than three decades later? Something links you to her." He paused, as if to digest the implausibility of that statement. "In any case, this is a highly suggestive document."

The lights above snapped off. We'd sat talking for too long. "Does that happen often?"

"A fair amount, yes," Horace said. "I don't mind. It gives me a minute to think."

We stayed quiet. Thinking.

"You must seek her out," Horace said at last.

He was right.

The lights snapped on again, revealing Horace on his feet, caught mid-gesticulation. "It takes a bit of a leap to wake them up." He straightened. "Bring the menu. I'll make you a copy."

We walked back the way we'd come, resynchronizing with the present.

From the disarray in the corridor, and from the bright sticky notes affixed to the shelves and boxes and walls and floor, overlapping in places and fluttering like feathery lichen as we passed, it became clear: this was not a sleeping archive. Horace had a project under way.

"What are you doing with all this?"

"I am following the path that the archive of John Eliot Sinclair set me on. I have come to believe that food is history of the deepest kind. Everything we eat tells a tale of ingenuity and creation, domination and injustice—and does so more vividly than any other artifact, any other medium. There are histories of food, of course. I have them all here. And yet . . . something is missing. So, I am trying to write a book."

He sighed.

"And even if I fail—this is always the archivist's consolation—perhaps I will have laid a foundation for someone wiser."

We walked farther.

"I gave this place its name, you know. I said it to Lily. I said, 'This man, our benefactor, he works powerfully in secret like a lump of marrow.' She repeated it to him, and the next thing I heard was that the place was called the Marrow Fair! And then, to his chagrin perhaps, he became Mr. Marrow. It's a wonderful word, isn't it? From the Old English *mearg*, the innermost core. The hidden heart! It makes our blood in its secret chambers. That is Mr. Marrow's ambition, I believe. The production of new blood."

The end of the corridor was in sight; across the concourse, a grow room glowed pink.

"Is he succeeding?" I asked.

"It is no small thing to change a culture," Horace said simply. "But I think interesting things are growing here. Lucrative enterprises. Provocative tastes. Perhaps, even, if you can imagine it"—he pranced into the light—"this book of mine."

Out in the concourse, among the shelves I now understood were only the tip of a vast project, Horace hunted and reached and produced a grip of books.

"Here," he said. "This is your education."

The stack contained *The Candide Cookbook* and *The Next Candide Cookbook*, both with plain black covers, along with *California Table: The Café Candide Story*, large and glossy, and finally a floppy paperback titled *Tend Your Garden: Charlotte Clingstone and the Making of a Perfect Place*.

That last volume showed on its cover a woman, broad-faced and serene, standing in a garden wearing very comfortable pants. A sense of recognition circled the runway, came in to land: I knew Charlotte Clingstone after all. She had been part of the panel at the Ferry Building. She was the central deity. *That will be all.* I had no doubt: she was the one who'd said no.

IN YOUR MESSAGE, you told me about your family, how you don't have any traditions. The first time I read that, it made me sad, but then I thought about it for a while and I started to feel jealous. Lois, think about it! No one cares if your restaurant has tables. You can build robots, or bake bread, or do something else entirely. You're unencumbered by culture. You're . . . light!

We've arrived in Berlin. This apartment is bigger than the last one, but it's really dark. Shehrieh says it's fine. I still haven't told her about my restaurant.

Chaiman wants me to tell you he misses your city by the bay. As for me, I miss your voice on the phone.

THE LOIS CLUB (CONTINUED)

I'D SKIPPED A MEETING of the Lois Club, not because I consciously decided not to go, but because I'd been so busy it had escaped me completely. I sent an apology to Hilltop Lois a week late and promised I had not forsaken them. *We missed your bread!!!!* she replied. She seemed to use more exclamation marks every time.

When I entered, bearing six loaves of bread—one to eat, the rest to distribute as gifts—the Loises all fell silent. I'd expected a hero's welcome; instead, they looked at me strangely.

"What?"

"It's just—you look so different," Professor Lois said.

"You look wonderful!" Compaq Lois said.

"Do I really look that different? What do you mean?"

"You just—" Professor Lois searched for words. "You're in great shape. Have you been doing yoga?"

"You're making us feel bad!" Old Lois cackled. "Here we are, all the same as ever. Of course, for some of us, that's an achievement . . ."

To fill the silence, I started to unspool the story of the last month. They didn't know about the Marrow Fair. I told them everything.

"Can I shop there?" Compaq Lois asked. "It sounds fabulous."

I explained that it ran previews early on Wednesday mornings, but by invitation only, and that it would be opening to everyone soon.

"And you're going to Café Candide?" Professor Lois asked. "How wonderful. My husband and I went there years ago. Our twentieth wedding anniversary."

"Hope you saved your pennies," Old Lois said. "I hear it's pricey."

"I'm not going to eat," I said. "Just to investigate."

"I saw her speak at the Commonwealth Club," Professor Lois said. "Charlotte Clingstone. Very impressive woman."

"I saw her in a documentary on KQED," Hilltop Lois interjected.

"I met her at a fund-raiser," Compaq Lois said. "For the turkey vultures."

They had started and it seemed they couldn't stop. Their fascination surprised me; but as they spoke—

"She spent three years in France, you know."

—I realized—

"Yes, she met her husband there."

—Charlotte Clingstone presented a kind of ideal. She was bohemian but accomplished. Worldly but rooted.

"Her *first* husband. Now she's married to a poet."

Who wouldn't want that life?

"Oh, yes. I have his book. He dedicated it to her."

"That was his first one. The second, he dedicated to her plums."

"Her plums!"

"No, he really meant it. In the back, in the garden behind the restaurant, I guess there's this amazing plum tree . . ."

"Her *plums,*" Old Lois crowed.

"I'll see if I can spot the tree tomorrow," I said.

"Yes," Old Lois said between snorts. She couldn't stop laughing. "Watch for those plums!"

THE HUB, THE HEART

SAN FRANCISCO IS SHORT ON GREENERY and the streets have a bare brightness. Berkeley runs wilder. Walking from the North Berkeley BART station to Café Candide, I had to circle around huge hedges that surged and blocked the sidewalk. There were no lawns. Instead, residents cultivated behemoth planter boxes; personal citrus groves; gardens of meaty succulents that seemed to glow with an inner light. The streets were quiet, but I sensed eyes through gauzy curtains. A fat squirrel shadowed me for a block.

In one place, a massive willow tree's roots had split the pavement. Its leaves brushed my head.

I pulled out my phone to double-check the restaurant's address, but I didn't have to search for it: Café Candide was preemptively inscribed on the map, like a government office or a natural landmark.

When I emerged into the quiet shopping district I saw the rim of the hills looming above, a dark cutout now turning pink in the evening light, the steep wooded slope crusted with houses whose windows flashed white in the sun.

I found the restaurant smashed between a hardware store and a mobile phone outlet peddling a brand I didn't recognize. Both store and outlet looked like they belonged on this block; Café Candide, not so much. That impression was wrong, of course. Café Candide had stood here for decades while businesses flashed through the storefronts on both sides.

It was a house of darkest gingerbread, odd-angled and enormous, seeming to lean slightly on its neighbors. Yes, Berkeley Nuts-n-Bolts and Air Zero were definitely providing significant structural support to the old restaurant. Café Candide's roof was densely shingled and sharply slanted. A short chimney tossed up a ragged streamer of smoke

It was very clearly a witch's abode.

The house/restaurant was set back from the sidewalk, guarded by a stubby fence of wrought iron, the gate currently open. My heels *thwapped* across a patio paved in slate. The door was a slab of dark wood with an iron handle that matched the fence. The wood was carved with a mazelike pattern; I wanted to plunk my finger down and find my way through it. The maze's channels shone smooth and glossy, so maybe I wasn't the first person to feel that impulse.

There was no sign that said CAFÉ CANDIDE. There was also no doubt that this was the place.

I knocked, or tried. My best effort produced barely any sound; it was like knocking on a mattress. So I took the door by its handle, hauled it open a crack, and before it could close again, I slithered through.

Inside, a young woman in a linen smock was pushing a mop across gleaming floorboards. The soap smelled dense and spicy.

"Excuse me," I said. Her eyes snapped up. "I'm here to see Charlotte Clingstone. I called this morning."

The smocked mopper nodded and beckoned for me to follow.

She glided through the cool, dark dining room. The tables and chairs matched the paneling on the walls and the boards beneath my feet; the room could have been carved from one great block of wood. Everything was soft and smooth, polished by use. I saw myself reflected in the floor. A warm shadow.

The smocked mopper led me through a swinging door into the kitchen.

According to Horace, this was it. The hub, the heart. Sanctum sanctorum. The quiet workers before me—currently chopping, cleaning, carving, prepping, planning, all in matching smocks—would in time open restaurants, host TV shows, write bestselling cookbooks. I had penetrated the innermost crèche of California cuisine.

Where, as in Chef Kate's kitchen, hip-hop was playing on a whoomphy Bluetooth speaker.

The smocked mopper glided through the kitchen and I followed her path as precisely as I could, wary of getting in anyone's way. I kept my head down.

Then I saw the oven.

It was epic, with a pale stone dome, walls of black-lacquered brick, and a yawning mouth with a flicking, forking tongue of fire. The heat was palpable from across the kitchen. As I passed, a red-faced baker twirled a long wooden paddle—her arms were enormous—and sent it slicing into the oven to slip beneath two loaves at once. With a snap of her shoulders they were out, rough and crackly, uppermost edges singed black. Her bread looked even more rustic than Everett Broom's, like some primordial ancestor from a harder epoch—one that required more armor. As I watched, she dropped the loaves into a line that was forming on the counter-top, then gave the paddle another twirl, tossing it into the air as she did, a confident flourish intended for no one but herself.

"Awwwesommme." I groaned it out loud without intending to. She heard me, and a wicked grin flashed across her face.

I spotted the baker's starter sitting on the countertop in a widemouthed plastic tub. Its name was written on a band of peeling tape: CLINT YEASTWOOD.

The smocked mopper waited at the next door, impatient with my awe. I followed into a dark hallway lined with coats on pegs and shoes and boots on the floor, past a small wash-room, around a corner.

We came to a door, slightly ajar. The smocked mopper knocked gently, and when the reply came—a crisp command to enter—she left me to discover on my own what waited within.

THE ROOM WAS LONG AND SKINNY, set up against the back of the building, with tall windows that offered a panoramic view of the restaurant's backyard garden filtered through a veil of beans that climbed lengths of string pulled taut across the windows, their leaves softening the light that fell into the study.

Through the beans, I saw figures moving in the garden, filling baskets with greens. More acolytes, serene in their linen smocks.

At a small desk, Charlotte Clingstone sat in dappled bean-shadow. Before her were a laptop, an enormous pile of documents, and not one but three phones. She was poking at one of them as I entered. She glanced up with a look of annoyance.

It was definitely her: the central deity from the Ferry Building.

"Someone named Lawrence," I said. "I talked to him on the phone . . . He said you would have time to see me. Around now."

"Lawrence is very accommodating," Clingstone said. She lowered her glasses and a look of recognition flitted across her face. "I know you. How do I know you?"

I hadn't expected her to recognize me, but maybe the fact that I had presented her pantheon with something other than pickles had earned me a single sparking neuron.

I told her I was Lois Clary. I'd tried out for the Bay Area farmers markets . . . all of them . . . and been rejected.

"Oh, I hope you're not here about that." Pity and impatience mixed in her voice. She fiddled with her phones, moving them into a neat line. I wondered if she had a panic button mounted on the underside of her desk to call for help in case of confrontation by spurned farmers and/or simpering gourmands.

"I came to show you something." I crossed the distance between us and extracted the copy of Horace's menu from my bag. "This."

She hitched her glasses up and peered at the menu. "Goodness."

"Do you remember it?"

"Well, give me a moment." Her eyes flitted across the

152

paper. "I've made quite a few of these, you know. Hmm . . . 1979. This is ancient." Her eyes scanned farther down, and something crossed her face. A softening. "Oh, yes. I do remember." She looked up at me. "Where did you find this?"

"A friend of mine. Horace, he's a—"

"Portacio. Of course." She clucked. "It's quite a hoard he's gathered. I didn't know I was part of it."

"He has all your cookbooks, too."

"A lot of people have my cookbooks. No one has these menus anymore. I wish I did."

"I wanted to ask you about something specific. About this meal."

"Go on."

"The bread. Sourdough à la Masque. What was it? Where did it come from?"

Outside, the acolytes moved in the garden.

"It's the most interesting thing on the menu, isn't it?" Clingstone mused. "I don't think that's obvious. Am I remembering correctly—you're a baker? Yes, I can see why you might be curious about this. Well. All right."

She stood, slipped a manila folder under her arm, dropped a phone into each of her jacket's pockets, leaving the third on the table. "Come along, then. I'll explain."

She led me out through the warren—past the washroom, the coats—and back into the kitchen, where it was a different thing entirely to enter in the presence of Charlotte Clingstone. Nothing outwardly changed—not one knife skipped a chop—but a crackling field of attention snapped into existence.

"Where's Lawrence?" Clingstone called out. "Someone find Lawrence, please. His memory is required."

Acolytes zipped out every door.

Clingstone glided over to the burly baker. "Mona," she said sweetly. The baker glowed. Clingstone turned to me. "This is Lois. She bakes."

Mona's gaze cooled. I was an intruder in her domain.

Clingstone lifted one of the loaves from the line, tapped it on its back. "Lovely," she cooed. She returned it to the line and lowered her glasses. "I've always thought the starter's influence was overstated. People tell these wild stories— 'Oh, I got it from such-and-such, it's been going strong since, you know, Sister Brunhilde began it in Gothenburg a hundred years ago,' that sort of thing—but it's all basically the same."

"I agree," Mona said. As if she had any choice.

"But," Clingstone said, "there *was* an exception. Years ago. Look at this." She handed Mona the menu I'd brought. "From 1979, you see? We were just starting. This was still Harriet Grayling's house, and we were her wild young friends"—Clingstone seemed to apply some retroactive skepticism to this—"throwing these enormous dinners in her parlor. This kitchen was different. It was tiny." She snapped her head around. "*Where* is Lawrence? I need him to remember something."

Two more acolytes went scurrying.

She turned back to Mona and me. "It was becoming a bit of a flophouse. Harriet didn't mind. She was having the time of her life. It was that summer, I think, when Jim Bascule wandered through. A friend of someone's . . . I can't remember who. Lawrence!"

Another acolyte gone.

"He'd been in Europe. He'd met someone. They'd lived

together in Brussels. She was a wonderful cook, apparently. She baked bread. He fell in love. Then she left, and he ran out of money. He showed up here with nothing but a beat-up old guitar and the sourdough starter she'd left behind."

Around the kitchen, those acolytes who had not gone in search of Clingstone's quarry tilted themselves to hear the story. This was precious history. Indoctrination.

"Jim Bascule played his guitar all day, singing sad songs. He might have been in a band. I can't remember. I need Lawrence! But"—she clucked—"here was the surprise. Every morning, Jim baked. His lady had taught him well. The bread was wonderful, but also . . ." She paused. Looked from Mona to me with eyes that dared us to question what came next. "There's no getting around it, is there? There were faces in the crust. These strange . . . sharp-edged . . ." She curled her fingers and made a face. An ecstatic mask. I recognized the spirit of it immediately. Her features returned to normal. "We ignored them. Those weren't the strangest things we saw back then. Jim baked that bread every day for . . . six months? We paid him what we could. He saved it all up, until he had enough for a ticket back to Europe."

Mona was fully caught up in the story. "To go after his lady?"

"That was the idea. We threw him a going-away party." She held up the menu: A FEAST FOR THE UNREQUITED. "Back then, we could get away with names like this." She smiled and was lost for a moment. "Someone—I can't remember who; where's Lawrence? He knows all these things—someone tried to keep the starter alive, but it just . . ." Clingstone made a limp gesture. "We all said it died of a broken heart."

An acolyte burst into the kitchen trailing a man, wiry and bald, Clingstone's age, cradling a bottle of wine under each arm.

"*There* you are!" Clingstone cried.

His hair rose up in a frizzy halo around his skull. "What is it, my love?"

"I needed you for a story. But now I'm done with it. Do you remember Jim Bascule?"

"I certainly remember Jim Bascule's *bread*, darling."

Clingstone offered the man the old menu for his inspection. He leaned close, and while his eyes scanned the page, she said to me, "This is my husband, Lawrence. Although he wasn't my husband when this menu was written."

Lawrence looked up and said drily, "I was only her lover then."

"In any case," Clingstone said, "I haven't thought about that bread in years. It was wonderful."

It was clear that Mona, the baker, would have preferred for this story to be recounted to her exclusively. She addressed me. "You're a professional? Do you work for Broom, or . . . ?"

Here I was at the wellspring, the source, and this baker was checking my credentials—her curious gaze joined by Clingstone's now, and Lawrence's—and I wanted to impress them.

"I'm the baker at the Marrow Fair," I said. "The market on Alameda. Have you—?"

Charlotte Clingstone's expression closed like a gate crashing down. She started to speak, but only made a clucking sound. Currents of annoyance swirled across her face.

"The Marrow Fair," Lawrence repeated, trying the name on for size. "Do you know it, darling?"

"I do," Clingstone said. "I've heard about it. From Portacio, and others."

"Ah, Horace!"

"He's my friend," I said. "He found this menu." For Lawrence's benefit, I explained: "It's a new kind of market."

"Very . . . forward-thinking," Clingstone said lightly. Other possible adjectives played across her lips. "Its founder thinks our restaurant here is quite retrograde. Even a bit silly."

I felt waves of opprobrium from the acolytes. If Clingstone ordered them to beat me to death with rolling pins and stale sourdough, there could be no doubt: they would do it.

I sputtered, "I'm sure he doesn't. I mean. I don't really know anything about him. I only make bread. I have a robot."

Mona looked at me with pity.

One of the phones in Clingstone's pocket buzzed. She peeked at the screen and said, "I'm sorry. I'm late for a call." Retreating back into the warren of the restaurant, she paused a moment, then turned. Her gaze was chilly and complex. "Now I wish I hadn't told you that story."

Lawrence escorted me out of Café Candide, and, on the way through the dining room, he swiped a bottle from inside a white cardboard box. "Take this to Horace. He'll like it. Sorry about Charlotte. Well, not really. This Marrow Fair place sounds wretched." He said it with winning diffidence. "But it's all changing, isn't it? No matter. We'll stay the same. You should come for dinner sometime. We have tables available next spring, I believe."

I T'S STRANGE TO HEAR the starter might have reached San Francisco once before! Mainly I'm surprised it wasn't a Mazg who brought it. Actually, I think I might be a little bit scandalized. Who was this Jim Bascule guy?

Chaiman finished his album. It has seven tracks and he calls it *The Mazg Tapes*. I don't think he's ever touched a tape in his life. Shehrieh is super worried about it—she doesn't want him to use the word "Mazg"—and that is *very* good news for me. I told her about my restaurant and she barely blinked. Sorry, Chaiman!

I'll attach the album. I like some of the tracks more than others (it gets *oonce*-y . . .), but mostly, I'm proud of my brother for making something that's truly his.

BOONVILLE

THE EXPEDIENT SEARCH ENGINE revealed that Jim Bascule had, sometime between the mid-1970s and today, become a winemaker in Mendocino County. On the website for a winery called Tradecraft, I found his picture. He looked to be in his sixties, scruffy at the chin, blond hair gone gray curling down to his shoulders. There might be more than one Jim Bascule in the world, but this image reassured me. He looked like the kind of person who might have taken up residence at a turnip restaurant in Berkeley.

The drive was long, three hours. I listened to the radio until the signal faded and then switched to Chaiman's Mazg remix album, which steadily increased in tempo as it proceeded from track to track. When it got to be too much, the sad Mazg voices all warped into the chipmunk register, I stopped the album short and went back to the beginning, where it was slower, with undistorted crooning buoyed by a spare accompaniment, which seemed to fit the landscape better.

Fog became mist, which accumulated in sheets on my windshield. I drove very, very slowly, occasionally pulling into turnouts to allow pickup trucks to roar past me, sending up high plumes behind them. My car moaned pitifully as I crawled over a steep switchbacking rise, then coasted with palpable relief down a long and lazy slope toward my destination.

Boonville was a short strip of shops and restaurants huddled along California State Route 128 where it dropped into the golden fold of Anderson Valley. There were wineries on both sides of the road, some with ramshackle tasting rooms. The local brewery maintained a hopyard, pale buds clinging to long wires parallel to the road. I passed a broad-faced hotel that seemed to preside over the tiny town. I thought about stopping. Maybe on the way back.

My phone had no signal here, but it had already loaded the map I needed and my GPS showed the way. I turned off the highway onto a hard-packed dirt road, now mottled with puddles, and followed it for a mile until I saw a wooden sign for TRADECRAFT.

The driveway plunged through the scrim of eucalyptus and dipped to cross a wide bridge over a rushing creek. The planks went *thump-thump-thump* beneath my tires. My car's engine groaned a little as I pushed it crunching onto a gravel parking lot. There were two other vehicles parked there in the rain.

The winery was a long building with a log-cabin look. A small sign advertised the tasting room. Inside, I found a middle-aged woman sitting on a stool behind a countertop, absorbed in a Thomas Pynchon novel. She set it aside when she saw me.

"Welcome to Tradecraft! Not the nicest day for wine tasting, is it? Anyone else, or just you?"

I told her I was alone, and that I was here to see Jim Bascule.

"He just went to drop a couple cases off at the hotel. He'll be back soon. Can I offer you a taste while you wait? I'm Barbara."

I acquiesced, peeled off my jacket, and set it down with my tote bag containing a loaf of bread. (I was always carrying bread these days.) I sipped samples of three red wines and two whites as Barbara probed me gently, learning that I lived in San Francisco ("I love the city") and worked as a programmer ("Is everyone a computer person now? It seems that way") but also baked bread ("Have you been to the bakery across from the hotel? They make the best scones. The *best*"), and I had, in fact, brought a loaf for Jim Bascule.

"How nice! Well, he should be back any minute. Let's finish with this, the Tradecraft Gewürz. It's what we're known for."

She uncorked a slender bottle and poured a trickle into a narrow glass. The wine shimmered thickly.

"Have you heard of botrytis?" She said the word carefully, *bo-try-tis*. "They call it the 'noble rot.' These grapes actually get moldy on the vine. On purpose, I mean. It gives the wine a flavor—you'll see."

I took a sip. The wine felt heavy in my mouth. It was very sweet but also tartly acidic, and the taste lingered for a long time. Barbara poured a glass for herself, nearly full-size, and her eyes were closed when she lifted it to her lips.

We were both quiet, sipping, when I felt a draft of cold, wet air. Barbara's eyes fluttered open. "There he is!"

JIM BASCULE WAS SHORT AND LEAN, a sixty-year-old man with the bearing of a boy. His chin bristled with blond whiskers and his hair was pulled away from his shoulders into a neat ponytail.

I introduced myself and he shook my hand, looking plainly puzzled.

"Are you the Jim Bascule who baked at Café Candide?"

His eyebrows leapt. "I'm not sure if I am . . . But I remember him, sure. How do you know about that?"

As explanation, I hauled my tote bag onto the countertop, drew out the loaf of bread, and thumped it down.

He looked first at me, then at the bread. He smiled. And, of course, the bread smiled back.

I followed him out of the tasting room into a cluttered kitchen. Cases of wine were stacked haphazardly. There were also miscellaneous wheels of cheese and thin sausages hanging on strings like torpid bats. A slab of wood supported an array of jams as well as what appeared to be a loaf of bread, its brown bottom peeking out from underneath a towel patterned with blue flowers.

Bascule swept the towel back. The loaf underneath was round and thick-crusted with a burnish to shame Everett Broom. That crust didn't show a face, but instead an intricate spiral.

"Did you do that yourself?" I asked.

"I think you know I didn't," Bascule said.

Here's what he told me.

When he was preparing to reunite with his love in Europe—or so he thought—Jim Bascule left the starter with his parents in Santa Rosa, and he shared with them his suspicion: that it needed music to flourish.

"Things didn't work out in Brussels," he said. "Oh, gosh. She lived in this little apartment overlooking an alley . . . she had a balcony where she grew herbs. She knew everyone, and she was always helping people. Little favors, and big ones, too. I was smitten. There's no question I built her up in my mind while I was away. By the time I returned, she'd met someone else. This gorgeous Greek guy. I didn't stand a chance. So I wandered a bit, got involved in some other things."

What kind of things?

"Oh, things. I didn't come back to the States until 1985. When I returned, I discovered my dad still had the starter going. That whole time"—Bascule started to laugh—"he'd been playing it the Grateful Dead!"

So here I was seeing the hippie spiraling crust of a Deadhead starter.

"I still play it the Dead every night. There's a lot of bootlegs."

But how? Why?

"Here's my theory, honed over decades of bullshitting to myself. This starter, it uses music as a kind of . . . synchronization. It helps the little yeasts and whatever-elses to do the right things at the right times. You've gotta be careful, though."

Careful how?

Bascule laughed drily. "I used to play around with other music, just to see. You know that classical tune 'Flight of the Bumblebee'?" He whistled a bit of the breakneck melody. "I left it alone for fifteen minutes, no more. When I came back inside, it had spilled out of its container. It was *everywhere.*" He eyed me sharply. "You seen anything like that with yours?"

I confessed I hadn't. The Clement Street starter was well behaved.

"Well, be careful. I think the music matters. After that happened, I thought I'd finally killed it. Stuff barely bubbled for weeks. Now I just play it the Dead. Good vibes."

I traced my finger around the maze, an inch above the sourdough's crust. "Don't you find this . . . really exceptionally strange?"

Bascule shrugged. "I've done a bit of reading. The way these things work together . . . It's unbelievable. I'm sure you've heard all this stuff about the bacteria in our gut, how they're like a second brain? There's a lab—this was just published recently—there's a lab where they've got some yeasts hooked up to the internet. You can log in and reprogram their DNA."

That sounded like a terrible idea.

"My point is, there are things in this living world plenty weirder than this. If you want proof, just come back and visit us in the fall. See the grapes."

"The ones with the fungus?"

"You ever heard of a suitcase clone? No? Well, okay. Come back in the fall."

Before I left the winery, I asked one last question.

"Who was she? The woman in Belgium who gave you the starter?"

Bascule shook his head. "She had the strangest name."

ON THE WAY OUT OF TOWN, I stopped at the Boonville Hotel. Inside, I walked down a shadowed hall to claim a stool at the short bar—I was the only one there—and when the bartender appeared, who was also the hotel's manager, I ordered a glass of the Tradecraft Gewürtztraminer.

Through an open doorway, I watched a small kitchen staff working quietly, preparing that evening's meal. I wondered how one of General Dexterity's robot arms—with kitchen skills!—would fit in here on the side of California State Route 128. Would it ruin that kitchen, or improve it? I genuinely didn't know.

I sipped my wine slowly.

I pondered the egg problem.

I wondered what other music I could play for the Clement Street starter. Was there any album, any composition, that would encourage a crust that looked simply . . . normal?

The bartender/manager came back out and asked me if I'd be joining them for dinner. I asked him what they were serving, and he reported: roasted chicken, accompanied by a panzanella salad with tomatoes from the garden and croutons from homemade sourdough.

I told him I had to get back to the office.

YOU SHOULD HAVE SEEN my mother's face when Chaiman and I asked her about Jim Bascule. She told us she hadn't thought of that name in thirty-some years.

Apparently, when he appeared again in Brussels, Shehrieh was shocked. She refused him, and she told us she felt bad about it, but he was too short, and he couldn't cook anything. Well, he could bake bread, but she'd taught him that. And there was another man, he was Greek . . . this was before Leopold. (My father wasn't home when we were talking about all this, and I think that was probably for the best.)

But I understand what she means about the cooking. It's crucial in Mazg relationships, especially in the beginning. How do you even get started if you can't woo the other person with your spicy soup?

<FROM: BEO>

THAT WASN'T A EUPHEMISM!

THE EGG PROBLEM

DURING MY SENIOR YEAR OF COLLEGE, at the urging of a professor who specialized in the history of the assembly line, I had embarked on a self-directed project to identify the first use of a computer program in a manufacturing process. After a semester of digging through libraries in East Lansing and Ann Arbor, I had scrounged a few early examples, but I failed to convince either Evelyn Simmons or myself that I had succeeded in my task. Nevertheless, she gave me a 4.0 and told me I'd learned a useful skill.

I used it now.

I was going to be the one to solve the egg problem.

I read up on anatomy and physiology. I acquired textbooks for students of physical therapy and DVDs for students of dance. I tracked down software from a company called Anatomix that could accurately simulate the flex of skin and muscle, and I inspected every menu, every command. Horace became my research assistant: he scoured the internet and brought me three new kinesiology papers every day; dropped them on the countertop still warm from the laser printer.

Sometimes, when I was sitting at the long picnic table

reading and rereading the papers, sipping endless cappuccinos provided by Naz, I paused to wonder: Who paid for all this?

The master of the market, the figure known universally as Mr. Marrow, was an enigma. Horace hypothesized that our patron was the scion of an old San Francisco family that had earned its fortune feeding the Barbary Coast. Naz was more paranoid, and said Mr. Marrow walked among us. "He could be Horace, for all we know." I heard from others that Mr. Marrow was obviously Anthony Bourdain; definitely Ferran Adrià; indisputably Sergey Brin.

Every day, I carried a carton from the open pantry and placed it before the Vitruvian. One by one, it lifted the eggs, and one by one, it ruined them.

I imagined Mr. Marrow looking at a rapidly growing outlay for pasture-raised eggs and wondering, *What the—?*

I had watched the Vitruvian make a hundred attempts without any apparent improvement. At the Task Acquisition Center, identical arms had ruined probably thousands of eggs. (What happened to those eggs? Did we, the Dextrous, eat them as breakfast scrambles? I hoped we did.) The problem wasn't the training. There was something about this task that eluded ArmOS, even when it had mastered so many others. It could assemble a phone, but it couldn't open an egg.

Could I criticize it, really? My own egg-cracking experience was extremely limited—a cookie-baking spree during my senior year of college; everything but the egg and a little butter was already in the box—and in that time I had certainly never attempted to do it one-handed, which was what was required of the Vitruvian. Even with the benefit of two hands, my egg-cracking had been fumbling, borderline disastrous—a gentle rain of eggshell into the cookie mix, shards removed carefully one by one.

If I was going to have any hope of teaching the Vitruvian, I would have to master this skill myself.

I opened the expedient video-sharing website on my laptop, searched for "how to crack an egg," and was rewarded with thousands of results. I selected the first and watched a disembodied hand crack an egg against the rim of a clear glass bowl and pull its halves apart, two fingers forward, two fingers back. The gesture was almost obscenely elegant. I tried to copy what I saw on the screen, and was rewarded with a smear of yolk across my palm.

I felt a surge of kinship with the Vitruvian. We were starting at the same level.

But there was a difference between us: I learned fast.

Thwack, crack, pull—after only a few attempts, I could do it as neatly as my faceless tutor. *Thwack, crack, pull.* There's a technical term for this: "one-shot learning." You see something once; you can do it. Programmers who work on artificial intelligence and robot locomotion regard it with nearly mystical awe.

Having mastered the elegant, one-handed egg-crack in if not one, then maybe three shots, I set myself to the deeper task of understanding it. I pushed all my awareness into my hands—muscles, tendons, finger pads. *Thwack, crack, pull. Thwack, crack* . . . another smear. As quickly as I had learned it, I unlearned it. *Thwack* . . . The egg didn't even crack. My fingers trembled.

I repeated this cycle every afternoon for a week. Every session contained, at its peak, a few perfect, satisfying cracks, with the broken shell levered apart by the subtlest workings of my fingers and palm. But the sessions all ended the same way, with me so lost in amped-up self-awareness—proprioception!—that I was dinging the eggs harmlessly off the bowl, or demolishing them entirely, just like the Vitruvian. Our performance converged. I had nothing to teach it.

After this happened, I would angrily dispose of the broken eggs, feeling stupid and wasteful, then stomp up and down the concourse in frustration.

And I would watch other people work.

When Naz used his espresso machine, it was musical: *clack* of portafilter, *hiss* of steam, *gurgle* of milk, *clink* of saucer. When Anita worked her cricket flour into dough, she stared into space, thinking with her hands. That's what I wanted to achieve. Even Jaina Mitra: when she shuttled samples between her great microbial menagerie and the DNA sequencer, her fingers and feet moved of their own accord. *She* was elsewhere, gaze clouded, brain churning. She could have done it with her eyes closed.

That, of course, was it.

I ran back to my workstation, opened my laptop, and made sure I was synchronized with the latest changes to ArmOS. It was going to be so simple. It was going to be so huge.

To date, my contributions to the codebase had all been tiny refinements—painstaking embroideries in the tight tapestry of Proprioception. I had also written a related debugging panel for Interface, but I would never admit to that.

Now I created a module from whole cloth. It was concise, not even a hundred lines of code, built in perfect symmetry around a single action. One by one, in exactly the right order, I suspended the arm's motor control loops. Then I loaded the action directly into the PKD 2891 Stepper Motors, which most

171

people didn't realize you could do; they all had their own MCUs, with just enough memory for what came next. Then, one by one, I brought the motor control loops back online.

I finished my new module, named it, tried to compile, was informed of several embarrassing syntax errors, corrected them, compiled again. I flashed the Vitruvian with the new code and said aloud, "Try again."

It plucked up an egg, moved it lightly into position, paused, and *thwack*ed the egg against the rim of the bowl. Just after the *thwack*, my new module took over. The motor control loops went dark. The arm wasn't running blind; it was more like . . . a blink. Not even a hundred milliseconds, during which my new module said: *Just go for it.*

In the ArmOS codebase, as part of the Control package, I had created something new—a tiny space without feedback or self-awareness—and I had named it Confidence.

The yolk flowed out with the albumen while the shell came apart cleanly in the Vitruvian's six-fingered grip. The arm swiveled and dropped the shell neatly into the small bowl I had set up for that purpose—the bowl that had never before this moment actually been needed.

I had solved the egg problem, and I had done so in the simplest way possible: not by adding code, but by taking it away. During the blink, the Vitruvian was no longer caught in a wash of continuous feedback. It was no longer second-guessing its second guesses a thousand times every second.

I bundled my new module into a pull request and sent it upstream, straight into the master branch of ArmOS. I didn't even write a commit message. The module's name would suffice. I waited for the emails. My heart was pounding.

"Do that again," I told the Vitruvian.

Thwack, crack, pull.

My laptop pinged. It was a message from Peter, composed entirely of exclamation marks.

Confidence!

ELEPHANTS' ARMPITS

HORACE'S E-NEWSLETTER brought with it a schedule of classes—the expertise of the Marrow Fair shared freely. Aeroponics with Kenyatta on Monday; cheese tasting with Orli on Tuesday; bug husbandry with Anita on Thursday; and on Friday, Jaina Mitra would teach a workshop on DNA sequencing.

I recruited Horace and we went together.

A very small group gathered at noon in the center of Jaina Mitra's lab. Naz from the coffee bar was there, as well as Clay from NewBagel, and Kenyatta, one of the pink-light farmers.

Jaina Mitra offered a plastic dish. "Who wants to spit?"

Horace raised his hand and expectorated neatly.

"Okay," Jaina Mitra said. "So there's a whole lot of things living in a human mouth, and we might want to know what they are. You want to know, don't you, Mr. Portacio?"

"You have no idea!"

"Biologists have become very interested in *communities* of microorganisms," Jaina Mitra said. "Characterizing the community in a sample like this used to be a laborious process, but now—watch."

Her machine was enormous, as big as a refrigerator, with a round-cornered plastic carapace, glossy white with black accents. A line of letters on the front edge named it the ILLUMINA HYPER CENSUS.

Jaina Mitra pressed a button on its belly and the machine released a tray. She laid the dish of Horace's spit into place, and when she pressed the button again, the machine pulled the tray back into itself and began to hum.

"What's it doing?" Naz asked.

"First, it denatures the sample. It heats the microbes up to make them . . . relax. Then it mashes them up using tiny beads. It's quite a massacre."

I raised a finger. "Won't that mix all the different DNA together?"

"Yes, but they can't hide. Organisms share a lot of genes, but there's one that's unique between species. Sixteen-S. It's like a fingerprint." Jaina Mitra grinned wolfishly. "So we'll pick through the body parts to find the fingertips."

We all thought about that for a moment while the machine whomped and whirred.

"While it's mashing," Jaina Mitra said, "I'll show you my collection."

She led us to an enormous refrigerated cabinet stocked with trays, each holding dozens of tiny vials.

"This is why I came here," Jaina Mitra said proudly. "Mr. Marrow promised me a subscription to the Global Microbiome Survey. It's not cheap."

Horace, gravitationally attracted to collections of all kinds, put his face up against the glass. "What do you have in there?"

"Environmental samples. The National Science Foundation sends students all over the world. I did it one summer

175

in grad school. It's a bit of a boondoggle, really. You pick the wildest place you can imagine. I went to Greenland."

"You went to Greenland . . . on purpose," Naz said.

"It was very interesting, microbially. I sent back huge tubs"—she circled her arms around an imaginary barrel—"full of ice and mud. Rainwater, too."

"So this is a catalog of puddles," Horace said. His breath was fogging up the glass.

"Among other things. There's a bit of the Great Lakes in there. The Great Pacific Garbage Patch. Swamps. Volcanoes. There are samples scraped out of caves, and birds' nests, and elephants' armpits. New samples are coming in constantly. I just got one from an Arby's in Clearwater, Florida."

We all shuddered.

"How many labs have a subscription like this?" I asked.

"Thirty, thirty-five? Like I said, it's not cheap."

"What do you *do* with it?"

Jaina Mitra's face took on a hungry look. "Think of it as raw genetic ore. All the subscribers are on a mailing list. When a lab identifies a new species, they send out an alert. I just heard that an organism in the Mono Lake sample has some interesting enzymatic regulation properties, so I'm going to see if I can isolate it and—" The sequencing machine interrupted with a low and commanding chime. "Oh, here we go." Jaina Mitra tilted the laptop beside the Illumina Hyper Census.

"Anyway," she said, "let's hope Mr. Portacio's saliva isn't as mysterious as those samples." On the laptop's screen, she swiped the cursor with the ease of long practice, summoning the machine's results.

Horace frowned. "I expect it to be strange and wondrous."

On the screen, a spiky line appeared, utterly unremark-able. It could have been the price of a stock or the tempera-ture in a midwestern city. Then another layer of information arrived: a label for each of the spikes.

Jaina Mitra read them off: "*Veillonella . . . Prevotella . . . Porphyromonas gingivalis*, but not too much. Oh, and *Strep-tococcus*. That's what gives you strep throat, but it's also what they use to make Swiss cheese. You have a very healthy oral microbiome, Mr. Portacio."

Horace looked disappointed.

Kenyatta was growing agitated. "I don't understand how you use this information," he said. The tone of his voice indi-cated he did, in fact, have his suspicions, and he didn't like them.

"My work is all about microbial communities," Jaina Mitra said. "If you want to know how your plants are doing, you need to look at them, right? This is how I look at my communities."

He narrowed his eyes. "So you're just reading DNA. Not editing it."

Jaina Mitra pursed her lips. "I've experimented with CRISPR protocols, of course. Those colonies all collapsed, but—"

"Seriously?" he sputtered. "You need to come *here* to do that?" He clutched his head and walked in a little circle. Disbelief. "I thought this place was supposed to be for *new* ideas, but, I don't know, Dr. Mitra, this sounds a lot like the same old GMO shit."

"It's really not—"

"Did you get rejected from DuPont, or what? No? Maybe you should take this there. They'd be all over it."

"You have a problem with Lembas," Jaina Mitra said flatly, "but I'm not sure what it is."

"This approach—everything you're doing, the *scanning*, the *editing*—it's the height of hubris. Like, the *height*. Look around. I'm sorry if it sounds mean, but, we—don't—need you—to work on this. The plants are way, way ahead of you, Dr. Mitra. Do you *really* think—"

"Mr. Marrow supports my project."

Kenyatta snorted. "I wonder what he'd say if I told him it was either your lab or our grow rooms. We make half of the food that goes out the door here." He started to stomp away, then caught himself and turned back, made a final plea. "I'm no traditionalist. I mean, pink LEDs—come on. But there's a difference, right? Plants have developed over millions of years. They just *work*. What you're doing—it's not natural."

Jaina Mitra clicked her tongue. "Nothing is natural."

AFTER THE SEQUENCING SESSION WAS OVER, I walked with Horace through the grove at the heart of the concourse.

"These are Meyer lemons," Horace said as we passed the trees. "Named for Frank Nicholas Meyer. Dutch by birth, but an agent of the United States government. He worked for the Department of Agriculture's Office of Seed and Plant Introduction before the First World War. I thought of him when Jaina Mitra spoke of her microbial survey. Meyer and his cohort were hunters for larger prey. They canvassed the world and sent back living samples of plants thought to be useful to the advancement of the American economy. Meyer worked in China. He sent the first soybean to America. And persimmons! Any persimmon grown in this country today comes from that lineage. And of course, there are these lemons—named for him. Meyer died in China. He drowned in the Yangtze, pushed from a riverboat."

I looked at the trees with new appreciation.

"He sent these across the Pacific, and the Spanish sent tomatoes to Italy in the sixteenth century, and the Portuguese, chilies to India. And maybe a comet brought it all to Earth—who knows? I quite agree with Jaina Mitra."

He plucked a lemon from a tree.

"Nothing is natural."

A LONG-AWAITED ANNOUNCEMENT

THERE ARRIVED FROM HORACE a special, urgent edition of the Marrow Fair e-newsletter: there would be, the next morning, a convening of all the vendors, because Mr. Marrow intended to address his market.

Did that mean I'd finally see him?

Lily Belasco's eyes were merry when I asked. "In a manner of speaking."

"How often do *you* see him?"

She dug in the pockets of her slouchy jacket. "He's pretty hands-off, but I keep him in the loop." She produced a wide phone and waggled it. "Encrypted messages. He keeps the bank account full. What more can you ask for?"

Wandering the workstations, I heard rumors. Mr. Marrow was moving the market to Los Angeles. To Tokyo. He was shutting it down. He had run out of money. He was being pursued by the SEC. The yakuza. The Department of Health. (This last possibility seemed, to me, the most plausible.)

In the early morning, an hour before the preview was set to begin, all of us gathered in the lemon grove. Some loitered among the trees, others sat at the long picnic table. I found a seat with Orli, Naz, and Jaina Mitra. Jaina slumped, head propped up by one hand, her cheek smooshed, eyes half-lidded. She looked utterly spent.

Belasco had wheeled an enormous TV out to face the long picnic table and was now fiddling with the laptop at Naz's coffee bar, patching her phone into the sound system. The TV glared bright, basic blue, the words NO SIGNAL migrating slowly across it.

Mr. Marrow wasn't going to be here at all.

"He lives in China," Orli whispered. "It's already nighttime there."

Naz looked dubious. "No, he's here with us." He lowered his voice to a hiss. "Do you see Horace anywhere? He's Horace."

"Okay, folks," Belasco called out. The depot's soundtrack went quiet and was replaced with the buzz of a phone line. At the same time, the TV showed a painted still life: a feast set up on a pockmarked table with a deep blue curtain hanging inexplicably behind it. On the table were a heel of bread and a bowl of plums. A curved knife protruded from a rump of cheese. On a bright platter there was a whole fish, its mouth frozen in an eternal yawp. Everything in the scene gleamed as if lacquered.

A voice boomed out over the speakers.

"I haven't met all of you," the voice said, "but I've tasted everything you have to offer." Its tone was deep, digitally disguised. The long space smeared it with echoes. It was as if the concourse itself were speaking to us. This was the voice of Mr. Marrow.

As for his face: with every syllable, the fish in the painting moved its tiny mouth.

"I've gathered you here for a long-awaited announcement."

The juxtaposition—the booming voice, the tiny fish—was weird and hilarious. I looked around. No one was smiling.

"We've been here for a little over a year. Lily Belasco opened the doors and wheeled in the lemon trees. Some of you joined shortly after. Others have only been here a few weeks. We've been running previews all summer, and I know most of you are wondering: When do we open to the public?"

Murmurs of assent. I'd been more than busy enough serving the customers who showed up for the previews, but others were apparently ready to reach a larger market.

"There is a great realignment coming," the fish intoned. "It will be equal to the upheaval of the 1950s. You have heard me say this before. In those years, the entire experience of eating in America was remade. Packaging, refrigeration, the interstate highways—you can trace it all back. These systems were invented by particular people, at particular times, in particular places." The fish paused. "Times like now." Its glittering eyes scanned back and forth. "Places like this." Another pause. "We can build a new system."

The shiver of pleasure that ran through the assembled vendors was so intense I felt it like a rattling gust. They believed the fish. The fish was their prophet.

"On both sides, they've failed us," the fish said. "Of course, we know about the industrialists. Their corn syrup and cheese product. Their factory farms ringed by rivers of blood and shit, blazing bonfires of disease barely contained by antibiotic blankets. These are among the most disgusting scenes in the history of this planet."

Murmurs of agreement and apprehension at that.

"But on the other side . . . the organic farms, the precious restaurants . . . these are toy supply chains. 'Farm to table,' they say. Well. When you go from farm to table, you leave a lot of people out." The crowd was silent. "I think more poorly of these people than I do of the industrialists, because *they know better*. They know it's all broken, and what do they do? They plant vegetables in the backyard."

The fish would get along with Andrei.

"So that leaves *us*."

Wait, *was* the fish . . . ?

"The doors of the Marrow Fair open to the public not this Wednesday but the next."

The vendors exploded with agitation and excitement.

"That's too soon!" someone cried.

"Is there a plan for parking?" asked someone else. "I think we need a plan for parking."

The fish closed its mouth, lidded its eyes, and the painting was still. The TV went blue again, and after a moment, Naz's soundtrack resumed.

There were whoops and groans, smiles and nods, high fives that snagged the branches of the lemon trees.

Across the picnic table, Jaina Mitra looked stricken.

To no one in particular, she said, "I'm not ready yet."

QUITTING

THE MARROW FAIR was happening for real, and soon my two jobs would not coexist so comfortably. Lily Belasco expected the market's foot traffic to equal the Ferry Building's, eventually. That meant thousands of people a day. It was time to choose.

I visited General Dexterity's website. The Vitruvian 3 was calmly listed for sale at forty thousand dollars, or forty-eight with a two-year support package.

My salary was hefty, but my Cabrillo Street rent was commensurate. However, I spent basically nothing on food, transportation, health care, or entertainment, so after a year in San Francisco, my savings account had swollen to a little over ten thousand dollars.

Employment at General Dexterity carried with it a small allotment of stock options, and of those, a quarter had vested and were officially mine. The company was still privately held, almost entirely by Andrei, so I couldn't sell them directly, but there was a standing offer to impatient Dextrous from a Qatari prince who would buy our options at a slight discount. (When I first heard about this, it seemed breathtakingly exotic, possibly illegal, but the cold-eyed wraiths all shrugged. Apparently every tech company had a prince waiting in the wings.) I cashed out my options, which brought my total to thirty-seven thousand dollars.

I almost had enough to buy the Vitruvian outright, but mindful of the need to also eat and pay rent, I decided to seek additional financing.

I explained it first to Lily Belasco. "Just like he bought Jaina's sequencer," I said. "And her subscription to the microbe thing."

"How much are we talking about?"

I told her, and Belasco nodded slowly. "I'll check."

Later, she appeared at my workstation. She watched the Vitruvian work for a moment. "Forty thousand dollars, really?"

"The cost is mainly in the pressure sensors," I said. "They have twenty-four-bit resolution, and the sample rate . . . Anyway, they're expensive."

Belasco initiated a call, switched her phone to speaker mode, and placed it on the ping-pong table. In another moment, the modulated voice of Mr. Marrow squawked through the little speakers. He wasted no time with a preamble.

"The problem, as I see it, is that you've done the crucial work—here in my market, I should add—as an employee of another company. Your employer owns that work, correct? So what does my investment get me?"

"I'm quitting General Dexterity." It was the first time I'd said it out loud. I felt as renegade as Beo with his restaurant. "There's so much more to do. So many skills! Knives, food processors, frying pans . . . the arm could reach right into the oil. There's a marketplace for ArmOS extensions, and I'm going to sell kitchen skills."

Mr. Marrow was silent. Then I heard a modulated sound that might have been a laugh. I looked at Belasco and mouthed, *Is he laughing?*

Mr. Marrow composed himself. "I don't understand half of what you said, which makes me think you might be onto something. Keep your savings. I'll buy the robot in exchange for twenty percent of . . . whatever this is going to be." The modulated voice was silent a moment. "Are you sure this is what you want?"

I was sure.

"Belasco, cut the check. Lois—make it work."

The phone went silent. Until that moment, I hadn't realized how much I cared about the opinion of an anonymous benefactor who sometimes inhabited the body of a painted fish. But I did.

At General Dexterity, Peter did not seem very surprised.

"We'll miss you on Control," he said, "and I know the guys at the Slurry table will miss you, too. Have you tried the latest formulation? Revision G mark . . . five, I guess? The glycemic index is unreal."

I ducked into the cafeteria to reassure Chef Kate that I would keep her supplied with sourdough even though I was leaving the company. In the kitchen, I found her robot arm wheeled out of the corner, reactivated, cracking eggs merrily alongside her sous chefs.

"I heard we have you to thank for this," Kate said drily. Her expression was complicated.

"I can't tell if you're happy about it or not," I said.

She sighed. "Neither can I."

As I was shepherded around the office, enduring various last-day-of-work rituals, I was accosted first by Arjun and then by Garrett.

"There's something you need to know," Arjun hissed as I was walking out of the HR debrief.

"There's something you need to know," Garrett whispered as I was preparing for the Proprioception handoff.

"Garrett's in love with you."

"Arjun's in love with you."

I told them both I didn't have time for this bullshit, and if anybody wanted to ask a lady out, he could do it via text message like a normal person.

Across Townsend Street, I walked the length of the Task Acquisition Center, headed for the desk of Deborah Palmer-Grill, where I would make my arrangements to purchase the refurbished arm. I peered across the rows and tried to spot the bearded chef, but of course, he was gone. I'd made him obsolete. Confidence.

DPG rose to meet me. "You did it." She reached for my hand, giving it not a mere shake but a hearty rattle. She was grinning. "I think I'm going to get a raise because of you. Andrei was obsessed with the eggs!"

I bent across her desk to reach her keyboard and tap my payment information into a digital form.

"Are you sure you don't want to stay?" DPG said. The purchase order floated on her monitor. "You could join me over on this side of Townsend Street. We would make a good team!"

I looked back at the arms and their trainers. There were fewer than before. It wasn't just the bearded chef who was gone. General Dexterity was making progress.

I shook my head. "I think I want to get a little labor in while there's still a chance."

I walked out of the robot factory into bright sunlight with my belongings in a small box. My tablet and stylus; my picture of my parents; Kubrick the cactus. It was the middle of the day and I'd deployed no office chaff. Odd parts of me, my chin and my heels and the soft backs of my arms, felt tingling and buoyant. I was light.

THE NOVICE'S GRACE

ANOTHER WEDNESDAY CAME, and with it the final market preview. Soon, our secret kingdom would open to the world. Every customer whom I'd ever seen was here this morning, snapping photos to post on the expedient image-based social network. This was their last chance to prove to the world they had been one of the elect.

I had forwarded Chaiman's album along to Naz, and this morning he played it through the concourse. Stretched out by echoes, the songs of the Mazg were sweetly sad. Valedictory. They were perfect.

There was at least one new customer on this, the last of the Wednesdays. I recognized her. Charlotte Clingstone.

"So, here you are," she said.

A trio of acolytes clustered behind her, eyes roving the concourse warily. I recognized them, too, from the kitchen at Café Candide. They all noticed the Vitruvian at once. It was mixing placidly. They stared.

"That's quite a contraption," Clingstone said. "Is it really necessary?"

"It's helpful," I said.

She lifted a loaf from the ping-pong table, faced the smiling crust squarely through her glasses. "It looks different than I remember it."

I offered her a taste. Her contingent, too.

The acolytes chewed dutifully. Clingstone sniffed the bread, raised her eyebrows, and took a nibble. "It's very competent," she said. "Do you bake anything else? Croissants? Pizza dough?"

I did not.

"You do remind me of Jim with his mystery starter. He had the novice's grace, perpetually. It was maddening." She nibbled her sourdough sample and continued, sounding very casual. "I have a proposal for you. Leave the robot behind. Come join us at Café Candide." It took her acolytes a moment to process what they'd just heard. When they did, their eyes went wide, and they looked at me with bewilderment and horror.

Clingstone continued. "Bring the starter back to the café. You'll apprentice under Mona Rahut. You met her. There's no better teacher."

I felt the disorientation of a generous offer that in no way lines up with anything you want to do: like a promotion to senior alligator wrestler, or an all-expenses-paid trip to Gary, Indiana.

"That's very kind of you," I said, "but I have a business here. They're about to open the market. It's going to get a lot bigger."

My reply pinged off Clingstone's calm countenance without leaving a mark. She chewed the last of her sample and swallowed. "Many young people wait years to be offered an apprenticeship at Café Candide." The smoldering hatred in the acolytes' gazes indicated they had recently been those people.

"I just don't see myself working in a restaurant," I said.

Clingstone's gaze was even. "It's really quite a bit more than a restaurant."

"No," I said. "Thank you." Firmly. "I've learned a lot on my own."

She *hmm*ed, and it was almost musical. She looked from me to the Vitruvian to the starter in its crock, and back to me again. "I wonder if that's true? Some days, that bread of Jim's . . . it seemed almost to bake itself."

I was going to protest, but Clingstone turned and shepherded her acolytes back onto the yellow-tape road. "Thank you for the taste," she said. "Though I do think you should try pizza dough. A killer sourdough crust. Can your robot do that?"

More customers passed by. I was reaching into the Faustofen when I heard a voice I recognized: "Lois! Proprioception!"

It was Andrei, linked arm in arm with an older man.

"What are you doing here?"

"I was invited," he said. He started to laugh. "I didn't expect to see a Vitruvian! This is the one you bought."

"She's one of your employees?" the older man asked. He was very handsome, with an old sea captain look to him.

"Was. Gregor, this is Lois Clary. Originally from Michigan. She worked with us on the Control team for . . . fourteen months?"

Those flash cards were good.

Andrei looked down the concourse. "You quit . . . to work here?"

"This is where I solved the egg problem," I told him. "I wouldn't have been able to do it at the office. I bake bread now, and I'm going to put some things up for sale in the ArmOS marketplace."

Andrei smiled at that, but still seemed perplexed. He and his companion said farewell and continued along the yellow-tape road. I told them to sample the Lembas cakes with an open mind.

Watching them walk away, it occurred to me again: Could Andrei be Mr. Marrow? They were both so deeply impatient with the world as it was . . .

Later, Charlotte Clingstone and her acolytes passed by on their way out. The acolytes looked exhausted; worn down by novelty. Clingstone spoke to them, and while they proceeded up onto the airfield, she returned to my workstation. I was afraid she was going to try again to recruit me, but she only thwapped a book down on the ping-pong table.

"From Portacio's collection," she said.

It was *Candide.*

"I read it when I was a little younger than you, and it was a formative experience. Thus, the name of the café."

I inspected the book. It was very slender.

"I think you might enjoy it," Clingstone said.

I wondered if this market was all silly gimmicks to her, or if she'd found anything at all that she actually liked.

"Yes. The mushroom grotto is interesting, isn't it? We're going to try those hen-of-the-woods."

"Did you see the Lembas cakes?"

Charlotte Clingstone smiled and winced at the same time. "It's a very impressive project, but I fear it's a bit too far ahead of the curve for Café Candide. That woman still has things to prove. But one day? Who knows. Maybe we'll start a dinner with her little cathedrals."

<FROM: BEO>

HERE'S A STORY about how the starter came to us.

The first of the Mazg, before we were the Mazg, was a man named M., who was pressed into service as a slave. He rowed aboard a ship crossing the sea. (Which sea? The story does not specify, of course!) There was a storm; the ship capsized; and this man M. washed ashore onto a great rocky island that, even though it stood along many trade routes, was uninhabited because there was no place to grow anything, and so anyone who settled there would be dependent on others for their food, and that was a losing proposition in those times, on that sea.

M. cursed his luck. His refuge was barren. There were pools of condensation in the rock, and he sipped from these while little crabs snatched at his nose.

On the third day, starving, he considered his options, which were (1) attempt to swim elsewhere, or (2) throw himself off the great rocky island's tallest outcropping. Two kinds of suicide.

Then he discovered a cave. Its opening was the narrowest crevice, invisible from any but the closest angle. He would not have discovered it if there had not been a smell emanating from inside—very faint, but in his starved state it drew him like a lure.

Lois, you know this smell.

I will write more later.

DEFLATION

AS THE MARROW FAIR ACCELERATED toward its launch, a crisis unfolded, first slow, then fast.

To ensure I could make enough loaves to sell five or six days a week, I was testing myself, with the Vitruvian slinging dough double time and the Faustofen's burners roaring nonstop. I ordered the fancy flour in bags larger than I'd known existed. To match all that flour, to mix dough in the volume I required: I needed more starter.

It felt like a kind of surrender, but I transferred the Clement Street starter from its ceramic crock into a wide plastic tub. When I began to bake, I prepared a prodigious amount of floury paste for fuel. But in its new tub, the Clement Street starter grew slowly, almost reluctantly. I put the music of the Mazg on repeat and turned up the volume; it didn't have any effect.

Worse: the loaves that resulted were deflated. Upon reflection, it had been happening for some time, just too gradually to notice. Now there was no denying it: the loaves were not as round as before, and when I tapped them on their backs, I heard unappetizing thuds. Inside, the crumb was different:

heavy and dense. The smell was off, too: less banana, more acetone. And the faces that peered up from the crust were flat masks of resignation.

I was asking a lot of the starter, I realized. But I was treating it well; I was offering it a daily feast of the finest wheat sugars! This was a partnership, a symbiotic relationship, and the starter had a job to do. The Vitruvian and I were doing ours.

I tried to negotiate with it. "What's the matter? What do you need?"

No gurgles. No puffs. No phenomena at all. The Clement Street starter seemed . . . depressed.

Each day, the starter took twice as long to double in volume. I was accustomed to the mathematics of exponentiation working in my favor; now I worried that it had turned against me. If this trend continued, there wouldn't be enough hours in the day to get what I needed for the day's loaves. The Marrow Fair's opening was approaching.

I began to quietly freak out.

It was possible I was overthinking it. The problem might be mundane. A search of Global Gluten revealed that, yes, starters sometimes lost their mojo. The customary recommendation was to throw it out and start over, but I couldn't do that. I wanted to bang on the keyboard: *WHAT IF YOUR STARTER WAS GIVEN TO YOU BY MYSTERIOUS SIBLINGS FROM AN UNKNOWN COUNTRY AND WHAT IF IT'S IRREPLACEABLE??*

Naz at the coffee bar noticed my mood. "This might be more than a cappuccino can fix," he said. I ordered one anyway, and while he was preparing it, I explained that my sourdough starter was exhibiting a pathology I couldn't diagnose.

Naz nodded sagely. "This thing"—he clonked his espresso machine on the head—"is fantastic, but it's totally temperamental. I always struggle with it. You know who turned out to be the Marzocco whisperer? Anita, with the crickets. She rebuilds old motorcycles." He clacked a cup down into its saucer and slid it across the countertop. "This place is a magnet for weirdo geniuses. Somebody at the Marrow Fair can help you. Just put a note in the newsletter."

I composed my query, stared at it on my laptop's screen for ten minutes, then sent it to Horace for inclusion in the next day's dispatch.

In the morning, Jaina Mitra found me at my workstation. I was sitting in the folding chair, waiting for a batch of dough to very slowly rise.

For once, her hair was down. It was impossibly thick—definitively a different substance than what was attached to my scalp. She was wearing a T-shirt, not her usual lab coat, and she seemed more relaxed than I'd ever seen her before. Maybe things were going well with Lembas.

"I saw your note in the newsletter," Jaina Mitra said lightly, "and . . . I have an idea. I could run your starter through the sequencer. Find out what's in there."

I got the sense she was just looking for reasons to use her amazing machine. I thought about the sequencing process as she had described it—the pulverization of the cells, the divination of their entrails. What good would it do me to know about the starter's dead DNA? It was its living behavior I needed to understand.

"I'll think about it," I said. "It's nice of you to offer. Thanks."

"Of course. Tell me what you decide. And you should come

over and try the new batch sometime. It's better! I think it's better. I'm almost there."

Nothing was happening at my workstation. The dough was going to take a very, very, very long time.

I rose from the folding chair. "Can I try it now?"

Over at Jaina Mitra's lab, I bit into one of the new Lembas cakes. The gluiness had improved, but there was a new flavor—deeply metallic. It tasted uncomfortably like blood. I winced, and I could see the disappointment in her eyes. She took a bite herself, and cursed. "Something changed. It wasn't like this last night . . ."

"It's really hard, what you're trying to do," I said. "You're inventing something totally new. Everyone else here, we're taking things that are established and . . . putting a twist on them. Even *then*, it's impossible. Trust me."

Jaina Mitra nodded absently. "I think maybe the problem is the molybdoenzymes . . ."

I walked to Naz's coffee bar and requested a glass of water to wash the coppery flavor out of my mouth, then sat at the long picnic table to check my email. Replies to my query in the newsletter were accumulating, and in their recommendations they were unanimous. Unequivocal.

Talk to Stephen Agrippa, they said.

Ask Agrippa.

Agrippa the cheese maker.

Agrippa knows more about microbes than anyone.

Agrippa, up on the airfield.

Agrippa, with the goats.

So, WHAT NEXT? M. wormed his way through the narrow crevice and found a scene from a dream. Inside, the cave was forested with fungus, their stalks as thick around as trees, with fluttering ribs and wobbling tendrils. The wind across the crevice played a whistling song. (Remember this.)

M. knew that mushrooms could be deadly, but what choice did he have? He feasted. And guess what? They were great! The fruits of the cave sustained him.

Weeks later, a sharp-nosed ship ventured close enough to the great rocky island for him to signal, waving his arms atop the precipice from which he might before have jumped. When the ship approached, he climbed aboard and . . . was immediately pressed into service, a slave once more. He told no one of the cave and its hidden sustenance.

Five years later, he had earned his freedom, and five years after that, he had acquired a ship of his own, slow and leaky, but large enough to carry not only his own small family but also the families of the men beside whom he had rowed and suffered.

This part of the story feels true to me.

AGRIPPA

BEYOND THE OLD HANGARS there was the expanse of abandoned airfield, cracked and overtaken by tall grasses. A line of low, rounded bunkers rose at the asphalt's edge, and beyond them it was just dark water.

I carried a sample of the Clement Street starter in its original ceramic crock across the broken landscape, the Marrow Fair beneath my feet.

The man and his alpaca were out there guarding their herd.

I approached slowly, both of them watching me as I crossed the concrete.

"Stephen Agrippa?" I called when I was close enough. "We met before . . . never mind. I work in the market." I pointed dumbly into the ground. "Everyone said I should talk to you."

The man nodded slowly at this.

"I have something strange," I said. "It's a sourdough starter, but it's not— Hey!"

A goat was gnawing on my pant leg. I danced away. Agrippa laughed; a high, echoing bark.

"Come on," he said. "Bring your something strange. Don't worry about Hercules. He's cool." His voice was wry and reedy. He turned and ambled away. I followed, circling wide around the hungry goat and the watchful alpaca, whose name was apparently Hercules.

Agrippa led me toward one of the bunkers, set deep into the ground, its rounded top thick with vegetation, inky green and rusty red. The bunker's face was a half-moon of white. There was a ramshackle Airstream set up next to it with an awning that extended to one side.

In the shade of the awning, Agrippa reached into a plastic cooler and retrieved two bottles, both unlabeled. He cracked their caps with his molars. "Want one?"

I accepted my beer from the master of microbes and spun the blank bottle. "Home brew?"

"It's from Algebra, around the way." He motioned back toward the brewery. "Quintuple-hopped. Experimental. I help 'em out sometimes."

"People say you're a microbe whisperer."

He took a swig from his bottle, looked out across the water. "They do say that. I try to discourage them, but then they ask me what I *am*, and I can never quite say it right. So then I just shut up."

"You make cheese."

He made a deep *Mm-hmm*, jerked a thumb at the bunker behind him. "That's the cheese cave. Used to hold nukes." He took another swig of beer. Grinned. "And now it holds some *truly* advanced technology."

A nervous itch spread across my scalp. "Is it safe to be here?"

"Do you drive here in a car?"

"I take Carl's ferry."

"Well, it's safer than that."

"I mean, is it radioactive?"

"Everything's radioactive. It's fine. Mutation's a good thing."

I had no idea if he was serious or not. He seemed like the kind of person who cultivated that ambiguity—who reveled in it.

Generally I don't enjoy those kinds of people.

I hefted the Clement Street starter in its crock and held it out to Agrippa for inspection. He eyed it, then me.

"Oh, I can't do anything about that."

"What?"

"You think I'm a sourdough mechanic, and you just drop it off? No, ma'am. I will tell you what I know. How you apply that knowledge to *your* particular technology there is up to you."

"You keep calling it technology."

"Technology it is. Come on. I want you to see the cave."

INSIDE THE BUNKER, the air was clammy and dense, heavy with a ripe ammoniac smell. It seemed to crawl up inside my nose and elbow other odors away. The bunker was narrow but deep—deep enough, at least, that the light from the open door did not illuminate the back wall and instead only petered out into darkness.

Wire shelves ran straight down the long space, like an art school demonstration of perspective and foreshortening. The shelves were laden with huge wheels of cheese that I recognized from Orli's table at the Marrow Fair. They were veined with bright colors: blue and turquoise, flame orange, hot pink.

Agrippa carried a basket under his arm as he walked slowly through the bunker, scanning up and down like a value-conscious shopper scouring the shelves at a grocery store.

"If you sit here in the dark," he said absently—and it was no stretch to imagine him doing so—"and wait a long time . . . you see yellow flashes. That's vitamin B_2 fluorescing."

"And you are one hundred percent sure it's not dangerous."

"It's beautiful."

That was not a satisfying response.

We passed a shelf where a wheel of cheese had exploded into some kind of fungal overgrowth. Tall, mushroom-like fruiting bodies rose up and swayed slightly in the air disturbed by our passage. I sucked in a sharp breath.

"Is that . . . there . . ." I pointed. "Is that all right?"

Agrippa nodded. "Oh, it's fantastic. An empire is rising, lifting up great works."

He picked up a wheel on the next shelf, held it close to his nose. Then he fished a tool out of his pocket, some kind of metal syringe, and plunged it into the wheel. He extracted a slender core sample, popped part of it into his mouth. Offered me the other part. I hesitated for a moment, then accepted it. Satisfied, he turned around and headed for the exit.

"*Culture*," he said. "The word meant *this*—making cheese—before it meant *that*—art and opera. And before it meant anything, it just meant working the land. That's a better definition. That's who we are. Not our music, our books. *Psh*, books. They're all dead. We're alive. We eat, we grow. But, but but but, here's the thing! We're amateurs."

We emerged back onto the airfield. I was happy to be out of the bunker.

"Amateurs!" Agrippa repeated. "Compared to what you just saw? This is the key to my cheese, to that beer, to your sourdough, to anything and everything. I'm going to say it, and you're going to nod like you get it, but you won't. Not yet. It doesn't come easy."

He took a breath.

"In that cave, empires are rising and falling. There are battles under way. Wars. More soldiers on both sides than in all the wars of human history combined. And they are *struggling*. They are taking territory, making it safe. Building fortresses." He lifted the wheel he'd chosen out of his basket and hefted it. "There is a saga in here to put our whole history to *shame*."

His eyes were a little defocused now, lost in the grandeur of his rant.

"In every wheel of cheese, there's revolution, alliance, betrayal . . . Can you feel it?"

I told him the truth: I could not.

"Nope. You're honest, I appreciate that. Of course you can't. I couldn't, not at first. We're blind to it. But this is their world, not ours, and their stories are greater."

I frowned. "They're just bacteria. They don't think or plan. They just . . . exist."

"Just *exist*? They do things we only dream of. They are fecund and potent, they can speak to one another with chemicals and light, they can form teams—oh, the teams they can form. Millions strong, all working together perfectly. If we could cooperate like that—if we could even get close—we would have all of our problems solved. They can live at the bottom of the ocean. They can live in volcanoes. They can live forever."

Well: my comrades below had sent me to the right person. This was a man who loved microbes.

He looked at me, eyes blazing. "This is all I have to offer you. If you can understand this—if you can not only hear what I'm saying but *believe* it—then you'll know what to do with your starter."

We were both silent a moment. Then I ventured: "Can you at least give me a hint?"

He laughed. "Sure. What I'm saying is, first you have to respect it."

He spun his wheel of cheese around and sniffed it, sucking in a great deep breath. Then he held it out, turned it a degree either way, inspecting, and the look on his face showed more than respect. It showed awe.

<FROM: BEO>

ON THE GREAT ROCKY ISLAND, M. built a kingdom! His friends and family feasted on the fruits of the cave and they were well nourished. They built a long jetty, a place where ships could pause on their journeys across the sea. To feed the sailors, the Mazg brewed beer and baked bread. The fluttering, wobbling culture of the cave, they kept secret.

This is a pretty good story so far, but maybe you're wondering, Why haven't I heard of M.'s great rocky island? Why is it not a wealthy maritime state? Why are Beo and his cousins hidden away in all the second-story apartments of Europe?

Because, of course, there was a problem.

Their port was very successful, and the population of the Mazg (we can call them that now) grew rapidly in just a few generations. They became beer-drinkers and bread-eaters themselves, because the culture of the cave thrived nowhere else, not even in other caves on the island. For a long time, they wondered why. Most shrugged. Then a girl of the Mazg, a genius, simply opened her ears. The whistling song across the narrow crevice was linked somehow to the life of the culture. Through experimentation, she determined the crucial tones and sequences. This is the origin of the songs that the Mazg sing today—the songs on your CD.

This girl became the governor of the great rocky island, and she transformed it, bringing the culture out of the cave. Now the Mazg had beer and bread and something else, too. Sailors who tied up their ships and walked ashore to rest and trade were well fed and well treated, but they were not allowed behind the walls of the fortresses in which the culture of the Mazg was propagated and the songs of the Mazg were sung.

Behind those walls, the language of the Mazg grew in upon itself and lost its kinship with other languages.

AGRIPPA (CONTINUED)

IRETURNED TO THE AIRFIELD the next day because the others had spoken the truth: Agrippa was a genius. Maybe also an asshole. But I believed he had something to teach me; I believed he understood the starter in a way I didn't, or couldn't.

The cheese is not the thing, he told me. The cheese is just the territory, the battleground. The bacteria are the thing. They are the actors on a milky stage.

Most plants have at least one bacterial symbiote, he told me. He pronounced it carefully: *sym-bi-ote.* He looked out across the airfield, at the scrubby red and green plants. All those? Infected. But that's not the right word, he said. Infected means there's something wrong. This is all right; it's partnership. Some plants are infected by bacteria that are themselves infected by a virus. Wheels within wheels. Clockwork.

You have four pounds of bacteria in your body, he said. You don't feel it. He bounced on his heels. I think I'm starting to feel it. I think I can talk to them.

Talk to them?

Yes, he said. Send them messages. Chemicals. Hormones. What I want to do next is learn how to listen and hear their reply.

He held one of the wheels of cheese under my nose and instructed me to breathe deeply. I did. The smell was dense and close, but there was also the suggestion of citrus—a far-off orange.

What would it be like, he asked, to smell our whole world at once? Our whole history? If this wheel were *us*, what would it smell like? Agrippa thought it would smell like engine exhaust.

He seemed barely to eat, and the things he did eat were strange: extremely funky yogurt, strained and thickened, along with tiny wild radishes foraged in the far corners of the airfield.

Once, I asked him: Do you . . . shower? He shrugged and said: The last time I showered was before I arrived here. Almost a year ago.

A year without a shower! The idea of it made my skin crawl. And he did have a ripeness to him, but like the cheese he created, it wasn't unpleasant. Agrippa had achieved equilibrium. He had won the inhabitants of his underarms to his cause.

One day, Agrippa said: I dream of a great council of fermentation. Beer. Sauerkraut. Kimchi! Have you had kimchi? I love kimchi.

My phone reception was terrible on the airfield. It was an uncanny spot: really truly in the center of everything—with San Francisco's skyline visible across the water, the great bustle of the Port of Oakland across the channel, Oakland's own downtown rising in the other direction, the Marrow Fair beneath us—yet it felt utterly desolate and disconnected. It was amazing to see the goats grazing here in the calm eye of a storm of trade and transit.

I came to visit again the next day, and the next. Mainly, I listened to Agrippa talk. When he didn't talk, I followed him around, enjoying the silence. I followed him into the bunker, tried to see what he saw in the developing wheels of cheese. Mostly, I failed. I tried to be helpful. He would show me how to do something, and I would do it.

I milked a goat.

I learned how he made his cheese. He painted it. Literally: He painted bacteria and fungi onto the wheel. Dipped a brush into a scummy pool of some culture, dragged long wet strokes across the curd's pale surface. In the cave, after weeks of development, these strokes took on texture and color, became deep blue or hot pink or flame orange, or even exhibited a ghostly bioluminescence.

I had my first tiny breakthrough when I looked at one of his painted wheels and saw not a lump of milk by-product inoculated with bacteria, but a *map*, color-coded just like an atlas. For a moment, I saw the battle lines. There were mighty armies on the march, billions strong or more, deploying biochemical matériel, fighting a war that was going to take, on their timescale, millennia or more, maybe millions of years, because it was for them an evolutionary timescale. They could change. The organisms that won the war might not be the organisms that began it. For a moment, I saw it. Blue and pink and orange.

I found Agrippa farther back in the bunker.

"I saw it," I told him. That's all.

He looked at me—his face changed, eyes narrowed, then

opened again—and he nodded once. "Good. Now you know what to do with your starter."

Did I?

I sat with the ceramic crock in the deck chair next to the Airstream. It was nighttime, past ten. The sun was down, but the Port of Oakland lit the airfield with a purgatorial glow. I wondered how the goats handled the strange light. They must have adapted.

Agrippa and I were sipping experimental beers. I was a little bit drunk.

"I think . . . my starter needs a warrior spirit," I said.

"It *has* a warrior spirit," he said. "It was born with it."

"Then what's the problem?"

"You need to give it something to fight."

"Like what?"

"A rival. Another culture. Something from Big Sourdough." He paused. "Is there such a thing as Big Sourdough?"

I considered the question. The answer came to me.

"I can use King Arthur," I declared.

"That's flour, right?"

"Yes, but, but but but"—I was getting excited—"they also sell a starter, they say it's a hundred years old . . . They ship it to you. It's really popular. They must make it by the barrel."

"Ohhhh," he said. "Perfect. Get some of that. Put them in the arena together."

"What if the King Arthur wins?"

"Hey now! You gotta believe in your starter," he said. "It can hear you. It's right there. *You* need to have a warrior spirit, too! Lead the way!"

I stood up. Stared down into the crock. The pale gray

scum was no less pale, gray, or scummy than ever before.
"Are you ready to fight?" I asked it.

"There you go," Agrippa said.

"Are you ready to fight?" I cried.

"There you go!"

"Are you ready to fight?!"

I held the crock over my head and stomped my feet. A starburst of shadows spun around me, cast by the lights of the bridge and the port and the city and the brewery, all the lights of civilization.

Agrippa got up, too, and started howling and dancing along. The goats stayed on the far side of the airfield—wisely—but Hercules the alpaca wandered closer, curious.

WHAT NEXT? Beyond the great rocky island, the world was shifting, and now the richest trade routes crossed other seas. Fewer ships stopped at the jetty; fewer sailors bought beer and bread. But the Mazg were still full of ambition! They had hardly begun their story. They used their accumulated wealth to acquire ships of their own, and armed themselves, and became pirates.

For a while, this was extremely successful. When Mazg pirates stormed a ship, they had the advantage, always, for while the other crew was sick from moldy rations, the pirates were strong from rations made of mold. The great rocky island was now a single enormous fortress-pantry, teeming with the fluttering, wobbling culture that sustained the Mazg. They sang their songs louder. They sang them faster. They were hungry. They were unstoppable!

They didn't realize the danger they were in. Something important had been lost. In case it's not obvious—it's easier to communicate this when you tell the story out loud, like my uncle does—this story wants you to think that maybe that something was humility.

After a long season of piracy, one of the roving ships of the Mazg returned to the great rocky island only to find that the great rocky island was gone. In its place there was a floating forest of fungus with fluttering ribs and wobbling tendrils, many times larger than the great rocky island had ever been. While they watched in horror, it fluttered and wobbled and . . . burped.

Lost was the kingdom of the Mazg—eaten, in the end, by its own food.

That last ship fled to land. The Mazg aboard carried in their crocks the culture of the cave, and in their memories the songs. Everything else was lost.

It's just a story. There's another one, about a girl named Mazga who steals the culture from the queen of the dead. In that story, the songs are the memories of sad souls, and they are needed to trick the culture into believing it's still in the underworld. Shehrieh likes that one better.

Me, I like the pirates.

THE FALL OF CAMELOT

THE KING ARTHUR FLOUR COMPANY began as a Boston-based importer in 1790 and introduced its own American-grown wheat flour in 1896. Since 2004, it's been one hundred percent employee-owned, which is pretty cool. The company's headquarters, now located in Vermont, is an enormous twelve-sided building called Camelot.

From Camelot's website, I ordered the King Arthur sour-dough starter (a single ounce) and paid extra for expedited shipping. The UPS driver delivered it to Cabrillo Street in a plain brown box. Inside, there was a very small plastic tub with a white screw-on lid.

I carried the King Arthur starter to Alameda, transferred it into a larger container, and began to feed it on the same schedule as the Clement Street starter. It grew eagerly, bubbling and expanding. Where the Clement Street starter smelled faintly of bananas, the King Arthur smelled strongly of flour, with maybe a touch of vinegar. I got the sense that's how sourdough starter was supposed to smell. Its surface was wet and gloppy; there was no suggestion of the silvery tautness that was the signature of the Clement Street starter's occasional sentience.

I tried to see it through Agrippa's eyes—imagined the King Arthur starter a civilization on the rise. Was it bland, a bit boring? Maybe, but so was my own human civilization. I imagined myself as a cell down there among the teeming trillions. Maybe I was happy. Maybe I was excited for the future.

Then I carried the King Arthur starter across my workstation to meet its neighbor. It was time for an apocalypse.

I portioned off a section of the Clement Street starter, noting its despondence, and dropped it into a fresh tub—a great arena—then added the King Arthur and swirled them together. The mixture turned an even gray. For just a moment, I wondered if I had made a miscalculation, and if the King Arthur, with its Protestant work ethic, might be the stronger substance.

I whispered encouragements to the home team. "You're Alexander the Great. Rising China. Everybody better get out of your way."

The starters spasmed in slow motion. The tub frothed with gas, emitted gouts of scent new and strange: not only bananas and flour but also orange peel, Earl Grey, gunpowder. Was I detecting signal flares launched above a vast battlefield? Or was it the wreckage of war—the broken remnants of armies cleaved apart? Was I smelling corpses?

It took an hour. By the end of it, the scent of flour was gone, and the Clement Street starter was frothing, victorious. I hadn't seen it so lively since the early days, before the Marrow Fair, before anything.

I added this rampant culture to a tub with flour and water and salt and I mixed the dough myself. It bucked and surged; it was uncanny. I formed a loaf and nothing stuck to my fingers. Silvery and taut, this was sourdough on a war-time footing.

The finished loaf emerged from the Faustofen perfectly round and buoyant. Its face bore a new expression: an even, distant look, hollow-eyed like a statue from antiquity. It was a face full of grim purpose. When I tapped it on its back, I heard an echoing boom.

Lois! I haven't heard from you in a while. How is your robot doing? How's the starter?

TEND YOUR GARDEN

THE CLEMENT STREET STARTER had changed, perhaps irrevocably. Before, I sustained it with inert flour. Now it would accept only living fuel, and only in large quantities.

Every morning was a new conquest. The starter was jubilant, and I was back on track, production-wise. I had the volume of starter I needed, which meant I could mix the amount of dough I required, which meant I could bake enough bread to supply Chef Kate every day and, with luck, meet the demand that was imminent.

But as the mornings passed, I grew uneasy. The floury scent of the King Arthur starter was so innocent. When I scooped up the little utopia and dropped it into the arena with the Clement Street starter, I felt a twinge of . . . something. More than a twinge. It was as if trillions of voices suddenly cried out in terror . . .

Agrippa's logic had led me to this strategy, and to the survival of the Clement Street starter. But Agrippa's logic also demanded that I see it this way: not as a simple kitchen operation, but as a clash of civilizations.

It seemed silly to attach such a grandiose label to something so small . . . but was it really small? There had to be a scale somewhere—the scale of stars, the scale of far-off cosmic super-beings—upon which we ourselves, we humans with our cities and bridges and subterranean markets, would look like the lactobacilli and the yeast.

To them, I was the cosmic super-being, and what did I wreak with my vast and implacable powers? Total war. Utter annihilation.

I oscillated between finding this vision totally ridiculous and finding it deadly serious.

The bread had never been better! The faces in the crust were stoic and satisfied. Some of the scent of domination lingered in the finished loaves. Lily Belasco noticed the difference. "It's a bit . . . peaty," she said. "How do you do that?"

What I thought was: *Well, every morning, I sacrifice a teeming civilization to the Clement Street war machine.*

What I said was: "Who knows! Ha-ha! Sourdough is complicated!"

Agrippa had solved my problem, and he had created a new one.

I'd known the Clement Street starter wasn't normal, of course, but I honestly hadn't realized the depth of its strangeness until now, because the King Arthur starter was *very* normal. It was happy and dopey like a big brown dog. It had no special high-maintenance desires. It just wanted to grow.

I let it.

Every day, the Clement Street starter required a larger sacrifice. It was absurd: I was brewing the King Arthur starter in garbage bins. Now, instead of adding the King Arthur to the Clement Street, I did the reverse. Only the tiniest trace of the culture of the Mazg was required. I tipped a cup over and deployed a dollop of hunter/killer starter, potent and relentless. In just fifteen minutes it would sweep through the whole bin, destroying/consuming/reproducing, venting plumes of banana and gunpowder. When it was finished, nothing of the happy floury folk remained.

AS I WAS DOING THIS, I was also reading the book that Charlotte Clingstone had selected from Horace's library and left for me, *Candide*—her café's namesake.

It was, unexpectedly, a screwball action comedy. The hapless main character, whose name was Candide, traveled with a band of companions from Europe to the New World and back. Along the way, characters were flogged, shipwrecked, enslaved, and nearly executed several times. There were earthquakes and tsunamis and missing body parts.

One of Candide's companions, Pangloss, whose name I recognized from the hundred-dollar adjective he inspired—I'd never known the etymology—insisted throughout that all their misfortunes were for the best, for they delivered the companions into situations that seemed, at first, pretty good. Until those situations, too, went to shit.

The story concluded on a small farm outside Istanbul, where Candide plunked a hoe into the dirt and declared his intention to retreat from adventure (and suffering) and simply tend his garden.

The way the author told it—the book was written in 1759—it was clear I was supposed to think Candide had finally discovered something important.

I could see why the book appealed to Charlotte Cling-stone. It was a rejection of ambition; a blueprint for her small, perfect, human-scale restaurant—a safe space set apart from the scrum of the world.

NOW THAT THE CLEMENT STREET STARTER was back on track, even if distressingly, I had to contend with my other limitations. The Vitruvian was working as fast as possible, but not fast enough. I needed another arm, but that wasn't in the budget. Not yet.

So I joined it.

We stood side by side. I watched it work, every so often adjusting my motions to match its hyperefficiency. The student became the master.

Other vendors, in the days before the market's public launch, had started to stay overnight. They unrolled sleeping bags in the lemon grove and slept there. I joined them.

The depot sustained me. I wolfed down cricket cookies and tube-fish tacos and Lembas cakes, which had somehow gotten even worse—now both gritty *and* gluey—but they kept me going. I drank ten coffees a day. When Naz wasn't around, I operated the espresso machine myself, and my drinks were quadruple shots.

I was working more hours than I ever had at General Dexterity, but here, I was ecstatic. I hardly worried about anything; for days I would enter states of perfect flow, eating/drinking/feeding/folding/baking/sleeping. While I slept, the Vitruvian still worked.

Then, one morning, I overslept beneath the lemon trees. I

must have looked mildly postapocalyptic as I sprinted up the concourse: hair wild, eyes dimmed, clothes stale with bits of cricket cookie on them.

When I reached my workstation, I discovered the tub that contained the Clement Street starter tipped onto its side, and a taut, silvery tendril extending outward, reaching for the King Arthur where it waited in its garbage bin. The tendril flexed and flowed. The Vitruvian had retracted and was watching it warily. It wasn't programmed to handle this.

The sight jolted me out of whatever dream I'd been lost in. This was not okay.

I had to stop. I had to figure out what I was dealing with.

I ROSE FROM MY SLEEPING BAG in the middle of the night. The depot was quiet, powered down. The only light came from the grow rooms.

I carried the Clement Street starter in front of me—now transferred back into its ceramic crock, quarantined—and padded in my socks toward Jaina Mitra's laboratory.

There, I found the hulking sequencer, the ILLUMINA HYPER CENSUS, its plastic carapace gleaming in the darkness, a line of pinprick status lights rippling silently. It seemed to be twiddling its thumbs.

I fumbled around the lab, looking for one of the sample plates. I opened one cabinet, found the Lembas cakes assembling themselves, closed it. Opened another. *There.*

Jaina Mitra had only needed a tiny bit of Horace's saliva. I dabbed my finger into the crock and let a dollop of starter ooze onto the plate. I pressed the button to open the machine, and its tray extended, along with a wash of blue light from its glowing heart. I put the sample plate into the tray and pressed the button again. It was simple; there was only one button to press. This machine that could crack the code of life was easier to operate by far than the Faustofen, or even my microwave.

The machine reclaimed the tray and began to hum.

I whispered an apology for the massacre to come. Then I sat on the floor.

Minutes passed. The hum gave way to the pulse of abrasion, then a high-pitched whine. Then silence.

I would take the information I gleaned from this machine and enter it into an expedient internet search engine. There would be something, surely, about this organism. A warning. A remedy.

I was waiting for the machine to chime, but there was no chime.

I wandered through the sleeping depot, carrying the Clement Street starter with me in its crock.

I wandered through Horace's library. Up and down the vehicle ramp. Through a loop of corridors I'd never found before, which deposited me back near the door to the tiny pier. Then I followed the corridor toward the cricket farm. I could hear them chirping.

This time, I pressed ahead.

They lived in row houses made from corrugated cardboard and superfine netting. I saw them milling around, climbing on top of one another, jumping and flickering, chittering and chirping.

What were the epic sagas of the cricket kingdom?

From back in the concourse, I heard a low and commanding chime.

HUNGER

L ATER THAT MORNING, with the first light of day peeking
in through the skylight above the lemon grove, I was
forming one set of loaves while the arm mixed a batch of
dough when Jaina Mitra appeared, fully suited up in her lab
coat again.

I curled my face into the beginning of an apology, but she
held up a hand preemptively. "I'm not angry," she said.
"Well, I am. You should have just accepted my offer and let
me help you. But it doesn't matter."

I stood there with a cold lump of dough in my hands.
"Is that all, then?"

Jaina Mitra's nostrils flared. "Not by a long shot." The
slashes under her eyes seemed darker than usual. She tossed
a printout onto the countertop. "I've never seen anything
like it."

I recognized the spiky cascade from the screen attached
to the sequencer; it was exactly what I'd seen in the middle of
the night, found inscrutable, emailed to myself, and, after
reviewing it in the morning, still found inscrutable. This
printout was wildly annotated in bright green ink—little

blobs and whorls and, above the graph, an exclamation in Jaina Mitra's blocky handwriting: *WOW!*

"Listen to what I'm saying," she said. "Sourdough starter is a community of organisms. You know that, right?"

"Yes. Of course." Everett Broom taught me that.

"Generally, there are two or three different species living together. That's what they say at the bread lab."

"There's a bread lab?"

"Washington State. They do very good work. *Maybe* four species can live together in a stable community. But this is the sequencer's report on your starter. You saw this?" I nodded, and Jaina Mitra snorted lightly. "I almost cried."

She smoothed the printout flat on the countertop and pulled a green-barreled pen from her lab coat.

"This here"—she indicated the graph's broadest peak with the pen's tip—"this is the yeast. And this"—she indicated another peak—"is *Lactobacillus sanfranciscensis*." She pronounced it carefully. "These—" She danced the tip of her pen along a series of sharper spikes. "These are matches for bacteria in the Global Microbiome Survey. It adds up to a lot more than four, obviously." Then she traced a wide box around the series of spikes that rippled along the graph's floor. "And these—there are so many of them—these are novel." She raised both eyebrows.

Apparently that did not impress me as much as it should have.

"*Meaning,*" she went on, "there are no matches in the library. That, by itself, isn't so strange; like I told you, my cabinet is full of novel organisms. What's strange is finding this many taxa, known and unknown, living together in an apparently stable community." She paused. Looked at me. Over at my workstation. Back at me. "It *is* stable, isn't it?"

It felt like she was asking about me, not the starter. "I've been baking with this starter for months. I got it from a baker who had it for—years? Yes, it's stable."

She tsked. It was a tsk of awe. "There must be a hundred constituents! The smallest spikes might be noise—it's hard to tell. But even so, this many! It's a scale and complexity of commensal behavior beyond anything I've ever seen or read about." Jaina Mitra looked like she wanted to shake me. "It is *unreal*."

WE SAT WITH OUR ESPRESSO CUPS beneath the lemon trees and I told her the starter's story. Jaina Mitra did not make a good audience; her gaze was hard and hungry, and she scrawled notes as I spoke, page after page of them in green ink. She made me nervous.

I finished by explaining the starter's decline, my consultation with Stephen Agrippa, its resurgence, and my concern that I'd taken it too far. Because I didn't understand what I was working with.

Jaina Mitra stared down at her notes. "Everyone in my field is obsessed with identifying new organisms," she murmured. "It's like a treasure hunt. But I already have the organisms I need. I just can't put them together." She looked up, staring into space. "How do their communities work? I try . . ." She sighed raggedly. "When I move one piece, the others don't fit anymore. When I turn one knob, the other knobs eat it for dinner. My new batch is worse than ever. Do you know what makes it so sticky? It's not the enzymes.

It's what the enzymes *produce*. Dead cells. Lysed bacteria. Corpses!"

The gluey taste of death. Great.

Jaina Mitra was showing me something real, and it ran a little ragged, and it made me like her a little more. Like, two percent more.

She laid her hands flat on her notebook. "I'd like to study your starter."

"I don't think it's going to solve your problem." I said it as lightly as I could.

Her face was a mask of control. "It might. Please. We could work together." She was suddenly sweet and solicitous, and it was very strange. She should have stayed sharp and brusque. She should have commanded: *Let me work with that muck of yours!* I would have complied in a moment.

THE SLURRY FACTORY

IT WAS THE DAY BEFORE the Marrow Fair's grand opening, and I was relaxing at my workstation, satisfied with my ability to produce enough sourdough, wasting time on the internet, and still thinking about Jaina Mitra's offer when she appeared again to announce she wanted to show me something that could, or should, influence my decision. It involved a car trip, and could I take the afternoon off? I accepted. I had the feeling, suddenly, that I'd been down in the darkness of the depot for too long.

A year in California and I'd rarely been south of Daly City, never stepped foot in San Jose, and barely contemplated the existence of the San Joaquin Valley.

Driving down California State Route 99 in the passenger seat of Jaina Mitra's blue Tesla, the rightmost lane was taken up completely by semis hauling trailers, and beyond them endless orchards, silvery olive trees alternating with spiky almond trees, solid green to the horizon. The San Joaquin Valley's existence was confirmed.

We watched a pickup truck with a portable toilet in its

bed crawling along an access road, keeping pace with the pickers who were sweeping across the field in a loose line.

There were structures that poked out in places: immense, featureless white warehouses, like big-box stores before any branding had been applied. We saw grain elevators, smelled feedlots.

Jaina Mitra eased onto an exit ramp and turned onto a long, straight road called Avenue 16. We passed a neon-green tractor lumbering on the shoulder and I waved to its driver, who waved back. Farther up, we watched a small plane fly in low arcs over a vast field of pistachio trees, leaving a trail of pink vapor. I fumbled with the Tesla's control panel and set the AC to recirculate.

We turned off Avenue 16 onto Road 23. There were too many long, straight roads out here to bother with names.

A semi was rattling up the road, coming in the opposite direction. The trailer it hauled was painted bright green, and as it passed, I saw a familiar logotype rendered in crisp white. That semi was hauling nutritive gel.

This was Slurry country.

The facility was ahead. It was enormous, one mile square, a tangle of towering vats with pipes and valves embroidering their surfaces, all of it bounded by loading docks where more bright green trailers were waiting. Train tracks ran straight through the facility; Slurry could be lowered in containers directly onto freight cars and hauled away to Chicago or New York or the Port of Oakland and points beyond.

Olive trees lined the long driveway that led from Road 23 into the facility. Beneath the trees, fruit rotted in dark piles.

"THIS FACILITY USED TO BELONG TO GALLO," Jaina Mitra said. "They made like ten percent of the country's wine here."

A man was crossing the parking lot to meet us. He was tall and bald and frighteningly gaunt, waving energetically, his lips pressed flat in an enthusiastic smile.

"Dr. Mitra! Yes! And our guest of honor!"

"This is Dr. Klamath," Jaina Mitra said. Her face was cheery but her eyes betrayed a sense of duty. "Founder and CEO of Slurry."

"I prefer Chief Nutrition Officer!" He gave Jaina Mitra a feather-light hug, then offered his hand to me. Taking it, I encountered a palm of extraordinary dryness.

"Come in, come in," he said. "See the sights. Dr. Mitra told me you're a Slurry subscriber—well, it all comes from here."

"I *was* a subscriber," I said. "I haven't had it in a while."

He grinned, unbowed. "It's getting better all the time!"

Inside, the air was dense and smelled slightly sour. Every surface, walls and ceiling, was braided with pipes painted primary colors, some as skinny as my wrist, others fat enough to admit Jaina Mitra's Tesla, all connecting an array of enormous vats marked with cryptic identifiers. It looked like a power plant or a refinery. In a way, it was both.

Klamath spun around and continued to speak as he led us, walking backward, toward one of the vats. This was not his first tour.

"Farmers in Fresno talk about yield per acre. That's economic, not human. So what if you're growing four tons of alfalfa per acre? Talk to me about *people.* How many people's lives are you supporting? How many *healthy* lives?"

That seemed like a reasonable question.

"Slurry is one hundred percent vertically integrated here, so I can tell you, this unit"—he patted a mammoth vat affectionately—"supports two thousand people every week. *Two thousand!*"

Two thousand students lived in my college dorm. I imagined all of them lined up in front of the vat, bowls in hand, waiting to get their daily ration of dystopia.

"We put in just five thousand dollars' worth of raw ingredients. As Dr. Mitra can tell you, it used to be a lot more. We're making it more efficient. You know what my goal is? Everybody says this is crazy, but I say it's physics. An average person uses about three kilowatt hours of energy every day. Just to live. You know the price of three kilowatt hours in California? Forty-five cents. That's our goal. It ought to be just like plugging yourself into the wall."

"That sounds pretty robotic," I said. "And I say that as someone who likes robots."

"I just want everybody to be healthy," Klamath said. His bulldozer enthusiasm faltered; I detected a note of weariness. "We should be way past this already. I want people to have time to do the things they want, rather than work to make money to buy food, or scrounge around in the kitchen."

He stopped, and steepled his fingers theatrically.

"But I know people don't want to eat gray goo. I do. That's why Dr. Mitra's work is so important. That's why we want to acquire Lembas."

Ah. It came into focus.

Klamath was leading us through the vats, toward the far-thest corner of the facility.

"Those fields you drove through? That whole system? It's a dead end."

It seemed like a rather large and vibrant dead end.

"Here, we can program a yeast to make anything. Gaso-line. Heroin."

Hummus?

"Not yet. But damn it, we are *close*. Dr. Mitra's work is the key. Right now, I can get one organism going . . . a yeast, or a bacteria like *E. coli*. But we want more complex products. We need to assemble and train whole communities."

Like Lembas.

"Like your starter," Jaina Mitra said lightly.

Listening to Dr. Klamath talk, hearing him slam the old system, seeing the resources he commanded, it struck me: Was I speaking to Mr. Marrow?

THE VAT WAS THE SAME SHAPE as the one in Jaina Mitra's lab, but ten times as large, a monstrous egg of shining stainless steel. A neat sign on the front read COMMUNITY PRODUCTION TEST, which sounded sort of nice. Healthy.

Klamath patted the vat affectionately. "It's cute, right? We run our wacky experiments in these little ones. I want to give it to Dr. Mitra. And this, too." He stepped over to a plastic-clad box the size of a mini-fridge—another flawlessly anonymous piece of biotech gear. "This is brand-new, which is why it looks like shit. It can build microorganisms from scratch. We hollow out a yeast, squirt in some new DNA, boot it up."

I frowned. "You just hollow . . . out . . ."

Dr. Klamath gave the box a quick caress, let his hand linger. "It's a printer for life."

Jaina Mitra extended a finger to touch it, too. Their affection for this anonymous machine was palpable. "These are impossible to get."

I looked up and considered the vat. It was bigger than my apartment.

"You can't just feed my starter flour and water," I said. "Not if you want to make this much. It likes King Arthur." I paused. "You can get it online."

"Or we could try feeding it Slurry," Jaina Mitra said, and Dr. Klamath nodded gamely. Would the Clement Street starter eat Slurry? Possibly. Would its farts be as fragrant as mine had been? Probably.

Dr. Klamath squared himself to me. "Here's the thing. Before I give Dr. Mitra the go-ahead to get this revved up, we need some legal protection. No big deal, just something that says you give us the right to exploit this biological IP that you control, et cetera, et cetera. I've got the contracts ready. I want to make it worth your while, and give you a stake in the outcome of this project. If you have questions, that's why we're here. I hope you find this as exciting as we do."

Jaina Mitra's face grew solemn. "My deal with Mr. Marrow was that he got twenty percent of Lembas. If this is as big as Dr. Klamath thinks it can be . . . that could mean millions of dollars for the Marrow Fair."

Hearing that sum, Dr. Klamath made a face as if he'd just eaten something bad. "We're not playing for pocket change here. We're playing for the whole future of food."

But was this deal exclusive?

Dr. Klamath rolled his eyes. "What? No. Keep baking.

It's great. I mean, I don't eat bread, but Dr. Mitra says it's great."

Walking back toward the lobby, I considered the vastness of the facility. If Jaina Mitra's work was successful—if she used whatever talent was hidden in the Clement Street starter to stabilize and support Lembas, to make it viable—it was possible that all of these vats might be turned over to its production.

This was scale.

It was two thousand people sustained by a single vat.

For the Clement Street starter, it would be a conquest unimaginable.

ON THE RIDE HOME, Jaina Mitra explained that if I agreed to license the Clement Street starter to her, I would receive fifty thousand shares, or five percent, of Lembas Labs, an LLC set to be acquired, soon, by Slurry Systems of Fresno, California.

"Those shares could be worth a lot of money," she said.

There was my nineteen million dollars. I could split it with Beoreg—his reward for sharing the starter—and his restaurant could have very nice tables, indeed.

I thought about it all the way through Madera, Patterson, Tracy, and Livermore, and when Jaina Mitra pulled her Tesla onto the airfield in Alameda, I had my answer.

"I'm sorry. I can't."

Her face crumpled. "Were we not clear? You have something very, very important."

"I just don't feel like it's *mine* to give. In fact, it's the other way around. You don't understand, because you haven't worked with it. And I heard a story about it—a warning." I paused. "I'm going to get rid of it."

"Please, please, *please* don't do that."

I cracked the passenger-side door. "I'm sure you'll find another way to make your stuff work. A better way."

"Let's keep talking about this!" Jaina Mitra called as I stepped out of the car. She was reaching over, her seat belt cutting into her shoulder, her expression pleading. "Keep that starter. Keep it alive!"

THE ISLAND OF THE MAZG

THAT NIGHT, I SLEPT ON MY FUTON on Cabrillo Street, satisfied with my decision. There were paths ahead that didn't require the Clement Street starter. I still had the Vitruvian, and I had become possibly the world's leading expert on the use of robot automation in kitchen processes.

In the morning, I was startled awake by a bad dream that melted away as soon as I tried to remember it. It was dark outside. I decided I would go to the Marrow Fair and make my peace with the starter. It felt like it should be a private affair.

I rode my bike to the pier and waited for Carl to arrive. The atmosphere was close and clammy, heavy clouds hanging low. Some days, working in the Marrow Fair, I missed the sky, but this would not be one of them. It would be cooler down in the depot.

The *Omebushi* approached the pier, chugging merrily. Aboard, Carl's mood matched mine.

"Haven't seen you in a while," he said, his voice still sticky with sleep. "People said you were spending the night." He poured us both some coffee and launched his boat again.

We cleared the Bay Bridge and rounded Yerba Buena Island on the way to Alameda. Then, we both saw it at the same time.

Ahead, the silhouette of the island had changed. A hazy bulge loomed in the center of the airfield. There was a new structure there—vast, round, and somehow built overnight.

Was this part of Mr. Marrow's grand opening?

The *Omebushi* brought us closer.

Though it was as large as one of the hangars, it wasn't a proper structure, but rather an organic form with a swollen, gaseous look. It might have been a rising hot-air balloon or a crashed dirigible.

Or, as I considered it, an enormous panettone.

Carl muttered a curse. Keeping one hand on the wheel, he dug in the compartment beneath his seat, produced a pair of binoculars, and tossed them into my lap.

Through the binoculars, I could make out the texture of the structure, and a sick feeling bloomed in my gut.

The forgotten lemon I'd discovered in my explorations of the depot's dark corridors—I had picked it up, only to discover that the bottom was fuzzed over with fungus, velvety to the touch. Out of sick curiosity, I'd held my breath and peeled the lemon's skin away to discover that the fungus had padded its interior with airy filaments.

Through the binoculars, I saw that, but huge.

The billowing surface looked velvety like the underside of the lemon, and in the softness there was a pattern of ridges and depressions, and in that pattern, there was the unmistakable swirl of faces.

I put the binoculars down.

I knew those faces.

The *Omebushi* bumped roughly against the tiny pier. "Better get in there and see what's happening," Carl said.

I waved my bone-key token in front of the bay-side door. It called me skinny and unlocked, but when it opened, there was no depot.

Instead, I stared at a wall of the same material that bloomed on the airfield. Pale, creamy, billowing, and patterned with familiar faces. They were variously ecstatic and anguished and accusing and calm.

Up close, the smell was overpowering. Banana and gunpowder.

For a moment I was hypnotized. Then, tentatively, I extended a finger and poked at one of the faces. The substance yielded like foam.

It had the consistency of Lembas.

It *was* Lembas.

Carl was at my side, holding an oar. "Careful there," he said. He prodded the ballooning substance with the butt of the oar and it fell away; behind the Lembas was more Lembas. The depot was full of it.

AGRIPPA'S GOATS WERE CLUSTERED at the edge of the airfield, clearly perturbed by the apocalyptic puff pastry that had invaded their domain. Their keeper stood among them; he looked more placid.

"Agrippa!" I called. "How did this happen?"

"Don't ask me," he said. "The goats woke me up. They were freaking out."

"Have you called anyone?"

"Nope."

I wanted to sputter in protest. I remembered who I was dealing with.

I ran to the control tower, descended the spiral staircase, and waved my bone key. The door opened—*STILL—TOO—SKINNY*—revealing the concourse.

Just inside, my workstation was safe, unaffected. The Vitruvian wobbled apprehensively. The Clement Street starter was quiet in its tub. But farther down the concourse, where Jaina Mitra's lab had been, the Lembas had formed a massive trunk that reached up to grip the ceiling. There, it splayed out in a dramatic many-fingered star, and one of its fingers had found the skylight above the lemon grove and pushed its way through to form the base of the bulbous structure rising on the airfield. Below it, the lemon grove had been consumed entirely. A few dark leaves were suspended in the Lembas like feathers on the nose of a cartoon cat.

The great bloom of Lembas blocked the skylight, so the only illumination came from the grow rooms, which cast their pink glow across a rippling scene that also had a soundtrack: Chaiman's album was playing, and not the spare overture but the later tracks, the ones in which he had accelerated the songs of the Mazg and overlaid them with rising sirens, bursts of noise, and a driving *oonce-oonce-oonce.*

It was a fungal party hellscape.

The Lembas was not finished. Around the absorbed lemon grove, it was growing in hungry surges. Was it obeying the *oonce*s? I watched it bulge sickly in time to the music.

Then a figure darted into view. It was Horace: wielding a wide book, charging forward, poking at the Lembas, slashing it, gaining ground.

Just beyond the grove was his library.

Horace was holding the Lembas at bay.

His shouts echoed. *"Back!"* he hollered. *"Back!"*

I kicked at the brakes on the Vitruvian's wheeled base, spun it around, and pushed forward. We coasted together down the yellow-tape road, the arm's momentum almost overbalancing it as we caromed into workstations and refrigerators before reaching the place where Horace was making his stand. He had his heels set, swiping with the book as the Lembas encircled him, *oonce* by *oonce*.

I locked the Vitruvian's brakes and grabbed at Horace's shirt. "Let the arm do it!" Then, all my scorn for the programmers on Interface drained away as I shouted, "Arm, *change task! Say hello!"* and the Vitruvian began to swing in a wide, slow arc. Where Horace's book had been making scratches, the arm made great gouges. It was tireless. The Lembas could not pass.

I heard a howl and turned to see Stephen Agrippa emerge from the depot's vehicle ramp. He was running, Hercules the alpaca beside him, and all the goats a pace behind. Agrippa urged them forward with feral hoots and yips. Hercules spat.

The Lembas was vast but brittle; where its growth had slowed, it left an airy matrix, like the crumb of one of my loaves but scaled up massively. So, when we struck it—the Vitruvian with its great fist, Hercules with his hooves, Agrippa and I taking swipes with fingers curled into claws—it broke away in ragged chunks that tumbled and bounced to be consumed by the ravenous and, frankly, terrifying goats.

The goats feasted. The Lembas shrank. I reached out, gently now, and brought a sliver of the substance to my tongue. It didn't dissolve into slime or stick to my teeth. This Lembas was a light, crispy bread with a deep well of flavor.

It was . . . really good.

Horace was still swinging with his book, enraged, protecting his archive. I unlocked the Vitruvian's brakes and pushed it slowly forward on its base. Its great swipes sent chunks of Lembas the size of beer kegs arcing slowly through the air.

At last, it was too much. The Lembas could not hold. A thin crack crept up the trunk, then spiderwebbed out, and it all began to fracture, glacierlike, huge slabs coming unstuck. The giant top, deprived of its foundation, came tumbling down—but gently. I tucked my chin into my chest, covered my head with my hands, and held my breath. The collapse was nearly soundless; just the whisper of a Rice Krispies Treat moving against itself.

I peeked. I was covered in the stuff. Everything was covered in the stuff. The smell of bananas was overpowering.

LATER THAT MORNING, the people of the Marrow Fair surveyed the damage in a deep, padded silence. Sometime during the scuffle, Chaiman's album had reached the end of its *oonc*ing and the playlist, mercifully, had not been set to repeat.

The Lembas had filled much of the depot, and Agrippa

was going corridor by corridor with his insatiable goats. Hercules, however, had reached his limit. The alpaca was sitting in the ruin of the lemon grove, apparently asleep.

Horace had successfully defended his archive, and the cricket farm had resisted the Lembas without assistance; there, the wave front stopped abruptly, ragged-edged, gnawed to a standstill by thousands of tiny mouths. The crickets chirped contentedly.

I looked around the depot and for a moment I saw it with Agrippa's eyes. These were the ruins of a glittering, overnight civilization. There were aeons packed into those hours.

More people were milling around the depot now and the spell was breaking. I heard cries of alarm and dismay, and then, increasingly, laughter. Vendors dug out their workstations, checked to see what had been wrecked and what was intact. Our bodies were all coated gray-green with a dusting of Lembas. We might have been made of Lembas ourselves.

Lily Belasco arrived, her lips curling in disbelief that such a disaster could have unfolded on the day before the market's public launch. She conscripted Orli and me to help Naz excavate the coffee bar and return the espresso machine to operational status.

"Quick," she urged. "Quick quick quick."

WE ALL WORKED TOGETHER, hauling the Lembas away in slabs, piling it up like firewood. Finally, we reached the epicenter, and there we found Jaina Mitra, who had scratched out a little cave for herself. I'd expected panic. Instead, she was exultant.

The bioreactor told the tale. The metal twisted apart in a wicked pucker. It had been breached from the inside.

Through the broken skylight, I heard sirens on the airfield.

"You used the starter," I said. "You just took it."

Jaina Mitra nodded, unrepentant. Her eyes flashed white and wild beneath a mask of Lembas dust.

THE FIRE DEPARTMENT blocked off the airfield and set up a perimeter around the control tower, clearing us out of the depot, but there was a languor to their efforts. The bloom was quiescent. In its great leap into the world above, the hybrid Lembas and Clement Street starter seemed to have burned itself out.

The firefighters stood around, not sure what to do. A helicopter hung low overhead. I waved.

"You can eat it," I heard one firefighter say to another.

"*Eat* it?" the other said.

"Yep. Not that I'm gonna. But you can."

All the vendors of the Marrow Fair stood in a loose ring around the control tower, chatting and checking phones.

I saw Jaina Mitra coming around the side of the brewery, leading a scrum of people in lab coats. I recognized one of the figures, tall and scary-skinny: it was Dr. Klamath from Slurry Systems of Fresno, California.

"You're in charge of the market?" he said to Belasco.

"That's right," she said. She was on her fifth espresso and seemed finally to have found her equilibrium.

"I need to assert our intellectual property rights in this matter. We have a claim under the Budapest Treaty . . ."

My Klamath-as-Marrow theory was dashed.

"You'll have to work that out with Mr. Marrow," Belasco said. "I'll pass along your . . . assertion?"

"Please. We have work to do here."

"Work to do!" I rounded on Jaina Mitra. "Did you do this on *purpose*?" I waved at the city-scale panettone.

"Of course not," she said flatly. Her face was still dusted gray-green. "I was terrified. But . . ." She had that Jaina Mitra look in her eye. The gleam. "Consider the *physics* of it. The efficiency . . . I estimated the mass and, even accounting for gas inflation, it's at nearly the thermodynamic optimum. Don't you see? Almost *perfect* conversion."

"Cool, but did you see your bioreactor? It *exploded*."

Dr. Klamath waved his hand dismissively in the direction of the bloom. "We'll build a stronger one. We have to tame it, yes . . . but—that's the breakthrough. We have something to tame! Dr. Mitra found the key."

Did she.

They both looked at me with eyes hard and bright while the tower of pale Lembas behind them glittered in the rising sun.

"Yes, I did." Jaina Mitra said it with the confidence of recitation. "I cultured it myself from freely occurring bacteria in the environment. That's how sourdough starter works, you know."

BECAUSE THE HYBRID LEMBAS was safe to eat, the bloom was ruled not a biohazard, and therefore not subjected to the various quasi-military quarantine procedures that would otherwise have been triggered. The CDC had nothing to say about snacks the size of houses.

The weekend following the bloom, the bridges and tunnels into Alameda were crowded to a standstill and the ferries were packed full with curious residents bringing their families to inspect up close the phenomenon they'd seen from across the bay.

They parked wherever they could find space, cars spilling onto the airfield, and walked across the cracked asphalt to break off a piece of the Lembas and tentatively put it between their lips. A thick swirl of people circled the bloom, levering off large chunks, which were broken into smaller pieces and handed down to children, who liked it most of all. The whole scene was very *Cloudy with a Chance of Meatballs*. Very *Strega Nona*.

An intrepid falafel truck pulled up and began to fry bits of the bloom into a new kind of fritter.

Agrippa and his goats watched from a distance.

Below, the market had its grand opening. It wasn't the one Mr. Marrow had planned; it was ten times better. Fifty thousand people came to Alameda that day.

People sampled cricket cookies and tube-fish tacos and pink-light kale. Every teenager on the airfield gripped one of the smoothies with . . . *things* swimming inside them. I never did find out what those were.

A week passed. Traffic across the Bay Bridge resumed its normal speed as drivers got their fill of the sight. The bloom sagged on the airfield, depleted but still enormous. Even the assembled nibbling power of the Bay Area had left it largely intact.

Klamath's team erected a field laboratory beside it. They were trying to reverse engineer the bloom, determine what had activated it so they could do so again, this time in Fresno, inside a stronger vat. A bigger one, too.

I saw Jaina Mitra stalking the bloom's perimeter, gazing up at it with a hungry expression.

THE LOIS CLUB (CONCLUDED)

IT'S INCREDIBLE," said Hilltop Lois. She held up a newspaper, the struggling local edition, and rattled it for emphasis. On the front page there was an aerial photo of the bloom, and below it, the headline: CLINGSTONE'S MARKET EXPLODES.

Clingstone's . . . ?

"Can I read that?"

I snatched the paper away without waiting for a reply. The whole story of the Marrow Fair was unfurled. The reporter, after some digging in the Alameda County records office, had worked her way through several shell companies to divine the identity of the market's owner.

"Charlotte Clingstone," I read. "This whole time."

"Amazing, isn't it?" Hilltop Lois said.

As I made my way through the story, my stomach gradually unclenched. I'd been expecting to see my own name, but there was no mention of local baker (and/or irresponsible microbial steward) Lois Clary. The story said the source of the "nontoxic environmental disruption" was a runaway experiment by Lembas Labs, which, it explained, had been recently acquired by Slurry Systems of Fresno, California.

Unfortunately, that put Slurry on the hook, liability-wise; several people had gotten sick gorging themselves on Lembas fritters, and a collision on the Bay Bridge was being blamed on the visual distraction of the bloom.

"Are you okay over there?" Compaq Lois called.

I put the paper down and looked at the Loises. "Can I tell you a story?"

In the kitchen, over glasses of port, I unspooled it. I told them about Clement Street Soup and Sourdough and the food I'd loved so intensely, so briefly.

"They gave me something when they left," I said. "It was a gift."

I told them about the starter's growth, and Agrippa and his goats, and the trip to Fresno with Jaina Mitra.

It took an hour to tell it. The Loises listened, rapt.

At the end, they each had a different opinion.

"Maybe you can get your old job back," Professor Lois said.

"Open a new bakery, is what I say." Hilltop Lois thumped her fist on the countertop. "Down in Cole Valley. It's a great neighborhood!"

"What about stock in that company?" Compaq Lois asked. "What was it called? Sludgy? You could sue for that."

Old Lois pursed her lips. She was either annoyed or amused; I couldn't tell. I prodded her. "Well? What do you think?"

"Oh, it's obvious." She smiled smugly. "You must go visit this young man. Beoreg? Yes. Beoreg."

That I did not expect.

"Somebody get a mirror. Lois the Baker, if you could see your own face when you talk about your messages back and forth, you'd know it, too."

Professor Lois started to speak, but Old Lois held up a hand, exquisitely wrinkled, to silence her.

"She needs to go."

There was a vibration in her voice that told a whole story, of Most Respected Elder Lois and some other soul, and a risky journey, long ago. And . . . a reward? A disappointment?

"Go," she said. "It will be worth it." A reward, then.

Hilltop Lois sighed limply. "Well. There are Lois Clubs all over the world."

Old Lois cackled at that. Then another Lois was laughing, and another, and then it was all of us Loises laughing together in a dark-shingled house on the hill behind the hospital with a view of the park and the ocean beyond.

MR. MARROW

I CONFRONTED CHARLOTTE CLINGSTONE in her garden behind Café Candide as she squatted beside a grid of bushy arugula, picking the widest fronds, leaving the others to grow larger.

"It was less a lie," she said languidly, "and more of a considered omission."

She didn't look like the secret impresario of an underground market, dressed now in sturdy jeans and a pink linen shirt with a banded collar, her hair swept back behind a pink headband.

I should have known Mr. Marrow was the kind of person whose headband matched her top.

"Was it just a game?"

Her expression was firm. "I believe everything I ever said as Mr. Marrow. I believe, also, that this restaurant is a precious place. Can't I believe both? I think I can."

"What about 'tending your garden'?"

Clingstone smiled distantly. "Oh, what *about* that book? I still love it. But I also wonder how it could possibly have resonated so powerfully with a twenty-three-year-old who had seen so little of the world. Now that I've actually suffered, I find it somewhat . . . theoretical."

"But why do it all in secret?" Surely, a market known to be organized by Charlotte Clingstone would be a huge deal. Overnight, the Ferry Building itself would have a rival.

Clingstone's gaze turned inward, and more gently she said, "It never occurs to people that maybe I'd like to be the reckless one. The disrupter! As the years have passed, I have discovered in myself this . . . energy. Is it anger? A touch of spite? I'm not sure." She looked back toward the restaurant. The beans on their strings were rippling on a breeze so gentle I couldn't feel it. "I can't be reckless with the café. We directly support twenty-seven farms and ranches. Almost four hundred people! And there's my staff, of course." She looked at me wickedly. "I wanted a place to break things, and that place is my Marrow Fair."

"So what happens now?"

"Now the market is open. We see what succeeds. Oh, and guess what? Through my investment in Jaina Mitra and her Lembas Labs, I now own three percent of a company called Slurry Systems. Isn't that interesting? They say it might be worth a billion dollars." She stood and brushed off her jeans. "You should join us here at the café."

"You can't be serious."

"Why not? Learn from Mona. She'll teach you how to make that sourdough pizza crust we were talking about. You're beyond the novice's grace now."

She wasn't wrong, but this wasn't the place I wanted to learn.

"And I paid for that robot, don't forget. What were the terms again? I think I own twenty percent of your company. If there is a company."

I walked out through the café's burnished dining room, the acolytes setting tables, their shadows moving in the dark wood. It really was a beautiful place. There was a bowl of plums sitting alone on a table. I plucked one out and ate it on the way to the train.

THE BEGINNING

O N FOOD BLOGS and in social media posts, the eaters of the Bay Area rendered their first judgments of the Marrow Fair; these ranged from deep appreciation to utter bafflement. Some people said Charlotte Clingstone had betrayed everything she ever stood for; others said she was plotting a commendable course for the future. Everyone agreed the bookstore at the back of the market was a gem.

Horace, spooked by the near loss of his archive, finally pieced together a book proposal and sold it to a publisher in Berkeley. He was to write a wide-ranging literary history of eating. It was to be finished in two years. His face was pale when he told me.

Jaina Mitra and Dr. Klamath retreated to Fresno with a sample of the substance that had bloomed above the Marrow Fair. They would become acquainted with the Clement Street starter now, and record their own catalog of phenomena. They would learn a lot using their sequencers and bioreactors, but would they ever suspect the crucial role that music played? Maybe I'd send them a clue. Maybe not.

In Berlin, Beoreg had opened his restaurant. He sent me

a picture of the space he'd leased in Kreuzberg. It was no larger than my apartment, but it faced a busy street, and inside, there were three tiny, glorious tables. The process had not been without intra-Mazg drama, but Beo was undeterred.

Out of necessity, I read the very first chapter of *The Soul of Sourdough*, the one I'd skipped, about capturing a wild starter. Following Everett Broom's instructions, I set a dish of flour and water on the windowsill and watched it closely. Within a week, it was bubbling. And that's all it did, ever. This sourdough starter was a party of two, just yeast and lactobacillus, like every other starter in the world except for one.

I returned to the Jay Steve Value Oven in the backyard. In my absence, the Cabrillo Street cats had made it into their lair. I shooed them away and built a fire. Cornelia came outside and watched me learn to bake again for the first time. Mainly, we sat in companionable silence. Then, one morning, after we'd pulled a couple of particularly plump loaves from the Jay Steve, I told her I was leaving.

"A lot of people have lived in that apartment," she said, "but none of them ever fed me before you came along."

I told her I'd leave her some of the starter so she could bake her own bread.

She narrowed her eyes. "What am I getting myself into? Is it high-maintenance? I don't like high-maintenance."

"Not this one," I said. "It's boring."

THERE'S A CRATE HERE at the restaurant in Kreuzberg. It's enormous, and it's addressed to NUMBER ONE EATER. Is it a mistake? Are you inside the crate? I banged on it and called your name, but there was no reply. Then I pried it open (sorry), but there was just another box inside. This one is bright blue, with a lightning bolt.

Lois, what's going on?

BEO! Inside that big blue box there is a refurbished Vitruvian 3 robot arm, partially disassembled, loaded with software I helped create. That robot and I have been through a lot together. I have things to teach it still.

I'm coming to Berlin.

I'm starting a new business, and I need your help. I want to learn how to use knives correctly, and which vegetables are which, and how to make my own spicy soup. (That's not a euphemism.) (It could be a euphemism.) If you can teach me, I can teach the Vitruvian, and then those skills can be shared in a new way, thanks to my former employer. The world is going to change, I think—slowly at first, then faster than anyone expects. It's going to be a weird time, but along the way I think I can get rich. *We* can get rich.

Beo, I'll bring plenty of Fresno chilies.

I also want to learn how to bake sourdough the way you did on Clement Street. Honestly, mine was never as good. But I have one condition, and you might not like it.

Let's not use the starter of the Mazg.

It almost caught me, Beo. And then it caught someone

else. It starts out very sweetly, doesn't it? The songs, the smiles. One night, I saw a dusting of pinprick lights. Luminous powdered sugar. That feels like a long time ago. Maybe, if you're lucky (or if you're you), the starter of the Mazg stays sweet. But if you're not, it sneaks up on you—the ambition, the impatience, the *hunger* . . . I'll tell you the whole story when I get to Berlin. There aren't any pirates in this one, but it does feature a great rocky island, along with some very heroic goats.

This time, I'm bringing *you* a starter: authentic San Francisco sourdough, native citizen of Cabrillo Street. I captured it myself. I will decant it into a plastic container small enough to take through airport security. If challenged, I will claim it's moisturizer.

In Berlin, it will grow

It will make no faces and sing no songs, but I guarantee you, it will do its part. And, Beo, working there with you, I will set myself, at last, to the task of learning mine.

A Note About the Author

Robin Sloan is the author of *Mr. Penumbra's 24-Hour Bookstore.* He grew up in Michigan and now splits his time between the Bay Area and the internet.

35674057273592